MW00442187

LUFTWAFFE ACES

German Combat Pilots of World War II

Franz Kurowski

Translated by David Johnston

STACKPOLE BOOKS

0 11557 03177 5

Library of Congress Cataloging-in-Publication Data

Kurowski, Franz.
  Luftwaffe aces : German combat pilots of World War II / Franz Kurowski ; translated by David Johnston.— 1st ed.
    p. cm. — (Stackpole Military history series)
  Translated from German.
  Originally published: Winnipeg, Man. : J.J. Fedorowicz, 1996.
  Includes index.
  ISBN 0-8117-3177-4
  1. Germany. Luftwaffe—Biography. 2. World War, 1939-1945—Aerial operations, German. 3. Air pilots, Military—Germany—Biography. I. Title. II. Series.
D787.K89 2004
940.54'4943'0922—dc22
                                        2004011439

Table of Contents

Hauptmann Helbig after receiving the Oak Leaves, January 1942.

Joachim Helbig:
The Ju-88 Ace of the Mediterranean

It may be said without exaggeration that Joachim Helbig was one of the outstanding officers of the German bomber arm in the Second World War. He joined the Luftwaffe in 1936 and began his war service in the Polish Campaign as a bombardier in the 1st Training and Demonstration Wing (*Lehrgeschwader*), the unit with which he was to serve throughout his entire career. In May 1940 Helbig became commander of the 4th Squadron of the 1st Training and Demonstration Wing. Effective November 1941, he commanded the 1st Group of the the 1st Training and Demonstration Wing. Finally, in 1943, he became the wing commander of the highly successful wing, from whose ranks came twenty-eight recipients of the Knight's Cross.

Helbig saw his first combat operations in the campaign in Norway and in the war over Western Europe in the spring of 1940. His formation was also fully committed in the Battle of Britain, and he survived a disastrous mission from which his was the only aircraft to return in one piece. In the years that followed, Helbig and his formations saw action in the Mediterranean Theater. There, he and his group achieved great success against the British Fleet. It became the best-known bomber formation, not just on his own side, but on that of the enemy as well. His great success was founded in his polished tactics and coolness, combined with outstanding flying skill and exceptional courage.

In January 1943 Helbig became an inspector on the staff of the senior officer responsible for the Luftwaffe's bomber force. During his tour of duty there, he received ever-increasing positions of responsibility. In August of the same year Helbig was named the wing commander of the 1st Training and Demonstration Wing. Together with the 76th Bomb Wing, the 1st Training and Demonstration Wing was committed against Allied invasion forces that had landed in Italy. The combined force operated as Combat Formation Helbig. In the March–April 1945 timeframe, Helbig commanded an ad hoc combat unit on the Eastern Front consisting of ele-

1

ments of the 1st Training and Demonstration Wing and the 200th Bomb Wing. After the war ended he was captured by the British but managed to escape a few weeks later.

THE FIRST STEPS

To his comrades he was "Jochen." When war began Helbig was a young Oberleutnant (1st lieutenant); when it was over he was an Oberst (colonel), one of the youngest in the Luftwaffe at the age of thirty. His English opponents called him the "all-round bomber pilot" and his men were the "Helbig Fliers."

Helbig commanded a bomber pilot's entire repertoire. Every member of his squadron, group and wing tried to emulate him, as their success shows. But he remained at the top, flying special missions that no one else could pull off. He was a born warrior who evolved from a pilot into a highly capable unit leader. Someone characterized him and his men as the "extended arm of the artillery," and that is just what they were. From the first to the last day of the war Helbig exhibited nerves of steel. He was the personification of self-discipline and control.

Joachim Helbig was born on an estate in Saxony in the eastern part of Germany. Located in the Dahlen District, the estate was called Börln. After 1945 it became an agricultural collective of the German Democratic Republic. As a youth, Helbig's first love was horses. He decided to become an officer and soldier after completing his schooling; the only choice for him was the cavalry or, perhaps, the horse-drawn artillery.

Helbig received his initial training as an officer candidate with the 4th Artillery Regiment, but he was transferred to the Luftwaffe in 1936. The move was against his will, and the change from horses to aircraft was not to his liking at first. Very soon, however, "Jochen" discovered that he enjoyed flying as much as riding. In the end he became so enthused with his new branch of service that he even ignored riding in his free time so as to earn every Luftwaffe pilot certificate as quickly as possible. After attending officer candidate school, Helbig was posted to the bomber school at Lechfeld in the autumn of 1936. There he was trained as a bombardier.

In April 1937 Helbig joined the 152nd Bomb Wing's 3rd Group at Schwerin as a bombardier. At Schwerin he became good friends with Fritz Sohler and Gerhard Schröder, both outstanding pilots. While serving with the formation—which was redesignated as the 1st Training and Demon-stration Wing's 2nd Group in 1938—he was secretly and unofficially trained to fly, something that was not uncommon at that time. Without the benefit of formal training at a flying school, "bombardier" Helbig was taught to fly by his two friends. He was able to earn a C-Class certificate and a Class II instrument rating. Helbig's experience was unique in the entire Luftwaffe bomber force.

In the war against Poland Helbig served as a bombardier in a He-111 flying reconnaissance missions. On the third day of fighting the He-111 encountered a Polish reconnaissance aircraft, which was shot down by Hel-big after a brief skirmish. The next day he was injured in a motorcycle acci-dent and the Polish Campaign was over for Joachim Helbig.

After recovering from his injuries, Helbig was assigned to train on the Junkers 88, which was just entering service with the Luftwaffe. He became a pilot while still in the 1st Training and Demonstration Wing. That wing was the oldest formation in the Luftwaffe, having been established at Neubrandenburg and Greifswald in 1935. It served as the school forma-tion for the developing air force. The unit's peacetime bases were:

Greifswald: Headquarters, Headquarters Squadron, and 3rd Group
Barth: 1st Group (Heavy Fighter Group)
Schwerin: 2nd Group (Bomber Group)
Barth: 4th Group (Dive-bomber Group)

With the end of the campaign in Poland, the 1st and 4th Groups of the 1st Training and Demonstration Wing returned to their bases in East Prussia. A number of reorganizations and redesignations took place within the wing, and when Joachim Helbig joined it, his 4th Group was still sta-tioned at Tronsheim. The decision had been made at the highest level of the Luftwaffe command that the 1st Training and Demonstration Wing was to fight in the Mediterranean Theater.

By then Helbig was a full-fledged bomber pilot and a member of a close-knit fighting unit in which every man could depend fully on the oth-ers. Outstanding individual actions were not the order of the day; any suc-cesses achieved by the wing's formations were joint efforts.

General of Fighter Forces Dieter Peltz, who served in the General Staff, as the commander of the air forces attacking England, as the last Commanding General of the IX Air Corps (*Fliegerkorps*) and, in March 1945, was responsible for the air defense of the Reich, said the following in that regard:

Even in critical situations, confidence in the actions of one's comrades produced a feeling of security and belonging. The ability to depend on each other, even when the ultimate sacrifice—one's life—was demanded, was the basis of this arm's special ability to perform and of its professional demeanor. Though it is no longer obvious to many today, the roots of this strength and will to fight lay in a consciousness of belonging to the German people and to the Reich, something that was felt by everyone.

JOACHIM HELBIG ON THE JU-88

Anyone who, like the author, spoke with Jochen Helbig, found that he eventually ended up talking about the Ju-88. It seemed as if every conversation turned in that direction and, when it did, Helbig spoke enthusiastically about the Ju-88's qualities. It was not easy to fly, but next to the incomparable Ju-87, it was the best and safest aircraft in the Luftwaffe, perhaps even in the entire world, during the Second World War. That was especially true of medium bombers.

Joachim Helbig mastered the Ju-88 like a virtuoso. His aircraft, which bore the code L1 + AM, was well-known among the workers at the Junkers factory. Thanks to the tireless efforts of his chief mechanic, Rudi Behm, Helbig was able to log more than 750 hours in the aircraft on combat missions and in the course of 200 inspection flights. Helbig always flew the aircraft himself and never handed his machine over to another pilot. During the war this unique aircraft survived hazardous missions in the hands of its gifted pilot and braved sandstorms in North Africa and severe icing over the Alps. Helbig's Ju-88 survived damage inflicted by enemy antiaircraft fire and fighters by day and night over the Balkans, England, Malta, Africa, and Palestine.

In one dangerous escapade Helbig successfully flew L1 + AM from Tobruk to Tripoli on one engine, a flight lasting 4.5 hours. It even survived a general overhaul of the airframe after 1,000 hours. This gallant aircraft was never downed by the enemy in combat; instead, it met its end in an air raid by U.S. bombers against the airfield at Pordenone on the Po Plain.

After serving its crew faithfully for more than four years, Helbig's Ju-88 was destroyed by a direct hit. Looking at the wreck, Helbig's chief mechanic said consolingly: "It was only a machine." But Helbig, in reflection later on, added:

To all of us, the maintenance crew chief as well as the "black men" of the crew, it had become something alive. In that terrible moment in the midst of that bombardment, it said farewell forever to its four faithful friends. The only thing left was its cockpit and the fin marked with four victory bars—two day fighters and two night fighters.

NORWAY AND FRANCE

In October 1939 Oberleutnant Helbig flew several uneventful missions against the British Home Fleet as a bombardier. The great change in his military career came when the 2nd Group the 1st Training and Demonstration Wing converted to its new aircraft, the Junkers 88.

By the time the campaign in Norway began, Helbig had been made a pilot. He flew missions in support of the German ground forces, particularly in the Narvik area. For these missions the He-111s took off from Aalborg in Denmark and landed at a training area at Trondheim-Vernes on the return flight from Narvik. Among the attacks carried out by Helbig were several low-level strikes against British positions. In the course of one such sortie his flight engineer was severely wounded and the left engine of his aircraft was destroyed by antiaircraft fire.

Calling on all his piloting skills, Helbig brought the He-111 home on one engine in a flight lasting almost two hours. The He-111 crashed while attempting to land on a runway whose surface had been covered with wooden planks. Some Norwegian prisoners took advantage of the excitement caused by the dramatic landing to escape.

Not content with his flights over Norway in the He-111, Helbig managed to persuade his group commander and finally the wing commander to allow him to go hunting enemy shipping in the area southwest of Trondheim in the sole Ju-88 then issued to the 2nd Group. Flown from Schleswig on 21 April 1940, the anti-shipping sortie was unsuccessful. After landing Helbig received a dressing-down from his commanding officer, who ordered him to immediately fly the Ju-88 back to its base in Schleswig. But it was already 2200 hours. Too late, the group commander realized that Helbig's late departure would mean a night landing at Schleswig, a first for the Ju-88, then undergoing frontline testing. He tried to stop Helbig, but he had already taken off. At Schleswig the firefighting vehicles and ambulances as well as the local commanders had been placed on alert; there was great tension and excitement at the airfield. Then, suddenly, there was Helbig's Ju-88. In spite of the prevailing conditions—a black night with poor weather and a strong crosswind—the Ju-88 landed without incident. The spell was broken. Helbig's superiors acknowledged his skill as a pilot.

When the campaign against Holland, Belgium and France began in May 1940, Helbig was the squadron commander of the 4th Squadron of the 1st Training and Demonstration Wing, which was equipped with the Ju-88. Following the defeat of France he received an early promotion to Hauptmann and from that day on was called "Captain Fit." As a young squadron commander, it was Helbig's ambition to exploit to the full the capabilities of the Ju-88. Although it was a heavy dive-bomber, it was employed mainly as a horizontal bomber. This enthusiasm was passed on to his crews, and he carried on an intensive training program while continuing to fly all the combat missions assigned to the unit. These personal efforts by Helbig, coupled with his personal rapport with each crew, were to pay dividends; the 4th Squadron would achieve considerable success in the campaign in Western Europe in 1940.

✠

Helbig's aircraft was intercepted by enemy fighters over Dunkirk. He had just dropped his bombs on a armada of enemy ships off the coast when Franz Schlund, Helbig's radio operator, spotted the three fighters. Schlund immediately began calling out evasive maneuvers to his pilot. The Ju-88s machine guns returned fire and the first enemy fighter veered off, trailing smoke. The other two closed in and a deadly dogfight began that was to last twenty minutes.

Joachim Helbig used every trick he knew, jinking left and right before diving away and climbing steeply to avoid the bursts of fire from the enemy fighters. Then his flight engineer was hit. Schlund dressed the man's wounds. The gunner then took his place again behind his machine gun and fought off the next attack. Helbig was also wounded but not seriously. A heavy blow shook the airframe and Schlund reported he had been hit. He was tended to by the flight engineer. After fighting off numerous attacks, the ammunition was gone. The Ju-88 was badly damaged and its left engine had been knocked out. It was time for them to take to their heels. They were in luck because it appeared that the enemy was also out of ammunition.

Escaping on one engine was not so simple, however, and when a fourth enemy fighter approached it looked like the end for Helbig and his crew. All four airmen were sure they were lost, but the new arrival did not fire. Instead, he moved in close to the Ju-88 from behind. The enemy pilot saw the stationary propeller and then slid into position off the Ju-88s left wing—as if joining formation with it. Looking to his left, Helbig saw the

Ju-88 A-4s of the 1st Training and Demonstration Wing.

young face of the opponent who would surely deliver the coup de grace in a matter of seconds. The latter merely looked over at Helbig and continued to fly alongside the Ju-88 over France for more than five minutes. Then, suddenly, the enemy pilot raised his right hand to his flying helmet, saluted casually, turned away—rocking his wings as he did so—and then disappeared to the north.

When they had landed and the ambulance had taken the two wounded members of his crew to the hospital, the injured Helbig related the story of the mission and this completely surprising and fortunate incident. When he had finished speaking there was quiet in the room for a few seconds. Then his commanding officer declared: "This is your new birthday. You should mark it on the calendar in red. You'll never experience anything like this again, Helbig."

Then, after a moment of silence, the group commander took him by the arm.

"God's hand must have been upon us, sir," said Helbig modestly.

"Well said . . . and now off to the hospital!"

✠

Indeed, throughout his entire operational career it seemed as if someone were watching over Joachim Helbig, allowing him to make a number of miraculous escapes from seemingly impossible situations. In spite of the many combat missions he flew during the war, Helbig was never seriously injured.

The minor wounds the squadron commander suffered over Dunkirk at the end of May could not keep a man like Jochen Helbig in hospital for long. He returned to flying again within a few days. Tireless in action, he was an example to his squadron. Helbig was one of the most successful officers in the wing by then and, on 19 July 1940, the "Day of the Field Marshals," he received an early promotion. His comrades presented him with his new shoulder boards bearing the two stars of a Hauptmann.

Soon afterward, Helbig and his squadron joined what was to become known as the Battle of Britain. the 1st Training and Demonstration Wing flew its first sorties on the third day of the German air attacks on England. The attack that day proved a disaster. The Ju-88s of the 1st Training and Demonstration Wing took off from Orleans at 1645 hours on 15 August 1940. Fifteen minutes later, the 1st Group of the 1st Stuka Wing (*Stukageschwader*) under Hauptmann Hozzel and the 2nd Group of the 1st Stuka Wing under Hauptmann Enneccerus took off from Lannion in Brittany. The target for the the 1st Training and Demonstration Wing's 2nd Group was Worthy Down, a British seaport northeast of Southampton.

Over the coast the two attack groups rendezvoused with their escort, elements of 2nd Long-Range Fighter Wing (*Zerstörergeschwader*) under Oberstleutnant Vollbracht, the 27th Fighter Wing (*Jagdgeschwader*) under Oberstleutnant Ibel, and 53rd Fighter Wing under Major von Cramon-Taubadel. It was 1800 hours when the combined force of more than 200 aircraft, arrayed in several formations, headed north across the Channel. Within seconds, the Germans were spotted by British radar stations. Air Vice-Marshals Park and Brand, the commanders of the 10th and 11th Fighter Groups of the Royal Air Force, had placed their units on alert. They were thus able to hurl a force of 170 fighters against the formations of Generalfeldmarschall Sperrle's 3rd Air Force (*Luftflotte*). Fourteen British fighter squadrons rose to intercept the approaching bombers.

Among them were the nine Ju-88s of the 4th Squadron of the 1st Training and Demonstration Wing led by Hauptmann Jochen Helbig. His squadron flew at the rear of the group's formation. Just as the English coast came into view, the rearmost machine of the squadron reported: "Indians (enemy fighters) from behind!"

About eighty British fighters dove on the bombers. They had taken off and flown in a wide arc to position themselves behind the German bombers. The Spitfires opened fire as they roared through the squadron formation from behind and above. After completing their firing pass the enemy fighters streaked upwards.

"Where are our fighters?" one of Helbig's pilots complained bitterly. The fighters could not help, however. They were several thousand meters higher than the Ju-88s and were themselves engaged. The enemy had planned his attack well and was following through to the letter.

"Maintain course, don't become separated!" Helbig called over the squadron frequency. "Close formation!"

Maintaining a tight formation had the effect of concentrating the defensive fire of the Ju-88s. The Spitfires returned for another pass. They concentrated on the trailing machine and sought to separate it from the formation.

"Evasive action!" Helbig ordered.

That was the only alternative, but it also scattered the formation. The slower Ju-88s had to fight it out with the Spitfires individually. The latter dived on the lone Ju-88s and blazed away with their eight wing-mounted guns. The gunners in the bombers did their best; three of the enemy fighters were hit and dove away trailing smoke. Manning one of the machine guns in Helbig's aircraft was Oberfeldwebel (Technical Sergeant) Schlund. He called out the enemy fighters as they approached, allowing Helbig to take evasive action.

"Spitfire from five o'clock, range 400 . . . 300 . . . 250!"

That was the signal for Helbig to turn; the enemy fighter would surely open fire at any moment. Helbig hauled the Ju-88 around in a steep turn. The Spitfire opened fire but the burst passed to the bomber's right. At that instant Schlund opened fire with his machine gun. The pursuing Spitfire flew into the long burst. Flames pouring from its engine, it veered off. Helbig then swung the bomber back to the right. Unable to stay behind the Ju-88, the next Spitfire roared past. It was also hit several times and, like its predecessor, it veered off trailing smoke.

Jochen Helbig's L1 + AM had so far escaped damage from the enemy fighters, but as soon as it had dropped its bombs and reversed course it came under attack again. Only Helbig's aircraft and one other one of the squadron returned to Orleans. Both had sustained serious battle damage. The other five aircraft had been shot down. Thirty-two members of the squadron had escaped by parachute or had survived forced landings on the English coast. They became POWs. Of the fifteen Ju-88s of the 1st

Training and Demonstration Wing that had taken off, nine had been shot down. Only three reached and bombed the target, Worthy Down. Most of the pilots had been forced to jettison their bombs in order to lighten their aircraft and improve their chances of escape.

The official British claims for the day were 182 German aircraft shot down as well as 53 probables. These figures far exceeded actual German losses, especially since the entire attacking force numbered only 200–210 aircraft. Actual German losses were 55 aircraft, mostly Bf-110 heavy fighters and bombers. The claims made by the German command were likewise exaggerated. The Luftwaffe fighter units involved in operations that day claimed 111 certain and 14 probable victories. The British authorities admitted the loss of 34 fighters; however, any aircraft which could be landed by its pilot was not considered shot down, even if it subsequently had to be written off on account of battle damage.

✠

As the Battle of Britain progressed, Joachim Helbig developed into a specialist in attacking industrial targets. As a result of his success he received the Knight's Cross on 24 November 1940. Helbig had already earned the Iron Cross, Second Class during the campaign against Poland, the Narvik Shield in the fighting in Norway and the Iron Cross, First Class in the French Campaign. By the time Helbig received the Knight's Cross from the hand of his commanding general, he had flown 122 combat missions. He was also one of the very first Ju-88 pilots to win the coveted decoration.

HELBIG AS SQUADRON COMMANDER AND GROUP COMMANDER

While based at Orleans, Joachim Helbig took great pains to ensure that all the new arrivals were trained as well as possible, and he considered it his sworn duty to pass on to them the experience he had gained in several theaters of war. This attitude on Helbig's part goes some way toward explaining the low casualties sustained by the units led by him. He never forgot the disaster over England on 15 August 1940, when he was one only two pilots from his squadron to return safely to base at Orleans.

On 6 September the Luftwaffe's bomber force began night attacks on England. Helbig very soon came to realize that small-scale raids against pinpoint targets—industrial and port facilities, rail junctions and airfields—offered the best chance of success. He selected only the most qualified crews for these missions, and they must have volunteered in writing to the wing commander to be considered.

Helbig took full advantage of the prevailing weather in planning his attacks. In November 1940 he flew no less than eighty missions over England. Reconnaissance photos confirmed that he had destroyed or inflicted heavy damage on the important Eastham lock gate in the Manchester Canal. In another lone attack, Helbig inflicted serious damage on the administration building of Penrose airfield, a training base located south of Liverpool.

The group commander of the 2nd Group of the 1st Training and Demonstration Wing, Knight's Cross recipient and well-known German pentathlete Hauptmann Heinz Cramer, was shot down during a daylight raid on Warrington Propeller Factory near Liverpool. Jochen Helbig attacked the same target at dusk the following day.

WARRINGTON IN THE CROSSHAIRS

Helbig's success in surviving seemingly hopeless situations was due to the high caliber of his crew, which included Oberfeldwebel Franz Schlund. Schlund became the first Luftwaffe radio operator to be awarded the Knight's Cross on 30 August 1941. Schlund played a prominent role in three dangerous special missions flown by Helbig in 1940.

✠

The wing command selected Helbig and his crew for three missions against special targets in England. All were to be flown in daylight. The first attack was against the Warrington Propeller Works north of Liverpool. Taking off at dawn, Helbig's Ju-88 crossed the Channel without being intercepted. Schlund spotted the first enemy fighter over England. Helbig climbed toward a dense layer of cloud that began about 300 meters above them. He continued to climb, passed 1,500 meters and finally reached approximately 2,000 meters. When the aircraft emerged from the clouds Schlund called out:

"Indian behind us, veer right!"

Helbig threw the bomber into a tight right turn and dived toward the nearest cloud. Descending at an angle of 55 degrees, the Ju-88 quickly accelerated to more than 500 kilometers per hour.

"Indian from the left!" reported Schlund.

Helbig's evasive maneuver caused the burst of machine-gun fire fired by the British pilot to miss. Then the cloud swallowed them up and they

were flying through dense "cream soup." Helbig climbed; it was pre-
dictable where the enemy fighter would be waiting for them. When the
bomber emerged from the clouds at an altitude of 2,300 meters, the
enemy fighter was at least 500 meters behind them and to one side.
Schlund saw it straightaway and instructed Helbig to alter course toward
the northwest. The enemy fighter, which had been expecting the Ju-88 to
appear at the end of the cloudbank, was now left empty-handed.

Helbig congratulated his radio operator for a job well done in evading
the enemy fighter. Fifteen minutes later they were over Liverpool. Scattered antiaircraft fire rose to meet the Ju-88 and Helbig ducked back into
a cloud. Ten minutes later Helbig dived steeply through the cloud. The
first thing he and his crew saw was a huge factory installation. Helbig realized that this was the propeller works.

"Attention: Prepare for diving attack!"

Helbig swung the Ju-88 around so that he could approach the target
from the north or northeast; he knew from experience that the antiaircraft
guns were massed around the target in a semicircle from southwest to
southeast. Approaching from the north, Helbig put the Ju-88 into a dive
from approximately 1,800 meters. Not a round had yet been fired.

Then light antiaircraft guns opened fire from the left. Streams of
tracer reached out for the Ju-88, which picked up speed as it plunged

Helbig's Ju-88 at the time he was Staffelkapitän of the 4th Squadron.

toward its target. Helbig felt himself being pressed into his seat. The bombardier had the main factory centered in his sight. He pressed the release button and the bombs howled earthward toward the target. Meanwhile Helbig pulled the machine out of its dive and climbed away steeply, at the same time turning left to escape the British ground fire, which by then had grown heavy.

"Enemy fire shifting to the right!" reported Schlund.

The enemy antiaircraft guns soon found the range. An exploding round showered the Junkers with fragments. A heavy blow shook the airframe, but the courageous aircraft continued to climb and then disappeared into the nearest cloud. Aircraft and crew returned to base with no further contact with the enemy.

THE EASTHAM LOCK GATE

"Helbig, tomorrow morning you will fly a daylight mission against the Eastham lock gate, part of the Manchester shipping canal. If we can close the canal, the smaller ships that supply Manchester won't be able to reach the city."

Helbig acknowledged the instructions of his superior, who added: "But be careful. The enemy has positioned his best antiaircraft crews there and his fighters can get up quickly from the nearby airfield, as Schütte found out . . ."

Oberfeldwebel Schütte and his crew had been sent against the same target two days before. Coming home with a dead bombardier and a shot-up engine, Schütte, who had also been wounded, was forced to put his riddled Junkers down on the beach on the French side of the Channel.

"We'll watch out, sir," Helbig assured his superior.

That evening Helbig went to the quarters of the three noncommissioned officers who made up his crew. Referring to a map, he showed them the target. He said in closing: "This won't be a walk in the park. I suggest we go to bed early so that we'll be fresh in the morning."

This was the squadron commander that they knew. Helbig could sleep anywhere, even in the aircraft in flight if someone else kept watch. What they valued most in their commander was his coolness under fire, his concentrated attention in action and his aggressive spirit.

"We'll do that, sir," assured Schlund.

Pilot and crew were well rested for takeoff. The heavily laden machine took almost the entire runway before it finally left the ground and climbed away slowly. After flying a wide semicircle, they set course for the Channel. The Ju-88 was almost across when two fighters took off from the base at Great Yarmouth. Helbig immediately headed out over the sea and soon the two fighters were gone from sight. Half an hour later the Ju-88 turned back toward land in a gentle arc. According to calculations, they must be even with the target. Following another course adjustment, they should be able to attack from the south.

This time Helbig and his men had decided on a direct attack. In spite of the massed antiaircraft defenses, it offered a better chance of striking the lock gate effectively. The lone bomber had not yet been spotted when it arrived over the canal. Helbig rolled the Ju-88 out of a gentle right turn, lining it up directly over the canal. This time he descended to 450 meters to increase the chances of a direct hit. The Ju-88 was already in its dive toward the lock gate when the antiaircraft guns opened up. Only when the target filled his sight did the bombardier release the two heavy bombs. Climbing away steeply and veering to the right toward the Channel, the Ju-88 escaped the danger zone of the enemy air defenses. They had climbed several-hundred meters and were out of range of the direct blast wave when the bombs went off.

Schlund shouted joyfully: "Hit it!" Then, as he watched, a tidal wave of water rushed along the canal: "Clobbered it!"

Climbing to 3,600 meters, Helbig set course for home. Once again the return flight was uneventful, and they landed safely at their home base.

THE TARGET IS PENROSE

The third mission was the most dangerous—the pilot training airfield at Pellrose, south of Liverpool, was surrounded by a dense ring of antiaircraft guns. Furthermore, there were several fighter bases in the vicinity. Success depended on surprise. Helbig decided on a night takeoff. They would fly along England's west coast as far as possible toward Liverpool under cover of darkness and then make their attack at first light.

Once again, all went as planned. When daylight arrived they were already turning towards the target. Antiaircraft fire greeted the intruder and Helbig circled the airfield at a discrete distance until the bombardier located his target—the main building with the airfield control tower. He passed course corrections to the pilot and brought the bomber into attack position.

The Junkers plunged toward its target. A heavy blow shook the aircraft, but Helbig held it on course through the firestorm of antiaircraft fire. At the last second the bombardier dropped the bombs, and, as the Ju-88 veered off, Schlund reported that both bombs had scored direct hits.

Two-and-a-half hours later the Junkers landed back at its base; there were seventeen bullet and fragment holes in the airframe. After he had made his report, Helbig was lauded for his three outstanding bombing runs by the wing commander. His response: "I would like to see to it that my radio operator, Franz Schlund, receives credit for his actions. It was due to him that the missions were successes."

"I quite agree, Helbig. Consider it done," the wing commander answered. Franz Schlund was recommended for the Knight's Cross. However, it was not until a second submission was made that he received the decoration on 20 August 1941.

✠

When Helbig presented himself to the wing commander, Oberst Harry von Bülow-Bothkamp, before leaving to receive the Knight's Cross, he was wearing an old, battered cap that he had worn faithfully since the Polish Campaign. A talisman! However, his commanding officer, a cavalier of the old school, took offence to the battered peaked cap. He reproached the squadron commander harshly and, when Helbig left to meet the commanding general, he was wearing a new cap that someone had loaned him. Needless to say, however, he continued wearing his old cap for a long time to come.

TARGET MALTA

Between Christmas and New Year of 1940 the 2nd Group of the 1st Training and Demonstration Wing transferred from Orleans to Sicily. This flight over the Alps marked the beginning of a two-year period of action for the wing in the Mediterranean area—over Malta and North Africa. During this period Joachim Helbig was to fly more than 100 combat missions. The 1st Training and Demonstration Wing flew its first missions in the new combat zone in January 1941. These included air strikes against convoys in the Eastern Mediterranean, attacks on the aircraft carrier *Illustrious* and raids in support of Italian forces engaged during their rapid retreat through Libya.

✠

A dusk attack on Tobruk nearly ended in disaster for Helbig and his crew. Once again accurate British antiaircraft fire knocked out one of the Ju-88's engines as it dove on its target. It required all of Helbig's skill and experience to nurse the crippled aircraft home. Benghazi was already in British hands, which made Tripoli the nearest airfield. Helbig and his crew landed there after flying four hours on one engine.

✠

The First Battle of Malta, which lasted from January to May 1941, saw the 4th Squadron engaged in dive-bombing attacks on port facilities and airfields on the island fortress of Malta. Part of the reason for these raids was to take pressure off the German Africa Corps. As well as attacking Malta, the squadron also flew long-range missions against targets in the Eastern Mediterranean.

✠

The night of Good Friday 1941 saw the squadron carry out a moonlight attack against British shipping in the port of Piraeus. Helbig dive-bombed and sank al 10,000-ton troop transport. Over the Bay of Salamis the Junkers was caught by searchlights of a British air-defense unit. As soon as the searchlights pinpointed the Ju-88 the antiaircraft guns opened fire. Then the guns abruptly fell silent and a British night fighter opened fire.

By maneuvering on instruments at low altitude, Helbig was able to escape the night fighter and give the searchlights the slip. Flying at full throttle, Helbig left the most dangerous part of the trip behind. Below them, somewhat off to one side, was the British base at Eleusis, which was home to Beaufighter twin-engined night fighters.

It was radio operator Schlund who, alert as ever, spotted a second night fighter and shouted a warning to his pilot. He then opened fire with his machine gun and shot down the night fighter with his second burst. Looking back, the crew of the Ju-88 watched as the Beaufighter crashed and exploded. It was Oberfeldwebel Schlund's second kill; he had earlier shot down a Spitfire on "Eagle Day" on 15 August 1940.

Delayed by his encounters with the enemy defenses, Helbig was late returning. All the other crews had already landed and there was a mood of depression at the group's command post. Returning crews had reported seeing an aircraft crash and explode; it was assumed that it had been Helbig's Ju-88 and that he and his crew had met their end. The joy when Helbig and his crew turned up later that night was indescribable. It was as if Helbig had risen from the dead.

✠

In June 1941 Helbig flew his 150th combat mission, a sortie against Haifa on the East Mediterranean coast. It was also a success.

✠

Several weeks later Helbig attacked a group of British tanks south of Benghazi. Two enemy aircraft engaged the Ju-88 over the desert. Once again it was Oberfeldwebel Schlund who saved the day by shooting down one of the enemy fighters. The other broke off its pursuit of this combative Ju-88. As soon as they had returned to their home base, the flight engineer of L1 + AM, Feldwebel (Staff Sergeant) Behm, painted the fourth victory marking on the fin of the Ju-88.

By the beginning of May 1941 the group had been moved to Eleusis. Located near Athens, it was an ideal base for operations in the western as well as the eastern parts of the Mediterranean and over Africa. Furthermore, Athens offered officers clubs and recreational facilities in addition to its cultural attractions.

While based at Eleusis, Helbig and his men were called upon to support the paratroopers (*Fallschirmjäger*) fighting on the island of Crete. From 20–29 May 1941 the machines of the 2nd Group of the 1st Training and Demonstration Wing were constantly in action over the embattled island. In addition to sorties over Crete, the Ju-88s also had to carry out raids against Tobruk, then under siege by Rommel's forces. Further raids

A Ju-88 A-10 of the 1st Training and Demonstration Wing after a forced landing in the African desert.

were flown against the Suez Canal and the cargo ships using the waterway. Another frequent target was Haifa, with its port facilities and oil refineries.

The summer of 1941 also saw the Ju-88s of the 1st Training and Demonstration Wing engaged in numerous anti-shipping strikes over the Mediterranean. The following is an account of its actions against the British Mediterranean Fleet.

OPERATIONS AGAINST THE BRITISH FLEET IN MAY 1941

On the morning of 22 May 1941 the Ju-88s of the 1st Training and Demonstration Wing took off from their Greek bases to attack a unit of the British Mediterranean Fleet in the waters off Crete. This unit was holding station north of the island, waiting to intercept and sink a second group of German ships reported to be on its way to Crete to support the airborne forces that had landed there.

The first group of light vessels had almost been wiped out during the previous night. On board were troops of the 5th Mountain Infantry Division (*Gebirgsjäger-Division*) on their way to reinforce the paratroopers. The second wave of ships, with further mountain infantry on board, was to be dealt with in a similar manner, if the British had their way. Here are the events leading up to the Ju-88 attack on 22 May.

On 21 May 1941 British headquarters in Cairo had issued its daily public report, in which General Wavell, Commander-in-Chief of British forces in the Mediterranean, announced:

> Powerful German forces launched a heavy attack on Crete early Tuesday at dawn. A very large number of parachute troops jumped over Crete. The latest reports indicate that aircraft carrying troops have landed in the interior of the island. Several German parachute battalions were overpowered and taken prisoner. The fighting continues.
>
> There have been numerous air battles between the German Air Force and British and Greek fighter aircraft around and over Crete. Light units of the Mediterranean Fleet have put to sea as an attack by German and Italian motor torpedo boats is expected.

During the night of 20–21 May British naval forces sailed through the Strait of Kaso and the Kithera Narrows. They had received orders from Admiral Cunningham to patrol north of Crete, specifically east and west of meridian twenty-five degrees east. Force C was supposed to seal off the area around Heraklion, while Force D was assigned the same role in the

Malemes-Khania-Kissamo Bay area. During the night of 20/21 May Force C came upon six Italian torpedo boats in the Kaso Narrows. The antiaircraft cruiser *Kandahar* and the destroyers *Juno* and *Naiad* attacked. In the ensuing unequal engagement, four torpedo boats were damaged by rounds fired by the British vessels. The Italians withdrew.

When dawn came, Force A-l found itself 60 nautical miles west of the Anti-Kithera Narrows. It then took up a southeasterly course in order to rendezvous with Force D, which was returning from its patrol through the Aegean. All units were supposed to spend the day at readiness south of Crete before sailing north again with the return of darkness. While still withdrawing, these units were spotted north of Crete by reconnaissance aircraft of the VIII Air Corps and were attacked several times. Destroyer *Juno* was hit by bombs and sank within two minutes. The light cruiser *Ajax*, part of Force A-l, was seriously damaged by a near miss. By evening, three German bombers had been shot down.

During the coming night, however, the German 1st Light Ship Squadron, which had sailed once again from Milos for Malemes to deliver the soldiers of the 100th Mountain Infantry Regiment of the 5th Mountain Infantry Division to Crete, was intercepted by British warships at 2250 hours. Within thirty minutes, the squadron had been virtually destroyed; only a handful of light vessels escaped. The Italian destroyer *Lupo*, which was escorting the squadron, was hit seventeen times but managed to escape.

The German 2nd Light Ship Squadron sailed into the patrol area of the British warships in the early morning hours of 22 May. The Italian torpedo boat *Sagittario* laid down a smoke screen. Only a few ships were lost as the enemy began to withdraw to avoid being caught by German aircraft. However, it was too late. German morning reconnaissance had already reported their position.

Ju-87 and Ju-88 units, among them the 1st Group, 1st Training and Demonstration Wing, under Hauptmann Cuno Hoffmann, took off immediately. Helbig's squadron departed Athens-Eleusis at 0830 hours. Hoffmann, who personally led his group's attack, had received the Knight's Cross a few days before. He wanted to make this mission something special—and the chances were very good.

The English vessels put up a curtain of antiaircraft fire; however, Hoffmann and his crews ignored it and plunged toward the warships in fifty-degree dives, the maximum allowed for a Ju-88. The *Naiad* received two near misses and stopped immediately. The British admiral ordered a turn to the south. This saved the bulk of the 2nd Light Ship Squadron, which had appeared directly in front of the guns of the British warships.

When Hoffmann learned that some of his aircraft had not dropped their bombs he ordered a continuation of the attack. Reinforced by Do-17Z bombers of the 2nd Bomb Wing, they flew southwest after the withdrawing warships and attacked a second time. The *Naiad*, which had got under way again, was hit. The antiaircraft cruiser *Carlisle* was damaged; its captain killed on the bridge. The cruisers *Calcutta* and *Perth* escaped, but the destroyer *Greyhound* was sunk. The cruisers *Fiji* and *Gloucester* were also sunk while attempting to pick up survivors from *Greyhound*. One of the attacking units was the 4th Squadron under Hauptmann Helbig. He failed to hit any of the enemy ships in this action.

✠

Unexpectedly, it was announced that there was to be a group formation in early September 1941. The squadrons were drawn up in front of their aircraft when the Commanding General of the 2nd Air Corps, General Lörzer, arrived. Addressing the bomber crews, the general expressed his and Göring's appreciation for their accomplishments. Then Oberfeldwebel Schlund was called forward. General Lörzer presented him with the Knight's Cross. It had been officially awarded on 30 August; Schlund was the first radio operator in the Luftwaffe to be so honored.

Franz Schlund was born in Leinen near Heidelberg on 10 August 1913. In April 1935 he was summoned to the radio-operator school at Mannheim. After serving for some time in other units, he joined Helbig's crew on 18 May 1940. By the time he was awarded the Knight's Cross, he had flown more than 200 combat missions and had successfully fought off 13 attacks by enemy fighters. Helbig was the first to congratulate his faithful "Franzel."

LONG-RANGE FLIGHTS—OPERATIONS AGAINST DESTROYERS

In November 1941 Helbig assumed command of the 1st Group of the 1st Training and Demonstration Wing, succeeding Hauptmann Cuno Hoffmann. With 220 combat missions to his credit, he was one of the youngest group commanders in the Luftwaffe. In the meantime, the 1st Training and Demonstration Wing had received Ju-88 A-11s to replace its A-5s. A tropicalized version of the new Ju-88 A-4, the A-11 eventually became standard equipment throughout the entire wing.

In December 1941 the 2nd Air Corps under Generaloberst Lörzer was transferred to Sicily. The airfields of Catania housed five groups from three wings: the 54th Bomb Wing, the 77th Bomb Wing, and the 1st Training and Demonstration Wing. The 12th Squadron of the 1st Training and Demonstration Wing, employed as a strategic reconnaissance unit, was based at Barce and Derna and was under the direct control of the Senior Aviation Officer for Africa, Generalmajor Stefan Fröhlich.

The main mission of the 2nd Air Corps main objective was to soften up Malta's defenses as a prelude to invasion. An airborne assault on the island fortress—"England's best aircraft carrier"—was planned for early 1942. Oberst Deichmann, the chief of staff of the 2nd Air Corps, prepared a detailed attack plan which, though greeted with initial skepticism, was eventually accepted. The air offensive against Malta began on 20 March 1942 and, for the first time, attacks were made in squadron or even group formations instead of by small formations or even lone aircraft. A new type of bomb, the PC-1000, was employed against the island's hardened defenses. The PC-1000 was capable of piercing the roof of virtually any concrete emplacement.

✠

After the conquest of Crete and prior to the offensive against Malta, other targets in the Eastern Mediterranean had assumed a position of prime importance, especially the Suez Canal and the airfields along the vital supply line from Suez past Port Said to Alexandria. These long-range flights were often at the very limits of the Ju-88s endurance. Accurate dead-reckoning navigation, then the basis for all long-range flights, was of vital importance if the aircraft were to return to their bases. Radio bearings were a valuable aid in navigation, however, they had to be used with caution in the extreme conditions of the Mediterranean.

On the morning of 11 May 1942 five Ju-88s of the 1st Group of the 1st Training and Demonstration Wing took off on a maritime reconnaissance sortie. The aircraft fanned out over the Eastern Mediterranean. Suddenly, there was excitement aboard the commander's aircraft. A British destroyer unit had been sighted between Tobruk and Crete. It was made up of the destroyers *Jervis*, *Kipling*, *Jackal*, and *Lively*. Commanded by Captain A. L. Poland, the destroyers had sailed from Alexandria and were bound for Malta.

The 1st Training and Demonstration Wing immediately received orders to attack. The 1st Group, which had established a new base at Heraklion airfield in Crete, was already at a high state of readiness. The wing headquarters and the 2nd Group, based at Eleusis, were at normal three-hour readiness. The first attack by 1st Group with fifteen aircraft went in at approximately 1400 hours. The ships zigzagged and put up a heavy anti-aircraft barrage and no hits were scored. Immediately after the alarm was sounded Hauptmann Helbig drove back to Eleusis from a 10th Air Corps briefing at Kefissia near Athens. From there he flew to Heraklion.

The second wave of twenty-two aircraft under the command of Major Gerhard Kolle had attacked at 1800 hours, likewise without success. At about the same time Hauptmann Helbig was taking off from Heraklion with seven aircraft of his 1st Group. He had selected the unit's best crews to accompany him, veteran flyers like Oberleutnant Iro Alk, Oberleutnant Backhaus, Leutnant Brenner, and Oberfeldwebel Leupert. Soon they reached the British warships, which were accompanied by Beaufort torpedo bombers operating as long-range fighters.

The seven Ju-88s dived toward the destroyers from out of the already setting sun. In the space of ten minutes, they succeeded in sinking three of the modem vessels. Helbig selected the *Kipling* as his target. His bombs struck the destroyer amidships. The other bombers attacked the remaining destroyers. *Jackal* was hit several times. Attempts were made to tow the crippled vessel to a friendly port, however, it sank the next day. Captain Poland was forced to retire to Alexandria with only one destroyer left, the *Jervis*, from his original force.

Joachim Helbig had already been awarded the Oak Leaves on 31 January 1942 after his run of spectacular successes. The day after sinking the three destroyers, Helbig's unit received a large, well-packed box. The sender: "The Commander-in-Chief of the 2nd Air Force, Kesselring." The Generalfeldmarschall (Field Marshal) had sent the successful group a crate of twenty bottles of sparkling wine. Helbig's four bombs had sunk the flag destroyer *Kipling*. A German submarine fished one of the vessel's life preservers from the sea, and it was later presented to Helbig. It was given a place of honor in his command post, where it was hung over the map of the Mediterranean.

The German Armed Forces daily report of Wednesday, 13 May 1942 declared:

> The successful attack against British destroyers in the waters south of Crete reported in yesterday's report by the Wehrmacht High Command was carried out by a formation led by Oak Leaves recipient Hauptmann Helbig. Hauptmann Helbig himself bombed and sank one of the enemy destroyers.

The sinking of the three British destroyers in mid-May 1942, the scattering of a convoy in June and, finally, the destruction of a whole series of strongpoints and forts in North Africa came to be attributed to the "Helbig Flyers." Helbig and his men gained a fearsome reputation in the English press, which gave the impression that there was little chance of escape against these pilots and their commander.

It was said of the attack on the three destroyers that it was one of the worst ever experienced by British warships. Survivors from the sunken destroyers were picked up and taken to Alexandria. There they described to correspondents the tremendous accuracy of the unit that had attacked them and the helplessness of their fast vessels, in spite of the fact that they had had the support of British aircraft. In fact, two of the Beaufort torpedo bombers accompanying the destroyers had been shot down by the Ju-88s. For the first time the expression "Helbig Flyers" was used to refer to Helbig's group. Later, this nickname was even used by Churchill.

British antiaircraft defenses and fighters had failed to destroy Helbig and his group. Later, the British formed a special unit with just this task in mind. Following the events at Dieppe, the 2nd Air Force in Rome received word from agents that British special forces were going to be used against German air bases in the Mediterranean. These operations would

Evaluating reconnaissance photos. Helbig is second from right. Beside him wearing the white peaked cap is his gunner, Franz Schlund.

be timed to coincide with the sailing of British supply convoys from Egypt to Malta.

Helbig and his group had been transferred to Heraklion to counter those convoys. The group was then moved to Derna for a time so as to be closer to the convoy route. On the first night at Derna, however, the base was attacked by a British commando unit. By attacking at night and taking advantage of the element of surprise, the British hoped to be able to blow up the German bombers on the ground. However, the British unit was spotted by the German troops guarding the airfield and was engaged before it could do any damage.

The 1st Group of the 1st Training and Demonstration Wing flew two missions the following day, both of which were successful. After debriefing, at about 2300 hours, the group's crews made their way to their quarters. Helbig gave the sentries special instructions, as he expected a surprise attack again. Shortly after midnight, a small group of British bombers attacked the airfield. The 88-mm Flak opened fire on the intruders. About five to ten minutes later the sentries and the officers at the wing command post, which was located on the airfield perimeter, heard several small explosions.

At first they thought that the explosions were caused by small delayed-action bombs from the earlier attack, but this error was soon clarified. It was found that sixteen of the aircraft of the 1st Group, 1st Training and Demonstration Wing, which were parked in blast pens, had suffered considerable damage from explosive charges placed at their wing roots. The British special raiding force had scored its first success.

Hitler was furious and ordered an official investigation. The Luftwaffe's chief military judge arrived in Crete aboard a Ju-52. Once again, the old saying that "shit rolls downhill" was to prove true. In this case the one to get shat upon was the group commander, Jochen Helbig. The affair ended to no one's satisfaction, even though Helbig had pointed out the inadequacies of the existing security measures in February 1942.

While in Crete the military judge fell victim to pappadachi fever, which was common on the island. The fortress commander and his senior aide were relieved from duty. Helbig was supposed to be put on trial. Generalfeldmarschall Albert Kesselring did not set up an investigating commission, but he held a grudge against Helbig over the affair until the end of the war. Ten days after the raid three followers of de Gaulle and a Greek interpreter were captured in the nearby mountains. They had participated in the operation. They were subsequently brought before a German military court. However, the leader of the raiding party, an English major, had made good his escape, setting off from the south coast of Crete in an inflatable boat and subsequently being picked up by a waiting submarine. He arrived safely in Egypt and was decorated for his actions.

Not until 1971, during a visit with his former landlord, a lawyer named Michaeltakis, did Helbig learn some of the details concerning the commando raid on Crete. The raiding party had been spotted by crews just returned from a mission while on their way to the command post. In the darkness they identified them as persons in German tropical uniforms, assuming they were personnel of the field maintenance unit.

Helbig brought his group back up to strength in a very short time.

✠

The spring and summer months of 1942 were a very demanding time for every flyer in the Mediterranean Theatre, but it was the bomber crews who faced the most trying situations. Time and time again they had to fly difficult day and night missions at the very limits of their aircraft's endurance.

The embattled fortress of Tobruk, bitterly defended by the enemy, had to be softened up by bombing. Losses were heavy. For ten nights in a row, Helbig and his men set off from Crete for Tobruk. These missions lasted four to five hours, and the flight to and from the target was an overwater one with all its added risks. The aircraft carried a full load of fuel and bombs, often exceeding the maximum takeoff weight of 14,500 kilograms and often barely managing to get off the ground.

Concurrent with the Tobruk raids in the first half of 1942 were the nonstop attacks on Malta. Operation Hercules, the invasion of the island, had not yet been written off. The bomber crews were also called upon to support cargo ships sailing the supply route from Italy to Africa by searching for submarines of the British Malta Flotilla (the 10th Submarine Flotilla under Commander Wanklyn).

✠

In these difficult times Helbig was a tower of strength. His black hair did not go gray, his flashing eyes were not dimmed. During the pre-mission briefings he was always composed and deliberate. The following is a typical example of such a briefing:

Course Alex (the German air crews' name for Alexandria). No problems; wind the same as yesterday. No cloud cover; antiaircraft fire the same as yesterday. Obviously there will be night fighters there as well. Approach at 1,000 meters and dive on the target like yesterday. After pulling out alternate left and right turns until out of the antiaircraft zone. Time hack . . . that is all!

✠

In June 1942 the Royal Navy initiated a major fleet action in the Western Mediterranean in support of a supply convoy bound for Malta. It committed aircraft carriers and about forty warships of all types. Part of the German response was attacks by bomber units, including those of the 1st Training and Demonstration Wing, then based on Sardinia. The German air forces attacked constantly for two days and three nights and sank twenty-two of the convoy's twenty-four cargo vessels. The bomber force had achieved its primary mission in the summer of 1942. The shortest sea route between England and Egypt had been completely disrupted, while air and sea forces safeguarded Axis supply traffic from Italy to Africa.

THE "HELBIG FLYERS" DURING ROMMEL'S DRIVE ON EGYPT

On 21 January 21 Generaloberst (Colonel General) Rommel launched his new offensive toward the east; his initial objective was the recapture of Cyrenaica but his long-range goal was the Nile and Cairo. When the offensive began, Helbig and his men were constantly in action. Their objective was to deny the enemy supplies through the systematic destruction of his supply traffic. In addition, the advance through the desert by Panzer Group Africa had to be supported by timely dive-bombing attacks.

Helbig's Ju-88s were in action constantly, attacking enemy forces wherever they tried to stop and make a stand in the desert. The "Helbig Flyers" played a prominent role at Tobruk and Sollum, on the battlefield at Acroma and especially at Bir Hacheim, Sidi Barrani and Marsa Matruk. Erwin Rommel once said to Oberst Fritz Bayerlein, his chief of staff, that the success of the offensive would have been in doubt without the help of the dive-bombers. "In particular, the desert fortress of Tobruk would not have surrendered to us within twenty-four hours" (Fritz Bayerlein to the author).

During the assault on Tobruk, Joachim Helbig was one of the few to bomb the heavily defended desert fortress on ten consecutive nights. Taking off from Heraklion, Helbig flew against Tobruk until only he and his crew were left. For ten consecutive nights Helbig flew two missions a night to Tobruk. The effort exacted a great toll on him and his crew, for each mission lasted four to four-and-a-half hours, with the Ju-88 operating at its maximum allowable takeoff weight of 14,500 kilograms. Often the Ju-88 came back with antiaircraft-fire damage.

It is no wonder then that the number of available crews dwindled rapidly. Some were lost to fatigue and exhaustion, others to the "little malaria"—pappadachi fever—which lasted "only" three days. When the men reported for duty in spite of the fever—which was the rule—they were dismissed by Helbig and assigned to bed rest. The welfare of his men was always uppermost in Helbig's mind. That these measures caused displeasure among those "above" did not bother him. Helbig said in that regard: "I can only use crews who are in top shape. Anyone else will only end up as a loss report and I can't do that to the men or the ground crews."

Helbig attributed the fact that he alone remained healthy and ready for action to a recipe that he developed and continued to use after the war: "Every morning I drink two straight shots of Raki, a Greek liquor, on an empty stomach. My devoted Greek landlord has kept me well supplied with it through the years."

Helbig had another recipe for good health:

I tested this system on my long-range night flights of eight to nine hours over the Mediterranean, which I knew well and where I felt at home, for example to Haifa, Port Said, Suez and Alexandria. I also used it on missions from Catania to Suez with an intermediate landing on Rhodos. I forbade any noise in the aircraft: No talking, not even music from the radio. At my favorite altitude of about 4,000 meters I trimmed the aircraft, pumped the fuel tanks serving the engines full of fuel and lay back in my seat for at least an hour of rest. This procedure worked especially well with a four-man crew, one of whom always had to keep a lookout as "officer of the watch."

Joachim Helbig was not reckless by nature, but what man would never "feel his oats?" Here is an example. At the end of one of his "milk runs," Helbig provided ample proof of his ability to concentrate by shutting down one of the aircraft's engines for the last part of the flight and the landing, no easy feat in a Ju-88.

In the beginning these single-engine landings caused concern and anger among those on the ground. The maintenance personnel assumed that there was something wrong with the aircraft. The rescue personnel readied their vehicles at the edge of the runway and positioned an ambulance to pick up possibly wounded crewmembers.

When, after completing his landing, Helbig turned the aircraft and taxied toward the firefighting vehicles, he switched on the second engine, waved to the perplexed men with a friendly smile and rolled on to the squadron area. After leaving the aircraft, Helbig sat down to enjoy breakfast, his favorite meal. Not surprisingly, these antics resulted in warnings and, on one occasion, even a "dressing down with a threatening undertone," but it didn't seem to bother Helbig. The ground crew and mechanics were appeased with several bottles of wine.

It was universally acknowledged that Helbig was a terrific pilot, and that was why he was assigned the most difficult missions. But when he took command of a group doubts were expressed from many sides as to whether he would also be able to lead. Within a very short time all doubts were soon scattered like chaff in the wind. As a group commander, Helbig proved that as addition to being a gifted pilot he was an exemplary leader, with the welfare of his men at heart. He always weighed his chances before ordering his men to attack.

It was Helbig who set the standard, and he only asked of his men that which he was ready to do and had already done himself. His entire bearing had a positive effect on his group.

✠

The evening of 30 August 30 found Panzer Army Africa bogged down in front of Alam Halfa. After resuming its advance, the army had driven through an extensive minefield, which cost the life of Generalmajor (Brigadier General) von Bismarck and resulted in the wounding of General Nehring and General Kleemann. The Ju-88s were called in again to help break the deadlock.

✠

The "Helbig Flyers" were in the air constantly. By late 1942 Helbig had flown 450 combat missions.

✠

When the Allies dispatched another major convoy with supplies for Malta, the "Helbig Flyers" were committed against it. Codenamed "Pedestal," the convoy passed through the Strait of Gibraltar from 10–15

The crew of a Ju-88 A-4 at Eleusis, Greece, during operations to bomb Leros, 1943. J. V. CROW COLLECTION

August. It consisted of thirteen transport ships and a tanker guarded by four cruisers and eleven destroyers. The covering naval group included two battleships (*Nelson* and *Rodney*), four aircraft carriers (*Victorious, Indomitable, Eagle,* and *Furious*), three cruisers and fourteen destroyers. The fleet was capable of putting up a massive antiaircraft barrage against attacking aircraft.

German-Italian reconnaissance aircraft kept track of the convoy's position. U-73 commanded by *Kapitänleutnant* (Lieutenant) Rosenbaum sank the carrier *Eagle* and, on the evening of 11 August, the "Helbig Flyers" and He-111 units attacked. The fleet's antiaircraft fire repelled the attack. A second attack by nineteen Ju-88s was made the next morning, followed at noon by a third attack by thirty-seven Ju-88s. Six aircraft were lost in the morning attack.

On the morning of 13 August Jochen Helbig's men finally penetrated the curtain of antiaircraft fire. Helbig attacked the 8,982-ton freighter *Glenorchy,* which was loaded with munitions. Huge explosions tore the ship apart and it sank immediately.

The pitiless convoy battle, which claimed heavy losses on both sides, raged on until 15 August when what was left of the convoy—four merchant ships—finally sailed into Malta. It was the end of September. The total weight of enemy shipping sunk by Helbig's group then stood at 200,000 tons. His was the most successful Luftwaffe unit in the Mediterranean.

FAILED TO RETURN

At various times the Luftwaffe employed seven wings in the Mediterranean area. Some of the elite among German aviators were lost there. Such was the case of the crew of a Ju-88 that sustained damage in an attack on a heavily-defended convoy in the Eastern Mediterranean and was forced to ditch. The crew drifted in a life raft for three nights and two days, surviving on emergency rations dropped by fellow aviators. High seas prevented the air-sea rescue flying boat from landing to pick up the crew. When, after two days, the flying boat was finally able to land, all that was found was an empty life raft. The crew had apparently drowned.

The lost crew was that of Knight's Cross recipient Leutnant Brenner. Another member of the 1st Training and Demonstration Wing, he had flown more than 250,000 kilometers—equal to 150 times around the globe—in the course of numerous combat missions. In the end, however, he was claimed by the Mediterranean.

After successfully supporting Rommel's offensive in the summer of 1942 and the sinking of 180,000 ton of enemy shipping in the Mediterranean, Joachim Helbig became the 20th member of the German Armed Forces to receive the Knight's Cross with Oak Leaves and Swords on 28 September 1942. By then he had flown 330 combat missions. Helbig was one of only four bomber pilots to receive this decoration, the others being Baumbach, Peltz and Hogebach. In addition to the decoration, Helbig was given an early promotion to the rank of Major for bravery in the face of the enemy.

Joachim Helbig took off with eight machines of his group to attack the Cairo airfield. He and his men knew all too well what the situation was. The English, who had halted the German advance in front of El Alamein, were now obviously preparing to take the offensive. Their attack could not stop this offensive, but it could make things more difficult for the English.

As they flew over the Quattara Depression, which was being held by Paratrooper Brigade Ramcke, fog began to restrict visibility. By the time they reached the Nile, the fog had completely obscured their view of the ground. "It looks like we're out of luck today. If this dense cloud holds, we'll never find the airfield," declared Helbig, furious over their bad luck.

They had loaded their aircraft full of fuel and bombs and, with a takeoff weight exceeding 14,000 kilograms, had barely managed to get airborne. If they had to scrub the mission at that point, all that fuel would have been wasted. Unlike the Allies, every drop of fuel had to count, even at that stage of the war.

When one of the squadron commanders suggested turning back, the group commander replied: "We'll fly on . . . perhaps we'll get lucky." Then, a few kilometers from the target, the cloud deck suddenly dissipated. The moonlight was so bright that they could make out clearly every feature of the terrain below. Then the tower at Heliopolis airfield came into view, shining brightly in the moonlight.

"The airfield lights are on, sir," reported Schlund.

"It's a regular torchlight parade," observed the flight engineer. The airfield appeared to be crowded with aircraft. It looked as if British bombers were preparing to take off on a mission, probably against targets at El Alamein and in the German rear.

"All group aircraft! Two aircraft release their 250-kilo bombs over the airfield. The others attack the hangars and tower with the 1,000-kilo bombs as discussed. I'll take the apron in front of the hangars. There are several bombers sitting there."

The bombers were already in attack position when the antiaircraft fire began. Diving at 55 degrees, they plunged toward the airfield. Surprise was complete. Helbig swooped down on the apron. He dropped his two heavy bombs right on target. As he climbed away from the target he could see and hear the bombs dropped by the others exploding. There was a cascade of fire as the runway and taxiway were torn up by the 250-kilo bombs.

"Fires in ten, no twelve places! Now I see sixteen fires," reported Schlund as they turned and climbed westward, toward the sea and away from the antiaircraft fire. Four large fires were still visible from fifty kilometers as the attackers returned to base. Then two munitions dumps and several aircraft exploded in flames.

"That was a complete success!" Helbig called over the radio. All aircraft returned safely to base.

THE "HELBIG FLYERS" IN OPERATION TORCH

On 8 November 1942 the Western Allies landed more than 100,000 men at three places on the Northwest African coast near Safi, Mehadia and Fedhala. The German reaction to Operation "Torch" was to commit the Luftwaffe together with submarines in an attempt to hinder the landings or at least interfere with subsequent landings.

Several submarines were successful against the array of vessels involved in the landings or lying at anchor. U-130 commanded by *Kapitänleutnant* Kals sank three large transports and U-173 under *Kapitän zur See* (Captain) Schweichel accounted for a cargo ship. U-515, commanded by *Kapitänleutnant* Werner Henke, sent the depot ship *Hecla* to the bottom and torpedoed the destroyer *Marne* after several attempts.

The greatest success in terms of tonnage was scored by U-143 under the command of *Oberleutnant zur See* (Lieutenant Junior Grade) Poel, which sank the 20,107-ton troop transport *Warwick Castle*. Commander Piening of U-155 sank the carrier *Avenger* and the 11,279-ton troop transport *Ettrick* and torpedoed another transport. Further enemy ships were accounted for by other U-boats. Nevertheless, the handful of submarines in the area could never have effectively engaged such a huge convoy on their own. The convoy had sailed in three large columns with a multitude of escort ships.

✠

The Ju-88s of the 1st Training and Demonstration Wing went into action. Led by its commanding officer, Helbig's group attacked the ships wherever they were sighted. Off the Algerian coast Helbig scored three direct hits on a 10,000-ton transport, probably the US ship *Leedstown*. Loaded to the gunwales with munitions, the ship exploded in a towering cascade of flame.

The Ju-88s flew missions deep into enemy territory lasting four to six hours. Enemy searchlights and radar tried to track the bombers for their night fighters. Over the target the Ju-88s were met by heavy antiaircraft fire. On occasion, the bombers were intercepted by night fighters; escape depended on luck, flying skill and concentrated defensive fire. Long return flights in damaged aircraft were not uncommon. The return flight over the sea imposed a great mental strain on the crews; if they came down in the water there was little hope of rescue.

Joachim Helbig made further dive-bombing attacks on enemy ships off Bougie and Algiers and sank two of them, the *Karanja* and *Glenfinlas*. He was subsequently banned from flying combat missions; Göring and Hitler imposed the ban on all officers who had won the Swords in order to preserve them and their leadership qualities for the training schools and to use them as wing commanders.

When Helbig was banned from further flying, his total tonnage of enemy shipping sunk stood at approximately 180,000 tons. This included an auxiliary cruiser and two modern destroyers. He had also damaged other ships in attacks on Mediterranean ports and convoys bound for Malta and Alexandria. It should be mentioned that submarine captains usually received the Knight's Cross for sinking 100,000 tons of enemy shipping and the Oak leaves for 180,000 tons. Helbig's antishipping sorties were only *part* of his activities as a bomber pilot.

During the period lasting from 6 November to 25 December 1942, the 2nd Air Corps, to which the 1st Training and Demonstration Wing belonged, lost 201 crews in attacks on the Allied landing fleet. Under these conditions further operations were insupportable.

Joachim Helbig was forced to bid farewell to Heraklion, his home base, and his "flyers." It was January 1943 when he shook hands with his old comrades for the last time before leaving for Berlin to report to Reichsmarschall Göring before assuming his new position on the staff of the inspector general of the bomber forces. During a discussion with General of Fighters Peltz in January 1943 he was promised the job of inspector of bomber forces engaged against the Western Allies. In March 1943 Helbig received an early promotion to Oberstleutnant (Lieutenant Colonel) for bravery in the face of the enemy.

✠

Like all the other frontline officers condemned to staff work, Helbig saw first hand the often totally inadequate work done by the various command posts of the Luftwaffe, which were filled with officers completely blind to the situation at the front. He was soon having loud disagreements with senior commanders, right up to Field Marshals von Richthofen and Kesselring.

Helbig asked for a return to operational duties, as he had no wish to take part in the constant wrangling over weapons and personnel any longer. After his first brief but cordial visit with Göring, Helbig came straight to the point on his second visit to Karinhall, Göring's residence. He related directly to the Reichsmarschall all the failings and shortcomings he had identified, a topic which was a sore point with Göring. The result was a heated argument. Sparks flew and Helbig did not hold back, listing all his negative experiences. He later recalled that Göring jumped to his feet like a madman in response. Not surprisingly, he was blacklisted by Göring and transferred to the inactive officer pool.

Also responsible for this degradation was Generalfeldmarschall Wolfram Freiherr von Richthofen, at the time Commander-in-Chief of the 2nd

Air Force in Italy. Several incidents had taken place in Richthofen's area of command that had been justifiably denounced by Helbig.

A successful flyer like Helbig, one who was respected by his men as well as his former superiors for his great skill as a pilot, was not going to be left idle for long, however. With the 1st Training and Demonstration Wing leaderless following the death of its wing commander in the crash of a Fieseler Storch while on a reconnaissance flight, Helbig's old wing was withdrawn from operations for the first time in its history and was transferred to Wiener Neustadt in Austria to rest and refit. The wing had suffered catastrophic losses on Sicily and in Southern Italy after the Allied invasion, leaving it incapable of conducting operations. This gave Helbig cause to denounce the faulty decisions taken there.

A Ju-88 of the 1st Squadron at Aviano, Italy, February 1944. Note the distinctive "wave mirror" camouflage. J. V. Crow Collection

Joachim Helbig then went personally to the Chief of the Personnel office of the Luftwaffe and asked to be placed in command of his old wing, which he knew like no other. At first the request was flatly refused. He suggested that giving him the wing would be tantamount to a demotion, as he was being considered for the position of Inspector General of Bomber Forces.

Helbig made it clear that it was not a question of rank as far as he was concerned. He used honeyed words on the general. But the general could and would not see that Helbig's sure grasp of the overall situation and his intimate knowledge of the wing were solid reasons for him to give him command of his old formation.

If the wing were expected to regain its former high level of proficiency then a man like Helbig had to be placed at its head. This was the view expressed by group commanders and squadron commanders in letters to the Luftwaffe Personnel Office. All of this would have availed Helbig nothing, however, if someone who had previously sent him into a holding pattern had not reappeared on the scene.

When the Luftwaffe High Command announced that the 1st Training and Demonstration Wing was to be disbanded, it was Generalfeldmarschall von Richthofen—who had previously contributed to having Helbig sacked—openly admitted that he had been wrong in this regard and energetically called for the preservation of the wing and the return of Helbig as its commander:

I am convinced of the great significance of this wing to the conduct of the air war on the Southern Front and I am certain that there is no worthier commander than Helbig, whom I hereby recommend for early promotion to Oberst.

In mid-August Joachim Helbig became the new wing commander of the 1st Training and Demonstration Wing. He immediately began work to again make this battered bomber unit into a homogenous and effective instrument of air power within the shortest possible time. Helbig threw all his abilities and the force of his personality into the balance; his efforts received the support of every man of the wing—from the group commanders to every last member of the ground crews.

And so, after overcoming numerous obstacles, Joachim Helbig returned to the Mediterranean as wing commander of his beloved the 1st Training and Demonstration Wing in August 1943. He was to lead the wing longer than any other commander.

ACTION IN THE BALKANS—THE INVASION OF LEROS

Following a brief period of rest and refitting and the addition of a third group—the 3rd Group of the 1st Training and Demonstration Wing—there began a "new era" for the wing under Helbig's command. The wing first saw action in the Balkans and participated in the recapture of the island of Leros together with the army and navy. This was the first true amphibious operation carried out by the German Armed Forces. Its objective, the Island of Leros, was occupied by 2,300 English and 5,350 Italian troops. The island threatened to become "a second Malta in the Mediterranean."

As the men of the German Coastal Light Infantry Battalion (Special Forces) went ashore early on the morning of 12 November 1943, the Ju-88s of Helbig's wing attacked the main enemy positions. Enemy artillery positions that were holding up the landings were dive-bombed and put out of action. The Ju-88s aided the advance by the assault troops and paved the way for a drop by paratroopers. Sorties were flown against the British 8th Destroyer Flotilla commanded by Captain Thomas and the destroyer *Dulverton* was sunk. Attacks were carried out against a further British destroyer group during the night of 15 November, preventing the destruction of German supply ships.

Monte Meraviglia, the center of the enemy defenses, was bombed three times at noon on 15 November. Afterwards the mountain was stormed by paratroopers, the special forces personnel and the men of the 16th and 65th Infantry Regiments of the 22nd Infantry Division. By the evening of 16 November Leros was in German hands. Taken prisoner were 200 English officers and 2,000 soldiers, as well as 300 Italian officers and 5,000 men. The "Helbig Flyers" had played a major role in this victory.

AT ANZIO-NETTUNO AND OVER THE ITALIAN FRONT

After the successful invasion of Leros, the pace of operations picked up and, when the situation at the Anzio bridgehead became critical, Oberst Helbig received orders to intervene with his unit. On 21 February 1944 Helbig received orders to move his wing to the Anzio front in daylight. For his inexperienced pilots this was as good as a death sentence. The same applied to the ground personnel, who were among the best there was. They were supposed to be flown from Greece to Italy in Ju-52 transport aircraft and ancient Italian Savoia-Marchetti transport aircraft.

Acting contrary to orders, Helbig postponed the move by fifteen hours. He flew ahead to the new base of operations with his experienced crew, the unit operations officer, his maintenance officer and a staff clerk—seven men aboard a Ju-88. The weather was poor and the entire flight was made on instruments, proof of the correctness of his decision.

In Italy Joachim Helbig formed Combat Formation Helbig by combining his battered groups and those elements of the 76th Bomb Wing still based in the Po Plain. This combined formation was under the direct command of Generalfeldmarschall von Richthofen.

Helbig continued to participate in combat missions flown by his wing. His adjutants and officers took care of the paperwork, allowing him to devote his time to operational flying. As a result of his efforts, the 1st Training and Demonstration Wing was able to operate effectively, even in this difficult area of operations. It helped prevent a breakout from the beachhead by U.S. troops until mid-May 1944.

The "Helbig Flyers" repeatedly came to the fore in the ongoing fighting of May 1944. Two large-scale night raids were flown against two enemy airfields on the east coast of Corsica. Both missions inflicted major damage on the enemy. After the bombers left, huge fires could be seen from the mainland, visible proof of their success. Both attacks were mentioned in the Wehrmacht daily report of 13 May 1944.

The 1st Training and Demonstration Wing enjoyed further success in the weeks and months that followed. Missions against Anzio-Nettuno aimed at destroying supplies stockpiled there were successful, as were dive-bombing attacks on Naples harbor and roadstead, where supply ships were hit and sunk. By this time Combat Formation Helbig was as well known as the "Helbig Flyers." In the fighting near Valmontone, in the area southwest of Velletri, in the Giugliano Valley and near Ceprano, Helbig's bomber unit was able to halt the enemy's advance and prevented the shattered German lines from being overrun. On 28 May Joachim Helbig was mentioned in the Wehrmacht daily report:

Bomber units under the command of Oberstleutnant Helbig distinguished themselves in the fighting on the Italian Front.

During the defensive struggle in Italy, Helbig experienced one of the most painful moments in his career as a pilot. His veteran Ju-88— L1 + AM—was destroyed in a raid by American heavy bombers on Pordenone airfield in the Po Plain. He had flown the aircraft for more than three years, amassing more than 1,000 hours of flight time.

Senior commands, for example Luftwaffe Command Southeast (*Luftwaffenkommando Südost*), tried on a number of occasions to claim Helbig's unit for themselves. The commander of the bombing offensive against

England and the IX Air Corps applied to have the 1st Training and Demonstration Wing placed under their command, claiming that the wing was badly needed in France.

On 6 June, right after returning from a night mission, the 1st Training and Demonstration Wing was ordered to transfer to Belgium for operations over the invasion front. As there was an intense low-pressure area over Southern France and because the movement of the wing on the first day of the invasion would have resulted in a disaster at the hands of the swarms of Allied fighters operating in the area, Helbig postponed the movement.

Early the next morning Helbig, who had got no sleep that night, flew ahead to the unit's new base in Belgium. The 2nd Air Force accused the wing commander of disobeying orders, which could have resulted in a demotion for Helbig or possibly worse. Helbig summoned his wing as soon as the low-pressure area over Southern France dissipated. It arrived in Belgium at dusk without losing a single machine.

The court martial proceedings against Helbig, which had already begun, were dropped. It was shown that his actions had been of decisive importance in preserving the wing and its operational readiness. It was at that time that Helbig received the promotion to the rank of Oberst that Generalfeldmarschall von Richthofen had proposed some time earlier. The wing achieved a measure of success in the fighting against the invasion fleet, but losses were extremely heavy. Every attack by the handful of German bombers was met by swarms of Allied fighters.

On 10 September 1944 Oberst Helbig received orders to form a new Combat Formation. He was sent a Stuka group and a reconnaissance squadron to join his own wing in the new formation. The Combat Formation command post was established in Cologne. Its mission was to support German ground forces in their defensive struggle against American armored divisions driving toward the German border near Aachen.

On his first visit to the Stuka group at Vogelsang airfield in the Eifel Mountains, Helbig's car was strafed by enemy aircraft. Machine-gun bullets and cannon rounds riddled the car before it could reach cover. The driver and Helbig's adjutant were wounded. Helbig was also badly wounded and was forced to enter hospital for some time.

During Helbig's absence the formation was led by Oberstleutnant Hallensleben, the wing commander of the 2nd Bomb Wing. The latter was a recipient of the Knight's Cross, which he had received on 5 November 1943 while serving as the wing commander of the 76th Bomb Wing. Hallensleben was killed in action near Leipheim on 16 April 1945.

When Helbig returned from hospital he once again assumed command of the Combat Formation, which consisted mainly of the 1st Training and Demonstration Wing and elements of the 200th Bomb Wing. His command post was located at Schwerin/Zippendorf. Helbig had come full circle, for it was there that he had begun his military career.

✠

On 30 April 1945 Oberst Helbig was summoned to the command post of the 4th Air Division commanded by Generalmajor Franz Reuß. There he learned details of a special mission that was being planned. At least ten prominent members of the German government, people from Hitler's inner circle, were to be flown out of Berlin in Fieseler Storch aircraft. The commander of the 4th Air Division explained: "The formation will overfly the Russian lines west of Berlin through a selected narrow corridor with limited or no Russian antiaircraft defenses. It will land in Berlin-Wannsee, where the persons will be waiting. The aircraft can return directly the same night."

Generalmajor Reuß did not order Helbig to lead the formation, but the latter immediately declared himself willing to take on the mission: "I will assume responsibility for leading the mission, sir. But the planned take-off time is too early. We cannot expect moonlight until after 2300 hours and we need it in order to reach our objective. I therefore suggest that we take off right after midnight."

"Agreed, Helbig," replied the General.

This mission appealed to the Oberst, who had successfully carried out so many special operations. At midnight nine Fieseler Storch aircraft stood ready. The pilots had received their instructions and, at 2402 hours, Joachim Helbig took off on his most spectacular mission. It was rumored that the Führer and Eva Braun and the Goebbels family were among those who were to be flown out of Berlin.

The flight went off smoothly. They found the gap in the Russian defenses. "We fluttered through, low to the ground. We saw the flashes of the besieging artillery as well as the rounds impacting in the city." Helbig's Storch was the first one through the gap, followed closely by the others. They reached Lake Wann and circled over Berlin-Wannsee waiting for the agreed-upon light signal from the east shore.

Cursing to himself, Helbig looked at his aircraft's clock and saw that time was quickly running out. An hour had already passed and there was still no sign of life. As they circled the pilots could clearly see the approach roads and several streets that branched off from them, but there was no sign of a column of vehicles or anything else. Helbig suspected that the breakout attempt by the affected persons and their arrival at the Lake Wann Station must have gone wrong. He did not know, however, that Hitler and his wife as well as Dr. Goebbels and his entire family were already dead. When he approached the Lake Wann Station, Russian anti-aircraft guns opened fire on the Storch. Helbig turned away. The station was obviously already in Russian hands and the surrounding buildings were burning, set afire by Russian rounds.

With fuel running low, Helbig gave the designated signal to return to base. The aircraft landed safely at Schwerin at first light. The operation had been a failure.

On 2 May Helbig flew the same Storch back to his unit at Schleswig.

By this time Helbig had flown 350 combat missions. Because many of them had lasted more than six hours, a total of 480 missions were entered in his logbook.

✠

On 4 May 1945 Oberst Helbig was forced to leave his wing on orders from the Luftwaffe command. He had been selected to serve as a courier and fly to senior command staffs located in Czechoslovakia with secret orders. Helbig was able to reach those formations, which included an army headquarters, deliver his reports and, following his instructions, depart early on the evening of 8 May 1945, the day of the German surrender.

Helbig flew west until a lack of fuel forced him down. He was taken prisoner by the Americans who took him to Camp Senne, where he was interrogated several times. Helbig's treatment at the hands of the Americans was less than proper and he decided to escape.

On 9 June he succeeded with the help of an American officer who knew of his record and who accorded him all due respect—one soldier to another. Eventually, he returned to public life as a civilian. With all his customary energy, he built a new civilian existence from nothing and rose to become the manager of a well-known brewery in Berlin.

Heinz Bär accumulated 221 victories and won the Knight's Cross with Oak Leaves and Swords.

Heinz Bär:
With the 51st Fighter Wing
in the West and East

HOW ONE BECOMES A FIGHTER PILOT

In his youth Heinz Bär was what one would call a wild, crazy youngster, ready to engage in any prank. When he was twelve years old, he and several schoolmates took apart a wagon belonging to a farmer who had chased them from his turnip field. The boys had been trying to steal a few turnips to supplement their families' meager diet. During the night they lifted the parts onto the roof of the farmhouse using a block and tackle and there reassembled the wagon. The farmer was more than a little amazed when he suddenly found the wagon for which he had been so feverishly searching on the roof of the house.

When the same farmer refused to knuckle under and, on one occasion, even set his two dogs on the "turnip thief," a new plot was dreamed up. They removed one wing of the large barn door, dragged it to the village pond and placed two dozen of the farmer's hens on it. They then pushed the door out into the middle of the pond and anchored it there. The wild cackling of the hens and the crowing of the rooster soon woke the farmer. As he had no boat, he had to use a large zinc bathtub in his rescue attempt. The youths had anticipated this, however, and had bored a few small holes in the tub. By the time he had reached the middle of the pond, the farmer was soaking wet, much to the amusement of the youths, who were watching from behind some willows. From then on their turnip harvest was assured.

In the beginning, Bär had wanted to become a forester. Everything associated with the forests and wildlife interested him, but soon he discovered his love for all things technical. At school young Heinz, whom everyone called "Pritzl," developed an interest in aviation. He knew the names of the first balloonists and glider pilots and he watched with enthusiasm and astonishment as the new Luftwaffe appeared majestically in the skies over Germany.

The sight of the first Junkers transport aircraft in the skies of Germany convinced him that he would become an aviator, and he worked tirelessly toward this goal. His time came in 1935. Bär joined the Luftwaffe and passed all the training courses needed to obtain his pilot's certificate. During his training his superiors noted his iron discipline and his "loose tongue," though he was never offensive.

Bär's compact, powerful form and broad shoulders soon became a well-known sight. His large head with its bright, greenish eyes always bore an alert and calculating expression. Compared to his short legs, his arms were relatively long. He was physically strong and knew how to use this strength sensibly. He seemed to live up to his name, which meant "bear" in German. Many assumed that Bär was an easygoing and good-natured fellow. This was true up to a certain point, but when the line was crossed for Bär, the fun ended and offence was taken.

When pushed too far he was quite capable of taking matters into his hands, giving his opposite number a sound thrashing. Bär was a good-natured young man, but one capable of defending himself with his tongue and his fists to preserve his dignity and self-respect. An expression was soon coined referring to Bär: "Bär always hits what he shoots at!"

This expression became his motto. While a squadron commander in Russia, Bär became involved in an argument with the commander of the airfield's Flak (antiaircraft guns) over the shooting down of an enemy aircraft. The Major claimed the kill for himself and declared to Bär:

"It's true I saw you fire at this enemy aircraft, but then we brought him down."

"Mistake, big mistake!" countered Bär. "Bär always hits what he shoots at, you must realize that, sir!"

The Major relented. "Very well, Bär, it was you! Perhaps we damaged him, but you have the kill."

"Thank you, sir," replied Bär, conciliatory after he had got what he wanted.

Afterward Bär's victory claims were never disputed, for the word had got around: "When Bär fires, one of them goes down!"

THE 51ST FIGHTER WING:
ITS FORMATION, COMMANDERS, AND AIRMEN

When the commander of the Werneuchen Flying School, Oberst Theo Osterkamp, Knight of the Order of the Pour le Merite, was handed an official report by fighter instructor Cuno Wendt on an August morning in 1939, he had no way of knowing that it would fundamentally change his life. Osterkamp read the text: "Effective immediately, Oberst Osterkamp is to take over the 51st Fighter Wing as its commander. Site of formation is Lüttenheide."

Osterkamp's reaction: He threw his arms around his adjutant and shouted, "Hurray! Cuno, we're getting out of here!"

The next day Osterkamp took his leave of Werneuchen. He left fighter instructors Lützow, Wilcke, Roeders and Wendt behind, but he assured them he would soon see them again in his new unit.

A brief description of the formative days of this wing is appropriate, for it was this wing which made Mölders great and which allowed Heinz Bär to follow in his footsteps. At first the 51st Fighter Wing existed only on paper. It had to be created from the ground up. Osterkamp assembled a group of World War One veterans to serve in the wing headquarters, but when he arrived at Lüttenheide the wing still lacked everything. There were no pilots, officers or aircraft. All that Osterkamp and his staff had to deal with was paper: Activation orders, personnel orders, logistics orders, counter-orders, and secret and top-secret command matters. Theoretically, he was in command of the wing headquarters and three groups, each with three squadrons. Each group was supposed to have thirty-six aircraft, for a total strength of 108. In addition, there were wing and group headquarters flights. The wing thus possessed a total of 120 aircraft.

The 1st Group of the 51st Fighter Wing, which already existed, was not long in arriving at Lottenheide. The wing's 2nd Group was formed from the 2nd Squadron of the 71st Fighter Wing. The 1st Group of the 20th Fighter Wing arrived to become the 3rd Group of the 51st Fighter Wing, bringing the wing up to strength.

In January 1940 Oberst Osterkamp still had available only eighty-four Bf-109s. The number of operational machines was about seventy-five percent (sixty-three aircraft). At the beginning of 1940 the wing was based at the following airfields:

1st Group: Hocholt (Hauptmann Hrustelin)
2nd Group: Platlüne near Lingen (Hauptmann Handrick)
3rd Group: Höninghardt near Alpen (Hauptmann Trautloft)

The unit's pilots came from existing wings or were sent from the fighter schools.

As soon as daylight arrived, the wing headquarters staff set to work in Osterkamp's command post. The focal point of the command post was a large map, which was divided into quadrants. One morning the squadron

commanded by Oberleutnant Oesau was on standby alert. The air obser-
vation post at Hocholt sounded the alarm: "Enemy reconnaissance aircraft
east of Hocholt. Course south, height 3,500 meters."

Two minutes later the alert *Kette*—a formation of three to five aircraft—
whose pilots had been at cockpit readiness, took off. The small formation
was led by Hauptmann Trautloft and included the young Leutnant, "Pips"
Priller. When the Messerschmitts returned, Priller flew low over the field,
rocking his wings. "Pips" had scored the wing's first victory.

Initially the 51st Fighter Wing was the sole fighter unit under the command of the 2nd Air Force, which was commanded by General Kesselring.
When the German invasion of France and the Low Countries began on 5
May 1940, the 51st was given the task of providing air cover for the paratroopers during their airborne assault on Fortress Holland. However, the
wing lacked the resources needed to carry out its mission.

Just prior to the invasion, one of the wing's Bf-109s shot down the
Focke-Wulf 58 of the commander of fighters, Generalmajor von Döring, in
error. Luckily, no one was seriously hurt; the general escaped with a bullet
in his buttocks, while his adjutant, Hauptmann Harnekow, was hit in the
head by shrapnel. The incident had no repercussions for Oberst
Osterkamp. Indeed, one commonly heard remark at the time was:
"Osterkamp wants to become the commander of the fighter branch. He's
having everyone who outranks him shot down."

✠

Feldwebel Bär was on hand when all three groups took off to attack
Dutch airfields on the morning of 10 May. He flew in the 51st's 1st Group,
whose objective was Rotterdam. The next day Oberst Osterkamp shot
down his first enemy aircraft of the Second World War. After landing
Uncle Theo was carried across the field and there was sparkling wine to
celebrate the commander's success.

The wing soon moved from its pre-invasion base at Bönninghardt to
Eindhoven. In the days that followed, the wing's Messerschmitts flew escort
for Stuka dive-bombers. There was an encounter with enemy fighters and
Oberleutnant Philipp and his wingman each shot down a Hurricane.
Oberleutnant Oesau accounted for a third.

The German advance through France proceeded quickly. At the end of
May there were bitter aerial engagements over Dunkirk with an opponent
who had committed everything to bring his troops home from France. In

the first day of fighting over Dunkirk, Theo Osterkamp shot down three enemy aircraft: a Blenheim, a Hurricane and the first Spitfire.

✠

It was time to prepare for the coming air engagements over England. Oberst Osterkamp went to the Channel Coast and set up his command post at Wissant. When he returned he found that a squadron of British fighters had strafed the airfield. A pursuing Messerschmitt followed the British fighters and reported their position. Oberst Osterkamp committed every available aircraft. A glance at his watch showed him that the enemy must have just landed. They were probably refueling. That was reason enough to pay them a return visit.

His orders: "Attack the airfield, Trautloft! If there are no ground defenses, land!"

The 1st Group was first over the concealed enemy base, which was discovered thanks to the keen eyes of "Pips" Priller. Priller shot down an enemy fighter waiting to land and then the Messerschmitts roared over the airfield. The guns of the Bf-109s set ablaze the administration building and a number of aircraft.

Feldwebel Bär participated in the surprise strafing attack, which left two Hurricanes burning on the landing strip. A further eight British fighters lined up at their dispersal area were likewise destroyed. On the other side of the field, four Breguets and a Potez went up in flames. When all potential resistance had been eliminated, Trautloft and his headquarters flight landed. The rest of the group followed. The German pilots were shocked when they saw the antiaircraft guns on the airfield. Fortunately, the defenders had not had a chance to use them.

✠

The next base for the wing was Liegescourt. The second phase of the campaign against France had begun. On 12 June 1940 the wing received orders to escort the He-111s of the 27th Bomber Wing, which were going to attack military installations and airfields around Paris. All three groups took off for Paris on the morning of 13 June. The bombing by the He-111s was accurate. All the enemy aircraft that appeared in the sky were shot down or driven off. When the level bombers had finished, a Stuka group attacked.

Heinz Bär and his squadron raced over a crowded airfield. He took aim at the reconnaissance aircraft and fighters and opened fire with cannon and machine guns. As the Messerschmitts flew away they left behind fires and explosions. On the way home, east of Paris, there were several engagements with enemy aircraft. It looked like an entire wing of French fighters, but they had little chance against the Bf-109 E. Twenty-two French fighters were shot down; German losses were eight bombers and five fighters. The next day the wing moved to Buc airfield near Versailles.

Osterkamp pointed out the senselessness of the destruction wrought the day before when he remarked: "Yesterday, we wrecked all the airfields. Today, we're sitting in the rubble. Yesterday, the Stukas destroyed modern factories; today, we might need them. Yesterday, power stations and waterworks were our targets, and today we don't know what we're supposed to do without water and electricity."

✠

Heinz Bär was awarded the Iron Cross, Second Class at this time for his actions in the fighting in Western Europe. While the victory celebrations were going on in Paris, Oberst Osterkamp was hard at work at Le Touquet on the Channel Coast, laying down the necessary lines of communication together with the wing's signals unit under Hauptmann Hülsen and Oberleutnant Bredt. A backup command post was set up in Wissant on Cap Gris Nez. As it had a direct line to the radar stations on the coast, Oberst Osterkamp moved in there with his staff.

When all the groups had arrived, Theo Osterkamp summoned all the unit commanders for a conference: "For the time being, our wing is alone here on the coast," he told the assembled officers. Then he outlined frankly the difficulty of the situation: "Our opponent is the English fighter pilot, who is well known as a good fighter. You are to avoid uncertain chances and limit yourselves to really good attack opportunities. You will exploit your advantage quickly and then withdraw just as quickly. Everyone is to be kept together. Instead of individual successes by the more gifted pilots, the squadron, the entire group must be brought to the objective. And now, gentlemen, good luck in our fight against the noblemen!"

✠

The next day all of the 51st Fighter Wing flew over England for the first time in the Second World War. Flying at a height of 5,500 meters, the

Bf-109s penetrated as far as the Thames Estuary. Through their headsets, the Germans heard the voices of the British fighter controllers:

"Attention, bandits! Avoid combat! Do not attack!"

The wing operation came to nothing. Combat was limited to a few minor skirmishes south of London. In spite of this failed effort, the wing's tally of enemy aircraft destroyed stood at more than 150, which included aircraft shot down in the skies over France as well as those destroyed on the ground.

Reichsmarschall Göring arrived for a conference at the headquarters of the military commander of Holland, General Christiansen. Everyone was astonished to see that the "fat one" had donned a full-dress uniform for the occasion. Göring informed those present that the Führer had instructed him "to smash England with my Luftwaffe." However, Göring was shocked when he learned that the operational strength of the 2nd Air Force under General Kesselring and the 3rd Air Force under General Sperrle was no more than 700 combat aircraft. Dismayed, he murmured: "Is this my Luftwaffe?"

✠

The aerial engagements over England and the Channel developed into a costly struggle for the 51st Fighter Wing. The initial skirmishes cost the wing five airframes in return for six enemy aircraft shot down. Several days later, however, the unit claimed a major success: fourteen "kills" without loss. The wing's tally then stood at 175 victories against only 29 of its own machines lost. Albert Kesselring came to the Channel and informed "Uncle" Theo that Hitler had promoted him to Generalmajor for bravery in the face of the enemy. Then, only three days later, a thunderbolt struck the wing in the form of a Teletype from the personnel office in Berlin: "Hauptmann Mölders is to take over the wing effective immediately. Generalmajor Osterkamp is to place himself at the disposal of the 2nd Air Force."

Theo Osterkamp knew Mölders well. As his best pilot, he had sent him from Werl to the Condor Legion. Werner Mölders lived up to Osterkamp's expectations: He emerged as the top scoring German pilot in Spain and became the first member of the Luftwaffe to win the Knight's Cross. Together with Mölders, Generalmajor Osterkamp stepped before the assembled wing to say goodbye. His words were something akin to a bequest to all flyers, but especially to the men of the 51st:

If perhaps the time comes when you face an overpowering enemy and are at the point of despair before your impossible mission, then remember that fate has also given you the most beautiful thing it can give a free man: To become what all of you here before me today are. To continue to be where I have been with you: Closest to the sun as fighter pilots.

Osterkamp had a long personal discussion with Mölders in which he tried to pass on to the younger man who was taking his place his thoughts on the fight against England. The next day Mölders led his wing over England for the first time. Mölder's aircraft was shot up, but he managed to reach his airfield. The wing commander subsequently spent four weeks in hospital.

It was a reprieve for Oberst Osterkamp. He took off with his wing again on 13 July 1940 and shot down an enemy aircraft, his last. One of the blades of Osterkamp's propeller was holed during the engagement but, fortunately, it had little effect on the aircraft's performance.

By the time Osterkamp left the Channel, eight fighter wings had arrived there, as well as three long-range fighter wings. These fighter forces were concentrated under the control of the fighter commanders of the 2nd and 3rd Air Forces, Oberst Junck and Generalmajor Theo Osterkamp.

But back to the 51st Fighter Wing and especially to Unteroffizier Heinz Bär. As a member of the 1st Squadron, Bär had flown in some of the missions described earlier. The following is a description of Bär's activities in the period from the beginning of the war to the Battle of Britain.

UNTEROFFIZIER HEINZ BÄR IN ACTION

At the beginning of the war, Heinz Bär and his squadron saw action while patrolling Germany's western frontier. During one of these flights he found himself facing a French Morane fighter. It was 25 September 1939. Bär saw his first great opportunity. He turned toward the enemy aircraft, approached the Morane head on and held his course with iron determination. About 200 meters in front of him the French pilot pulled up and, at the same instant, Bär fired. The burst was on target and the enemy aircraft began to smoke. The Morane rolled onto its back and turned sharply. It then rolled horizontal again and raced away.

Bär's superior speed soon placed him behind the enemy aircraft. His second burst struck the Morane's left wing, which suddenly broke away and fluttered to earth like a dry leaf in the wind. Bär saw no one leave the aircraft. What had happened to the pilot? The Morane spun toward the earth and finally struck the ground in a flash of flame. There was no parachute visible.

✠

"Well done, Bär," called one of his squadron comrades. "That was your first!"

Back at the base Bär received a severe dressing down for breaking formation, but then the group commander made the following good-natured remark: "At least you got him. Congratulations!"

Heinz Bär had joined the phalanx of young pilots who scored their first victories in the early months of the war. Bär later recalled:

After several more "pleasure flights" to France, always with a warm welcome from the French air defenses, we arrived at the frontline airfields near Calais. France had been defeated and its airfields were at our disposal. The battle against England began.

✠

Bär was again in the thick of the action. He had been named a flight leader (*Schwarmführer*), a position he held throughout the Battle of Britain. During the Battle of Britain Bär shot down his next five enemy aircraft and was considered one of the group's rising stars.

Once, while over England with his flight, Bär and his men were bounced by nine Spitfires over Ashford. The enemy fighters opened fire on Bär and his wingman.

"Look out, Pritzl, behind you!" warned his wingman.

Bär instinctively pulled his aircraft into a steep, climbing turn. As he looked back he saw the enemy aircraft that had attacked him skid to the right. Bär completed the steep turn and positioning himself behind the Spitfire. The Spitfire could not match the speed of this maneuver by Bär. He opened fire and set the enemy aircraft on fire. Bär followed the Spitfire as it descended, preparing to administer the coup de grace and prevent it from carrying out a forced landing. Bär later recalled the rest of the engagement to his crew chief:

> I looked in the rearview mirror and suddenly saw all eight enemy aircraft on my tail. Tracers flashed by my crate to the left and right. Then my aircraft was hit. The damned English were using me for target practice and their aim was pretty good. My right wing was already riddled with bullet holes and the left one wasn't much better. Why those fellows concentrated on my wings and not the fuselage or cockpit, I do not know. But one Spitfire after another tried its luck and I wallowed back and forth in an effort to evade their bursts.

Bär had meanwhile descended to about two-dozen meters above the sea when, suddenly, a Spitfire appeared on his right flank and opened fire. Bullets smashed the Messerschmitt's instrument panel. Then the motor sputtered several times and finally stopped. Bär trimmed the aircraft and soon the Bf-109 pancaked on the surface of the water.

Bär jettisoned the canopy and climbed out. He pulled the ring cord and inflated his life vest. Although it was midsummer, the water was ice cold. Turning round as he swam away, Bär saw the fin of his Bf-109 disappearing beneath the water like a shark's. Feldwebel Bär was picked up by a He-59 of the recently formed Cherbourg Air/Sea Rescue Detachment. He returned to his group that evening, where he received a loud reception. He was forced to tell his story. After Bär mentioned the cold water, the group commander declared: "There are supposed to be two currents in the Channel, one warm and one cold."

Bär replied laconically: "Then I must have come down in the cold one, sir."

Later, after ending up "in the drink" a second time, Bär came back to the question of warm and cold currents in the Channel. He declared: "Obviously, I always land in the cold one."

✠

During a subsequent mission over England, Bär once again became involved with a superior number of enemy fighters that had scrambled to intercept the approaching German bombers and their escort. Bär saw that one of the Spitfires had latched onto his wingman's tail. The English pilot had already shot a large hole in the tail surfaces of his pilot's Bf-109 and

Joachim Müncheberg was Bär's wing commander in Africa.

was preparing to finish him off. The opposing fighters swung back and forth, both trying to reach a favorable firing position, but each time one opened fire, the other managed to escape the decisive burst.

Then, with his friend in an apparently hopeless position, Bär rolled halfway to the left and dove on the enemy fighter from behind. Before the English pilot could react, the Messerschmitt was on his tail and had opened fire. A stream of coolant vapor appeared behind the Spitfire. Faced with an imminent engine failure, the RAF pilot would have to bail out. Bär pulled alongside the crippled Spitfire. The English pilot raised his hand. His flight suit was smeared with blood and he gestured downward as a sign that he had also been wounded in the legs.

Obviously, he was too badly wounded to take to his parachute. Bär indicated to the English pilot that he should turn and fly east. The Spitfire turned and headed toward the coast of France; the stream of coolant thinned and then stopped. Bär and his wingman escorted the British fighter to their airfield at Calais and landed with him.

Alerted by radio, an ambulance was standing by. The British flight lieutenant shook Bär's hand. The latter had his ground crew chief fetch a bottle of cognac, which the English pilot took with him to the hospital with best wishes from the man who had bested him in combat. This was one of the many facets that distinguished Bär as an uncut diamond: He was one of those who gave a defeated enemy a chance to survive. Soon afterward, he was awarded the Iron Cross, First Class.

✠

Heinz Bär proved to be a born storyteller. While the pilots sat at readiness he regaled them with tales of his youth. Usually there wasn't a dry eye left when he was finished. A favorite story concerned a goat that had a penchant for eating from his family's vegetable garden. He played such a trick on the unruly animal and its owner that it never came back again.

Pritzl painted the goat's horns and beard red and drew thick black rings around its eyes. When the goat's owner saw the animal marked in this way and bleating loudly, it was the last straw.

✠

After his brief period as a prisoner of war in France—shot down near Compiegne on 5 June 1940—Werner Mölders assumed command of the 51st Fighter Wing on the Western Front on 27 July. Mölders immediately recognized Heinz Bär's potential:

> This young pilot has something that can make him one of the best. He is a fighter, a daredevil, but one who won't sell his hide cheaply. He has the eye and the piloting skill needed to make a proper fighter pilot.

From that point on, Mölders kept a critical eye on Bär. Bär had this to say about Mölders, whom his men called "Daddy" in spite of his twenty-seven years and who was only a week older than Bär:

> He was a man of the people, an example in regards to upbringing and courage. He became more than my revered mentor. We all tried to emulate him. He cared for us like a father and told us

everything we needed to know to become good fighter pilots like him: That was Werner Mölders. He was unquestionably one of the co-authors of the tactical doctrine of the modern fighter arm, even though Adolf Galland had similar qualities.

By the time Bär shot down his twentieth enemy aircraft in the West, he was one of the rising stars of the fighter arm.

WAR IN RUSSIA: BÄR'S STAR ASCENDANT

On 22 June 1941 Werner Mölders, wing commander of the 51st, became the second member of the German Armed Forces to be awarded the Knight's Cross with Oak Leaves. The wing had been in action from the first days of the Second World War.

By the end of June, Oberfeldwebel Bär had raised his victory total to twenty-seven and was promoted to Leutnant for bravery in the face of the enemy. On 2 July 1941 he received the Knight's Cross. As the days passed he rose nearer to the top of the list of the wing's aces.

The men around Mölders competed with their commander for victories. Before he was forced to leave his wing to take over the post of Inspector General of Fighter Forces, on 15 July 1941, Mölders raised his victory total from 73 to 101 in Russia. Bär also scored at a torrid pace and reached 60 victories by 14 August. Each day he returned from combat and waggled his wings as a signal to those on the ground that he had scored a kill. On 10 August he made two passes over the airfield and waggled his wings five times. This success was cause for a raucous celebration.

In the next four days Bär shot down six more enemy aircraft and his total of sixty victories placed him among the leading scorers. He became the 31st recipient of the Oak Leaves. Earlier, on 13 July, Bär had been named commander of the 12th Squadron by "Daddy" Mölders. He replaced Oberleutnant Gottfried Nordmann, who received the Oak Leaves on 1 August 1941 and was then assigned to other duties. Heinz Bär and his squadron became a well-known feature of the Eastern Front. Bär fought tirelessly. He was the first man off the ground when his squadron took off after the enemy and the last one to land.

THE RACE TO THE SWORDS

It was September 1941. In the fields behind the front, the harvest had not been brought in and the wheat rotted on the stalk. The 12th Squadron was on standby alert. The pilots sat in their deck chairs in the dispersal area while the mechanics finished preparing the aircraft for operations. Seven of the squadron's machines were reported operational. Standing on a wing of the most easterly aircraft in the lineup was the lookout. All of a sudden, he began waving both arms and the loudspeaker came to life: "Enemy fighters approaching!"

"Let's go, men. Simply follow me and you'll shoot something down too!" declared Bär good-naturedly. He raced to his aircraft and climbed in. A member of the ground crew helped fasten his parachute harness.

"Good luck, sir!" said the mechanic.

"Thanks, Tigges. But don't howl if I come back with a few scratches."

"Just as long as you come back, sir."

Bär smiled broadly. "You can count on that!"

The wheel chocks were removed. Bär slowly advanced the throttle lever and the Messerschmitt rolled to the takeoff point. The other six pilots reported that they were ready to go.

"Let's go and get them!"

The sleek fighters raced across the field. Bär was the first to lift off. Climbing steeply, he soon reached 700 meters and, in the distance, saw the Russian aircraft attacking a German column. One after another, trucks went up in flames. German soldiers fled the road to the left and right.

"Attack!" called Bär.

He dived on the low-flying Il-2s and shot down the first Russian on his first pass. The other pilots followed. The enemy aircraft abandoned their attack on the German column and turned away. They tried to escape by climbing, however, their rate of climb was far inferior to that of the German fighters. The seven Bf-109s pursued the heavily armored Soviet aircraft, which twisted and turned trying to escape. Bär shot down two more and his squadron took care of the rest.

When the Messerschmitts returned to base Bär rocked his wings three times as he flew over the squadron area. His mechanic took his forage cap from his head and tossed it into the air. Then he ran to the dispersal area and helped Bär out of his aircraft.

"Far fewer holes this time!" declared Bär.

"Looks that way, sir! Congratulations on your three kills. I'll have the squadron painter paint them on right away."

BEHIND THE LINES DISGUISED AS A RUSSIAN FARMER

A few days later the alarm was again sounded while the 12th Squadron was on strip alert. The Messerschmitts got airborne before the Russian bombers that had been sighted and reported by two Bf-110s reached the German positions. The squadron gained altitude rapidly, and the command post called to inform Bär that both squadrons of the 1st Group would be following immediately. Soon afterward the fighters flew over the front lines. Russian light antiaircraft guns opened fire, but the fighters were too high for them to pose a serious threat. Then they saw the large formation of Russian bombers, flanked by about twenty fighters. Leading the way was a squadron of Il-2 close-support aircraft.

"We'll pass them and swing south in order to attack from out of the sun!" Bär ordered.

As soon as he had given the order, he put his aircraft into a steep turn and headed into the sun, which was in the south. Bär led his squadron into another turn and then dived on the "fat cars," as the German pilots called the bombers, from directly out of the sun.

The Russian pilots still appeared oblivious to the presence of the Messerschmitts. The nose of Bär's aircraft was aimed at the first bomber, which grew rapidly in his gun sight. Bär pressed the triggers and the cannon and two machineguns roared, sending several dozen projectiles into the bomber. A jet of flame shot from the aircraft's fuselage; seconds later its right wing dropped and the Soviet aircraft plunged earthward, wrapped in flames. Four further bombers were shot down by the other members of the squadron. The Russian fighters, Ratas and Yaks, intervened and a wild dogfight began.

"Continue to attack the bombers!" ordered Bär. He already had the second in his sights. Two bursts from his guns were enough to set the enemy aircraft ablaze. Three Rata fighters turned and dived toward him. Bär turned and climbed at full throttle, evading the salvo of bullets. He turned, dived on a Rata from directly above and sent it to the ground with a single burst.

Bär's aircraft was hit two or three times in the process. Then a burst from another enemy fighter sawed off part of one of the Bf-109's wingtips. Suddenly, there was an Il-2 on his tail. He had gone too low. This was the first time in his career that Bär had engaged an Il-2 in a dogfight. The enemy pilot made him work and the engagement lasted a full ten minutes.

Bär could hear the calls of his comrades, but they sounded far away. His attention was riveted on his opponent. Bär's breakneck maneuvers allowed him to evade the bursts of fire aimed at him by the Soviet pilot. Then he climbed steeply, turned and came back down. As he raced past the Il-2 at full speed, Bär got off an accurate deflection shot. The burst of fire hit the enemy aircraft broadside. The Il-2's fuel tanks exploded and the blazing wreckage fell to earth.

Bär turned in the direction of home. Then, suddenly, two Russian fighters that had climbed above him during his duel with the Il-2 dived towards him. They hit the Bf-109 on their first pass. Bär heard glass shattering and, suddenly, his windscreen was covered with oil. He smelled a burning odor. His first thought was to get away and head toward the German lines. He allowed his aircraft to spin downwards. When he thought he had given his pursuers the slip, he recovered from the spin and raced lower. It was obvious that he would have to abandon his aircraft. At 300 meters he pulled the lever to jettison the canopy.

Bär placed the Messerschmitt in horizontal flight so as not to be thrown against the tail surfaces when he bailed out. He then released his straps and let himself fall clear. He fell several dozen meters before the parachute opened. The shock as the parachute deployed was painful, but he swung safely toward the earth. Looking west, Bär saw his Bf-109 strike the ground and explode several hundred meters away.

Heinz Bär knew that he was in Russian territory and that they would soon be looking for him. He landed safely and freed himself from his parachute. His first thought was to feel for his pistol. It was there, along with his emergency rations. He then began walking, but not toward the west, for that's where the Russians would look for him first. Instead, he headed south and walked several thousand meters through the bushes and along narrow forest paths.

When he came to a tiny settlement consisting of several huts, Bär veered into a tall field of corn. At first he followed a zigzag course. He then turned due south again, leaving the huts behind him. By his calculations, he had to be more than forty kilometers deep inside enemy territory. His flight map showed him approximately where he was.

Creeping along the edge of a forest, Bär heard the sound of an engine from the direction of a country road he had crossed earlier. He ducked into the forest and watched as a Russian armored vehicle turned straight towards him. Carefully, he withdrew several meters farther into the woods and took cover in a hollow overgrown with blackberry bushes.

The Russian tank came nearer and nearer and stopped a dozen meters from the edge of the woods. The crew climbed out and walked straight toward Bär's hiding place. He played dead, but he had already released the safety on his pistol that was now ready to fire. If need be, he would shoot it out with the four enemy soldiers.

However, there was no need, for the four men had only come to the edge of the forest to relieve themselves. One of the Russians farted loudly and they all laughed. Then they lit their *machorka* cigarettes and began to smoke. The Russians talked among themselves for about five minutes, until the driver, who had stayed behind in the tank, called something to them. Apparently, he had received new orders by radio. The Russians strolled back to their vehicle and, soon afterward, it rumbled back to the country road and disappeared.

Bär dared not leave the woods until it was dark. He had eaten several pieces of chocolate and was feeling thirsty. He set out toward the west, ready to leap into the bushes at the slightest sound. In the middle of the night, he came upon a squat cottage. He crept up to the house and noticed a well some distance from it.

Bär made his way cautiously to the well and began turning the crank to lower the pail into the water. He froze when he heard a noise from inside the cottage and then ducked behind the top part of the well. He waited ten minutes before daring to resume turning the crank. He heard the pail splash into the water. The water made a gurgling sound as it filled the pail. Carefully, he wound the pail back to the top of the well. Bär drank the water, which had a slightly musty taste, in long draughts and poured the rest over his head. Then he dried himself off with his neckerchief and went on his way.

When the sun rose Bär found himself in a small patch of woods in which he had taken cover in a dense thicket. He had hidden himself there at about midnight and fallen asleep. Bär first moved to the edge of the woods to have a look around, using some bushes as cover. He would have to cross several fields unless he wanted to make a huge detour.

Before setting off, Bär stopped by a marshy water hole. He knew that he had to change his appearance in order to avoid immediately being recognized as a German. First he mussed his hair and stuck several pieces of straw in it to make him look as wild as possible. Then he took off his leather jacket, smeared it with mud, and stuffed it with hay so that it looked as if he was carrying something in a rucksack. He packed all his belongings inside and tossed the jacket over his shoulder. His excellent flying boots did not fit the picture. He pulled them off and stowed them inside the jacket. Then he set off. Soon afterward, Bär passed several young girls digging potatoes in a field. They called something to him. Bär simply waved them away and continued on his way.

Bär went out of his way to skirt a Russian column at rest. When noon came he crept into the shadows. He was hungry and thirsty, but he dared not approach the houses that he passed. The enemy was too close; he could hear the sounds of engines and tank tracks. Toward evening the hunger pangs became more intense. He had eaten the last of his emergency rations that morning. In an effort to ease his hunger, he ate several raw potatoes he managed to dig up at the edge of a field. They tasted awful, but at least they helped end the hunger pangs and even quenched his thirst a little.

Barefoot, he continued on his way. Bär came to a stubble field. He was forced to cross it as it was impossible to go around to the left or right. The mild sprain he had suffered in bailing out now began to make itself felt. Not surprising in view of the strenuous march of the last two days. By the time evening came, Bär had covered about twenty-five kilometers by his own calculations and based on the large village he could see a kilometer to his right.

Cautiously, he took several sips of water from a pool at the edge of the woods. It was rather muddy tasting but, apart from that, it was most refreshing after a hot autumn day. Bär bathed his feet in the cool water, wrapped them in pieces of his scarf and then put his socks and boots back on. After one last portion of raw potatoes Bär set off again. By then it was pitch black.

At first he maintained a walking pace. After three kilometers he heard machine-gun fire flare up to his left. He veered slightly to the right but came upon an encamped Soviet unit. Bär returned to his previous course and decided to walk west come what may. Wearing his jacket again, he drew his pistol and slipped past a Russian supply column. Bär's affinity with the forest and his youthful woodsman games were standing him in good stead. He boldly crept past a combat outpost at a distance of fifty meters. When challenged by a sentry, Bär replied with a Russian curse and kept walking. Behind him he heard suppressed laughter.

The last 200 meters he covered by crawling. He passed a Russian machine-gun position and skirted to the left of a zigzag trench. Then he was in no-man's-land. Bär crawled toward the German positions. When challenged and asked for the password, he said in his best Saxon dialect: "Don't make me laugh! I am Oberleutnant Bär of the 12th Squadron of the 51st Fighter Wing, and I have walked forty kilometers in bare feet!"

"That's no Russian, it's a Saxon! . . . All right, come over here, but don't make any suspicious movements or we'll shoot!"

"May I move now?" asked Bär.

"Yes, come on," replied the voice.

Bär rose to a crouch. The German soldiers gasped audibly when they saw what appeared to be a Russian *mushik* wearing a German flight jacket, but then they saw the badges of rank and the Knight's Cross.

"Where did you come from, sir?" asked the Leutnant who was the officer of the guard.

"Direct from the other side. They shot me down three days ago."

"Then you are in fact Bär," declared the Leutnant. "I heard that you were shot down after destroying three of the enemy. When we're relieved we'll take you with us to the battalion. Our commander will call your group so that they can send a vehicle."

"Thank you, Leutnant! And now I have one wish. I need a cup of strong coffee and a few sausage sandwiches. I'm chilled to the bone and have had only raw potatoes to eat and muddy water to drink."

The Leutnant saw to Bär's request and, a half-hour later, the Luftwaffe pilot was in the battalion command post, where he was obliged to repeat his story. Then Major Jürgensen called Bär's group. Hauptmann Joppien, the group commander, was awakened and he shouted for joy when told that Bär was alive.

"Man, Pritzl, you're alive. And we were about to write you off."

Bär replied: "Don't be in any hurry to write me off!"

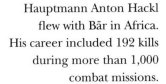

Hauptmann Anton Hackl flew with Bär in Africa. His career included 192 kills during more than 1,000 combat missions.

THE DEATH OF WERNER MÖLDERS

Werner Mölders, who was known to his men as "Daddy," assumed command of the 51st Fighter Wing on 27 July 1940 after following his return from a brief period in French hands as a prisoner of war. Mölders subsequently became the first fighter pilot to record forty victories on 20 September 1940. His sixtieth victory came on 26 February 1941. On 14 July 1941 he became the first fighter pilot in history to reach 101 kills.

The decorations came in rapid succession. Only 14 months separated the awarding of the Knight's Cross on 29 May 1940 and the Diamonds on

16 July 1941 (Mölders was the first member of the armed forces to receive this decoration). Following the awarding of the Diamonds and promotion to the rank of Oberst, Mölders was named Inspector General of the Fighter Forces and had to give up his wing. He was 28 at the time.

His successor as wing commander was Major Friedrich Beckh, who received the Knight's Cross on 18 September 1941. (Beckh was killed in action east of Kharkov on 21 June 1942 while wing commander of the 52nd Fighter Wing. He was posthumously promoted to Oberstleutnant.) Hauptmann Grasser, who himself was a recipient of the Knight's Cross with Oak Leaves, served as Mölders' adjutant during the fighting over the English Channel and Great Britain. His assessment of Mölders is typical:

Mölders was a good-looking man with an unusually firm character and a keen and logical intelligence. He always had an open ear for all of his men. Nevertheless, he insisted on discipline but without harshness. The only thing that made him angry was infringements against battle discipline.

Proof of his outstanding ability as a teacher and instructor lies in his many successful students, of whom Heinz Bär was to become one of the best. Many later admitted that they owed their survival purely to Mölders.

As Inspector General of the Fighter Forces Mölders remained in the East and eventually commanded a close-support air group consisting of Stukas, fighters and fighter-bombers. After the war, Günther Rall described Mölders' activities:

Every morning Mölders flew along the front in his Fieseler Storch. He landed among the infantry at the front and went to the most forward infantry trenches. There he used the radio he had brought with him to direct the activities of his close-support group. He pioneered the method of guiding his unit's aircraft precisely to the enemy positions and coordinating their attacks. In the evening, he flew back and held a commanders' conference. He discussed the day's operations and pointed out errors, but readily acknowledged when we had done it right. Three days before he flew to Udet's funeral he had encountered major problems in the delivery of munitions, fuel and replacement parts for the aircraft. It was his intention to fly to Germany and convince the High Command that the air forces had to be better supplied.

That was the situation when Mölders received news of Udet's death. Göring ordered him and seven other highly decorated aviators to Berlin to make up the guard of honor at the casket of the high-ranking Luftwaffe officer.

The weather was poor on the morning of 22 November 1941 when Mölders took off from Chaplinka airfield in a He-111 flown by Oberleutnant Kolbe. Kolbe had flown in the Condor Legion and enjoyed Mölders' complete trust. The unfavorable weather situation forced Kolbe to land at Lemberg (Lvov). There he tried to convince his passenger that they should not resume the flight that day, as every station between Lemberg and Berlin was reporting poor weather conditions. But Mölders was eager to resume the flight, because he wanted to use the visit to Berlin to get help for his pilots. As soon as the He-111 had been refueled, it took off for Berlin. The He-111 was buffeted by strong headwinds and Kolbe had to use full power to combat them. As they approached the city of Breslau, one of the overworked engines failed. Kolbe descended cautiously, guiding the He-111 through dense cloud toward the airport. The approach was too low and too short. Kolbe attempted to bring the remaining engine to full power, which caused it to fail as well.

Out of the murk there appeared cables which ran next to the airfield. Kolbe managed to clear the cable, but then the He-111 stalled and crashed to the ground. Mölders and Kolbe were killed instantly. The radio operator and Mölders' enlisted assistant were pulled alive from the wreck by those who rushed to the scene of the crash. The survivors were able to relate what had happened on the flight from Lemberg. The last paragraph of the Wehrmacht daily report released at noon on 23 November 1941 declared:

> As announced by the Armed Forces High Command, the Inspector General of the German Fighter Arm, Oberst Mölders, was killed in an airplane crash. The crash involved an aircraft not flown by him.
>
> The Führer has ordered a state funeral for this recipient of the highest decoration for bravery, the Knight's Cross with Oak Leaves, Swords and Diamonds.

Heinz Bär's return was marked by a tumultuous welcome from his comrades. He soon had a new aircraft, on whose tail were painted all of his victories, including the last three. Two days after his return, the injuries to his feet had largely healed and Bär went back into action.

Heinz Bär picked up where he had left off, racking up missions and victories. Multiple kills became more common. The recipient of an early promotion to Hauptmann, he continued to lead his squadron. Bär shot down every enemy aircraft that he encountered. There were LaGG-5s and 116s, Il-2s, and various types of bombers, even an R-5 and an I-153. The number of victory bars on the rudder of his aircraft increased rapidly.

There was a pause after the eightieth victory bar was added; Bär flew to Germany for his first home leave.

✠

It was still winter when he returned to Russia. On 11 February, after taking off from an icy runway, he sighted a formation of Russian fighters flying escort for several bombers. The German retreat from Moscow had begun by then, but it was stopped by Hitler's order to "hold at any price." This preserved the large airfields in the rear for use by the German fighters. From there they rose to intercept Russian bombers attacking the German defense lines.

Such was the case on 11 February 1942. Heinz Bär attacked the formation with only four aircraft. The Messerschmitts attacked the escort first. Bär shot down an I-16 and then turned his attention to a Soviet bomber. The Soviet aircraft sheared out of formation, jettisoned its bombs and headed for home. Bär did not follow. Instead, he dived on the next bomber, which opened fire, hitting the Bf-109. He dived beneath the bombers and then turned and climbed to attack the next one. He fired several bursts at the bomber, but it flew on stubbornly. Bär made a second attack, unconcerned by the enemy fighters, which were occupied with the remaining German fighters. This time his bullets damaged the bomber's tail surfaces and, after his third pass, it plunged to the ground in flames.

The enemy formation then jettisoned its bombs over open country and ran for home. When Bär returned to base he waggled his wings twice, indicating that he had shot down his 89th and 90th enemy aircraft. News of this success was immediately sent to the Luftwaffe High Command by Teletype. On 12 February 1942 the Wehrmacht Daily Report announced:

Hauptmann Bär, squadron commander in a fighter wing, has achieved his eighty-ninth and ninetieth air victories.

✠

On 16 February 1942 Heinz Bär became the seventh German soldier to be decorated with the Knight's Cross with Oak Leaves and Swords. His squadron, his group and especially his two ground crew celebrated with him—he was among the first ten to achieve that high honor.

Major Friedrich Beckh, Mölders' successor, shook his hand and said: "Thank you, Bär, you have done much for the wing."

Immediately afterward Heinz Bär was ordered to go to Führer Headquarters to receive the swords. There he received the coveted decoration from the hand of Adolf Hitler.

IN ACTION WITH THE 77TH FIGHTER WING

When Bär returned to his squadron at the end of March 1942 after receiving the Swords, he immediately threw himself into the bitter defensive struggle being waged by the German forces. Soon afterward, he was named commander of the 1st Group of the 77th Fighter Wing and had to leave his old wing.

Bär's transfer to the 77th was prompted when Hauptmann Ihlefeld, group commander of the that wing's 1st Group, was forced to leave the unit after receiving the Swords on 24 April 1942. Following promotion to Major, Ihlefeld became the wing commander of the 52nd Fighter Group. Bär was instructed to take over Ihlefeld's old unit. Hauptmann Bär attempted to get around this transfer. He wanted to stay with the men he had served his entire career with, but his efforts were in vain. A final order from "the fat one," as Hermann Göring was called by the fighter pilots, sent him on his way to the 77th, which was based in the Crimea.

Bär's arrival resulted in the turbulent operations that led to his 100th victory. On his arrival Bär discovered that his was the only group of the 77th in the Crimea. The 2nd Group was in the Kursk area and the 3rd Group had been transferred to the northern front, where it was to be based in the Krasnogvardeysk until September 1942.

FIVE KILLS IN ONE DAY

In the weeks that followed, Bär continued to fly in spite of a ban. His new group was behind him completely. His ninety-first victory came the day after his arrival at the 1st Group during a test flight. Two more kills followed the next day. When the Russians attacked the airfield where his group was based, Bär took off amid the falling bombs. He quickly closed in on the first enemy aircraft, which had already dropped its bombs and was running for home. The bomber fell to Bär's well-aimed bursts, struck the ground and began to burn. Three minutes later he shot down a second bomber. Setting off after the rest of the formation, which had by turned for home by then, Bär became involved in a duel with one of the escorting Soviet fighters. He soon realized that his opponent was an outstanding pilot. The engagement lasted ten minutes but, in the end, the Soviet fighter was shot down. Bär had raised his victory total to ninety-eight; the date was 18 May 1942.

The nineteenth of May dawned clear and promised plenty of action. Bär and his men took off, formed up and headed toward the front. The ground crews watched the commander's aircraft as it flew away and asked themselves: "Will he reach 100 today?"

However, Bär wasn't thinking about raising his victory tally. His thoughts were on the enemy. Where would he appear and in what numbers would he come? One of his men, who was flying ahead as lookout on account of his phenomenal vision, reported:

"Indians and Fat Autos. Altitude: Approximately 3,500. Range thirty kilometers. They're flying in 'V' formation."

"Break formation! Choose your own targets!" Bär called to his men.

Seconds later he spotted the bombers and, flying ahead of them, several Yaks and other fighters. Then he saw a further group of Red Air Force fighters above the bombers. Tracers flashed toward him. Quickly, he put his aircraft's nose down and the tracers passed overhead, striking nothing but empty air. The first enemy fighter swooped past over Bär's Messerschmitt. He raised the aircraft's nose, fired and let the enemy machine fly through his burst. The volley of bullets and cannon rounds struck the Russian's cockpit and fuselage; the Soviet aircraft plunged earthward in a steep spiral, wrapped in flames.

"Congratulations on your ninety-ninth, sir," called Bär's wingman enthusiastically. Meanwhile, a wild dogfight had developed between the other Messerschmitts and the enemy bombers and their escorts.

Bär then flew towards the bombers. He accelerated, took aim at the first one and pressed the triggers. A hail of rounds struck the enemy machine, which had taken no evasive action whatsoever.

"Number 100, sir!" shouted Bär's wingman. Then came a warning: "On your right, sir!"

Instead of turning to his left and flying into the sights of his opponent, as a beginner might have done, Bär pulled his machine into a steep climb. The Bf-109 nearly reached the vertical as it climbed and then swung about; the burst of fire from the Yak missed to the right. The 20-mm cannon barked and the two machine guns roared as Bär's third victim fell from the sky. The Soviet aircraft struck the ground and its fuel tanks exploded in a brilliant ball of fire. Bär's wingman positioned himself behind an enemy fighter that was stalking the group commander. He shot the Russian down, then roared past his commander's machine, waving and grinning. The aerial engagement was coming to an end. The bombers jettisoned their loads and fled for home. Bär moved toward the trailing bomber as it flew east; in position above and behind him was his wingman.

"You take him, Franz!" Bär called to his faithful wingman. At the same time he rammed his throttle forward against the stop. The Messerschmitt picked up speed and soon he had closed to within about 300 meters of the next Russian bomber.

The front lines appeared before him. He could see puffs of smoke from Russian antiaircraft guns, but they had opened fire too soon. Bär closed to 180 meters and opened fire. The enemy bomber fell from the sky, his fourth kill that day. In a wide, sweeping turn, Bär saw that his wingman had also shot down his bomber. Several parachutes opened above the doomed Soviet machine. He was pleased that the crew had got out; after all, they were aviators as well. As he turned toward home Bär spotted something flashing brightly in the sun far to the north. It had to be an aircraft and, given its course, it was Russian.

"Follow me, Franz!" he called to his wingman. Bär flew a wide semicircle until he was heading north and arrived in a favorable position from which to attack the Soviet reconnaissance aircraft—from an angle of ninety degrees. Bär fired two bursts that raked the enemy aircraft from its cockpit to the middle of the fuselage. The reconnaissance machine stalled and fell away. A further burst caused its right wing to separate from the fuselage, then it plunged vertically toward the earth.

"Number 103, sir!" called Bär's wingman, excitement in his voice. A glance at the fuel gauge showed Bär that it was high time to begin the flight back.

"Head for home," he ordered, and the two fighters set out after the group, which had already set course for base.

When they reached the airfield, wingman Franz gave way to his commander. Bär dropped low over the airfield and rocked his wings. Bär later learned that a crowd had gathered down below on the ground and counted loudly as he waggled his wings: "One, two, three!"

Bär flew over the field, made a wide turn and then flew past again and rocked his aircraft's wings twice more. After taxiing to a stop, Bär opened the canopy and sat still for two or three minutes. His ground crew was standing by but they didn't disturb him until they saw him stretch forward. Then they jumped onto the wing, removed his parachute and helped him out, which wasn't necessary. Bär was as fresh as ever in spite of the tension of five aerial engagements.

"Congratulations, Bär, that was simply terrific. Five kills, that means five times you didn't hesitate," called one of the group officers.

They carried him on their shoulders to the group command post. There a placard was hung around his neck; on it was painted a large number 100. The last zero had been crossed out and replaced with a three. At noon on 20 May 20 the Wehrmacht Daily Report announced:

Hauptmann Bär, group commander in a fighter wing, yesterday achieved air victories 99 to 103. As well, the 77th Fighter Wing raised its number of victories to a total of 2,011.

EAGLE OVER THE DESERT: BÄR WITH THE
77TH FIGHTER WING IN AFRICA

In July 1942 Bär's group and the wing headquarters were sent to the Mediterranean Theater. Bär continued his successful ways in North Africa, although the pace was not as furious as it had been in Russia. Nevertheless, the number of victory bars on the rudder of his aircraft continued to grow, and the unit "artist" had to adopt the practice of one broad bar for every ten kills instead of ten individual bars.

In the Mediterranean area Bär shot down fighters and bombers of the Royal Air Force and the United States Army Air Force, but his favorite targets were the enemy reconnaissance aircraft which sought to locate convoys carrying supplies to the German Africa Corps.

When Heinz Bär went to Africa with his group, he had already shot down more than 100 enemy aircraft. Bär had demonstrated his ability as a unit leader, having commanded a squadron as well as a group. His adjutant, Hauptmann Friedrich Geißhardt, a Knight's Cross recipient since 21 June 1941, took care of most of the paperwork. Nevertheless, as commander of the group, Bär sometimes had to wield a pen instead of the control stick of his fighter, which was not to his taste.

Bär had complete confidence in his squadron commanders. In command of the 1st was Oberleutnant Siegfried Freytag, a Knight's Cross recipient with seventy victories. The 2nd Squadron was commanded by Oberleutnant Thurz; however, Thurz was wounded during an escort mission over Malta soon after arriving in North Africa and was hospitalized. His place was taken by Oberleutnant Laube.

When the group arrived in Africa without ground personnel it was looked after by the ground crews of the Luftwaffe's veteran Africa wing, the 27th Fighter Wing. The "black men" of that wing accepted the added work without complaint as long as there were sufficient fighters to face the enemy, who was growing stronger day by day. On 19 October the Royal Air

Force had opened its great air offensive. Combating the RAF and supporting the German Africa Corps and Panzer Army Africa was the foremost mission of all Luftwaffe units in Africa.

The 28th of October saw the first machines of the second group of the wing, the 77th's 3rd Group, to arrive in Africa. In command of the group was Hauptmann Kurt Ubben, who had been awarded the Oak Leaves on 12 March 1942. The wing then had one other recipient of the Oak Leaves in its ranks in Africa. Eventually, the 2nd Group would join the wing as well. The wing commander, Major Joachim Müncheberg, had previously fought with success against the elite pilots of the RAF over the English Channel.

Hauptmann Huy scored the wing's first victory in Africa on 28 October. On the last leg of the transfer flight from Russia to North Africa, Huy spotted six enemy aircraft attacking a German column as he approached the North African coast. Together with Oberfeldwebel Herbert Kaiser, Huy dived on the enemy and fired a burst into the side of a Curtiss, whose pilot was still unaware of the new threat.

The enemy fighter rolled to the right and went down, exploding in flames on striking the surface of the desert. A second Curtiss was destroyed by Oberfeldwebel Kaiser. Huy then set off in pursuit of the remaining four enemy fighters and shot down another. These were Huy's forty-fifth and

Funeral for Joachim Müncheberg, who died on 23 March 1943 after colliding with a Spitfire on his 500th combat mission.

forty-sixth victories. However, Kaiser had also been hit and he was forced to land at Bir el Abd with his aircraft in flames. He returned to his unit on foot, carrying his parachute and a small suitcase.

Heinz Bär's first combat in North Africa occurred on 30 October. During an engagement over El Alamein, he shot down a Curtiss fighter with three short bursts. Bär and his group received repeated requests to provide fighter escort for Stuka units. One such mission took place in the afternoon of 2 November. The fighters were late and about thirty enemy fighters shot down ten Stukas before Bär and several of his men could intervene. Bär attacked the first enemy fighter from a slightly higher position and shot it down with two bursts from his guns. A minute later he had completed a steep turn and, as he later remarked, "blasted away and let the second enemy have it."

The airfield at Bir el Abd subsequently had to be evacuated when enemy tanks reached its perimeter. The group transferred to El Quotaifiya. That afternoon British fighters and bombers attacked the base, chasing the German pilots into their slit trenches. The British flew over the airfield at a height of only ninety meters and fired at everything that moved.

On 3 November Hitler issued his order to hold at all costs and the flyers had to return to Bir el Abd. There were numerous engagements on 4 November; enemy aircraft attacked the serpentine roads near Fuka and Marsa Matruk, over which rear-echelon units of Panzer Army Africa were retreating.

West of Alamein the German pilots enjoyed great success. The 77th Fighter Wing flew three missions that day. The airfield at Bir el Abd subsequently had to be abandoned for good and Bär's group moved to Haggag el Quasaba. When that airfield and then the next base at El Daba had to be evacuated, Heinz Bär had the following message painted in English on the wall of the dining room:

> "Welcome to El Daba!—Keep everything clean!—
> We'll be coming back!"

Unfortunately, for the Germans, this prediction did not come true.

On 9 November 1942 Major Müncheberg read aloud an order of the day from Reichsmarschall Göring. The Luftwaffe's commander-in-chief blasted his pilots for their lax behavior in Africa and declared that they were not only "slackers, but even cowards."

Bär declared: "Now it's supposed to be our fault that Rommel had to retreat. But we're of a completely different opinion. The blame belongs with those at the very top."

When Müncheberg regained his composure, he said: "My comrades, we'll probably never see Europe again." This prediction came true for Müncheberg, but not for Bär and his men.

✠

The defensive fighting went on. When a Tomahawk successfully evaded attacks by Leutnants Köhler and Brandt, Bär attacked from above and shot it down. When the 1st Group of the 27th Fighter Wing was transferred to Germany, it handed over all of its serviceable aircraft to the 77th. The wing command under Müncheberg set about reorganizing the unit. The wing resumed operations on 17 November 1942, when its 3rd Group shot down several enemy aircraft. All the units of the wing flew from the airfield at the Arco di Fileni with the exception of its 2nd Group, which was based at Nofilia/Merduma. On that day Bär's group possessed a total strength of eighteen Bf-109s. With thirty-five machines the 2nd Group was by far the strongest numerically. The 3rd Group had only seventeen machines.

The 2nd Group had only arrived in Libya on 5 December 1942. Until the beginning of November 1942 it had fought in Russia. From there it had flown to Sicily to Zazur airfield and was led by Hauptmann Mader. Mader's group had scored more than 1,300 victories in Russia and Mader alone had 50. The entire wing, which had fought so bravely in Russia, had arrived in Africa.

✠

An enemy aircraft shot down by Heinz Bär on 19 December 1942 was celebrated as the 1,000th victory of the wing's 1st Group. Then, on 21 December, another highly decorated German pilot presented his credentials by shooting down an enemy aircraft. He was Hauptmann Anton Hackl, who shot down two enemy fighters over the Syrte. Hackl was the commander of the 5th Squadron, which had just arrived at Zazur. On 2 August 2 of that same year Hackl had become the 109th recipient of the Knight's Cross with Oak Leaves.

At the end of 1942 the command structure of the wing was as follows:

Wing Commander: Major Joachim Müncheberg
Commander, 1st Group: Hauptmann Heinz Bär
Commander, 2nd Group: Hauptmann Anton Hackl
Commander, 3rd Group: Hauptmann Kurt Ubben

By this time Bär had already shot down twenty-two enemy aircraft in Africa.

✠

By 5 and 6 January 1943 the situation of the Axis forces in Tunisia had stabilized. Generaloberst von Arnim, commander-in-chief of the 5th Panzer Army, had divided the fronts into four sectors. He told the Armed Force High Command: "The 5th Panzer Army is capable of holding the Tunisian bridgehead by itself. The 5th Light Africa Division can remain with Panzer Army Africa."

✠

The 77th Fighter Wing carried out attacks against the enemy airfield at Hamraiet on 5 and 6 January. Bär destroyed several British fighters and two bombers that were parked there. The attack was repeated on 12 January 1943. Twelve Spitfires that scrambled to intercept the approaching Germans ran into five Bf-109s led by Hauptmann Hackl. Hackl and Leutnant Reinert, one of the top scorers in Africa, each shot down a "Spit" while Oberleutnant Burckhardt accounted for a third.

On another occasion, Major Müncheberg led every available aircraft in a scramble to intercept sixteen Baltimore bombers and their escort of twenty-two fighters. The Baltimores were familiar opponents of the German fighter pilots. In the ensuing dogfight, Hauptmann Bär, Oberleutnant Freytag, and Major Müncheberg each shot down a Baltimore, but it was Anton Hackl who was the star of the day, downing four enemy fighters.

On 14 January Heinz Bär shot down two B-25 medium bombers while Leutnant Berres destroyed a third. Led by Müncheberg, the wing intercepted a second enemy attack that day. Bär fired his guns three times and destroyed three enemy aircraft.

On the afternoon of 19 January there was a turbulent aerial battle against a formation of P-40s flying escort to B-25 bombers. Soon afterward twenty P-38 twin-boomed fighters attacked a German convoy on the coastal road, destroying sixty-five vehicles. Bär, who had stayed behind on account of severe stomach pain, took off with his wingman and raced to the scene of the massacre. The two pilots suddenly sighted about twenty enemy aircraft, which were still busy attacking the road. Bär dived on the enemy fighters, which were much lower. He called to his wingman: "Follow me! Follow me and fire, Franz!" The two Messerschmitts raced through the enemy formation. Bär shot down two from low altitude. Both enemy pilots succeeded in making forced landings but their aircraft caught fire and were destroyed.

The last German troops left Tripoli on 23 January 1943. As they withdrew toward the Tunisian frontier they were pursued hotly by the British Eighth Army. The airspace above the retreating German forces was the scene of bitter engagements, in the course of which Bär shot down an enemy aircraft. The 77th's 1st and 2nd Groups achieved further successes in the period from 25–27 January. Hauptmann Bär was fully involved and shot down his 148th and 149th enemy aircraft. Bär should have received the Diamonds at this point, and he was recommended for the award by Generaloberst von Arnim. However, Göring had heard unfavorable stories about Bär from someone and turned a blind eye to reports of his outstanding achievements.

FROM "SPECIAL DELIVERY II" TO "CAPRI"

The Allied Operation "Special Delivery II" began on 31 January 1943. The commanding officer of the 10th Panzer Division, Generalmajor Wolfgang Fischer, was killed on the second day of the operation when his vehicle ran over a mine, the explosion blowing off both legs and one arm. On 1 February the U.S. Army Air Force undertook five missions into the Sened area in support of its infantry. Stukas of the 3rd Stuka Wing's 3rd Group were intercepted and five Ju-87s were lost in spite of an escort of twelve Bf-109s of the 77th Fighter Wing.

On 3 February the 77th's 1st Group moved to Fatnassa airfield, situated eight kilometers west of Gabes. The base soon became a target for enemy bombers. Ten P-38s of the American 1st Fighter Group were assigned to protect the bombers. The bombers' approach was reported in time for German fighters to get airborne. Bär and Hackl, the first to get off the ground, each destroyed a B-17. Hackl brought down another bomber but was then wounded. His motor began to sputter and emit smoke.

"Get down!" called Bär to his comrade.

Hackl carried out a successful forced landing near Matmata, which saved his life. By then he had shot down fourteen enemy aircraft in North Africa. Soon afterwards he was to receive the Swords. The Americans then raided Gabes airfield with thirty-three bombers escorted by eighteen P-38s. Only three of Bär's pilots got off the ground. Heinz Bär was forced to remain on the ground. That was also reported to Göring, however, the reason behind it was left out.

Bär was there when the Allied airfield at Thelepte was raided on 15 February 1943. Every available aircraft of the 1st Group took part. The Messerschmitts dived out of the sun and silenced the antiaircraft guns

guarding the field. Nevertheless, the attack was not a success. The failure
of the morning rankled Bär, and he had "fire in his belly" that afternoon
when the group returned to Thelepte airfield. In a furious dogfight over
the airfield, Bär shot down two Spitfires.

✠

Leutnant Reinert's star rose rapidly in the fighting over the Mareth
Position. He followed his earlier successes by shooting down a Spitfire over
the Kasserine Pass during Rommel's advance aimed at cutting the enemy's
supply lines. The same afternoon he fought a half-hour engagement with
enemy aircraft in the same area and brought down three more. Leutnant
Berres accounted for two enemy aircraft in the same action.

In spite of his impressive accomplishment of bringing down four
enemy aircraft, Leutnant Reinert was not the hero of the day. Once again,
that distinction fell to Heinz Bär. He engaged enemy aircraft four times
that day. In each of the first three dogfights he downed a Kittyhawk, which
he followed up by shooting down two more in the fourth engagement. Still
he was not rewarded with the Diamonds.

✠

In the first days of March Bär's group fought from the airfield at Fatnassa. The group had been issued the Bf-109 G. The pilots flew multiple
sorties each day, and the airfield was a constant target for enemy bombers.

Before the 77th's 2nd Group moved to La Fauconnierie, Ernst Wilhelm Reinert, the "Africa Ace," shot down a B-26 and two P-38s. It was Bär
who continued to lead the way for the 1st Group, adding a Spitfire to his
list of victories on 1 March. That evening General of Fighter Forces Adolf
Galland arrived unexpectedly at Bär's command post. He was welcomed by
Major Müncheberg, who introduced Pritzl Bär. It was the start of a friendship that was to last beyond the war.

✠

Early on the morning of 3 March Bär shot down the well-known RAF
pilot Flight Sergeant J. D. A. Wright. The British pilot parachuted from his
crippled fighter. Bär then circled the parachute until Wright landed safely.
That same day Fatnassa was attacked three times by Allied bombers. The
first was carried out by B-17s, the second by Baltimores. Five German pilots

were killed and a number of aircraft of the 1st and 3rd Squadrons of the 77th were destroyed in a third attack.

Bär and his group lived from hand to mouth, and he could be pleased if he had six or even seven serviceable aircraft. On Friday, 5 March, the Bf-109s of his group attacked Spitfires escorting bombers of the 1st Squadron of the South African Air Force. In the afternoon eight Spitfires were patrolling the front when they discovered a lone Bf-109 flying west. They immediately attacked this "fleeing" enemy aircraft.

Heinz Bär was the pilot of the Messerschmitt. On sighting the enemy fighters, he pulled back on the stick and climbed steeply. He outmaneuvered them and, diving from out of the sun, Bär then attacked the eight Spitfires. He flashed past the enemy fighters and shot down the Spitfire he had selected as his victim. The British pilot bailed out and the remaining Spitfires fled.

The next day Bär shot down a Kittyhawk that appeared over Gabes. On Sunday, 7 March 1943, Heinz Bär scored his 170th victory. Leutnant Reinert claimed his 130th the same day. That afternoon Hauptmann Bär downed his 171st enemy aircraft.

The wing's hunting grounds were the skies over the southern sector of the Tunisian Front. On 12 March Leutnant Reinert shot down six enemy aircraft in two sorties. When he landed he was met by Bär, who had not taken off on the second sortie.

"Reinert, my heartiest congratulations! You are certainly becoming one of the best. But be careful when attacking from the same altitude. You have several weaknesses when you do that." Bär explained what he meant and Reinert thanked him. Considering the period he had been in action, his 136 victories represented more than just a notable achievement.

Bär was also pleased that Freytag had meanwhile increased his score to eighty-seven victories. Bär knew: If I take part in every mission, the others will rally round me and I will be the shooter. Bär did not want to hog all the glory. He let his less-experienced pilots develop into first-class warriors of their own.

On 13 March a dogfight was conducted above Gabes between the German aces and their first-class opponents, namely thirty-four P-38s of the 57th Fighter Group. Bär was once again successful, as was Reinert, who accounted for two of the American fighters.

✠

Operation "Capri," as the large-scale raid through the Kasserine Pass to Thala was called, began on 6 March. It had to be called off on the afternoon of 8 March. Three days later Feldmarschall Rommel handed overall command in Africa over to Generaloberst von Arnim and flew to Führer Headquarters. There, on 11 March 1943, Hitler presented Rommel with the Knight's Cross with Oak Leaves, Swords and Diamonds. He was the sixth German soldier to receive the decoration.

✠

By 15 March the 77th Fighter Wing had only a handful of operational fighters left. Its bases were bombed several times daily and, when 20 March ended, all of Bär's aircraft had been destroyed or damaged on the ground. Not until 23 March were large-scale operations resumed. That day, Major Müncheberg engaged an outstanding opponent. He finally shot down the American-flown Spitfire, but pieces of flaming wreckage from the stricken machine struck Müncheberg's Bf-109. It crashed, killing Müncheberg.

When Heinz Bär heard of the death of his commanding officer, he turned chalk white. He immediately thought of what Müncheberg had said on 9 November: None of them would see Europe again. For Müncheberg, their eternally optimistic comrade, that gloomy prediction had come true.

THE LAST EIGHT WEEKS

The Allied aerial bombardment of Gabes continued. The 77th Fighter Wing received instructions to fall back to La Fauconnerie by groups. Bär's group was ordered to remain at Fatnassa for the time being. Following Müncheberg's death, the group commanders led their units as separate formations. The staff officers continued to lead what was left of the wing in Müncheberg's spirit, pending the arrival of his replacement. Once, the 1st Group was caught by a bombing attack just as it was about to take off. Two aircraft sustained serious damage and two pilots were injured.

The 26th of March saw British ground forces attacking between Djebel Tebaga and Melab. The wing put all available fighters into the air. When the 2nd Group was forced to return to base on account of fuel, Heinz Bär and his group dove into the fray. In the subsequent dogfight, Bär shot down his 175th enemy aircraft. That afternoon eight Spitfires approached Gabes. They were spotted by Hauptmann Bär, who had taken off alone to watch for enemy aircraft. In a situation that normally would have called for an immediate return to base, Bär did exactly the opposite. He accelerated to maximum speed and roared through the Spitfire formation, shooting down the aircraft of Sergeant Sales. This victory was confirmed without a witness, as the time given in the enemy's account of the loss matched the time reported by Bär to the minute.

The last German fighters at Fatnassa left that afternoon and flew to La Fauconnerie. There the German pilots were met and briefed by the wing headquarters. On Sunday, 28 March, the men of the wing not on watch gathered for a small celebration. All that was left of the unit's meager larder was set out in the officers' mess to celebrate the occasion. Heinz Bär was promoted to Major, while Freytag and Omert got to add a second pip to their boards when they were promoted to Hauptmann. A round of drinks followed and, when asked by an administrative officer, how it felt to be a Major, Bär remarked: "Actually, the same as yesterday, only with a heavier load, like a caterpillar tractor." (He was referring to the braided shoulder boards).

Reinert increased his score on 29 March and again the next day. He shot down two Curtiss fighters and then took on a squadron of A-20 bombers, from which he brought down two.

With the beginning of Operation "Flax" on 5 April 1943, the Allies committed strong fighter and bomber forces. Prior to this, however, Bär shot down several enemy aircraft in the turbulent air fighting of 23 March, including a Warhawk and a Kittyhawk. He also attacked and shot down a straggling B-25. Finding himself under attack from another aircraft from the left, Bär dove away, evading the enemy's fire. He immediately initiated a climbing turn toward his attacker and set the enemy aircraft, a Hawker Hurricane IID, ablaze with two bursts from his guns. The enemy pilot crash-landed his burning machine.

On 24 March Bär spotted two P-40s beneath him. They were flying close together for mutual support and trying to escape to friendly territory. He observed several German fighters circling the enemy aircraft and making unsuccessful firing passes. His anger grew as he watched. Then Bär had had enough. Furious, he shouted over the frequency: "Let me have a go, you idiots!"

The fighter that was next in line sheared off to the left and Pritzl Bär dived on the two Americans at a steep angle. His first burst left the first P-40 in flames and, a minute later, the second exploded in a ball of fire. That was Bär! Only Bär could shoot down an enemy in seconds in such a situation—with his bravado, iron discipline, his good eyes and precisely calculated angle of deflection. When the shamefaced men asked him after landing how he had done it, he merely said:

"You approach boldly, but you still lack one thing: You must do the right thing purely instinctively and do it at the right time."

Further aircraft were lost when the group's base was again attacked by enemy bombers—once again the "stubborn eighteen" of the Baltimore group—and when Sbeitla was bombed during the night of 25 March. The group next saw action when seven Hurricanes of the 6th Squadron were reported attacking German armor in the El Hamma area. Bär attacked with three aircraft and each of them knocked down one of the enemy. The next day enemy bombers continued to seek out the handful of German airfields and bombed the assembly areas used by the German armored forces. This pattern was continued in the days that followed. There simply were not enough fighters available to cope with the enemy's numerical superiority.

Leutnant Berres was shot down on the afternoon of 2 April. He made a safe landing by parachute and made his way back to his group on foot, returning the following morning. This time Bär also let his emotions show, almost hugging Berres on his return.

An attack on La Fauconnerie by the 47th Bomb Group with a fighter escort from the 31st Fighter Group was spotted in time, allowing about twenty Bf-109s to get airborne before the bombers reached the airfield. A number of A-20s were shot down.

On 3 April a Stuka unit, the 3rd Group of the 3rd Stuka Wing, escorted by fourteen Bf-109s, was severely mauled by enemy fighters. The enemy claimed a total of thirteen German aircraft shot down. Captain N. MacDonald and Captain Vinson claimed a total of nine kills between them. Vinson was subsequently shot down by a Bf-109. In the afternoon, while scrambling to intercept an incoming attack, Leutnant Hemmersdorf's aircraft struck one of the stones bordering the strip. The Messerschmitt veered off course and collided with an aircraft of the 3rd Squadron. Both machines went up in flames and Leutnant Hemmersdorf was killed.

Leutnant Reinert showed his best side again on 4 April, shooting down three enemy fighters in four minutes.

Major Bär stayed behind at the command post when the new wing commander, Major Steinhoff, was expected to arrive. Steinhoff did in fact arrive that day and immediately made himself at home by shooting down a Spitfire of the American 52nd Fighter Group.

Johannes Steinhoff was no stranger to the 77th, having served with the wing in 1939. He received the Knight's Cross with Oak Leaves on 2 Sep-

Major Bär inspects a B-17 that
he forced down near Rheine.

tember 1942 while group commander of the 2nd Group of the 52nd
Fighter Wing. Shortly before being leaving Russia to become the wing
commander of the 77th, he shot down his 150th enemy aircraft. On the
morning of 8 April, the 1st Group took off from its new base at La Smala
on a *freie Jagd* (hunt and destroy) mission. Major Steinhoff led a *Schwarm*
as far as the Kairouan area. On their return, the fighters landed at yet
another new base, at Korba north of Nabeul.

On 13 April Bär's badly depleted group received new aircraft. They
were the G6 variant of the Bf-109, each armed with two additional 20-mm
cannon mounted in gondolas beneath the wings. With their increased firepower, they were intended for use against enemy bombers, however, this
modification made the fighter slower and no longer capable of meeting
the fast enemy fighters on even terms. Bär's group spent all of 14 April flying fighter escort missions. It then moved from Korba on the west side of
the Bon Peninsula to Solimane (South).

Following a lengthy hiatus from combat caused by illness and the
"bloody paperwork," Major Bär returned to action. After Leutnant Reinert

downed an enemy aircraft, it was Bär's turn. He pursued a Spitfire that dived away from him. Bär caught up with the enemy machine only a few dozen meters above the sea. The Spitfire began to smoke after the first burst and, after the second, it fell into the sea.

On Monday, 19 April, Leutnant Reinert of the 2nd Group achieved his 150th victory. Major Bär also shot down an enemy aircraft that day.

✠

On the evening of 19 April 19 the British Eighth Army attacked all along the front, focusing its efforts on the southern front near Enfidaville and Fadeloun. It was obvious that the end was near in Tunisia. Earlier Generalmajor von Arnim had asked Generalfeldmarschall Kesselring, who had just arrived at his headquarters: "What chance exists at present of eliminating the enemy troop concentrations with our air force? So far this hasn't happened to a sufficient degree."

Kesselring replied: "What could be done was and is being done. However, the number of enemy concentrations in the various places is so great that engaging them all must lead to a fragmenting of the few forces we have. That will continue to remain the case if several targets have to be attacked simultaneously."

This dialogue was also part of the reason why Reichsmarschall Göring summoned a number of prominent Luftwaffe officers to his residence at Karinhall after the end came in Africa, ostensibly to determine the causes of the Luftwaffe's failure. One of the officers summoned was Heinz Bär.

✠

On Tuesday, 20 April, Bär's group took off from Solimane (South) and became involved in an engagement against a numerically far superior group of enemy aircraft. The entire wing was still in Africa under Major Steinhoff, where it fought alongside the three groups of the 53rd Fighter Wing, the several remaining squadrons of the 27th Fighter Wing, elements of the 2nd Night Fighter Wing, and a handful of heavy fighter and Stuka squadrons. By this time the enemy air forces were able to fly up to 2,500 sorties per day.

Leutnant Berres shot down another enemy aircraft on 22 April, however, the attack by the enemy on the airfield destroyed more of the dwindling stock of German fighters.

Over Bou Arada Major Heinz Bär shot down his last enemy aircraft in Africa. On Easter Weekend, 25 and 26 April, the fighters of the 77th flew on escort and fighter-bomber missions. Steinhoff prepared the wing for the flight back to Sicily, where the wing was to occupy new bases. The first elements of the wing arrived there on 1 May. The rest continued to fight on in the ever-diminishing airspace over Tunisia.

A main body of the wing left Africa on 7 May and, on the morning of the next day, the senior Luftwaffe officer for Africa, General Seidemann, arrived at the wing's command post and declared: "Africa must be evacuated today, Steinhoff! We need you and your aircraft in Sicily." The flight back to Sicily was the wildest the men of the wing had ever experienced. A total of three men were packed into the single-seat Bf-109s. During the flight to Sicily, Ernst Wilhelm Reinert shot down an enemy naval fighter with three men in his Bf-109.

The wing's struggle in Africa was over. It had shot down a total of 333 enemy aircraft there. Heinz Bär's group had accounted for 140 of these. Ernst-Wilhelm Reinert shot down 51 enemy aircraft in Africa. Heinz Bär obtained 39 confirmed kills in the skies over Tunisia. Earlier, in November and December 1942, he had shot down 22 enemy aircraft over Libya. With 61 victories, he was the wing's top scorer in Africa. After Reinert, he was followed by Rudorffer with 27, Schieß with 23, Tonne with 21 and Anton Hafner with 20 victories. Several weeks after the end in Africa Major Heinz Bär was ordered to Karinhall to report to Reichsmarschall Göring.

THE INTERLUDE: HEINZ BÄR AND THE REICHSMARSCHALL

When Heinz Bär reported to the Reichsmarschall at Karinhall, Hermann Göring stared at him silently for a while. Then he came two steps nearer, still gazing fixedly at the highly decorated flyer.

"I must tell you one thing, Bär. You and the rest of the fighter pilots made a mess of things in Africa. You were slack, if not to say, cowardly. According to reports I received, you failed to take part in a number of missions."

"That's correct, sir," replied Bär. "I was sick and should have been relieved. That was also the opinion of the wing flight surgeon. But I remained with my men, because I was better below on the airfield than a replacement commander in the air."

"That's not all, Bär. You didn't trust yourself over water and left the convoy escort missions you feared to others." When he heard that, Heinz Bär, the recipient of the Swords to the Knight's cross and the victor in more than 150 air engagements, blew his top.

"Sir, I have come down in the water twice. I know very well what it means to fly over water."

In Göring's eyes this was open insubordination and the "fat one" immediately leveled another accusation at Bär.

"You left the interception of bombers attacking your airfield to others. You flew missions only reluctantly and . . ."

"Sir, I don't know who gave you this information, but I shot down sixty-one enemy aircraft over Africa. Find someone else apart from Marseille who can say that and I will admit that I was a lazy dog."

"And how was it that bombers and fighters appeared over your airfield and no one approached them?" continued Göring, showing that he had all the tales told to him about Africa.

"There was a wild dogfight over the airfield and none of my men was able to finish off one of the enemy, but they also failed to lose any of their number. Then, in spite of a flying ban issued by the wing flight surgeon, I also took off. In spite of the stomach pain, I called to the people in the air to hold the Tommies until I got there."

"And what was the result, Bär?" asked Göring smugly. "Did you scare off the enemy?"

"I didn't scare them off, sir, but I did shoot down four within ten minutes. Apparently, they didn't tell you that . . . but I have brought you the combat report, sir. It was witnessed by everyone in the wing, all of whom watched from below."

Bär had outfoxed Göring. Nevertheless, the Reichsmarschall wasn't about to let go. He looked down his nose at Bär's Saxon accent. He felt betrayed by his informants and his full fury was directed at Bär.

"But you weren't successful enough! Compared to its success in Russia, only 333 aircraft were shot down by the 77th Fighter Wing in Africa."

"In Russia, sir, the men are based at airfields that are scarcely ever attacked by the enemy. In the last few months in Africa we endured as many as eight attacks each day, and we had to fight our way through an escort of at least thirty to fifty fighters to get at them. Add to that the sandstorms and the mud in Tunisia and the . . ."

"Enough Bär! Those are old wives' tales. You had machines and you were capable of taking off and pursuing the bombers."

"I brought with me the operational strength reports concerning my group, sir. In April, for example, we had a total of seven serviceable aircraft from an authorized strength of twenty-seven."

Then Göring pulled his last trump card from his sleeve: "And why was it that you always took off after your group and then followed them back on the flight home?"

"On many occasions I took off alone when the group was already under way and did not get a chance to fire its guns. When it was time to come home I was obviously the last. I had to do that, sir. The old saying "the devil take the hindmost" also applies to fighters. I was always the last one. As a result, I was able to save my men from the pursuing enemy. That was it!"

Heinz Bär had not gone down on his knees, not even before the Reichsmarschall. He had remained the Bär—the "bear"—everyone knew. He fought his own fights; in this case, they were right on target. It was obvious that this did not please Göring and that Bär could have emerged from the affair better if he had sweet-talked Hermann Göring—but that was Bär, the fighter pilot and the warrior.

At the close of the discussion there was no Golden Flying Badge with Diamonds as his comrades had hoped for him and the Diamonds were right out of the question! There was a strong dressing down and, in conclusion, Göring uttered the decisive sentence: "Major Bär, stand at attention! For insubordination and dereliction of your duty as group commander I am demoting you to squadron commander."

Major Bär accepted this degradation stone-faced. He saluted and was dismissed. There was no further chitchat and no ride through Karinhall in the Reichsmarschall's carriage.

Bär went back to the airfield and climbed into a waiting He-111 which flew him back to his group on the Eastern Front, where he took command of a squadron. His men were glad to have him back again. He told them nothing, but slowly word filtered down from above about what "Heinz, the bear" had done during his visit with the Reichsmarschall.

"You wanted to pick up the fat one on your arm, Heinz," said his adjutant and friend from the African days. "But you strained yourself—he's too heavy for that!"

"I didn't really intend to pick him up," observed Bär. He then smiled as he thought of the corpulent Göring. Some time later Bär was ordered to Rheine to assume command of a squadron there. He was assigned to the 1st Fighter Wing. A short time later the Luftwaffe psychologist, Professor Dr. Paul Skawran, visited the wing to check up on Bär and, if necessary, help restore him to health, but he found Bär as he had always been. Soon after Skawran's arrival an order from the wing command arrived for the squadron, which Bär was leading in place of a wounded comrade. It was a directive on how to attack the large formations of heavy bombers that were attacking the Reich. At first Bär read out loud, then his voice became ever lower. Finally, he merely shook his head.

"It's all rubbish," was his comment when he had finished reading the message. He crumpled the wing order and threw it into the wastepaper basket. Then he turned to his pilots: "Men, just follow me and you're sure to shoot down something!"

Professor Skawran knew that "Heinz, the Bear" was still the same man and this was confirmed by a slogan on the long wall of the squadron barracks, which he noticed for the first time: In My Crate, I'm the Commander!

IN MY CRATE, I'M THE COMMANDER!

When the squadron briefing was over, Bär turned to the professor, whom he had met previously and whose company he valued.

"Yes, professor, take a good look at the brand-new squadron commander," he said with only a trace of his Saxon accent, slapping the keen-eyed, slightly built scholar on the shoulder with such force that he almost went to his knees. The following is a brief extract from Dr. Paul Skawran's account on this meeting with Bär:

> We had scarcely exchanged a few words in Bär's barren office when the telephone rang. Bär stared in amazement at the phone, as if he couldn't believe that such a small thing could make such a spectacle. He picked up the receiver, identified himself and said, "Jawohl, sir!"
>
> The lecture seemed to go on forever. Only occasionally was the frightful monologue interrupted by Bär's: "Jawohl, sir!"
>
> After one last time, Bär hung up with a sigh of relief.
>
> "Yes, old buddy, it's like this every day," he related. "I already know what he's going to say. I don't need to go on hearing it. He just wants to let me have it. The fat one's already made all that clear to me."
>
> Bär grinned and reached for the wine bottle in his locker. He poured each of us a glass of the vintage Bordeaux left over from the supply "Uncle Theo" Osterkamp had sent to Bär when he received the Swords.
>
> "So how was it in Africa?" I asked. "Was it really so miserable?"
>
> "It was shit, real shit! The fat one was right about that. But he hadn't the faintest idea why it was so. For one thing, we were bombed eight times a day. We had no aircraft and no fuel and when one of the old-timers was put out of action there was no one to take his place." Bär's face darkened. "But Hermann didn't want to hear about any of that. The many young men, still almost teenagers, who came to us half trained, were very soon shot out of the sky."
>
> We drank to each other's health, and Bär's face brightened when he recalled one episode from Tunisia.

"You know, professor, we also had fun. We needed it after all the combat. For example, we went gazelle hunting south of Sbeitla. That was great! You know that I always wanted to be a forester. But the way the others did it was rubbish. They piled into a Kübelwagen and set off after the gazelles. Then they opened fire when they thought they were close enough. It was like the navy: Broadside left and broadside right. Of course, they didn't hit a thing."

Bär took a drink.

"That's not how you hunt gazelle. They run low over the ground and, if you want to shoot one, you must hide in their path behind a camelthorn bush or an almond tree. Then, when they come to their waterhole you get one, allowing the correct amount of lead just like shooting in the air. And you must choose the right one, not a young animal or a powerful buck.

"Anyway, Müncheberg and I almost came to grief over a waterhole. Müncheberg, God rest his soul, knew where there was a large lake surrounded by marsh. It was far to the rear in no-man's-land—a salt lake beyond Gafsa. We set out long before dawn and, after a long trip, we arrived at a large lake just in time to see the geese land. The geese paddled about in large groups. We opened up with our borrowed hunting rifles and, afterwards, we had to wade in our high rubber boots through the knee-deep water that covered the salt bed of the lake.

"I can tell you, professor, we stank to the high heavens. Only wet camel dung could smell that bad. We fired at thirty geese and got them all.

"On the way back, we drove along the northwest road. We were about to turn north when we spotted an American armored car behind us to our left. I pushed the gas pedal to the floor, but the armored car moved cross-country and drew ever closer to us.

"Müncheberg wanted to get out and fight to the death with the submachine gun he had brought with him, but I drove even faster so that he couldn't jump out. Then the armored car passed us, blocked our path and turned its machinegun on us. And who do you think looked at us out of the hatch, professor? It was a stupid Oberleutnant, one of our own. When he saw who we were, he turned around and returned to his outpost position."

I smiled. That was my old friend, the one whom nothing could shake.

"But that wasn't all, professor," Bär continued. "A short time later General Seidemann, the senior air commander in Africa, crossed our path. He asked what we had been doing and, when we mentioned the goose hunt, his face lit up.

"Müncheberg asked: 'Would you like a few geese, sir?' And when Seidemann nodded we tossed about twenty birds into his car. The general was somewhat amazed. Then he asked, 'Where did you get so many geese?' We explained and his eyes grew wide.

"'Good Lord,' he shouted, 'you were miles behind the American armored spearheads!'

"That's how it was, professor. We had some fun too, but mostly it was a big mess like the fat one said."

The next morning Bär and I had just finished breakfast when Bär mentioned that they had wanted to take away the squadron cook.

"This stupid idea was hatched by some ops person. But I cut him short. I told him that a few of my men would catch it tomorrow or the day after and they should at least have something to eat first."

Soon the telephone rang again. Bär picked it up and answered, then fell silent at once as a torrent of noise spouted from the receiver. When the storm subsided, he said softly:

"I must have missed it yesterday in the noise of the engines, sir. Jawohl, sir, I'll come at once!"

Bär threw the receiver down on to the cradle. He hadn't realized that he had been ordered to report to the wing commander the day before. He set off a little worried.

Once again all turned out well, however. Bär was to take command of his old group again. There was simply no better man for the job and, in spite of all the mistrust of this highly decorated soldier's nonmilitary behavior, the wing commander was of the opinion that a qualified commander should occupy the position. He therefore gave Bär a chance in spite of his anger and annoyance.

Several months later when the wing commander of the 1st Fighter Wing was put out of action, Bär was named its commander. He was fully rehabilitated. However, the animosity toward him on the part of Göring remained, as the last year of the war was to show Heinz Bär.

IN ACTION WITH THE 1ST AND 3RD FIGHTER WINGS

Heinz Bär was one of the pillars of the 1st Fighter Wing. He succeeded the great Walter Oesau, who had been shot down and killed over the Eifel Mountains on 11 May 1944. Into the place of this man, the third German soldier to receive the Knight's Cross with Oak Leaves and Swords, was

Bär's Me-262 A-1 "Red 13," with which he shot down his 206th enemy aircraft on 19 March 1945.

Heinz Bär. Oesau's predecessor as wing commander had been Oberstleutnant Hans Philipp. Philipp died over Nordhorn on 8 October 1943 in action against enemy heavy bombers. Serving in the unit were a large number of recipients of the Knight's Cross and the Oak Leaves.

Heinz Bär made his mark as wing commander from the very first day. He accompanied the unit on its missions and shot down his first heavy bomber.

✠

When, in September 1944, the 3rd Fighter Wing "Udet" was transferred back to Germany from the invasion front, it was assigned to the defense of the Reich after resting and refitting. Oberstleutnant Heinz Bär received orders to take command of the wing. He flew to his new post immediately and, when he learned that the group under Hauptmann Moritz had been attached to another wing, he categorically demanded its return. This took place in October 1944 and the 3rd Fighter Wing once again had four groups.

The 3rd Fighter Wing took part in all the major operations that followed, and Heinz Bär led the wing with elan and an iron hand. On 2 November 1944, the 4th Group of the 3rd Fighter Wing under Hauptmann Moritz was part of a force that intercepted 383 heavy bombers headed for Central Germany. The bombers were escorted by 600 Mustangs. Five hundred German fighters took off to meet the enemy incursion. The 4th Group of the 3rd Fighter Wing and the 2nd Group of the 4th Fighter Wing achieved great success. Their total of sixty-one armored

Fw-190 A8/R2 fighters shot down thirty heavy bombers, but at a cost of thirty of their own machines.

Over Bitterfeld, Oberleutnant Werner Gerth, the squadron commander of the 14th Squadron of the 3rd Fighter WIng, rammed a Boeing Flying Fortress. The B-17 went down in flames. Gerth's aircraft was severely damaged and spun toward the earth. Werner Gerth got out, but his parachute failed to open. At the time of his death, he had thirty victories to his credit. After landing at Schafstädt, the 4th Group found that fifteen of its pilots were missing. Four had managed to bail out and return to their unit, eleven were killed.

Also shot down in the fighting over Central Germany that day was Feldwebel Bilek of the 3rd Squadron of the 3rd Fighter Wing. He was injured when he crash-landed his damaged aircraft. The commander of the wing's 1st Squadron, Oberleutnant Zwittning, was shot down over Halle in his Bf-109 G14. Unteroffizier Machalosowitz suffered the same fate, but both men escaped by parachute. Hauptmann Kutscha, commander of the wing's 2nd Group, had to report the loss of thirteen of his pilots to his wing commander. According to the records of 1st Fighter Corps, total losses were ninety-eight machines, including thirty fighters from the two aforementioned groups.

Aschersleben, Dessau and Halle, the home bases of the wing's groups, witnessed the disaster that befell the 3rd Fighter Wing. The wing was operationally withdrawn to rest and refit. Momentous events were casting their shadow before them.

THE BLOODLETTING OF DECEMBER 1944: OBERSTLEUTNANT BÄR AND THE 3RD FIGHTER WING

An analysis of the Allied attacks and the German defense carried out at the beginning of December 1944 revealed that the units of the 1st Fighter Corps under Generalleutnant Schmid had lost 404 aircraft in shooting down 155 enemy machines.

In November 1944 alone, 244 day-fighter pilots had been killed or listed missing, and these were only the operational losses. The German fighter arm was fighting for its very survival. Written off by their commander as "cowards," the fighter pilots of the Luftwaffe were engaged in a frightful battle of attrition unlike anything seen before.

✠

On 2 December 1944 the USAAF attacked Cologne and Bingen. Later that night the RAF dropped 1,802 ton of bombs on Hagen. The 3rd

Fighter Wing under Oberstleutnant Bär fought a bitter action against the daylight raid. Bär, who remained in his command post in Störmede that day, stayed in constant radio contact with his 1st Group.

Even before the unit landed he knew that Hauptmann Wirges, one of his old friends from Russia, who was in command of the 1st Group, had been shot down. He heard reports of further victories, but after the last machines had landed he found himself facing the almost unbelievable fact that his wing had lost a total of nineteen pilots killed and five wounded and nineteen aircraft destroyed in this one air battle. He discussed the disaster with his staff.

"Gentlemen, if this continues we will not have a single aircraft left by the end of the month, especially if the Fourth Group under Major Moritz stays attached to the Wild Boars."

After these losses Heinz Bär worked to obtain new aircraft and pilots to fly them as quickly as possible. In the days that followed he brought his wing back up to strength, which bordered on the miraculous. On 12 December Bär found himself in action over the Ruhr with his 1st Group against a force of RAF heavy bombers. He shot down one of the bombers before it could drop its bombs on Witten. Four of the group's pilots were killed in action.

✠

When the Ardennes offensive began—Hitler's last offensive in the West—there were twelve fighter wings engaged in the Defense of the Reich, including Bär's. Forty fighter groups were under the command of Luftwaffe Command West, whose headquarters was in Limburg (Lahn). As part of the beginning of the neutralization of General Galland by Göring, command of all fighter units was handed over to the General in Command of Bombers, Dietrich Peltz. This decision on the part of Göring unleashed a great wave of bitterness among the commanders of the fighter wings. In spite of his obvious bravery—evidenced by the awarding of the Knight's Cross with Oak Leaves and Swords—Peltz was no fighter pilot.

A great blow was planned for a massed attack on the enemy bombers with every available fighter. Rumors had already reached the leaders of the fighter wings concerning the strike. However, instead of attacking bombers in the air, which was the primary mission of the fighters defending Germany, orders were issued for low-level attacks on Allied ground targets in support of the German offensive.

The fighter attack was to have been launched on 16 December 1944 to coincide with the Ardennes Offensive. However, the fighter squadrons were unable to take off on account of dense fog and steady rain that day. The attack did not begin until the next day, when the 3rd, 4th, 11th, 26th, and 27th Fighter Wings took to the air, along with the Me-262s of the 51st Bomber Wing. The four groups of the 4th Fighter Wing, under commander Gerhard Michalski (667th Oak Leaves recipient on 25 November 1944), lost eleven aircraft on that day. Three others were forced to carry out crash landings.

The 3rd Fighter Wing fought between the Bonn area and the Ahr Mountains on 17 December. Unteroffizier Werner Thiel was shot down over the village of Nierendorf near Remagen. Though wounded, he managed to parachute from his Bf-109 G14. Leutnant Rolf Lane and his Fw-190 A8 were listed as missing. The 3rd was still on strip alert on 18 December when an aerial engagement broke out in the Cologne area between the 27th Fighter Wing and a numerically superior enemy force. Heinz Bär cursed softly to himself about the sluggishness of Luftwaffe Command West, which had placed him on alert an hour after becoming aware of the situation.

"They must know where they're going to send us by now! All I can say to you is this: Stay close to me and you'll shoot something down." Then, in closing, he said: "Langer, it's your turn!"

The order to scramble came moments later. All four squadrons took off from their bases south of the Teutoburger Wald with Bär in the lead. Visibility was poor, as the weather was awful, but Bär had to send his men into battle. The Ruhr was still the weapons forge and fuel depot of the Wehrmacht and had to be defended. While en route to the Ruhr region, Oberstleutnant Bär was instructed to change course in the direction of Cologne, which had been identified as the target. Bär was the first to sight the enemy on reaching the area south of Bonn.

"Fat autos from the northwest. Indians with them. Indians are approaching rapidly!"

Soon afterwards the fight began. The fighters were American P-51 Mustangs, fast escort fighters. In the ensuing dogfight Bär managed to evade a determined attack by three enemy fighters. He pulled up steeply, half-rolled and then dove on an enemy machine. Two brief bursts from his guns, and he pulled up again. As he climbed away, Bär saw that the enemy aircraft was burning. Its dive became steeper and steeper. Finally, it crashed and exploded.

Three more enemy aircraft, including one heavy bomber, were shot down. The cost was eight fighters shot down. Two of these made forced landings; three were listed missing. After they had landed, Bär waved for

Langer to come over to him: "Langer, that was a hard blow for us. We can't carry on like this."

Claims for twenty-four enemy aircraft shot down were offset by losses of twenty-one pilots killed and twelve wounded. One of those lost, Leutnant Karl Willecke, the squadron commander of the wing's 11th Squadron, was irreplaceable.

✠

The 23rd of December saw part of the wing in action against the second wave of a 400-strong bomber group of the USAAF escorted by 400 fighters. It was flying toward the Wester Woods. The elements of the wing were part of a mixed force which included elements from the 2nd and 11th Fighter Wings. In the course of this action, the American 398th Bomber Group lost sixteen of its Marauders. Oberstleutnant Bär was among the successful German pilots. The elements of the wing paid for this success with eight aircraft shot down between Adenau-Meckenheim-St. Vith. Four pilots escaped by parachute, including the young officer candidate Adolf Tham who, after his weapons failed, flew straight toward a Marauder and rammed it, causing the American aircraft to crash. Though wounded, Tham was able to take to his parachute and returned to action in the final weeks of the war.

Heinz Bär summoned the young officer candidate and pinned the Iron Cross, First Class on his breast. As he did so he remarked to him: "Easy does it, Tham. Otherwise, you'll be getting a wooden cross very soon and I wouldn't like to do that to your mother!"

Tham promised to be careful.

Altogether, the flying formations charged with the defense of German airspace lost more than sixty-five machines on 23 December. Personnel losses, including those wounded and missing, totaled ninety-eight pilots.

✠

On Christmas Eve the Allies sent 2,034 bombers and more than 700 fighters to attack eleven German fighter bases in the Gießen, Frankfurt and Darmstadt areas. Led by Brigadier General Frederick Castle, this huge force, the largest aerial armada Europe had ever seen, flew east inexorably. Bär had ordered a strip alert. Prior to that, he had assembled his squadron and group commanders around him. He said laconically: "No one can miss. They're as big as barn doors . . . This time we also have our rested

Fourth Group with us and we'll see to it that it is used correctly as part of the wing. It will lead the way and batter a way through for us."

The leaders of the assault squadrons nodded in agreement. They would attack the enemy bombers in their potent Fw-190 A8 fighters and spoil their flight. The leading squadron of the 4th Group of the 3rd Fighter Wing spotted the enemy near Liege. The report was passed back. Because the enemy fighter escort was not on station, Oberstleutnant Bär ordered an immediate attack. The fighters stormed toward the B-17 formation, concentrating their fire on the cockpits of the enemy aircraft. Four B-17s blew apart at once; the wreckage, some of it burning, spun earthwards. Five more bombers fell out of formation, engines smoking, and descended steeply in order to find a place to crash land. Encouraged, Bär called to his pilots:

"Well done, assault group, keep it up!"

Bär downed a B-17 with three bursts from his guns. The enemy bombers turned away. Hauptmann Kosse, commander of the of 3rd's 13th Squadron, was hit by return fire as he pulled away from the bombers. His aircraft dove away from the scene of the combat. He was posted missing in action, as was Oberfeldwebel Egon Schulz, who was hit during the first pass. Five other pilots were shot down by the bombers' defensive fire or by the escort fighters, which finally arrived on the scene. All five pilots bailed out successfully and, after landing, were taken prisoner.

The 3rd's 1st Group lost Leutnant Franz Ruhl, the commander of the 4th Squadron. He had been awarded the Knight's Cross on 27 April 1944. Ruhl was promoted posthumously to the rank of Oberleutnant as the result of a special request by Oberstleutnant Bär. In one of the shot-down Flying Fortresses was the commander of the mission, Brigadier General Castle. When his bomber was hit and began to burn, he gave the order to abandon the aircraft. However, Castle was unable to get out; he was still aboard the B-17 when it struck the ground and exploded.

The fighters of the 3rd stayed with the American bombers as they flew east. Heinz Bär downed two more and his pilots four before they could drop their bombs. Over Aachen the fighters of the 27th Fighter Wing's 1st Group and all three groups of the 6th Fighter Wing joined the clash. The fighting became even more intense. The approaching German fighters had to fight their way through British fighters—Spitfires, Typhoons, and Tempests of the 2nd Tactical Air Force—before they could come to grips with the bombers. The last to arrive on the scene was the 1st Group of the 26th Fighter Wing. It made contact with a formation of about eighty bombers guarded by Lightnings. The group was able to shoot down only a single Lightning while losing five of its own machines.

Among the losses suffered by the 52nd Fighter Wing, which had been transferred west only several weeks before, was Major Johannes Wiese, recipient of the 418th Knight's Cross with Oak Leaves. He bailed out, however his parachute only half opened. The wing commander was seriously injured when he struck the ground, but he survived.

Hauptmann Lothar Baumann, commander of the 52nd's 1st Group, was killed. A total of forty-four heavy bombers were destroyed, as well as a number of escort fighters. On the German side eighty-five fighters had been shot down. Most of their pilots were dead or missing. Another twenty-one were wounded but managed to bring their aircraft home. Bär's wing lost seventeen men.

✠

On Monday, 25 December 1944, the 1st Group of the 3rd Fighter Wing was placed on strip alert at 1204 hours at Paderborn. Equipped with the Bf-109 G14, the group was to provide air cover for German armored units approaching Liege. However, just before takeoff, the formation was instructed to intercept a small formation of Mustangs that had split off from a larger formation south of Bonn. All the remaining aircraft of the 1st and 3rd Fighter Wings attacked a 422-strong bomber formation of the American 2nd and 3rd Air Divisions. The 4th Group of the 3rd Wing was led by its new commander, Hauptmann Weydenhammer, who was killed in the attack. All told the that group lost seven pilots. Total wing losses amounted to eleven aircraft.

✠

The next major defensive action took place on Wednesday, 27 December. The US 8th Air Force sent 1,000 aircraft to hit transportation targets in the Koblenz area in an attempt to cut the lines of communications to the German armies in the Ardennes. Heinz Bär and three of his groups battled the escort fighters between Cologne and the Ahr Mountains. The wing lost a total of thirteen pilots while shooting down only four of the enemy.

In the days that followed there was relative quiet for the German fighter units, especially the 3rd Fighter Wing. Something big was imminent. In the space of three days the wing was brought up to full strength. It was to play a decisive role in the forthcoming operation entitled *Bodenplatte* ("Base Plate").

OPERATION BASE PLATE

The big strike—a massed assault on the Allied bomber fleet by every available German fighter—was the brainchild of the Inspector General of Fighters, Adolf Galland. Scheduled for 1 November 1944, it was shelved in favor of preparations for "Watch on the Rhine," the German codename for the Ardennes Offensive.

It appeared to the Allies that the Luftwaffe was no longer capable of mounting large-scale operations. But that was not so! Operation Base Plate was to be carried out no matter what the cost, even after the losses suffered in the Ardennes Offensive. That despite warnings from many wing commanders that such an attack would lead to the demise of the German fighter arm without influencing the course of the war in the slightest.

The Luftwaffe senior command was willing to accept the loss of 400 fighters as long as an equal number of enemy fighters and bombers were destroyed on the ground. Placed in charge of carrying out the operation was Generalmajor Peltz, the Commanding General of the 2nd Fighter Corps. He had also commanded the fighter units during the Ardennes Offensive after General Galland had been "sent into the desert" for good. The operation was scheduled for Monday, 1 January 1945. The wing commanders were very late receiving the necessary aerial photos of the targets they were to attack. Furthermore, for security reasons, they were not permitted to brief their squadron and group commanders until twenty-four hours prior to takeoff. The latter were then to brief their pilots immediately before takeoff.

In overall command of the operation was Luftwaffe Command West under Generalleutnant Schmid. The three operational groups of the 3rd Fighter Wing were assigned as targets the Allied airfields at Eindhoven in Holland. All in all, ten fighter wings with thirty-three groups along with several night-fighter and close-support formations were dispatched against the eleven major targets. Each machine carried a 300-liter drop tank for increased range.

At the time of the attack, the wing's 1st Group was based at Paderborn. The 2nd Group was at Lippspringe, and the 4th Group was at Gütersloh. On the afternoon of 31 December 1944 Bär left his command post at Störliede together with his staff and flew his Fw-190 A9 to the 1st Group at Paderborn. He had moved to Störmede with his staff from Erfurt (Bindersleben) at the end of November in order to be closer to the scene of the action. (It was while flying from Störmede that Bär had shot down his 200th enemy aircraft. At the time, he had been the group commander of the 2nd Group of the 1st Fighter Wing. The date had been 21 April 1944 and his victim had been a B-24 Liberator of the 8th Air Force.)

Heinz Bär wanted to go to Paderborn to meet with his group commanders in preparation for this important mission. Its aim was the destruction of the enemy's fighter arm. If it succeeded, the greatest threat to the German fighters would be eliminated for many weeks and they could again concentrate undisturbed on engaging the enemy bombers.

It was late on the afternoon of 31 December 1944 and Bär had assembled his group commanders.

"Gentlemen," he began, "Operation Hermann begins tomorrow morning at 0900 hours. We will be attacking airfields in Belgium and Holland which are occupied by enemy fighter forces. These are to be destroyed on the ground. This has precedence over air combat, however, the latter is not to be avoided."

Bär continued: "Our target is the airfield complex at Eindhoven. The flight plan is contained in the operations plan, as are the takeoff and attack sequences. Effective immediately, all groups are confined to base and there is to be no drinking. Lights out at 2200 hours. And one more thing: We will carry out several passes until everything is destroyed. Radio silence will be maintained throughout the entire mission!"

The maintenance company and the "black men" (ground crews) worked at a high tempo to repair three machines which were still unserviceable. All FuG-25 radio sets (IFF) were removed under the supervision of the electronics chief to avoid them falling into enemy hands.

A SUCCESSFUL MISSION

On the morning of 1 January 1945 the wakeup call came at 0530 at all three of the wing's bases. There was a briefing after breakfast, at which the pilots received their final instructions. Only then did they receive the maps depicting their course and turning points. On each map the target was circled: Eindhoven.

The squadron commanders instructed their pilots: "The airfield is full of Spitfires. Therefore, be careful! Approach straight away, descend and fire everything you have. It's probable that some of these speedy bees will be in the air and waiting for us over the attack area. Two passes is the absolute minimum."

These were the final instructions. At 0825 hours the pilots went out to their aircraft. The ground crews reported all aircraft ready to go. Some had not yet had breakfast, but they could go and eat at that point. The

The 3rd Fighter Wing's 3rd Group achieved great success in the defense of the Reich. It was commanded by Hauptmann Langer, who received the Knight's Cross in April 1945.

takeoff flag was lowered at 0830. Oberstleutnant Heinz Bär took off with the wing headquarters, which had flown with him to Paderborn.

At the same time, the fifteen serviceable Bf-109s of the 10th, 11th, and 12th Squadrons of the 3rd Fighter Wing lifted off from Lippspringe as did the three Squadrons under Leutnant Müller at Gütersloh. Led by the headquarters flight, Müller's aircraft climbed into the morning sky. All six flights formed up into squadron formation in the assigned quadrant, from where they continued on toward the target.

Each group commander satisfied himself that everyone was present. If a group arrived even a few minutes late it would allow more enemy fighters to take off. The wing joined formation over Lippstadt and flew west at heights of only thirty to sixty meters to avoid detection by enemy radar. It followed the route pencilled in on the flight maps. No one was allowed to say a word on the radio; it might be overheard and warn the enemy.

A few kilometers from the Rhine the headquarters flight sighted the Ju-88 that was to guide them to Holland. Sitting in their cockpits, the fighter pilots stared at their instruments and at the aircraft beside and in front of them. The lead formation kept its eyes on the Ju-88 in front of it. Even the most experienced pilots felt a chill when they thought of what might be awaiting them. Nevertheless, they were certain that the attack must succeed.

In extended formation, yet only seconds apart—the interval between squadrons within the groups was only about 200 meters—the fighters crossed the Dutch border twenty-five kilometers north of Venlo. They had been airborne for twenty minutes. So far not a sound had been heard. The level of discipline was extremely high; everyone knew that a single false step in this area could put the entire operation at risk. On reaching the Sonse Heath the unit turned south in accordance with orders. The wing flew around Eindhoven in a wide arc so as to be able to attack from the southwest. The airfield that was its target was between the Eindhoven-Tilburg road and the town of Zells.

Heinz Bär later described the operation to his friend, Professor Skawran:

I feared that we would be spotted prematurely purely by chance and recognized. That would have turned the attack on the airfield into a hellish flight. But there was still no sign of the enemy. I saw the half of the squadron assigned to attack Gilze-Rijen veer off from the main formation and head due west. A number of aircraft from the 27th Fighter Wing were also assigned to Gilze-Rijen.

We could already make out the outlines of the airfield buildings when the antiaircraft fire suddenly opened up. To my right I saw one of my aircraft go down steeply, trailing a banner of smoke behind it. Everyone just hold your course and then have at them, I thought.

Several antiaircraft rounds exploded in front of me. It was here that we lost our officer candidate, the always cheerful Uwe Naumann, a member of my wing's 11th Squadron.

What I didn't know then was that two of the Typhoon squadrons based at Eindhoven had taken off early in the morning on a weather reconnaissance and several other machines were engaged in an armed reconnaissance flight. A third formation was just about to take off. We dove down on them. The aircraft were led by Flight Lieutenant Gibbon. The latter shot down one of my aircraft while climbing steeply; seconds later, he was hit simultaneously by two or three of my machines. His aircraft lost a wing and crashed to the ground not 200 meters west of the airfield.

Then I was over the runway. I saw the Typhoons lined up and opened fire with all weapons. I saw flashes as the cannon rounds struck home and then fires. To my left and right the entire force went to the attack. The din was frightful. I saw Spitfires as well as the Typhoons. After the first pass I pulled up, made a knife-edged turn and raced down at the airfield for a second attack. I could clearly see two Typhoons set on fire by my A9. They were my 203rd and 204th enemy aircraft destroyed. I can't say that these two victories were easier than those I achieved in aerial combat. The enemy antiaircraft fire was well, and they were ready for us when we made our second attack. One of my pilots swung too wide during his second pass and, as he told me later, spotted several Mitchell bombers at the side of the airfield, obviously waiting to be refueled. He fired at that "furniture van" of a fueler, which exploded in an orange-colored fireball. One or another of the Mitchells may have been damaged in the explosion.

It is certain that the wing destroyed numerous aircraft belonging to 137th, 181st, 182nd, and 247th Squadrons of the RAF, all equipped with Typhoons. In addition, Spitfires of the 400th, 414th, and 430th Squadrons and Typhoons of 438th, 439th, and 440th Squadrons of the RCAF were also destroyed. All but two of 438th Squadron's Typhoons were hit and some destroyed. At the end of this dramatic surprise attack, the 440th Squadron had only two serviceable aircraft. Following minor repairs, the four squadrons of the 124th Wing RCAF (430th, 438th, 439th, and 440th Squadrons) had a total of only twenty-four serviceable aircraft. The 2nd Tactical Air Force lost numerous Spitfires in addition to almost a complete Typhoon wing.

The enemy aircraft that had taken off on the early-morning sorties returned during the second pass by the attackers. They at once dove into the fray, shooting down the commander of the 12th Squadron, Oberleutnant Graf von Treuberg. Oberfeldwebel Hameister shot down a Spitfire that was on the tail of one of his squadron mates. Almost immediately, Hameister was fired on from behind by another Spitfire and his aircraft caught fire. The young pilot made a successful forced landing and was captured the next morning while trying to make his way to the German lines. It had been his first mission with the wing.

After twenty minutes over Eindhoven the aircraft of the 3rd Fighter Wing flew back to their bases. They left behind a great pile of wreckage that had once been Eindhoven airfield. Aircraft, refueling trucks and hangars blazed fiercely.

For many pilots of the wing, the return flight was their last. West of Helmond the wing ran into four Typhoons coming home from weather reconnaissance. The Typhoons, aircraft of the 439th Squadron of the RCAF, and two Spitfires attacked the 15th Squadron of the 3rd Fighter Wing and engaged it in a five-minute dogfight. Unteroffizier Schmidt, who had destroyed two Spitfires on the ground at Eindhoven, then shot down the Typhoon of Flight Lieutenant Angelin. His aircraft was subsequently hit and Schmidt was forced to crash land. He was also taken prisoner and survived the war.

Bär heard some of his men calling for help. Then he also broke radio silence: "Head east!" His second and last call: "Disengage!" The attack by the wing was the only one to enjoy complete success, but the cost had been high enough—ten pilots killed and six missing, most of the latter having been captured.

The other flying formations suffered even heavier losses. The 1st Fighter Wing *Oesau*, whose target was Maldegem airfield, fifteen kilometers east of Brugge, lost twenty-four pilots. All told, the wing destroyed only thirty-two enemy aircraft at Maldegem and Denis-Westrem (a secondary target). Oberst Ihlefeld, one of Germany's most successful fighter pilots, was bitter over the heavy losses; he lost almost half the machines committed by his unit.

The 2nd Fighter Wing "Richthofen," which began the day with an operational strength of ninety aircraft, was led by Hauptmann Hrdlicka. He was another skilled and successful fighter ace. His target was St. Trond in Belgium, which until recently had been used by German night fighters. En route to the target, between Aachen and Liege, the wing was supposed to be joined by the 3rd Group of the 4th Close-Air Support Wing based at Cologne (Wahn). That close-support group was led by Oberst Alfred Druschel, an experienced close-support pilot who had won the Knight's Cross with Oak Leaves and Swords on 19 February 1943 while acting commander of the 1st Group of the 1st Close Support Wing with the rank of Hauptmann. (Druschel failed to return from that catastrophic operation. The wing commander flew with his 3rd Group of the 4th Close Support Wing that day.)

The 2nd Fighter Wing lost twenty-three pilots killed. Ten more abandoned their aircraft and took to their parachutes. Another four brought their damaged aircraft home. The wing's losses amounted to forty percent of its authorized strength. The operation by the 4th Fighter Wing was a complete failure. Under the command of wing commander Major Gerhard Michalski, also a recipient of the Knight's Cross with Oak Leaves, it was supposed to take out Le Culot airfield, fifteen kilometers northwest of Brussels. Part of the wing mistakenly attacked St. Trond. Of fifty-five aircraft that took off, only thirty returned.

The same thing happened to the remaining wings. It was not until years later that the true extent of the losses suffered became known, because both sides minimized their losses and played up their successes.

The German day fighter arm lost 214 pilots and their aircraft in this operation. A further eighteen pilots were wounded. Losses among command personnel were very high. Among those killed were two wing commanders, six group commanders and ten squadron commanders.

It is likely that approximately 300 of the 900 German fighters used in the operation were lost. A portion of these, about twenty machines, were shot down by Flak because their route led them straight through Flak corridors. The Flak gunners knew nothing of the mass operation by German fighters.

Referring to the success of Operation Base Plate, the Luftwaffe High Command report of 27 January 1945 declared that aerial photos of the eight target airfields had revealed 279 aircraft destroyed on the ground. The fighters had also claimed sixty-five certain and seventy-five probable victories in air combat, and another 123 enemy aircraft were seen to have been wrecked at seven other airfields. Together with 114 damaged aircraft at all the bases attacked, this brought total Allied losses to approximately 477 aircraft destroyed and 114 damaged. This was a loss the enemy could replace within fourteen days.

Oberstleutnant Bär accurately summed up the entire operation when he commented at the time of the deactivation of his wing: "The madness of Base Plate has broken our neck."

THE FINAL VICTORIES: COMBAT IN THE ME-262

The pilots of the 3rd and 4th Groups of the 3rd Fighter Wing flew several more missions in the first two weeks of January 1945. When Hitler finally realized that the German day fighters could no longer engage the vastly superior Allied air forces in the West without being completely destroyed in a few days, he ordered seven day fighter wings withdrawn from the West and transferred to the Eastern Front on 15 January 1945. The Luftwaffe High Command carried out the move in such a way that the 1st, 3rd, 4th, 11th, and 77th Fighter Wings were transferred to the east without their former commanding officers.

Heinz Bär also had to leave his wing. He was named commander of the jet fighter replacement training group based at Lechfeld in Bavaria. Bär's superiors hoped that they had finally shunted him off to the side. But Heinz Bär was cut from different wood than his enemies in the upper echelons of the Luftwaffe command. He set about training experienced Bf-109 and Fw-190 pilots to fly the new jet. Heinz Bär mastered the Me-262 in a way that few of his contemporaries could equal.

He had heard the comment made by Adolf Galland after his first test flight in the Me-262: "It's as if an angel is pushing." Like Heinz Bär, Adolf

Galland was firmly convinced that they should keep fighting in spite of the desperate situation. While Bär trained pilots for the Me-262, Galland set about forming a jet fighter unit, the 44th Fighter Formation. While Galland had to pull every possible string to obtain aircraft, pilots, ground personnel and equipment for his fledgling unit, Oberst Johannes Steinhoff had been officially tasked with forming the 7th Fighter Wing, the first Me-262 fighter wing, at Brandenburg-Briest. Steinhoff was prevented by his superiors from assisting the 44th Fighter Formation in any way, but here too they bit down on granite. He and his men did all they could to support Galland's efforts.

All of Galland's and Steinhoff's efforts did not seem to help; the plan continued to be sabotaged from above. Finally, Galland took the unorthodox step of reporting the state of the jet fighter unit to Göring by way of Oberst von Below, Hitler's Luftwaffe adjutant. The "fat one" suddenly realized what was involved. He gave the order for the 44th Fighter Formation to be provided with aircraft immediately.

Oberstleutnant Bär sent retrained pilots directly to Galland's unit. The Commander of Luftwaffe Fighter Schools, Oberst Trautloft, also sent the best men to the 44th Fighter Formation. From the Russian Front came Major Barkhorn, with 300 victories to his credit. He was soon followed by "Graf Punski," as Walter Krupinski was known to his comrades. Krupinski's victory total stood at 197. Another highly decorated pilot who joined the 44th Fighter Formation was Günther Lützow. Lützow had been banished to Italy after confronting Göring during the Luftwaffe conference at the Gatow School of Air Warfare in November 1944.

Galland almost succeeded in winning over "Bubi" Hartmann for the 44th Fighter Formation; however, Hartmann didn't want to leave his old comrades on the Eastern Front. He paid for his loyalty with ten years in Russian captivity. The men who made up the 44th Fighter Formation had more than 1,000 victories to their credit, a unique situation for a new flying formation.

Heinz Bär was confident in his ability to fly the Me-262. The 44th Fighter Formation had flown its first sorties against enemy heavy bombers from Munich (Riem) at the end of March and had met with success. On 27 March Bär was expecting a visit from Oberst Walter Dahl, the wing commander of the 300th Fighter Wing. With him on his arrival in Lechfeld was Oberst Gordon Gollob, the new Inspector General of Fighters, an experienced fighter pilot with 150 victories to his credit. Gollob wanted to inspect the new-equipment training unit.

At this time, Oberstleutnant Bär's victory total stood at 206 enemy aircraft, including a number of heavy bombers. It was obvious that he had done an excellent job organizing the operation at Lechfeld. Every pilot sent to a frontline unit from his group had completely mastered the Me-262.

Bär quickly answered all of Gollob's technical and tactical questions. Then, almost casually, he remarked: "I'll be handing the group over to my successor tomorrow or the day after."

Shocked, the Inspector General stared at Bär. "Why then, Bär? We're all very satisfied with you!"

"With one exception, and that is me," came the reply. "I won't send my pilots away from here without having been there myself."

"If that's the case I'll see to your relief," promised Gollob. He kept his word. Subsequently, Bär and Dahl went out to the ramp where two Me-262s were waiting. Dahl described his first flight in the jet fighter in his book *Rammjäger* ("Ram Fighter"):

> I was placed on the leash by Heinz Bär and flew my first circuits exactly as he instructed. I soon had everything well in hand and landed after six circuits so that the machine could be refueled.

During his second flight Dahl shot down his first enemy aircraft with the Me-262, a P-47. He reported the victory by radio and the first voice he heard congratulating him was Heinz Bär's. Soon afterward, he shot down a second Thunderbolt.

Bär also scrambled from Lechfeld. He swept over the field in his Me-262, climbed swiftly and found himself in the midst of a gaggle of Thunderbolts that were swarming about the airfield. He raced through the enemy formation at tremendous speed, fired at the right moment and saw a Thunderbolt fall. Bär reversed course and shot down a second P-47 . All the bullets meant for his Me-262 were wide of the mark. The enemy pilots were unaccustomed to the fast German aircraft and its 200 kilometer-an-hour (approximately 120 miles per hour) speed advantage. Bär attacked again in his incomparable style, and a third Thunderbolt paid the ultimate price for its flight into Germany.

Bär rocked his wings three times as he flew over the airfield and then carried out a textbook landing. Jubilation broke out at Lechfeld. That was Heinz Bär—their mentor, their friend and comrade. He taught them all something and, in return, he enjoyed their complete respect. Two days later, Oberstleutnant Bär reported to Adolf Galland for duty with the 44th Fighter Formation. Galland said: "We now also have with us Oberstleutnant Bär, who is already a flying legend."

THE FINAL BATTLES

In April 1945 Oberstleutnant Bär took off with the other pilots of the 44th Fighter Formation to intercept Allied aircraft, mostly bombers of the U. S. Army Air Force attacking targets in Southern Germany. On his very first sortie, Bär swept through a column of bombers and shot one down. He dove away and raced around the mass of bombers at breathtaking speed like a sheepdog around its herd. The Me-262 approached the bombers from below. The four cannon roared and another four-engined bomber fell from the sky.

After Bär landed, Adolf Galland came up to him and said: "You do it the way I'd like to."

"That can't be," replied Bär, "I learned from you."

The two aces complemented one another; that was certain.

The next scramble again found them intercepting an approaching U.S. bomber formation. The jet fighters climbed swiftly. Altogether there were more than 1,000 Allied aircraft from all three tactical air forces in action over the Western Front.

Bär closed with the enemy at almost 900 kilometers per hour. Occasionally he heard Galland calling instructions, but his attention was fixed on the tiny dots in the distance in front of him. The swarm of mosquitoes grew in size rapidly and became aircraft, enemy aircraft. The altimeter showed 6,000 meters and Bär was already above the enemy. Suddenly, he spotted a flight of Mustangs to his right; but they were not the target. He advanced the throttles until the jet engines were at full thrust. Flames shot from the rear of the jets and soon he had cruised past the Mustangs.

Then he saw the bombers. They approached as if in parade formation. The EZ-42 automatic gun sight lit up. Bär armed all his guns; a slight touch would be enough to unleash the devastating firepower of the Me-262s four 30-mm Mk-108 cannon. Then he could see the dense condensation trails behind the engines of the Flying Fortresses. A vast network of interlaced bluish-white contrails followed the huge formation.

The sight in front of Bär's face was trained on the nose section of the leading heavy. Range was still 2,000 meters . . . then 1,000. Bär pressed the triggers. All four cannon roared. The aircraft trembled from the fourfold recoil. Four streams of tracer streaked toward the enemy aircraft. The first hits shattered its cockpit. Shells from the two starboard cannon struck the B-17's wing root. There were flashes on the bright metal and then the starboard wing broke away. Bär made a slight correction and swept past the huge fireball that marked the end of the B-17.

Bär pulled back on the stick. The Me-262 swept upwards and was pulled into a steep turn by its masterful pilot. Halfway through the turn

Bär saw the wreckage of the B-17 falling in flames. After completing his turn, Bär saw another flight of Mustangs. He swept past the enemy fighters as if they were standing still in the sky. Beneath him he saw the bombers; they flew on unperturbed, even though at that very moment two more bombers were being shot out of the other side of the formation.

Bär pushed the stick forward. The nose of the Me-262 dropped and he took aim at another bomber. The indicator needle of the airspeed indicator was touching the 900 kilometer-per-hour mark when Bär reached firing position. He saw the bomber growing larger; he also saw the streams of pearls from the machine guns in the dorsal turret, but they lagged far behind his Me-262. Then it was time. The four cannon roared and the bomber was torn apart by the explosion of its own bombs. Bär rolled the Me-262 on to its back and dove away. He then turned south and raced toward his base. His ground crew threw their forage caps into the air when they saw him rock his wings twice as he came in to land. Bär opened the canopy and was literally lifted from the cockpit by his men.

In the days that followed Bär continued his run of success. His comrades acknowledged that he was the best there was. Bär's exploits in the final months of the war should have been enough to earn him the Diamonds, but the decoration was not forthcoming. This didn't bother "Pritzl" Bär; he was used to this unfair treatment. He trusted the sure instinct of his comrades and they celebrated him.

When Oberstleutnant Bär took off for the final attack against the Allied bomber armadas on 26 April 1945, he had shot down a total of fifteen four-engined bombers. Generalleutnant Galland was the most successful jet pilot on that day with two victories. Three others, including Heinz Bär, downed one enemy aircraft each. This brought his total to 220 victories. With sixteen kills flying the Me-262, Heinz Bär was the most successful jet pilot in the 44th Fighter Formation.

Though wounded in the knee, Galland managed to bring his Me-262 home. The nose wheel of his Messerschmitt had been damaged and the aircraft made a crash landing. Galland jumped clear and hobbled to the nearest bomb crater. Galland had several splinters in his knee and had to hand over command of the 44th Fighter Formation. As Günther Lützow was reported missing in the Donauwörth area two days earlier and was presumed dead and Johannes Steinhoff had been put out of action with severe burns suffered in a takeoff accident, Heinz Bär took over the 44th Fighter Formation as its last commanding officer.

It fell to Bär to move the unit to Salzburg. Galland was in hospital in Bad Eibsee. Several days later Bär telephoned from a villa at Lake Tegern. Speaking with his unique Saxon accent, which Göring so hated, he told

Galland the latest news concerning the 44th Fighter Formation. It was also Bär who had to carry out Galland's last order to destroy all the fighter unit's Me-262s.

An offer made to the enemy on 1 May 1945—to hand over the entire unit in order to keep it together—had come to nothing. With tears in his eyes, Heinz Bär watched as his faithful Me-262, in which he had achieved his final triumphs, was blown up. Invincible in air combat, it had become expendable with the end of the war.

✠

Heinz Bär could not return to his home. After a lengthy trek he settled in Braunschweig, where he was able to involve himself with aviation again. He became active as a test pilot in the field of sport aviation, testing the aircraft before they went on the market. While carrying out a routine flight check in a light aircraft, he put the sport machine into a flat spin, the final step in the test process. The aircraft spun down to fifty meters. Bär was unable to recover, and the machine crashed. Heinz Bär died one month before his forty-forth birthday.

✠

With sixteen confirmed kills with the Me-262 in the skies over Germany, Bär was the Luftwaffe's most successful jet fighter pilot. Bär never received the Diamonds. He was submitted for the Diamonds for the third time after the successful attack on Eindhoven on 1 January 1945. "Pritzl" Bär received the Knight's Cross with Oak Leaves and Swords on 16 February 1942 after his 90th victory. He subsequently added 131 kills to his total, achieved in more than 1,000 missions, including twenty-one four-engined bombers and one twin-engined Mosquito. No other German fighter pilot who enjoyed comparable success waited so long to receive the Diamonds. But Heinz Bär never received the richly deserved decoration. That was the extent of Göring's revenge against an airman who had served his country from the first day of the Second World War to the last.

Otto Weiß while commander of the 2nd Close-Support Group.

Otto Weiß:
Close-Support Aviation

Very soon after the expansion of the Luftwaffe began, the German aircraft industry was requested to design and develop an aircraft that could effectively attack pinpoint targets. With the aiming equipment then available, the required accuracy could only be achieved by diving directly at the target.

The result was the formation of a dive-bomber group in the autumn of 1935. In 1935 the 132nd Fighter Wing (*Jagdgeschwader*) in Döberitz began dive-bomber training, in addition to fighter training. A fighter unit was thus the parent unit of the later dive-bomber formations, the first of which was the Schwerin Aviation Group (*Fliegergruppe*) that later became the 162nd Dive-Bomber Wing (*Sturzkampfgruppe*).

This brief account of the genesis of the dive-bomber is included because several dive-bomber formations later became close-support formations or were required to provide elements for the formation of additional close-support groups. The first German close-support formations had their baptism of fire in the First World War. The Field Aviation Detachments (*Feldfliegerabteilungen*) provided support to the infantry, especially the storm troops employed in the latter stages of the war, including the German offensive of 1918.

Originally intended solely for reconnaissance and defensive roles, the "infantry fliers" of those field aviation detachments were employed in concentration as close-support formations with the beginning of the great battle in Flanders in autumn 1917. Between four and six close-support squadrons were combined to form a close-support wing. Those squadrons achieved great success in an offensive role, as the bitter battles of the German offensive of early 1918 showed. The close-support wing flew ahead of the infantry in massed formation, attacking enemy positions and clearing a path for the advancing ground forces. In many cases, the enemy abandoned the field in the face of such attacks.

✠

The first specially designed close-support aircraft, the Hs-123, saw service in Spain with the Legion Condor, where it proved highly effective. In Spain, the air and ground forces worked closely together. The most widely used close-support aircraft was the He-51. On 2 April 1938 the then Leutnant Priebe destroyed a Russian tank near Tervel with six 10-kilo bombs dropped from his He-51.

During the crisis over the Sudetenland, which lasted from August to October 1938, the Luftwaffe formed several close-support groups as alert units. Among these was 20th Air Group (*Fliegergruppe*) in Tutow. During the crisis it was stationed in Breslau and was moved back to Tutow on 1 November 1938. In Tutow the group was reequipped and reorganized as the 2nd Close-Support Group of the 2nd Training and Demonstration Wing (*Lehrgeschwader*). Equipped with the Hs-123, this close-support group was to be the Luftwaffe's sole close-support group until early 1942.

With a nominal strength of forty Hs-123s, the group fought in Poland—often with Stuka units—in support of the army. It was a role in which it achieved great success, especially in the battles of encirclement near Radom and at the Bzura River. The pilots of the group flew up to ten sorties per day during that phase of the campaign.

The campaign in Western Europe saw the group, then under the direct command of General von Richthofen's VIII Air Corps (*Fliegerkorps*), provide support for paratroopers (*Fallschirmjäger*) at Maastricht and Eben Emael. It also helped the Sixth Army cross the Meuse River. It was involved at Liege and Namur and supported the armored drive to the coast. Near Cambrai the close-support group, which was commanded by Hauptmann Weiß, smashed an advance by French tanks which could have threatened the German advance. The close-support pilots and antiaircraft guns together destroyed forty enemy tanks. Further sorties followed.

The start of the Russian Campaign saw the 2nd Close-Support Group of the 2nd Training and Demonstration Wing with three Bf-109 squadrons and one of Hs-123s again under the command of the VIII Air Corps (which had become a tactical air corps). The group earned lasting fame in the double battle of Vyazma-Briansk and in the fighting in the Kalinin area. It was there that Otto Weiß became the 52nd member of the German Armed Forces to win the Knight's Cross with Oak Leaves.

The 2nd Group was disbanded at the beginning of 1942 because of the heavy losses it had sustained. The surviving personnel were sent to Werl (Westphalia) and Lippstadt. There they formed the core of the first close-support wing (*Schlachtgeschwader*), along with a large number of new personnel. When the wing was activated, it only had a single group, however, a second group was soon formed.

The Luftwaffe's new close-support wing was equipped with the Bf-109, Hs-123, and Hs 129. In May 1942 it was sent to the southern sector of the Eastern Front. There the squadrons saw intensive action at Sevastopol, on the Kerch Peninsula, in the Caucasus and on the Don and Chir fronts. Led by Oberstleutnant Weiß, the wing achieved great success, upholding the reputation of its predecessor, the 2nd Group of the 2nd Training and Demonstration Wing.

Weiß stepped down from command in June 1942 to become the Inspector General of Close-Support Aviation. In that position he would use all of his practical experience as a tank "buster" and group and wing commander to bring the arm to the peak of its effectiveness. Standardized tactical and operational guidelines were issued to the close-support units. The man who led the way in this area was Otto Weiß.

✠

In September 1942, the Luftwaffe had activated its second close-support wing. That wing also had two groups. At this time the organization and equipment of the close-support wings was standardized. Each group consisted of three squadrons equipped with the Fw-190 and one with the Hs-129 B-1 (later B-2).

The 1st Close-Support Wing fought in the southern sector of the Eastern Front in 1943. In the Kuban bridgehead it was often called upon to clear up difficult situations for the infantry. It enjoyed great success in operations near Novorossisk, where its targets were mainly Russian strongpoints and positions, as well as at Myshako Mountain, on which units of the Red Army had dug in.

Operation Citadel saw the wing committed in an antitank role. In subsequent fighting near Orel and at the Mius River as well as in the Donets Basin, the wing provided welcome support to the hard-pressed German infantry.

✠

On 18 October 1943 all tactical wings—whether dive-bomber, high-speed bomber, close-support or antitank aircraft—were redesignated as close-support wings. As a result of the reorganization of 18 October, the two existing close-support wings were merged with the various new formations. (The 1st Close-Support Wing had been sent to Africa where it fought to the end in Tunisia.)

The former 1st Stuka Wing (*Stukageschwader*) became the new 1st Close-Support Wing and thus had nothing to do with the first incarnation of the wing. The following is a list of the close-support wings formed as a result of the reorganization:

> 2nd Close-Support Wing "Immelmann" (formerly 2nd Stuka Wing)
> 3rd Close-Support Wing (formerly 3rd Stuka Wing)
> 4th Close-Support Wing (formerly 2nd Close-Support Wing)
> 1st Group, 5th Close-Support Wing (formerly 5th Stuka Wing, it was redesignated as the 3rd Group, 200th Bomber Wing on 10 January 1945)
> 9th Close-Support Wing (antitank wing)
> 10th Close-Support Wing (formerly 1st Close-Support Wing)
> 77th Close-Support Wing (formerly 77th Stuka Wing)

✠

The "flying tank destroyers" represented something completely new in the history of air warfare. The force was created because the army no longer had available sufficient antitank weapons and Soviet tanks were able to break through the front in many places. As bombs had been shown to be relatively ineffective against lone tanks, the new Hs-129 close-support aircraft was equipped with the 30-mm MK 101 cannon. An antitank squadron was tested as part of the 1st Close-Support Wing. The cannon-armed Henschels demonstrated their effectiveness during the Battle of Kharkov, destroying twenty-three Soviet tanks.

This success prompted the Luftwaffe command to form two further antitank squadrons in September 1942: the 4th Squadron of the 2nd Close-Support Wing and the antitank squadron of the 51st Fighter Wing. In December 1942 the 8th Squadron of the 2nd Close-Support Wing was deployed to Tunisia with its Hs-129s. This brought to two the number of antitank squadrons in the area; after the fall of Tunisia both squadrons were transferred to the Eastern Front, where the 8th Squadron was already serving as an antitank unit.

In late 1942 an antitank test detachment was formed at the Rechlin Testing Station under Otto Weiß. Initially, the unit experimented with Ju-87s armed with two 37-mm cannon and Ju-88s equipped with a 75-mm Pak (antitank gun). Tests were also carried out with the Bf-110 and the Hs-129.

In April 1943 the test detachment was sent to the Eastern Front, where it saw action against the Red Army in the Kuban bridgehead. It became clear that neither the Ju-88 nor the Bf-110 were suited to the antitank role. On the other hand, the Ju-87 and Hs-129 were an unqualified success. The test detachment—of which Hans-Ulrich Rudel, the most highly decorated member of the German Armed Forces, was also a member—destroyed no less than 1,000 Red Army troop-carrying vessels in the lagoons of the Kuban.

The experimental unit was disbanded in June 1943, and the two Ju-87 squadrons were attached to the 1st and 2nd Stuka Wings. As early as the beginning of February 1943, the 4th Air Force had created its own anti-tank unit, Antitank Detachment Weiß (*Panzerjagdkommando*). Under Ober-stleutnant Otto Weiß' skilled and energetic leadership, the detachment was able to halt several serious armored penetrations and breakthroughs by the Red Army.

For the first time in history—during Operation Citadel in July 1943—Weiß' forces were able to wage a battle against an enemy armored force solely from the air without support from the army and deal it a destructive blow. The 4th Group of the 9th Close-Support Wing was created from five antitank squadrons equipped with the Hs-129. Led by Hauptmann Bruno Meyer, a veteran of the 2nd Close-Support Wing of the 2nd Training and Demonstration Wing, the group achieved great success in the antitank role.

With this brief overview in mind, let us now take a closer look at the leading pioneer of the fledgling close-support combat aviation forces in the Luftwaffe—Otto Weiß.

PIONEER CLOSE-SUPPORT PILOT AND FIRST TO RECEIVE THE OAK LEAVES: THE ROAD TO CLOSE-SUPPORT PILOT

Otto Weiß was born in Breslau on 25 September 1907. After leaving school in early 1926 he entered the Frankenstein Police School in Silesia, where he trained to become a police officer. In 1931 Weiß became an officer can-didate and, in 1933, he was promoted to Police Lieutenant. On 1 March 1933, at his own request, Weiß was detached to the Oerman Research Insti-tute for Glided Flight in Braunschweig. There he underwent all phases of pilot training and proved to be one of the most talented "flying police-men." His instructors soon realized that the born flyer Weiß had found his element and they pushed him to excel.

On 1 October 1934 Weiß was promoted to Oberleutnant of the police and was taken into the Luftwaffe at the same rank. Weiß later remarked to a friend: "I was happy finally to belong to an arm that had appealed to me since childhood. I was then a career officer in the right place!" From October 1934 until October 1936 Oberleutnant Weiß served as a maintenance officer in an army tactical reconnaissance squadron. Following a promotion to Hauptmann, he served as a staff officer with the 134th Fighter Wing *Horst Wessel* from October 1936 until July 1938.

Weiß was a competent staff officer, but he longed for a position in which he could fly, train young people and better prove himself. He submitted several requests for a transfer to flight duty. Finally, in July 1938, he was relieved of his staff duties and became a squadron commander in the 40th Air Group. On 1 November 1938 the group, officially became the 2nd Close-Support Group of the 2nd Training and Demonstration Wing.

The group's commander, Major Werner Spielvogel, had earlier spoken to Weiß and a number of other good pilots and convinced them to join him. Along with Weiß, who assumed command of the 5th Close-Support Squadron of the 2nd Training and Demonstration Wing, came Oberleutnant Freiherr Horst Grote and Oberleutnant Wolf-Dietrich Peitsmeyer. The commander of the first close-support group comprised the following:

2nd Close-Support Group: Major Spielvogel
4th Close-Support Squadron: Oberleutnant Freiherr Horst Grote
5th Close-Support Squadron: Hauptmann Otto Weiß
6th Close-Support Squadron: Oberleutnant Wolf-Dietrich Peitsmeyer
3rd Close-Support Squadron: (effective September 1939) Oberleutnant Egon Thiem

✠

The aircraft flown by the close-support group was the Hs-123, a biplane with an open cockpit, the only such aircraft still in frontline service with the Luftwaffe.

The Hs-123 was designed at the beginning of the '30s. It had been inspired by the success of similar dive-bombers in the USA, such as the Curtis Hawk. More than anyone else, it was General Udet who brought the dive-bomber idea to Germany and helped promote it. He was the Luftwaffe's Inspector General of Fighters and Dive-Bombers and, starting in June 1936, the Chief of the Technical Office in the Air Ministry. Later he was to become the Chief of Procurement for the Luftwaffe.

The Ju-87 G-1, the anti-tank version of the Stuka armed with two 37mm cannons.

Development of the dive-bomber in Germany was not without its problems, however. When the later Generalfeldmarschall Wolfram Freiherr von Richthofen took over the Technical Office's Development Department, he and his advisors rejected development of a dive-bomber, arguing that a diving flight below 2,000 meters was madness.

In spite of this setback, several engineers continued work on this development. The Henschel Firm built the Hs-123 and demonstrated it to Ernst Udet in early 1935. The latter was enthusiastic about the project, especially since he had flown a Curtis Hawk "dive-bomber" in the USA.

On 8 May 1935 Udet himself demonstrated the diving ability of the Hs-123 at Johannisthal, but it was a year before the air ministry invited tenders for a dive-bomber. The Hs-123 was not considered, as the general concept for a dive-bomber had changed. The robust biplane was then introduced into the Luftwaffe as a close-support aircraft.

✠

Here are some specifications concerning the Hs-123, an aircraft that was well-liked by Otto Weiß and all of his comrades:

- Single-engine dive-bomber and close-support aircraft.
- Single-bay, unbraced biplane, two-part upper wing with two spars, one-piece lower wing with continuous main spar.
- Wings of all-metal construction, wing undersides partially fabric covered.
- Fuselage: All metal monocoque with oval cross-section.
- Empennage: Conventional braced structure. Metal structure, metal-covered stabilizers, fabric-covered control surfaces.
- Undercarriage: Conventional cantilever undercarriage. Main wheels on robust, faired legs with Uerdinger annular spring shock absorbers. Non-retractable, castoring tailwheel, faired.
- Power Plant: One BMW 132 D air-cooled nine-cylinder radial engine producing 880 horsepower for takeoff. Three-bladed metal variable-pitch propeller.
- Crew: pilot seated in open cockpit.
- Armament: 2 x 7.9-mm MG 17 in the forward fuselage firing through the propeller arc. One 250-kilogram bomb beneath the fuselage. Underwing racks for four 50-kilogram bombs.

✠

The reliable and well-liked Hs-123, with its outstanding unimproved field performance, was to see service until mid 1944, even though its replacement, the Hs-129, began entering service in 1942. The latter type featured an armored cockpit and carried a standard armament of two 20-mm MG 151/20 cannon and two 7.9-mm machine guns. Those were complemented by various underwing stores. Frontline trials with heavy-caliber cannon began in the summer of 1942. The Hs-129 B-1/R2 was armed with a 30-mm cannon mounted under the fuselage. Armament of the Hs-129 B-2/R3 consisted of two 20-mm MG 151/20 cannon in the fuselage nose and a 37-mm BK 37 cannon under the fuselage, while the B-2/R4 carried a 75-mm cannon.

WAR SERVICE: CLOSE-SUPPORT PILOT
IN THE POLISH CAMPAIGN

Major Werner Spielvogel had gathered the squadron commanders of his 2nd Close-Support Group around him. The 1st of September 1939 was just two hours old and the assembled officers knew that war with Poland was imminent.

"At 0415 hours our group will attack the Polish border fortifications. We are under the direct command of the Commander of Special-Purpose Air Forces, General von Richthofen, and our mission is to support the breakthrough by the 10th Army."

The group commander stepped up to the map on the wall of the staff building. He picked up a pointer and gestured toward the Polish defensive positions marked on the map.

"Beginning from the left, the Fourth Squadron will take out the two flanking bunkers and silence the antiaircraft guns behind them. The Fifth Squadron will subsequently attack and put out of action the adjoining machine-gun positions. To the right the Sixth Squadron takes out the other machine-gun positions and the Polish command center believed to be in the town."

Major Spielvogel looked at his men one by one. There was the commander of the 4th Close-Support Squadron, Hauptmann Weiß. His face expressed a grim determination. Spielvogel nodded to the experienced aviator. He knew that he could depend on Weiß no matter what the situation. The same applied to Hauptmann Thiem, who commanded the 5th Squadron and Oberleutnant Peitsmeyer, the commander of the remaining squadron. The pilots went to the canteen for breakfast; on the airfield, the ground crews were still working on the aircraft and making their final inspections of weapons and ammunition.

"How do you think today will turn out, Wolf?" Egon Thiem asked his friend Peitsmeyer.

"Good, I think. We've flown these open crates enough."

"And you, Otto?" said Thiem, turning to Hauptmann Weiß.

"I think we will attack, fill the Poles' pants full of lead and then drive back to base," replied the oldest of the three squadron commanders.

At 0410 hours everyone taking part in the operation was ordered to cockpit readiness. Otto Weiß walked out to his Hs-123 and nodded to the two ground crewmen; he had earlier come out and exchanged a few words with them before the group commander held his briefing.

"All clear, sir!" reported Unteroffizier Körtning.

Weiß thanked the noncommissioned officer, climbed into the open cockpit and put on his parachute. The Unteroffizier standing on the wing helped fasten the straps.

The distinctive voice of Major Spielvogel sounded over the frequency: "Drake to all ducklings: Ready for takeoff!"

All three squadron commanders confirmed that they were ready to go. Takeoff clearance was given at 0430 hours and the Hs-123s began to roll. The biplanes lifted off after reaching the prescribed takeoff speed and climbed into the pale morning sky. The group circled the airfield twice while it formed up into the designated formation and then turned east. It was 0445 hours and everyone in the group knew that the infantry's attack was beginning. It was time for them to join the fray as well.

"Target ahead!" reported the group commander.

Ahead and below them they saw the marshy banks of the Liswarthe River. Weiß also saw the dense groups of advancing tanks belonging to the 1st Panzer Division, the spearhead of the 10th Army.

The enemy positions appeared out of the morning fog. The enemy guns opened fire; the gunfire could be heard clearly by the pilots in their open cockpits.

"To all aircraft: Attack!"

Otto Weiß directed his squadron a little farther to the left, then he gave the order to attack. His twelve aircraft nosed down steeply as they began their approach to the target. The slipstream howled in the bracing wires as the Hs-123s picked up speed.

Otto Weiß saw the bunker on the left flank. Behind it two Polish light antiaircraft guns fired at the Henschels. He steepened his dive. The wings of his aircraft vibrated. Then he had reached the most favorable bombing position. Weiß released his two 250-kg bombs and pulled the aircraft out of its dive. The protesting Hs-123 screamed as it gained altitude in a climbing left turn in order to escape the enemy antiaircraft fire. Looking down, Weiß saw his bombs explode in front of the bunker and shake it to its foundations. The machine-gun fire coming from the bunker's embrasure ceased.

Weiß turned his aircraft to the right and positioned himself to attack the enemy antiaircraft guns, which were still firing. Bombs exploded to his right; the squadron's attack was having the desired effect.

The defenders then concentrated their fire on Weiß in an attempt to stop him. Rifle fire joined the light antiaircraft weapons. Weiß evaded the fire by sliding to the left. He then dove a second time on the enemy. He opened fire with his two 7.9-mm machine guns and watched as cascades of dirt sprang up in front of the two antiaircraft guns. He then walked the fire into the two positions and silenced the antiaircraft fire.

When he pulled up from his firing pass, Weiß noted that there was no more resistance. The position, which had been selected as the point at which 1st Motorized Rifle Brigade of the 1st Panzer Division under Generalmajor Kirchner would break through, was then open to attack.

Major Spielvogel called his pilots and ordered them to head for home. The Henschels flew over the attacking units of the 1st Panzer Division to their two bases and landed safely.

✠

"Get everything ready for the next mission," Weiß instructed his two ground crew. He was certain that the second mission would not be long in coming.

At the debriefing in the group command post Major Spielvogel wasted no time on empty praise. Everything had gone smoothly, but he warned his pilots: "Just don't think it will always be like that. This time the element of surprise was on our side. The second attack will be different."

The advance of the 1st Panzer Division advance progressed smoothly. Then one of the neighboring divisions reported that it was being attacked by Polish cavalry and had to withdraw. The 4th Squadron took off for the second time that day. This time Hauptmann Weiß was at the head of his squadron. He was the first to reach the scene of the fighting and saw the second attack by the Polish cavalry unit. He was shocked to see that the attack was being made over completely open terrain. He clenched his teeth and ordered his pilots to spread out.

Once in position—with a lateral spacing of sixty to eighty meters—the Henschel biplanes dove on the enemy cavalry on a front of one kilometer and opened fire. The Polish horsemen fell under the dense machine-gun fire; they looked like toy cavalry being knocked over by the fist of a young boy. The attackers passed over the decimated cavalry and pulled up about 2,000 meters behind them. Then they reversed course and once again opened fire. The attack by the Polish cavalry collapsed. None of the pilots said a word after they landed. In their minds they could still see the awful slaughter, the result of the senseless Polish cavalry attack.

During the next three days the close-support aviators repeatedly assisted in the ground fighting, whenever the enemy resisted at a river crossing or fortified town. During the crossing of the Warthe River near the villages of Plawno and Gidle by the 1st Panzer Division, an attack on a Polish line of resistance by Otto Weiß and his squadron helped get the attack of 4th Motorized Reconnaissance Battalion moving again.

During the advance of the 1st Panzer Division between Tomaszow-Nortb and the Pilica, the close-support squadrons under Major Spielvogel struck a number of blows at the enemy. The attacks in support of the storming of Ujazd by the 1st Panzer Division resulted in a difficult situation for Otto Weiß. While flying very low he was caught in a storm of enemy machine-gun fire. His Hs-123 was hit several times and a bullet grazed his shoulder.

Weiß went even lower. He flew under the enemy machine-gun fire and returned safely to base, where be had his wound tended to. He was sent by Major Spielvogel to the forward aid station with instructions to first have his wound seen to and then rest for several days. But that was not the way of Hauptmann Weiß. Three hours later, at supper time, he returned to his group and reported himself ready for duty.

The city of Krakow fell on 6 September. That evening, Weiß and his comrades listened to a special bulletin:

> Wednesday afternoon German troops moved unopposed into Krakow. The commanding general of the corps in front of Krakow and the commander of the division that entered Krakow paid their respects at the grave of Marshall Pilsudski. An honor guard has been posted.
>
> The bridges over the Vistula there are intact. Bromberg has also been taken by German troops. The Netze was crossed to the south in the Bromberg area. At 1400 hours on Wednesday our

Hs-123s of the 2nd Training and Demonstration Wing's 2nd Close-Support Group at Cognac, France, in 1940. J. V. CROW COLLECTION

forces crossed the Lask-Unyewo road in the direction of Lodz. The important road and rail junction of Lielce at the foot of the Lysa Gora was occupied by our troops this morning.

"There's not much left for us to do then," declared one of the young officers.

"We have successfully completed the first and perhaps the most important part of the Polish Campaign," answered Major Spielvogel. "The important thing now is to prevent the enemy from getting back to his feet. I am certain that if that happens we will reach Warsaw in the next few days and the campaign in Poland will be over. That would surely also force the French and the English to come round."

"Possibly," interjected Wolf-Dietrich Peitsmeyer. "In any case, neither of Poland's allies have done a single thing to help her."

"And if they wait another week we'll be finished here and then we can move all our forces west and seal things off there," added Egon Thieme.

THE DEATH OF THE GROUP COMMANDER

The 7th of September found the 4th Panzer Division advancing at high speed toward the northeast. For the first time in the campaign it caught up with its neighbor, the 1st Panzer Division. Generalleutnant Reinhardt had a radio message sent to Guderian's corps headquarters: "The enemy is on the run! Division is pursuing!"

By evening the village of Babsk had been reached; the 4th Panzer Division had covered 40 kilometers in one day. In his division command post Generalleutnant Reinhardt leaned over the map. He found Babsk with the notation: "Forty kilometers to Warsaw!"

That day Spielvogel's group flew ahead of the 1st Panzer Division and attacked the enemy positions which flanked Tomaszow to the west and southwest. Otto Weiß and his squadron reached the target and the nine aircraft dropped their bombs, effectively clearing the way for the 1st Panzer Division to storm Tomaszow.

On the way back to base Otto Weiß spotted an enemy column to the south. It was moving toward the northwest, probably hoping to establish contact with the retreating Polish units beyond Tomaszow. If it did so, it would significantly strengthen the Polish forces there.

"To group commander: Have sighted large enemy column. Request permission to engage."

"Permission granted. I'm sending the 5th Squadron; the 6th Squadron keeps watch to the north and northwest."

Weiß ordered his squadron to turn and descend. The enemy column grew larger rapidly. Weiß called out targets to his men and then, racing over the column at barely 200 meters, he pushed the stick forward slightly to lower the nose of his aircraft and opened fire. The twin streams of tracer from his two machine guns ripped through the rows of trucks and horse-drawn artillery. Fires broke out; trucks veered to the side and crashed into the ditches. Behind him, Weiß could hear the guns of the other aircraft. He then saw the 5th Squadron joining them from behind and to the left.

"Be careful, Egon," Weiß called to the colleague of the other squadron. "Don't shoot any of us down."

"Don't worry, we're attacking the rear of the column; we're three kilometers behind you."

Weiß flew over the head of the column, pulled up into a climbing right turn and, after reversing course, dove on the Polish column again, this time from the front.

Weiß was almost out of ammunition when he saw tracers from several machine-guns arcing toward him. Just as he was about to veer out of the line of fire, he heard bullets striking his machine. There was a blow in the front section of the Hs-123 and, seconds later, the engine began to sputter.

He called to his squadron: "I've been hit in the engine . . . trying to reach our lines."

Weiß heard the voice of Leutnant Chalupka, who had joined the squadron just before the outbreak of war: "I'll cover you, sir."

"Understood, Siegfried," acknowledged Weiß. The squadron was still hunting down the last vehicles in the column. Otto Weiß sought to gain altitude and managed to reach a height of about 400 meters. Looking around, he saw the young Leutnant in his wake.

"Another ten kilometers, sir," reported Chalupka.

"We'll make it for sure," Weiß called back. But it was not to be. Suddenly, the Henschel stalled and Weiß was just able to clear a small patch of woods straddling his flight path. On the far side of the woods he saw a level field that looked like a suitable place to land.

"I have to land, Chalupka. Send our Storch here."

Otto Weiß brought his machine down smoothly. He touched down gently and rolled to a stop. The Leutnant, who had observed the landing, was about to pull up and fly back to base, when he saw at least twenty Polish soldiers storm out of the woods. Looking down, Chalupka saw Otto Weiß dashing across the open field toward the cover of some bushes. The Polish troops opened fire at the Hauptmann as he ran for his life.

A determined Chalupka hauled his aircraft around and raced at low level toward the men pursuing his squadron commander. He opened fire with both machine guns and saw the Poles fall to the ground. Then he fired several long bursts into the forest. He pulled up just over the treetops and turned. He saw Weiß disappear into the bushes. Spotting movement at the edge of the woods, Chalupka fired one last burst into the trees. Then he flew a wide turn and headed toward base at high speed.

Major Spielvogel, who was standing at the edge of the airfield waiting for the last of his aircraft to return, saw Chalupka approaching to land. He waved to the young Leutnant who landed and then taxied to a stop only a few paces from his group commander.

"Where is Hauptmann Weiß?" Spielvogel asked.

"The Poles got him with a full burst. Hauptmann Weiß had to land about eight kilometers from here on this side of the woods near Bielcze. I chased the Poles out of the woods. He's waiting for the Storch."

"Get the Storch ready," ordered Major Spielvogel. He ran to the command post and emerged two minutes later wearing his flight suit and pistol belt. "Peitsmeyer, you take over until we get back."

"You're not going to bring Weiß back in that flea are you?" the Leutnant asked anxiously.

"You bet . . . it works and it's the fastest. There's no time to lose."

"I'll follow with two aircraft in case you run into difficulties." The group commander nodded. The Storch lifted off and disappeared in seconds behind a rise.

Peitsmeyer and Unteroffizier Honseleit took off in aircraft that had just been refueled and took up the course Leutnant Chalupka had quickly shown them. When Major Spielvogel spotted the characteristic narrow patch of woods ahead of him, he dropped low over the trees. He saw the green signal flare, the agreed-upon emergency signal.

Descending lower, he saw Otto Weiß half standing and pointing to a clearing. The Storch descended and landed safely. Spielvogel waited as Weiß dashed toward the aircraft. Weiß squeezed in behind the pilot. He had to hold himself bent far forward, half hanging over the pilot, as the latter took off and the light aircraft slowly gained height.

When they reached 200 meters the pair heard the engine noises of several aircraft behind them. Bullets ripped through the fabric covering of the Storch; then Spielvogel let out a loud cry when Peitsmeyer and Honseleit appeared ahead of them. The pair dove on their attackers and shot them down. The two Henschels then took up station ahead and behind the Storch and escorted it safely back to base.

The four men shook hands after landing and Peitsmeyer observed: "That could have turned to shit in a second."

But the group commander replied: "Well, that's why none of us can get life insurance."

✠

In the days that followed the close-support aviators flew as many as six sorties a day in support of the advancing army formations. Near Chynow, about 10 kilometers west of the Vistula, they attacked retreating Polish units. They were under orders from above to spare the two Vistula bridges at Opacz and Brzumin, which the 1st Panzer Division was to use to get across the river. Their targets were the Polish columns.

By the time night fell, the 1st Panzer Division had covered 100 kilometers, advancing past abandoned weapons and equipment. At that point, it was far ahead of the rest of Army Group South; the division reached the suburbs of Warsaw. The 1st Panzer Brigade (of the 1st Panzer Division) under Oberst Harpe had reached its objective in eight days.

On the left flank, the 4th Panzer Division also made rapid progress. Spielvogel's squadrons also flew sorties in support of the division on that day and helped break Polish resistance at Raziejowice and Wolica and at Secocin and Raszyn. General of the Cavalry Erich Hoepner had brought his XVI Motorized Army Corps to the gates of Warsaw. Oberst Harpe proposed to Hoepner that they exploit the situation and attempt to seize Warsaw without waiting for reinforcements. After all, the Polish government had declared Warsaw an open city. Consequently, no Polish troops were allowed in the city.

General Hoepner gave his consent, but there were large contingents of troops under General Karaszewica-Tokarewski inside Warsaw. The Polish commander had ordered his troops to defend the capital "to the last drop of blood."

Harpe's tank brigade began the assault on Warsaw at 1700 hours on 8 September. On reaching the city limits, the troops were met by rifle fire from behind Polish barricades consisting of overturned streetcars and vans. Oberst Harpe realized that the city was strongly defended. The attempt to seize the city had to be abandoned. Polish artillery fired from the suburb of Praga. The next morning, an advance by the 4th Panzer Division was stopped by fire from Polish antitank guns.

The three squadrons of the close-support group were sent into action. Otto Weiß and his men were assigned as targets the Polish gun positions in

Praga and the antitank gun positions at the entrance to the city. The Henschel biplanes dove through a hail of antiaircraft and small-arms fire and dropped their bombs on the Polish positions. They were put out of action, one after another. Feldwebel Steincke's aircraft was hit and went down. The pilot was able to take to his parachute, but he was never seen again.

Otto Weiß' Hs-123 was also hit several times, but it kept flying. After landing, his two ground crew walked around the aircraft and counted seventeen holes. The faithful "One-Two-Three," as the aircraft was known to its pilots, had absorbed the damage and brought its pilot home.

There was little time for repairs; two hours later the entire group took off on another mission. Warsaw had to be taken. On the morning of 10 September the commander-in-chief of the 10th Army, General of the Artillery von Reichenau, had told Hitler at his headquarters that the fall of the city was as good as assured. Furthermore, the Wehrmacht daily report released on the evening of 8 September:

> German troops entered Warsaw at 1715 hours on 8 September. Mobile forces have reached the Vistula near Sandomierz in Southern Poland and at Gora Kalwarja southeast of Warsaw.

However, Warsaw had not fallen. True, German troops had entered the city, but they had been forced to withdraw again. Hitler had to be told

Hs-129 B-1/R-2 with 30mm Mk-101 cannon in Russia, 1942–43. Note the sand filters and yellow nose. J. V. CROW COLLECTION

the truth, but it was sweetened by the addition of the news that General von Reichenau was in the process of bagging eight to ten Polish divisions that had been completely surrounded by the 10th Army.

The days that followed saw the initiation of the Battle at the Bzura, a desperate counterattack by Polish forces. The close-support squadrons were in the air almost constantly and assisting the hard-pressed German ground forces.

Flying from their base in Altsiedel—then from Witkowicze and Wolworz and later from Mazowszany and Zalesie—the pilots flew up to ten sorties per day in their open-cockpit biplanes. It was an absolute record.

Ju-87s from the 2nd, 76th, and 77th Stuka Wings destroyed the bridges over the Bzura, cutting off the Polish forward troops and stopping the attack. The Stukas and Henschels then pounded the isolated forces remorselessly. The Hs-123 pilots discovered that if engine revolutions were set at 1,800 rpm the sound of the engine was so loud that it terrified both men and horses during low-level attacks. The Poznan army was soon surrounded, and organized resistance collapsed on 18 September with the surrender of some 170,000 troops.

✠

On 13 September the Battle of the Bzura entered its decisive phase. The situation that morning was unclear, but soon one call for help after another was ringing out from the front. Major Spielvogel took off in the Fieseler Storch in order to personally reconnoiter the area. He intended to be gone thirty minutes at most. When an hour went by with no sign of the commander, Hauptmann Weiß decided to go looking for him. The others talked him out of it, however. As senior pilot he would have to take over if the group commander failed to return.

The search for Major Spielvogel was fruitless. The Fieseler Storch had been shot down; a few days later the burnt-out wreck of the aircraft was found, but there was no trace of Major Spielvogel.

Otto Weiß then took over command of the unit which, over the course of the next three days, participated in the desperate fighting at the Bzura River. Weiß' men urged him to remain behind while they flew the combat missions, but he refused to consider such a course of action.

Weiß flew four sorties on 15 September, destroying three enemy tanks with bombs and decimating a Polish vehicle column. During a visit to his sole close-support group, General Wolfram Freiherr von Richthofen personally pinned the Iron Cross, First Class on the tunic of Otto Weiß. Weiß had earlier received the Iron Cross, Second Class (4 September).

The 2nd Close-Support Group the 2nd Training and Demonstration Wing had successfully passed its baptism of fire in the campaign in Poland. Luftwaffe dive bombing and ground-attack forces played a significant part in the victory. The Hs-123s of the 2nd Group in particular achieved results all out of proportion to their numbers.

THE CAMPAIGN IN THE WEST: SUCCESSFUL CLOSE-SUPPORT AVIATORS RECEIVE THE KNIGHT'S CROSS

Under its new commanding officer, the 2nd Close-Support Group was in action from the very beginning of the invasion of Western Europe on the morning of 10 May 1940. Once again, the group was placed under the direct command of the VIII Air Corps commanded by General von Richthofen. The group's first sorties were in support of German forces taking part in the Battle of Maastricht and the paratroopers involved in the assault on the Belgian fortress of Eben Emael.

Hauptmann Weiß led his group against the Belgian relief force trying to reach Eben Emael in order to dislodge the German airborne forces that had landed on the plateau by glider. In several pitiless and quick attacks, the group was able to halt the enemy force short of its objective.

In the days that followed, the group moved up to bases in the area north of Cambrai. On the morning of 17 May 1940 a badly shot-up He-46 reconnaissance aircraft flew low over the airfield and dropped a message capsule which was immediately taken to Hauptmann Weiß. He opened the capsule, took out the message and read: "Observer seriously wounded. My report: North of your group's airfield are about 50 heavy French tanks and 150 trucks with French infantry approaching in attack formation. Immediate action required."

The alarm siren sounded fifteen seconds later. All the pilots ran to the group barracks carrying their equipment. There they found Hauptmann Weiß already wearing his flight gear.

"Gentlemen, we will scramble immediately . . . form up in flight heading north. Large numbers of enemy tanks approaching followed by infantry. Takeoff in five minutes."

While the pilots ran to their aircraft and checked their weapons once more, Otto Weiß called the 1st Group of the 21st Fighter Wing, a fighter group commanded by Hauptmann Ultsch and based at a nearby airfield:

"Ultsch, there are enemy tanks ten kilometers north of my base. Many trucks carrying infantry. Request you assist us in attacking them."

"Thank you, Weiß, I'm on my way!" replied Hauptmann Ultsch, who then slammed down the receiver.

Weiß then called the 33rd Flak Regiment's 1st Battalion, which was in the vicinity. The battalion commander promised to immediately send his guns to engage the enemy tanks. Weiß hurried outdoors. The first aircraft of the 4th and 5th Squadrons of the 2nd Training and Demonstration Wing were already in the air. The remaining squadron was preparing to take off. Hauptmann Weiß ran to his aircraft, which was flanked by the remaining machines of the headquarters flight. He nodded to his two mechanics and climbed into the cockpit. The engine sprang to life and the Hs-123 began to roll. The sturdy biplane picked up speed and then lifted off; it was followed closely by the other three aircraft of the headquarters flight.

Weiß increased speed and positioned himself at the head of the formation. Oberleutnant Thiem was the first to sight the enemy. He alerted the others: "Trucks ahead. In front and to the right of them a mass of enemy tanks!"

The second report came from Peitsmeyer. Then Otto Weiß spotted a wave of tanks. They were 1,000 meters ahead of the rest and were rolling straight toward their airfield.

"Fourth Squadron: Take the first wave. Fifth and Sixth Squadrons: The rest. Attack by squadrons."

They raced toward the enemy. The Henschels swooped down on the tanks meeting only sporadic defensive fire. Weiß was the first to drop his bombs. They landed right in front of a French tank and flipped the steel giant over.

Flames spurted from the interior of the tank. Weiß raced onward and reached the trucks. As he fired bursts of machine-gun fire at the fleeing vehicles, he heard the sound of exploding bombs and saw fuel tanks exploding in flame.

"Antiaircraft fire ahead, sir!" reported Oberfeldwebel Förster, a member of the headquarters flight.

"Turn right and avoid the fire; then attack the trucks!" Weiß ordered.

On its first pass his headquarters flight had destroyed four enemy tanks and damaged two, which were limping from the battlefield. Weiß dove on one of the damaged tanks from behind and fired a long burst from his machine-guns into its rear. In a matter of seconds, the engine burst into flames and the crew abandoned the crippled vehicle.

The remaining squadrons had also dropped their bombs. In the meantime, the Bf-109s of the 21st Fighter Wing's 1st Group under Hauptmann Ultsch had also reached the battlefield. They immediately joined the engagement against the French ground element. It was the first time in the Second World War that such an engagement had been fought exclusively from the air.

The 4th Close-Support Squadron of the 2nd Training and Demonstration Wing flew back to base and rearmed. Thirty minutes later, it was back in the air again. The proximity of the airfield made refueling unnecessary.

Once again, Weiß and his men dropped their bombs and went after the French vehicles, which by then had scattered and were seeking cover. Hauptmann Ultsch called out the hiding place of several tanks behind two squat farm buildings. Once again, Otto Weiß noted how pilots of open-cockpit aircraft heard everything much more intensely and clearly than in other aircraft. He swept over the fleeing French troops without firing. His target was a group of trucks sitting camouflaged behind some vegetation; the smoke rising from their exhausts gave away their position.

Circling around, Weiß attacked the group of trucks from the flank and shot up two vehicles. He then approached from behind and opened fire again, flying not ten meters above the French vehicles. His aircraft was hit several times by ground fire, but Weiß himself was spared.

The fighting raged for three hours. When it was over, a total of forty knocked-out enemy armored vehicles were counted on the battlefield. The attacks against the French infantry in their assembly positions in the rear went on for another two hours. By then, Weiß and his group had flown three sorties.

The small German force had succeeded in destroying a major enemy formation that was preparing to advance out of its assembly area in the Mormal Forest, drive a wedge between the onrushing German armored units and prevent them from advancing any farther.

Of the 40 enemy armored vehicles destroyed, 2nd Close-Support Group was credited with thirty.

✠

Hauptmann Weiß' initiative and tactical skill enabled him to defeat the enemy attack before it unfolded and avert a possible disaster for the German ground forces.

Hauptmann Otto Weiß became the first close-support pilot to receive the Knight's Cross on 18 May 1940. The night before he had been named in the Wehrmacht daily report. The following excerpt is taken from the award recommendation:

He is awarded this decoration on account of his personal bravery and the effective action of his group in intervening in the ground fighting in the Western Campaign.

Hauptmann Otto Weiß saved the narrow German armored sickle slicing toward the English Channel from an enemy flanking threat near Cambrai.

TO THE END OF THE FRENCH CAMPAIGN—NEW EQUIPMENT

The war in France went on. German air elements were committed against the British naval forces off Dunkirk and the ships picking up the troops from the beaches after Reichsmarschall Göring proposed that "the Luftwaffe should prevent the embarkation of the British Expeditionary Corps and its retreat to the British Isles."

Otto Weiß and his men once again played a leading role in the German effort. His dive-bombing attacks through the gunfire of the British destroyers on the Dunkirk roadstead were famous. These attacks by Weiß sank a number of enemy vessels.

After accompanying the armored formations to the sea, Weiß and his group also played a part in bringing the fighting there to a successful conclusion, even though Göring's assurances that the Luftwaffe alone could defeat the enemy proved unfounded. The Luftwaffe had far too few aircraft to succeed in such an undertaking.

The Battle of Dunkirk came to an end; the Luftwaffe had been unable to finish off the British Home Army alone. Admiral Ramsey succeeded in bringing 350,000 men back to the island. Instead of pursuing the disheartened enemy and risking the leap across to the British Isles (as proposed by Student the airborne general), the German Army stopped. It then turned to take up the pursuit of the French in the second phase of the campaign.

The pursuit to the River Seine saw the 2nd Close-Support Group heavily committed in support of the advancing armies. On 1 July Otto Weiß was promoted to Major for bravery in the face of the enemy. He and his men effectively silenced enemy fortifications on both sides of the Oise during the crossing of the river by the army.

The German advance continued. The Aisne front was broken with the help of the close-support group, after which the German infantry crossed the Loire. Oberleutnant Horst Freiherr Grote, who had taken over the 4th Close-Support Squadron from Otto Weiß, played a prominent role in the air-ground battle against French machine-gun and antitank gun positions.

Otto Weiß turned his attentions to the destruction of enemy tanks. On a number of occasions groups of French tanks attached to infantry units tried to halt the German advance. The number of enemy tanks destroyed by his group in these sorties approached the amount accounted for by the 10th Panzer Division. The pursuit of the enemy continued into Normandy and then through Brittany. Oberleutnant Peitsmeyer's 6th Close-Support Squadron and Hauptmann Egon Thiem's 5th Close-Support Squadron were constantly engaged against enemy positions and tanks as well as anti-tank and antiaircraft guns.

The group suffered four losses, which was all the more serious because they could not be replaced right away. In spite of the losses, Major Weiß was confident that his aviators would be able to respond to calls for support from the army as before.

The entire group flew ground-support missions for the army in the final phase of the campaign. The Henschel biplanes—looking like relics from an earlier period of aviation, but nevertheless highly effective—were always a welcome sight to the German ground forces.

✠

The campaign in France came to an end. By that time Major Weiß had submitted recommendations for the Knight's Cross for all three of his squadron commanders. His submissions were processed and General von Richthofen "warmly endorsed" each one.

On 21 July 1940 the close-support group was drawn up in formation. Standing in front of their squadrons were the commanders of each squadron. Major Otto Weiß presented the group to the commanding general, Wolfram Freiherr von Richthofen. (Two days prior he was promoted to full General, thus skipping the rank of Generalleutnant.) The General decorated Wolf-Dietrich Peitsmeyer, Horst Freiherr Grote and Egon Thiem with the Knight's Cross. After receiving their decorations, the three officers accompanied the General as he reviewed the assembled airmen.

✠

Following the end of the campaign in France the group was issued the Bf-109 E-4/B fighter-bomber at Braunschweig (Waggum). Beginning in September, the group carried out attacks with bombs and guns against

The highest decorations a flyer could win. ***Top center:*** the Knight's Cross with Oak Leaves, Swords, and Diamonds. To the left of it, the Oak Leaves; to the right, the Oak Leaves with Swords. ***Top right:*** the Oak Leaves, Swords, and Diamonds. ***Bottom left:*** the Pilot Badge in Gold with Diamonds. ***Bottom center:*** the Golden Combat Mission Bar Pendant for 2,000 missions. ***Bottom right:*** the German Cross in Gold.

coastal targets in Southern England from its base at Calais. Major Weiß also took part in these operations, carrying out a number of attacks against enemy port installations. On one occasion, Weiß' aircraft sustained major damage over England, and he just managed to return to base, where he carried out a forced landing.

Though flying the Bf-109 was less physically demanding than the Hs-123, the men repeatedly asked for their old aircraft back. In early 1941 the group received a squadron equipped with the Hs-123.

✠

Otto Weiß subsequently received word from the Luftwaffe personnel office to report to the School of Air Warfare in Berlin (Gatow) on 10 October. There he was to participate in a course for future wing commanders, even though he had already demonstrated his ability in practical terms. He would attend that course until February 1941. Weiß finished in the top of his class. Once finished with the course, he was assigned to a fighter division on the Channel as its operations officer in order to gain experience in staff work with a larger formation. That assignment lasted until May 1941.

During that same period the 2nd Close-Support Group—with its two Bf-109 squadrons and one Hs-123 squadron—was deployed to the Balkans. Major Weiß received enthusiastic letters from his friend Oberleutnant Dörffel describing the operations there. Dörffel, who had received the Iron Crosses, First and Second Class for his daring actions in France, commanded the 5th Close-Support Squadron (Hs-123) in Yugoslavia.

With the start of the campaign against Russia imminent, Weiß received orders to immediately return to his group on the morning of 21 June 1941.

When Otto Weiß rejoined his group at its new base on the old Polish-Russian border, he discovered that the formation had undergone a profound change during his months-long absence. The group had received another full-strength Hs-123 squadron in early 1941 and two squadrons of Bf-109s had been deployed to the Balkans in April, where they enjoyed success. There was a small party—the invasion of the USSR was to begin next morning—to celebrate Weiß' return to the group. After a few hours, Weiß felt as if he had never left his comrades, especially when he was welcomed by his old ground crew, Feldwebel Heinz Kortning and Unteroffizier Bäcker, like a prodigal son.

Once again, the group was placed under the direct command of the VIII Air Corps, which was positioned in the central sector of the Eastern Front. Its role was to support the 9th Army and the 3rd Panzer Group as they broke through the enemy's border fortifications.

THE CAMPAIGN AGAINST RUSSIA: THE 2ND CLOSE-SUPPORT GROUP DURING OPERATION BARBAROSSA

The German invasion of the Soviet Union began at 0330 hours on 22 June 1941. The German assault began with attacks on 66 Soviet airfields; 1,200 aircraft were destroyed, most of them on the ground. The same day Adolf Hitler left Berlin and traveled to his forward headquarters near Rastenburg (East Prussia), which had been code-named Wolfs' Lair (*Wolfsschanze*). On his arrival there, he learned that the most important river crossings had succeeded. The army had already established deep bridgeheads beyond the Bug, the Dubissa and the Memel and was continuing its eastward advance.

✠

The Bf-109s and Hs-123s of Weiß' group were in action from the very first day of Operation Barbarossa.

Whenever the 9th Army was stopped by Russian bunker lines and in-depth obstacles, it called in the "butchers." Under the skilful leadership of Major Weiß, the group destroyed seven bunkers and forty antitank and machine-gun positions in the first week while helping to clear the way for the infantry. Otto Weiß and his men were heavily committed during the battle of encirclement at Bialystok and Minsk and the subsequent pursuit in the direction of Smolensk. All of the group's aircraft were put into the air there to combat a mass of Soviet tanks that had broken through the infantry.

The Hs-123s and Bf-109s made repeated dive-bombing attacks against the Soviet tanks. Major Weiß flew seven sorties that day and destroyed no fewer than five tanks with bombs. Two others were damaged and forced to flee the battlefield.

When the 2nd Panzer Group crossed the Dniepr River it looked as if Hitler's intention of destroying the Soviet Union in six to eight weeks might be realized. Bialystok-Minsk had cost the Red Army approximately 40 divisions. 287,704 Soviet troops had been captured after the Luftwaffe closed the gaps in the encircling ring. The Wehrmacht daily reports reported the capture of 2,585 tanks, 1,449 guns, and 245 aircraft.

☩

It was at this point that Stalin pulled the concept of the "Great Patri-otic War" from the drawer of history in which it had lain since 1812. At the same time he called for the formation of partisan forces. The Soviet offi-cers who had escaped the disaster were arrested. As early as 1 July an NKVD (secret-police) detachment shot Generals Dimitri Pavlol and Alexander Korobkov. A short time later Generals Nikolai Klitsch, Vladimir Klinovskich and Alexander Kosublitski went the same way.

Hitler was already planning to conduct a "world blitzkrieg" against England and the USA, a point he stressed to the Japanese ambassador Oshima. The way the war was progressing seemed to be proving him right.

☩

In the meantime, the Battle of Smolensk had begun. The main forces of the 2nd Panzer Group and the 4th Army were battling the Red Army between Vitebsk in the north and Gomel in the south. The German infantry followed the armored forces in steps, providing the necessary support for the continuation of the advance. In the north of this main front, in the sector of the 3rd Panzer Group, the LVII Motorized Army Corps under General of Infantry Kuntzen drove ahead as far as Nevel in order to make contact with Army Group North. East of Vitebsk, the XXXIX Motorized Army Corps under General of Armored Troops Schmidt was able to advance farther to the east.

As the V and VI Army Corps were available from Vitebsk and the area to the northwest for deployment toward the north, and as the 4th Army under von Kluge had caught up with the 2nd Panzer Group by mid-July, von Kluge was able to commit his corps near Shlobin and Mogilev. The stage was set for a battle of encirclement around Smolensk. By the evening of 15 July strong infantry patrols had entered the southwestern suburbs of the city. The 2nd Panzer Group was deep in the rear of the Soviet army units.

Just as the commanders of the 2nd and 3rd Panzer Groups, Guderian and Hoth, met near Smolensk on 16 July to discuss a further joint advance by their forces to cover the last 150 kilometers to Moscow—a move which was entirely realistic and one that could have turned out to be the deciding act of the campaign against the Soviet Union—the army high command stepped in. It ordered substantial elements of the 3rd Panzer Group diverted north to support Army Group North. As far as the high command was concerned, having reached the land bridge at Smolensk, the advance of Army Group Center was ended for the time being. Thus Moscow, the most important objective of all in the war in the east, was abandoned.

The actions of the German high command gave the enemy the necessary breathing space in which to regroup its forces, reorganize them and move in reinforcements from the interior with which to strengthen its defenses. Forces under Lieutenant-General Yeremenko counterattacked on 19 July and succeeded in breaking through to Smolensk, where they bolstered the Soviet troops still fighting in the city. In the course of this reorganization phase, the 2nd Close-Support Group was moved to the northern sector of the Eastern Front to support the hard-pressed infantry there.

✠

The greatest successes were achieved by the veteran close-support aviators Dörffel, Dörnbrack, Druschel and Bruno Meyer. Otto Weiß continued to fly with his men, leading the way as the group went to the aid of the infantry, often providing decisive support that enabled them to withstand vigorous Soviet assaults.

These pilots all received the Knight's Cross on 21 August 1941 while fighting on the north flank of the Eastern Front. Dörffel had more than 200 combat missions behind him at that point. Dörnbrack had excelled in the missions to contain the pocket at Bialystok-Minsk. Alfred Druschel, who like Weiß came from the 20th Air Group, had not only made a name for himself as a fighter-bomber pilot, but had also shot down seven enemy aircraft. Bruno Meyer had been one of the most successful pilots against enemy tanks in the fighting at Vitebsk.

The group was in high spirits when the four pilots were decorated. As Weiß rightly stated, the decoration of four of its personnel honored the entire formation. In spite of his own great success in Russia, Weiß stayed in the background as far as further decorations for himself were concerned.

✠

Four weeks later Weiß' group was pulled out of the northern sector. Close-support aircraft were needed in the southern sector. The German ground forces there were locked in a struggle against the Soviet Air Force, which made repeated attempts to halt the German advance.

As part of the 4th Air Force under Generaloberst Löhr, the group was under the direct command of the V Air Corps. It was also attached to the IV Air Corps for a time. With the beginning of the double battle of Vyazma-Briansk at the end of September 1941, Weiß' group returned to the central sector. The battle became a decisive duel against enemy armored forces and antiaircraft units. The 2nd Panzer Group had instructions to advance through Orel and Briansk in the direction of Tula. On its right wing, the 3rd Panzer Group was to advance on Vyazma before setting out from there for Gzhatsk and Moscow.

This was the start of the group's most successful period of operations. According to the orders received by Major Weiß, the role of the group was to support the infantry in its advance through the enemy defense lines and engage enemy tanks. Otto Weiß led his group into action on every occasion. He and his pilots were involved at the focal point of the struggle and helped the infantry fight its way to Kalinin. The advance would never have succeeded without these missions.

The Hs-129s, the first of these faster and more heavily armed close-support aircraft to reach the front, repeatedly dove on the waves of Russian tanks. The Hs-129 B-I was armed with two 20-mm MG 151/20 cannon in the fuselage sides and two 7.9-mm MG 17s located in the wing roots between the two spars. The aircraft lacked the heavy-caliber weapons needed to destroy the well-armored Russian tanks from in front, so they attacked from the rear, concentrating on the more vulnerable engine and cooling systems.

When their cannon were armed with antitank rounds with tungsten cores, the Hs-129s could also penetrate the side armor of enemy tanks.

✠

Otto Weiß led the first six Hs-129s into action when the Battle of Vyazma was at its peak. Russian tanks had breached the German lines. Weiß spotted the tanks just as they were rolling through the forward German positions. "Circle and then attack!" he called to his men.

The Henschels flew around the tanks in a wide arc, taking fire from the antiaircraft guns the Russians had moved forward. The defensive fire was inaccurate, however, and the Hs-129s descended to attack height. They were then within range of Russian small-arms fire. Otto Weiß heard bullets striking his aircraft as he reached the minimum height of eighty meters. Then he called to his pilots: "Attack from left to right. Everyone take one!"

The tank he had selected as his target grew quickly. Weiß felt several blows against the armored canopy that protected the pilot of the Hs-129. He then pressed the firing buttons. Weiß saw smoke trails from the armor-piercing 20-mm rounds strike the engine compartment of the enemy tank and clouds of steam spurt from the ruptured cooling system before he flashed past twenty meters above the tank. He turned steeply to the right and set up for a second pass. Below him Weiß saw five tanks burning in the open area. Flames were pouring from the hatches of the vehicle he had attacked.

"Good work! Let's go again! This time the wave farther to the front!"

His pilots called out "target in sight." The Henschels raced over the burning enemy tanks toward the next wave. Wingtip to wingtip, the aircraft flew as if on a training mission. Almost as one, they opened fire on the rear row of enemy tanks. One aircraft was missing from the third pass. Hit by ground fire, it headed for home trailing a banner of black smoke.

With their 20-mm ammunition exhausted, Weiß instructed his pilots to attack Russian positions with their machine-guns. The Henschels worked over the enemy positions until their ammunition was gone. They then headed for home.

When Weiß landed, the group adjutant, Oberleutnant Steinweg, reported that the infantry had already sent a message of thanks. They had counted fifteen tanks knocked out by Weiß and his men; the rest had been put out of action by mechanized infantrymen armed with explosives. The eastern section of the ring around Vyazma and Briansk remained intact.

THE PRINCE OF KALININ

By the second day of the double battle, the 4th Panzer Division had already advanced to the outskirts of Orel, offering the XXXXVII Panzer Corps the chance to turn toward Briansk. The 17th Panzer Division under Generalleutnant von Arnim set out straight toward Briansk; the tanks rolled through the city and seized the bridges over the Desna. Several Soviet armies were encircled near Vyazma. The Wehrmacht daily report of 3 October 1941 reported:

> As announced by special bulletin, the deep penetration operations in the center of the Eastern Front have led to another major battle of encirclement. Attacked in the rear by strong armored forces, three enemy armies now also face destruction in the Briansk area. Together with the units encircled near Vyazma, Marshall Timoshenko has sacrificed the last fully capable armies of the entire Soviet front.

Bitter fighting raged in both pockets until mid-October, however, as the surrounded Soviet armies attempted to break out. Otto Weiß and his close-support group were constantly in action. Frequently flying the Bf-109, he destroyed eighteen Russian tanks in ten days. More were accounted for by his men. Army Group Center took advantage of the gaping hole in the front and, by 15 October, its formations had reached the line Mzensk-Kaluga-Borodino-Kalinin. There they were stopped.

In the weeks that followed, Weiß and his men fought a grim battle against Soviet counterattacks, defending their own base on occasion. It was here that Weiß earned the title "Prince of Kalinin." The close-support aircraft flew in terrible weather, taking off to attack Soviet armor when the visibility was only fifty meters. Weiß raised his total of enemy vehicles destroyed to thirty-one tanks and more than 200 trucks and other types of vehicles, as well as thirty antitank and antiaircraft guns and machine-gun positions.

Finally, the group accompanied the ground forces as they advanced on Moscow. Temperatures had dropped to minus-thirty degrees Celsius. Otto Weiß was in the air several times each day and, by mid-December, had flown more then 450 combat missions.

On 31 December Weiß became the 52nd member of the Wehrmacht to receive the Knight's Cross with Oak Leaves. He was the first member of a close-support formation to receive that decoration. The group still flew the Bf-109, which was also armed with 20-mm cannon, as there were not enough Hs-129s to permit a general reequipping with the aircraft.

Hubertus Hitschhold, who later rose to the rank of Generalmajor, also received the Knight's Cross with Oak Leaves (number 57) on 31 December. In June 1942 he was to become the wing commander of the 1st Close-Support Wing.

The launching of the Soviet counteroffensive on 5 December 5 had marked a change of fortune for the German forces in front of Moscow. It was at this point that Otto Weiß was called away from the front to take on an important new role.

THE LUFTWAFFE'S FIRST CLOSE-SUPPORT WING

In January 1942 Major Otto Weiß was named wing commander of the Luftwaffe's first close-support wing. It had yet to be formed. He flew to Werl in Westphalia, where his proven 2nd Close-Support Group formed the cadre of the headquarters and the 1st Group of the 1st Close-Support Wing. The wing's aircraft was officially the Hs-129, but it continued to fly Bf-109s as well, since the "tank buster" aircraft was always in short supply. At first the wing consisted of a single group, but the wing's second group was eventually formed at Lippstadt. Major Weiß worked wholeheartedly to train his new wing. The training plan included tank recognition and tactics for attacking tank formations and single tanks. The pilots practiced until every one of Weiß' pilots had mastered the tactics.

In May 1942 Otto Weiß received orders for his unit to move east. He had been promoted to Oberstleutnant by then. The wing was initially assigned to support Generaloberst Erich Manstein's 11th Army in the preparatory battles leading up to the assault on the fortress of Sevastopol. In the interim, however, Manstein launched Operation Buzzard Hunt, the conquest of the Kerch Peninsula. The 1st Close-Support Wing took part in this operation, earning a fearsome reputation. Although the Hs-129 pilots could attack the side armor of Soviet tanks with their tungsten-core 20-mm rounds, the preferred angle of attack—as was the case with the unit's Bf-109 Fs—remained the rear of the tank where the engine compartment was located.

For Oberstleutnant Weiß these were days filled with difficult missions; he always strove to be with his aviators at the front. He raised his total of enemy tanks destroyed to 47 in a total of 520 combat missions in the

Hs-123, Bf-109, and Hs-129. The 1st Close-Support Wing flew a total of 1,476 sorties in the operation against Kerch, of which 1,028 were flown by Bf-109s, 259 by Hs-123s, and 180 by the new Hs-129. Major Weiß also took part in those operations, flying sorties against land and sea targets in all three types of aircraft.

It was largely due to Erich von Manstein that the heavy fighting there resulted in the Soviet landings near Kerch and Feodosia being repulsed. The recapture of the Kerch Peninsula, whose key points included Parpach, Armi-Eli, Sem Kolodesej and Kerch itself, would not have happened so quickly without the 1st Close-Support Wing.

During the Kerch Peninsula fighting Hauptmann Freiherr Robert-Georg von Malapert, who had been decorated with the Knight's Cross after the winter fighting at Kalinin, became the 99th German soldier to receive the Oak Leaves.

✠

After the conclusion of the campaign on the Kerch Peninsula, the 1st Close-Support Wing began flying missions against the fortress of Sevastopol. During this period the commanding general of the VIII Air Corps, Generaloberst von Richthofen, visited the command post of Weiß' wing on a number of occasions. On 18 June 1942 Otto Weiß was forced to leave the men with whom he had served since the beginning of the war. General von Richthofen had already prepared him for the move:

"Weiß, we need knowledgeable, experienced people like you to build the close-support arm we are planning. Therefore, you must leave your wing to form and train the first airborne antitank detachment."

Oberstleutnant Weiß bowed to his fate.

On 18 June 1942 Weiß handed over the wing to his successor, Oberstleutnant Hubertus Hitschhold. Hitschhold had received the Knight's Cross earlier in the war while serving with the 2nd Stuka Wing "Immelmann." He later received the Oak Leaves with the same wing on 31 December 1941. The 1st Close-Support Wing got off to a good start with its new wing commander, however, he was to remain in command for only slightly less than a year.

Otto Weiß had led the 2nd Close-Support Group of the 2nd Training and Demonstration Wing and its successor, the 1st Close-Support Wing, during a decisive phase of the Second World War. Both units enjoyed a legendary reputation and the wing claimed the honor of being the last frontline unit to fly an open-cockpit aircraft in combat.

✠

The following were commanders in the wing (up to October 1943):

Wing commander: Oberstleutnant Weiß (13 January to 15 June 1942); Oberstleutnant Hitschhold (18 June 1942 to 10 June 1943); and, Oberstleutnant Druschel (11 June to 18 October 1943).

1st Group, 1st Close-Support Wing: Major Druschel (13 January 1942 to 10 June 1943) and Hauptmann Dörffel (10 June to 18 October 1943)

2nd Group, 1st Close-Support Wing: Hauptmann Freiherr von Malapert (13 January 1942 to 21 May 1943) and Hauptmann Darjes (21 May to 1 October 1943)

THE REMAINING WAR YEARS

With a promotion to Oberstleutnant, Otto Weiß became Inspector General of Close-Support Aircraft and Heavy Fighters. Drawing on his wealth of experience, Weiß promoted every technical project that might benefit the close-support formations and make them more effective. He personally flew every aircraft—those intended for the antitank role for example—and evaluated their equipment and weapons.

On his initiative, a test detachment was set up at Rechlin in late 1942 to investigate the destruction of tanks from the air. After a number of test flights Weiß reached the conclusion—shared by all the test pilots—that the Ju-88 P and the Bf-110, which had been selected for the antitank role, were unsuitable for technical reasons. He was enthusiastic over the Ju-87 D-1 and G-2 and the Hs-129 B-2, however, which had proved superior to all other aircraft in the course of testing. They offered better pilot protection and a higher probability of success against tanks.

By February 1943 Weiß was ready to test his theories in practice. At his urging an operational trials unit—Antitank Detachment Weiß—was created and assigned to the 4th Air Force in Chortitza. The small special detachment enjoyed great success against attacking armored spearheads and enemy tanks that had broken through the front.

Oberstleutnant Weiß led from the front until he was finally stopped by General Adolf Galland, who feared they might lose their expert in close-support flying. Galland placed Weiß in charge of all antitank squadrons and, a short time later, appointed him Inspector General of Close-Support Aviation on the staff of the General in Command of Fighters.

Weiß held the position of Inspector General of Close-Support Aviation from July until September of 1943, when Generaloberst Kürten introduced the new position of General in Command of Close-Support Aviation and Oberstleutnant Dr. Ernst Kupfer took over the post. On 6 November 1943 the He-111 returning Oberstleutnant Kupfer from Saloniki crashed into Mount Semer Kajasen in the Belasia Mountains in dense fog. A search was initiated at once, but Oberstleutnant Kupfer and the other five persons on board were not found until 17 November. Everyone on board the aircraft had been killed. The six men were buried together at the military cemetery in Arsakli near Saloniki.

On 1 January 1944 Oberst Hubertus Hitschhold, who in 1942 had succeeded Otto Weiß as the wing commander of the 1st Close-Support Wing, was named General in Command of Close-Support Aviation.

Otto Weiß was promoted to Oberst on 1 November 1943. On 1 December 1943 he was placed in charge of an airfield commission. In April 1944 he returned to the Eastern Front as Commander of Air Forces Danzig. Weiß' main concern there was the small number of close-support forces under his command, which he committed wherever the Red Army appeared to be planning a breakthrough. He had earlier served as Commander of Air Forces Polar Sea, but this position had not satisfied him. Weiß was always at the front with his forces during the major offensive efforts by the Soviets, especially the fighting east of Danzig.

In the final weeks of the war he was sent by the staff of the 6th Air Force to the threatened Teschen area. Weiß was able to prevent his close-support forces from being captured by the Russians by ordering them back to Germany only hours before the enemy overran his headquarters.

✠

Otto Weiß, one of the first and most outstanding close-support aviators: A great fighter, tactician and strategist, he was never forgotten by his old comrades. When he died in Kiel on 19 August 1955 following a lengthy illness, all the former close-support aviators who had survived the momentous conflict accompanied the casket as it was carried to the grave.

Fate did not allow Oberst Weiß to serve as commander of his beloved close-support forces—a position for which he was more than qualified on the basis of his abilities and experience—but he knew that his comrades would have wished it for him. Hubertus Hitschhold once said to him:

"You should be the General in Command of Close-Support Aviation. I would gladly step aside, but orders are orders."

Weiß replied: "No, it's time for the young to step forward. At thirty-six, I'm already one of the old timers."

✠

Otto Weiß died at Kiel on 19 August 1955 after a long illness. When he was carried to his grave, one of those present was his old comrade-in-arms, Hubertus Hitschhold. Standing by the open grave, he saluted the man who had become a legend and who in the course of 520 combat missions had experienced the highs and lows of German close-support aviation in the Second World War.

Wilhelm Batz rose to the top rank of German fighter pilots, scoring 237 kills in a combat career that did not begin until 1943.

Wilhelm Batz:
A Late Starter Wins the Swords

EARLY CAREER

Wilhelm Batz was born in Bamberg on 21 May 1916. After completing his schooling, he joined the Luftwaffe in 1935.

After basic training and a wide variety of courses, all of which he successfully completed, the people in charge of the weapons and training schools became aware of the somewhat serious, slim young man. All of his superiors considered him a gifted and level-headed aviator who demonstrated a natural ability for passing on the skills and knowledge necessary to a budding pilot and whose training made him an ideal candidate for instructor duties.

Batz began serving at various Luftwaffe training schools in 1937. Through his hands passed volunteers and "trained aviators," and he instructed officer candidates. Batz progressed from assistant instructor to flight instructor; promotion was slow in coming.

Thanks to his extraordinary abilities as a pilot, Wilhelm Batz was an excellent instructor on all current aircraft types. He played an important role in providing the young Luftwaffe with trained pilots for its first fighter units. The pilots trained by Batz were all good aviators by the time they left his hands; they knew their trade and became successful fighter pilots with the wings to which they were subsequently assigned.

Batz's activities helped ensure that the Luftwaffe received first-class pilots. Many who later won the Knight's Cross gave credit for their success to this thin man with the narrow, energetic face and the clear, brown eyes. He had brought them to the point where they could hold their own against any enemy pilot. They knew how to employ all their skills as a pilot, but he also pointed out each man's boundaries. He fixed the point in time at which it was necessary to break off an engagement in order to avoid being shot down and killed. Wilhelm Batz was not a proponent of staid tactics. He preferred clever tactical moves within a squadron or group. All this ensured his success—and survival—in critical situations in the operations to come.

With more than 5,000 hours of flying time to his credit, Wilhelm Batz longed to join the many aviators he had sent to the front—to fly and fight with them. It took two years and ten requests before his superiors relented and gave him what he desired. The Commander of Flying Schools ordered him released from his duties as an instructor and transferred to a combat unit.

It was December 1942 when Leutnant Batz packed his things and set out to join the 52nd Fighter Wing's 2nd Group, which was based in the Barvenkovo-Kerch area and in the approaches to Stalingrad. This wing was to be Batz's home for the rest of the war.

When the invasion of the Soviet Union began, the 2nd Group moved east from the Suvalki area and reached the gates of Moscow by way of Vitebsk, Kalinin and Smolensk. During the winter of 1941–42 the group undertook close-support missions, helping the German Army avoid being destroyed during its retreat from Moscow.

The entire wing was not deployed together. Its 1st Group did not move to the Eastern Front until October 1942; prior to the move the group was based in the Vlissingen-Esbjerg area from where it participated in the campaign against the RAF.

The 3rd Group took part in the airborne invasion of Crete in early 1941. Together with the wing headquarters, it was subsequently transferred to Romania. From there it moved east into Russia in July 1941. The group reached the area of the Lower Dniepr and arrived at Poltava airfield. From there it flew missions in support of the fighting in the southern sector of the Eastern Front. At this time the 3rd Group received a Croatian squadron (the 15th), which was followed in early 1942 by the Slovakian squadron (the 13th). Both squadrons remained with the wing until the end of 1943.

In early 1942, both the 1st and 2nd Groups had pulled out of action to rest and reequip. Roth groups returned to the Eastern Front in May 1942. The entire wing—with all three groups together in Russia for the first time—participated in the battle of encirclement south of Kharkov.

The start of the German summer offensive of 1942 saw the beginning of the phenomenal rise of the 52nd Fighter Wing. By the time Willi Batz arrived, the wing had become a typical "eastern wing." The wing already had a number of recipients of the Knight's Cross and Oak Leaves in its ranks. Its three group were based in different areas of the front. They flew fighter sweeps and escort missions, flew deep into enemy territory on reconnaissance flights, and intercepted incoming raids by the Soviet Air Force. A particular specialty of the wing was its low-level attacks in support of ground forces.

Batz was welcomed to the group by its commander, Hauptmann Johannes Steinhoff. Batz saw the Knight's Cross with Oak Leaves at the throat of the group commander. Steinhoff had received the Knight's Cross on 30 August 1941. Following his great success as commander of the 52nd Fighter Wing's 4th Squadron in Russia, he received the 115th Oak Leaves as a Hauptmann and group commander of the 52nd Fighter Wing's 2nd Group on 2 September 1942.

"Glad to have you with us, Batz. I think I'll have you serve as my adjutant first, before we turn you loose on the Russians."

"Sir," interjected Batz, "I want to see action more than anything . . . I want to test my skill in aerial combat."

"All in good time, Batz. You'll have plenty of that. I promise you that I'll get you out as my wingman as soon as possible."

"Thank you, sir," replied Batz, satisfied.

Batz's patience was severely tested in the weeks that followed. There were numerous combat missions, but the only positive result was that Steinhoff learned that his new adjutant was an outstanding pilot and wingman. Even when he tried, he was unable to lose Batz.

Wilhelm Batz made repeated requests to be released from his duties as adjutant. On 11 January 1943 the squadron commander of the 4th, Oberleutnant Gerhard Barkhorn, received the Knight's Cross with Oak Leaves after more than 120 victories. The 6th Squadron received a new commanding officer in the form of Oberleutnant Gustav Denk, also a Knight's Cross recipient. By now Batz was literally burning for an opportunity to show what he could do in combat with the enemy. In his own words, he was "downright hot to take off and fight."

On 13 February 1943 Oberleutnant Denk was shot down by Russian antiaircraft fire. Batz mourned the loss of a comrade who had taught him several practical tricks for use in combat.

Led by the wing commander, Oberstleutnant Dietrich Hrabak, the wing headquarters was moved to Kerch, where it was based at "Kerch IV" airfield. The 2nd Group followed, landing at muddy Slavyansk na Kubani airfield on 16 February 1943. The new airfield was grass-covered. That prevented the radiators of the aircraft from becoming clogged with mud during takeoff, which had been the main cause of a number of losses at the group's previous airfield.

Most sorties from Kerch IV were flown in a flight of four (*Schwarm*). The primary mission of the fighters was to guard German marine ferries and other vessels against enemy air attack while crossing the Strait of Kerch. A fresh flight arrived over the crossing site each hour. This ensured that there were always fighters in the air to intercept enemy aircraft in the event of an attack.

At this time the 2nd Group had thirty-five pilots. One of them was Leutnant Wilhelm Batz, who had succeeded in freeing himself from the position of adjutant.

THE FIRST VICTORY—BATZ ON COURSE FOR SUCCESS

Oberfeldwebel Willi Nernitz assumed acting command of the 52nd Fighter Wing's 6th Squadron as successor to Oberleutnant Denk. He was decorated with the Knight's Cross on 1 March 1943 but was shot down and killed over Anapa barely six weeks later on 13 April.

On 11 March 1943 Leutnant Batz flew a mission over the Strait of Kerch as wingman to Leutnant Haberda, the commander of the 5th Squadron. It was a clear morning and, as the two fighters neared their patrol position, Batz spotted several silvery objects about twenty kilometers away that grew rapidly in size. He reported this to his commander and Haberda advised Batz that they would approach the enemy aircraft while remaining above them.

The two German pilots recognized the enemy aircraft as four Il-2s, whose mission was obviously to attack German ferry traffic in the strait. By now Wilhelm Batz was familiar with Soviet aerial tactics. The four Il-2s were in a four-plane *zveno* formation. Other formations used by the Red Air Force included the *para*, which consisted of two aircraft, and the *gruppa*, made up of eight machines. A *gruppa* was usually accompanied by a *para*, which flew ahead of and about 350 to 800 meters above the leading *zveno*, providing top cover. The course they were flying suggested that this *zveno* of Il-2s had been sent to attack German marine traffic.

"I'll take the one in front," called Haberda. "You take the rear one."

"Understood!" replied Batz.

Wilhelm Batz rammed the throttle forward and pushed the nose of his Messerschmitt down. He felt the aircraft vibrating beneath him. The two fighters very quickly reached a position 1,000 meters above the enemy aircraft, which stubbornly maintained their course, seemingly unconcerned about the two German fighters.

Batz felt the excitement coursing through him. Now it was time to put into practice all that he had learned. He rolled out of a turn and saw Haberda carry out the same maneuver. Both German aircraft were then above and behind the Il-2s and flying in the same direction. The Messerschmitts quickly caught up with the enemy; the two pilots dropped behind their chosen victims, gaining speed as they did so. Batz saw the Il-2 wander into his sight and finally fill it.

Just before he opened fire, Batz saw flashes from the guns of his squadron commander's aircraft. Then he pressed the triggers and the two machine guns and the 20-mm MG 151/20 roared to life. There were flashes as the bullets and cannon rounds bounced off the armored flanks of the Il-2. Batz dropped lower. Glancing ahead, he saw Haberda's victim go down in a flat spin and explode as it struck the ground.

Batz followed the enemy aircraft, which had veered off when it was hit. In seconds he was again in firing position. Approaching from below and behind, he fired a long burst into the oil cooler of the Il-2. A dense stream of oil sprayed from the shattered cooler. The Soviet aircraft began to burn and plunged toward the earth like a comet.

Instinctively veering off, Batz avoided the stream of oil. Then the Il-2 pulled out of its dive. Batz closed in and fired again. This time the enemy aircraft exploded in mid air.

Batz turned away and, as he did so, he received a warning call from Leutnant Haberda: "Look out, behind you!"

Batz hauled his Messerschmitt into a steep turn, avoiding a burst of fire from an enemy aircraft, which was shot down by Leutnant Haberda seconds later. The fourth Il-2 had meanwhile left the scene and was headed home alone.

The attempt by the Soviet bombers to attack the ferries had been frustrated. An hour later the patrol was over and the pair of Messerschmitts flew back to base. For the first time Wilhelm Batz waggled his wings as he flew over the airfield, the signal to those on the ground that he had shot down an enemy aircraft. His ground crew received him with waves and shouts of jubilation. They helped him remove his parachute and shook his hand.

"Your first, sir. Continued good hunting!"

"Thanks, Hillers," said Batz, grasping the hand offered by the mechanic. Haberda, who had landed first, came over to Batz. "Your first kill was a textbook one, Wilhelm. There should be many more."

"Thanks for covering me," declared Batz.

"That's one of the finer points you'll achieve after you've done this a few times, Wilhelm."

During a briefing in the group barracks Hauptmann Steinhoff also praised Batz for his first kill. Wilhelm Batz received the Iron Cross, Second Class, the first war decoration to adorn his flight jacket. Whether even greater rewards would follow was still written in the stars.

✠

On 13 March the 2nd Group moved to Anapa in the Kuban bridge-head, where it was to remain until 4 July. Wilhelm Batz received promotion to the rank of Oberleutnant.

Oberleutnant Walter Krupinski had assumed command of the 7th Squadron on 1 March. He had earlier received the Knight's Cross on 29 October 1942 as a Leutnant serving with the 6th Squadron. The young Leutnant Erich Hartmann, who had just arrived at the front, became Krupinski's wingman. Within a very short time, he had achieved eleven victories.

Batz was able to shoot down three more enemy aircraft in the period from 1 April to 8 May 1943, for which he received the Iron Cross, First Class. Batz was proud of the decoration, especially since all of these victories were hard-won. Every pilot in the unit was convinced that the Russians must have deployed an elite unit to the area. Only later, when the first downed Soviet pilot was captured and interrogated, were their suspicions confirmed (more about this in the next section).

On 20 April 1943 the 52nd Fighter Wing achieved its 5,000th victory. The unit's 6,000th confirmed kill came only eleven weeks later. The obvious conclusion is that Soviet aircraft were easy prey for the German fighters, but this is contradicted by the losses suffered by the wing and other formations in the southern sector of the Eastern Front.

From left: Fritz Eisenach, Gerhard Barkhorn, and Wilhelm Batz.

Wilhelm Batz shot down his twentieth enemy aircraft in this period. On 8 May 8 1943 Oberleutnant Helmut Haberda was shot down in combat over the Kuban. Haberda was due to receive the Knight's Cross. The next day Oberleutnant Wilhelm Batz was named to succeed him as commander of the 6th Squadron. With the arrival of the wing's 1st Group in the Anapa area on 16 May 1943, the wing was finally back together again. This happy situation lasted only until 2 July, however.

The 2nd Group achieved its 1,650th victory the day that the 1st Group arrived. Leutnant Hartmann was making a name for himself. On 25 May he shot down a LaGG 5 then collided with a second Soviet fighter while climbing into position for a second attack. Hartmann regained control of his damaged aircraft and only his skill as a pilot allowed him to avoid crashing.

THE 52ND FIGHTER WING IN SOUTHERN RUSSIA

When Operation Citadel, the last German offensive in the east began, the wing headquarters and its 3rd Group were located at Ugrim in the Ukraine. The 1st Group was also withdrawn from the Kuban region and, on 4 July 1943, it arrived at Besenovka near Belgorod.

This was the beginning of an extremely successful period for these two groups of the wing. On 5 July Hauptmann Johannes Wiese, squadron commander of the 2nd Squadron, shot down twelve enemy aircraft in one day and raised his victory total to 88. Twelve days later his victory total reached the magic number 100.

The commander of the 8th Squadron, Hauptmann Günther Rall, was named group commander of the wing's 3rd Group on 6 July 1943. His successor as squadron commander was Oberleutnant Friedrich Obleser. Rall had been awarded the Oak Leaves on 26 October 1942. His success in the Belgorod sector contributed to his becoming the 34th German soldier to receive the Swords on 12 September 1943.

Günther Rall shot down his 200th enemy aircraft in this area. The 1st and 3rd Groups waged a bitter struggle against a numerically superior enemy during Operation Citadel and in the fighting that followed near Orel and Briansk. Leutnant Erich Hartmann shot down his 50th enemy aircraft on 2 August. In the next 15 days he shot down another 30 enemy aircraft and, on 29 October 1943, he was decorated with the Knight's Cross. The 2nd Group had held its position at the Kuban. It moved to Gostagayevskaya and spent several days on the southwest coast of the Crimea at Yevpatoria. It returned to Anapa on 14 July and, on 3 August 1943, it moved to Stalino. The Red Army had secured a bridgehead across the Donets River eighty kilometers east of Aremovsk and was then poised to launch an assault on Stalino.

The Soviets launched a second attack toward Melitopol from their positions on the Mius River with the objective of splitting the German forces. These Soviet attacks were carried out with heavy air support and the pilots of the 2nd Group had their hands full dealing with the Red Air Force.

Stalino was lost on 8 September 1943. All three groups of the wing were subsequently reunited; they resumed operations from Makeyevka—fifteen kilometers east of Stalino—on 24 August.

WILHELM BATZ ON THE VICTORY TRAIL

One morning eight Soviet Pe-2 bombers appeared over Anapa at first light. They roared over the airfield at treetop height, spraying machine-gun fire in all directions in an attempt to prevent the German fighters from taking off. The air raid alarm was sounded and everyone not on duty ran for the trenches. The first pass by the Soviet light bombers left several aircraft in flames on the ground. They overflew the base and turned for a second pass, ready to drop their 600-kilo bomb loads.

Oberleutnant Batz and his headquarters flight managed to get air-borne between the two attacks. The Messerschmitts climbed and turned out of the path of the enemy bombers as they approached for their second attack. By the time the Pe-2s had completed their third pass, Batz and his pilots were in position to attack them from above.

The enemy aircraft turned for home, leaving several Bf-109s blazing on the ground. Two tents had been swept away by exploding bombs. Luckily, no one had been inside.

Batz's four Messerschmitts followed the withdrawing bombers. They closed the distance between the two formations and then picked up speed as they dove on the Soviet aircraft. Wilhelm Batz closed to within 120 meters of his chosen victim, which was flying on the right side of the formation. He opened fire with all guns. The Soviet bomber began to burn, and its pilot pointed the nose of his machine toward the Soviet lines, hoping to carry out a forced landing. Batz, who had climbed to a position 250 meters above the Pe-2, turned behind the enemy aircraft and hit it with a full burst. The right wing of the Pe-2 separated from the fuselage, and the aircraft crashed in a huge ball of flame.

As he turned away, Batz came under fire from the Soviet lines. Several fragments from exploding rounds struck the fuselage of the Messerschmitt. One of Batz's men had shot down a second Pe-2. Two others were left on fire. When they landed, work was under way to repair the damage inflicted by the Soviet attack.

Barkhorn congratulated Batz on his latest success and remarked in closing: "I'm sure that you will soon equal and surpass the best of the wing. No one can match your skill as a pilot."

"It's still a damned long way to there," replied Batz with a grin.

Barkhorn was still confident: "You'll be at the top within a year!"

The first order of business, however, was to pay the enemy a return visit. Hauptmann Barkhorn selected the two headquarters flights of the 1st Group to carry out the raid. He discussed the attack with squadron commanders Batz and Lipfert. Stressing that the element of surprise was vital, Barkhorn instructed the two officers to be ready for a pre-dawn takeoff.

The total of ten aircraft took off at the crack of dawn. The sun had not yet risen as the fighters lifted off from Anapa airfield and climbed quickly to a height of 3,500 meters. There was no opposition; the Messerschmitts dived on the airfield that housed the Pe-2 squadron. It had been identified from aerial reconnaissance photos taken the day before.

Barkhorn ordered the attack to begin. Batz, who was flying on the right flank of his four-aircraft flight, saw the airfield buildings grow larger. A glance at the airspeed indicator showed that he had already reached 620 kilometers per hour. Batz raced directly toward a low building. Spotting a row of Pe-2s beside it, he made a course correction and fired a long burst into the enemy bombers. He raced over the last bomber and pulled up into a steep turn before beginning a second firing pass. Aircraft caught fire on the ground. The main airfield building had been riddled by the first *Schwarm.*

The airfield antiaircraft defenses recovered from the surprise and returned fire. A Messerschmitt was hit and turned for home trailing a dense banner of smoke.

Hauptmann Barkhorn and two of his pilots dived on the antiaircraft gun. The Soviet gun crew fell under a hail of bullets. A munitions dump exploded and, seconds later, the airfield' s fuel dump was hit by another Bf-109 and began to burn.

When the fighters assembled for the flight hone they left behind a chaotic scene; eleven Pe-2s were burning. Never again would they take off to attack German positions.

✠

Batz was confident of success when he took off on a morning patrol twenty-four hours later. His *Schwarm* climbed quickly and passed through a thin layer of cloud. Visibility above the cloud layer was excellent. Batz's objective was a Soviet fighter base. One fighter had been sent ahead as a decoy to tempt the enemy into the air. The ruse worked. Barely five minutes after the lone Bf-109 reached the enemy airfield, four I sixteen Rata fighters took off to intercept. These were later versions of the I-16; armed with two 20-mm cannon, they were not to be taken lightly, especially since the Soviet aviators in this area were first-class pilots.

Batz attacked from a superior altitude. He flashed past the enemy fighters on the first pass and his short burst went wide of the mark. Seconds later he approached a second I-16. He followed the enemy aircraft as it began to climb. Batz positioned himself behind the I-16 and opened fire. There were flashes all over the enemy aircraft. The I-16 went into a spin. It plunged earthward trailing a long banner of smoke and crashed.

Meanwhile, every aircraft of the *Schwarm* was engaged with an enemy aircraft. Excited voices shouted warnings or instructions over the radio. Batz saw an enemy fighter flying alone on the right. As soon as he dived on the next enemy, this fighter would attack. Batz instructed his wingman, Oberfeldwebel Koller, to attack the lone enemy fighter.

Koller acknowledged the order and Batz saw him turn toward the Red fighter. He also saw Barkhorn shoot down an enemy fighter. The remaining I-16s then turned away and tried to reach their base.

"After them," ordered Barkhorn. "Wille, keep an eye on the airfield. Report any takeoffs immediately."

The Messerschmitts dived after the surviving enemy fighters. Batz closed in on an I-16. He opened fire from a distance of only ninety meters and literally blasted the I-16 out of the air. The machine blew apart, scattering wreckage.

"Attention: Aircraft taking off from the enemy base. First Indians approaching from ahead. Height 1,200!" Wille reported.

Two seconds later Batz saw the first enemy fighter flying straight toward him. He changed course and pulled back on the stick. Batz sent the Messerschmitt climbing toward the sun at full throttle and outclimbed the enemy. He counted eight I-16s.

The other Messerschmitts intercepted the new arrivals and the engagement began. Turning tightly, Batz spotted an enemy fighter as it dove to the attack. Tromping down on the rudder pedal, he evaded the burst of fire. Batz tried to get on the tail of the Soviet fighter, but the enemy pilot veered out of the way. He realized that he was facing a skilled opponent who could really fly. But the enemy pilot had met an equally skilled opponent in Wilhelm Batz.

The German pilot never let the small, maneuverable Soviet fighter out of his sight for a second. He countered each move its pilot made and waited for the moment to strike. The two fighters twisted and turned, seeking to achieve an advantageous position from which to open fire. Batz began a loop in an effort to get behind the enemy fighter, but the alert Soviet pilot caught him with a burst as he hung inverted. Batz heard bullets striking his aircraft. Fortunately they did no serious damage.

The dogfight had been going on for seven minutes when Batz caught his opponent by surprise. A steep turn followed by a half-roll placed him above the enemy fighter. Rolling back to the horizontal he found the Soviet fighter in his gun sight. Batz fired at once and the burst sheared off the tail of the enemy aircraft. He waited a few seconds and fired again; the Soviet fighter began to burn. As Batz watched, it plunged earthward in flames. He turned away. Then he heard a sharp warning cry from Oberfeldwebel Koller, and Batz instinctively reversed his turn. He almost avoided the burst of fire coming from his left, but the first few bullets found the mark. Batz heard bullets striking his aircraft and knew at once: "This time you've had it. You're not getting out of this one."

But everything in him resisted the idea of giving up; he must get away!

Erich Hartmann, the most successful fighter pilot with 352 kills, was a close friend of Batz, who was a witness at Hartmann's wedding.

Batz cursed as he veered away. He attempted to escape the enemy by climbing; that might allow him to reach the German lines. Suddenly, the engine spat a cloud of oil. Things were now getting hot in the truest sense of the word. Nevertheless, he carried on toward the front. Batz's height was down to 500 meters when he overflew the front lines. Almost half the windscreen was now covered with oil, but he could still see well enough to carry out a landing. He then flew directly toward base and just managed to reach the edge of the airfield. Batz descended more steeply over the last 250 meters, urging himself to remain calm.

The Messerschmitt touched down with a jolt and raced across the grass. Braking harshly, Batz managed to stop short of the other side of the airfield. Batz undid his parachute straps and climbed out of the cockpit. As he jumped down, he saw the airfield fire/rescue personnel approaching. They put out the fire in the engine compartment. Fortunately, it was just smoldering.

"That was a close shave, Wilhelm!" said Barkhorn.

"Yes, it was very close," agreed Batz. "But it all ended well. I had an opponent who simply knew everything in advance. He must have been an old hand, one of the best they have."

"The intelligence folks report that the Red Air Force has put one of its best squadrons into action here," interjected the wing commander, who had just arrived.

THE ENEMY VIEW OF THE BATTLES AT THE KUBAN AND KERCH

The reader of Luftwaffe operational accounts is limited to the German view of events, which is understandable. The following description of the fighting over the Kerch Peninsula and the Kuban from the Red Air Force point of view is provided in an effort to present a balanced account. The material has been gleaned from a study of Soviet sources.

First, however, an overview of the German and Soviet air forces in the southern sector of the Eastern Front during this period.

✠

When extremely heavy fighting broke out at the Kuban in the winter of 1942–43, the Luftwaffe first sent Special Detachment Stepp—an anti-tank test detachment—with its Ju-87s armed with two 37-mm Pak. The detachment's leader was Hans-Ulrich Rudel, who would later become the most highly decorated member of the Wehrmacht and its most successful close-support pilot. His principal mission was to see to it that the Russian offensive northwest of Temryuk was stopped.

German reconnaissance aircraft reported sighting large numbers of open landing craft lying in the ports of Yeysk and Aktarsk, ready to ferry Russian assault troops through the marshy region. The Soviet boats made their way through the many canals and lagoons in the Kuban Region. The next morning found Rudel and his crews in the air over the Kuban. The cannon-armed Ju-87s went to the attack. Any vessel that showed itself on the water was shot up; Rudel alone destroyed seventy vessels in a few days. Flying one of the few Hs-129s issued to the detachment, Leutnant Rudolf-Heinz Ruffer was hit by Russian antiaircraft fire. He came down on one of the small islands and it was several days before he was picked up by a German infantry patrol.

On 1 April 1943 Hans-Ulrich Rudel was promoted to Hauptmann. On 14 April he was the 229th recipient of the Oak Leaves in the Wehrmacht.

The Soviet offensive operations in this area were nothing less than an attempt to encircle the 17th Army like the 6th Army had been encircled at Stalingrad. If they succeeded, they would trap all the German forces in the Caucasus. For this purpose the Soviet high command deployed a large part of its air force in addition to potent ground forces. The objective of the Soviet Air Force commanders was to achieve air superiority over the Luftwaffe for the first time in the history of the Great Patriotic War.

To achieve this objective, which General of Aviation Forces Novikov outlined to Stalin, the Soviet Air Force had to commit everything that could be spared from other fronts. This included the massed aviation units from the Stalingrad area. The sheer mass of Soviet aircraft deployed in this one area helps explain how the 52nd Fighter Wing was able to shoot down such a great number of enemy machines.

The 17th Army withdrew from the Caucasus via Novorossisk; Generaloberst Richard Ruoff kept an iron grip on the army and reached the planned objectives. By the end of April the 17th Army had reached a line extending from Novorossisk through Krimsk-Kiyevskoye-Krasny Oktyabr-East to Temryuk. It was closely pursued by the Red Army.

The 4th Air Force was fully committed during this period. It ordered the VIII Air Corps to halt the pursuing Soviet forces and support the army to the best of its ability. All available Stukas of von Richthofen's former tactical air corps attacked the Soviet ground units and airfields in an effort to put them out of action and spare the army surprise air attacks, especially by the Il-2s. It also attempted to destroy forward Russian armored spearheads by the cannon-armed aircraft of the new close-support formations

then being developed. These elements also included several weak fighter
units, the core of which was the 52nd Fighter Wing.

Repeated attacks were made against the large Soviet bridgehead at
Mount Myshako near Novorossisk. Vessels delivering supplies and troops
were also bombed. The 1st Group of the 3rd Stuka Wing bore the brunt of
the action in this area. The Luftwaffe met increasing numbers of modern
Soviet fighters. These and the Soviet bombers attacked the German forward airfields, especially those in and around Kerch and near Anapa. The
units of the Soviet Air Force had instructions from the Soviet high command to destroy all German airfields in the Kuban bridgehead. Other
units, especially the Il-2 *Stormavik* elements—as the close-support formations were then being called—were also heavily committed.

Here as in other areas of the Eastern Front, the Luftwaffe was too weak
to effectively protect the entire area. It received some assistance in the
form of the 9th Flak Division under Generalmajor Wolfgang Pickert, which
served in a ground role and defended the seaports on the Kerch Peninsula
such as Kerch, Taman, Anapa and Temryuk. There were also immense
logistical problems. Large quantities of supply goods had to be flown in.
One of the main tasks of the transport units was the evacuation of the
wounded. In short, there was too little to accomplish too much.

In April 1943 the 52nd Fighter Wing flew a series of Stuka escort missions in the Novorossisk area and to the south. The Stukas flew up to 15
times per day. On 19 April alone, sixteen groups of Ju-87s took part in a
total of 294 missions in support of the 17th Army in its struggle to contain
the large Soviet bridgehead. "Table Mountain" and "Sugarloaf" were hit
hard. One hundred sixty-five Ju-87s of the 1st Group of the 2nd Stuka
Wing and the 2nd Group of the 77th Stuka Wing saw action in a single day.

The fighters of the 52nd Fighter Wing were very successful in their
Stuka-escort role, destroying numerous Soviet fighters and keeping losses
among the dive-bombers to a minimum. Fifty-six enemy aircraft were shot
down on 20 April 1943 alone.

✠

The Red Army launched a new offensive at the end of April. Soviet
fighters, bombers and close-support aircraft attacked the German positions. On 29 April German fighters shot down sixty-three enemy aircraft.
The Soviet Air Force lost another thirty aircraft on 30 April and thirty-five
on 3 May. Luftwaffe units pounded Mount Myshako, inflicting heavy losses
on the units of the Red Army holding out there.

The high command of the Red Air Force assembled approximately 500 aircraft to meet these attacks, including 100 bombers. However, the main Soviet airfields were too far from the battlefield; improvised forward operating bases were too small to sustain large-scale operations.

In contrast, Luftwaffe units could reach the battlefield quickly from their forward airfields at Anapa and Gostagayevskaya, only about forty-five kilometers away. They could remain over Myshako and other Russian positions for at least fifty minutes. Nevertheless, Russian air attacks in the last third of April were highly effective.

On 21 April Soviet General Novikov visited a forward command post. He watched through binoculars as the Il-2 flown by N. V. Rhyklin of the 805th Close-Support Regiment was attacked by four German fighters. Rhyklin's gunner, Ivan Yefremenko, shot down two of the fighters. Then the Il-2 was hit and Rhyklin was wounded. The Soviet pilot nevertheless succeeded in bringing his damaged machine back to base, where he landed safely.

General Novikov, who was well known for his battlefield promotions, promoted Rhyklin to First Lieutenant and Yefremenko to Second Lieutenant. (Both men were later awarded the Golden Star of a Hero of the Soviet Union for subsequent exploits.)

Russian pilots claimed 182 German aircraft shot down and another 260 destroyed or damaged on the ground in the period between the 17 and 24 April. These figures were of course exaggerated. Nevertheless, German losses were high and many of the German kills were obtained by only a few pilots.

On the morning of 29 April 1943, 144 Soviet bombers and 82 close-support aircraft bombed and strafed German ground forces for three hours. 265 fighters guarded the bombers.

The 1st Air Corps, to which 52nd Fighter Wing was attached, committed all available resources. On 29 April an air battle began which lasted until 12 May 12. The following is a Soviet account of an air engagement on 29 April:

> The well-known Russian aviator Dimitri Glinka, in fourth place on the list of Russian aces with 50 victories, took off that day with six of his comrades. Their mission was to engage and destroy German bombers and Stukas. A group of Ju-88s and Ju-87s flew over the village and approached the front; Glinka and his six machines attacked. He first fired at the leading aircraft and, in the subsequent engagement, destroyed two more German bombers. This daring attack stopped a raid by sixty German machines.

According to Soviet sources, The 1st Air Corps lost an average of eighteen fighters and twelve bombers daily. This would suggest the loss of 252 fighters and 174 bombers in the fourteen days of fighting. The I. Fliegerkorps never had that many aircraft at its disposal, however.

✠

Compare the following two accounts of the same engagement that took place on 29 April 1944. The Soviet account is presented by Georgi Golubev, a wingman of the Soviet ace Alexander Pokryshkin, who ended the war in second place on the list of Soviet aces with 59 victories. Both pilots were members of the 16th Guards Fighter Regiment. This is Golubev's account:

> These combat missions demanded maximum readiness and iron stamina from each of our regiment's fighter pilots, who averaged four to seven missions each day in the course of which they were involved in two or three engagements. Dogfights developed very quickly in the crowded airspace over Krymskaya. The German pilots were the elite of the entire German Eastern Front. Most belonged to the 52nd Fighter Wing, and we knew that they never avoided combat. They attacked whether alone or in squadron strength and had shot down many of our comrades. There was no doubt that every member of this wing was a fighter and an excellent technician and tactician. They were masters of their aircraft and knew all the tricks needed to cope with our 16th Fighter Regiment, which had an excellent reputation and whose ranks included several of our best and most successful pilots.
>
> I once faced one of these German fighter pilots. As we sparred for more than five minutes, both waiting for a chance for the decisive attack, I recognized the phenomenal flying ability of this man. I only learned his first name, Willi or Wilhelm.
>
> Like me, he was a determined aviator, a tireless fighter and a pilot with few equals. We both scored hits on the other. He shot up one of my wings and I hit him somewhere near the cockpit. When we broke off the engagement, it was at the last second, otherwise both of us would have fallen at the same time.

Whenever a pilot found himself in such a swirl of opposing aircraft over Krymskaya, he was confronted with a confusing game of numerous engagements all taking place at once. The flash of tracers, the rattle of machine guns, the gun bursts from our own antiaircraft fire or the enemy's at his bridge sites, the wild confusion of aircraft at different heights—all this frayed the nerves.

> On that 29 April I approached a Me-109 that was flying close behind its element leader. It was my intention to shoot down this aircraft in order to have a clear path to the leader, certainly a well-known aviator. The pilot flying cover for his superior must have had eyes in the back of his head—quick as lightning, he veered left and avoided my first burst. He then carried out a reversal in an effort to get on my tail. I countered this obvious maneuver by turning to the right. Suddenly, we were flying straight toward one another. Nose to nose, we raced toward one another at 1,000 kilometers per hour. I saw flashes from his cannon and pushed the nose down slightly; the burst whipped over my canopy into thin air.
>
> Immediately raising the nose again by the same amount, I was able to get in my first burst, which struck the side of his aircraft near the cockpit and tore out a piece of the fuselage. My opponent dove away, then climbed inverted and half-rolled into level flight. Damned good flying! He had calculated that he would be able to fire at me from the side at that point.

Bf-109 G-10s of the 2nd Group at Neubiberg, Germany, 1945. "Black 7" has "Gigi" under the cockpit on both sides. J. V. CROW COLLECTION

I frustrated his move by also putting my aircraft into a roll. I turned away from him and, seconds later, came back following a steep, almost too steep, knife-edge turn. This time I caught him from the side and put a burst through the side of his machine. Part of the tail surfaces broke away. The Me-109 put its nose down and raced toward the earth. I was about to dive after the Messerschmitt to finish it off, when I was attacked by the element leader, who had just shot down one of my comrades. He hit me on the first pass. Diving away, I escaped only because two of my comrades fired at my pursuer from the right and forced him to break away.

Wilhelm Batz described what had to have been the same engagement on 29 April as follows:

The 5th Squadron under Helmut Haberda, finally promoted to Oberleutnant, was assigned to guard a Stuka unit that day. They flew in the direction of the Russian disembarking points at the Kuban. The formation was first attacked by Russian fighters on the way to the target. A large formation of Il-2s passed not three kilometers to the left of the Ju-87s, headed in the direction of Anapa, but the fighters were forced to stay with the Stukas. All that Oberleutnant Haberda could do was radio a warning to the squadron on strip alert that the Il-2s were on their way to attack the German landing site.

Then a formation of eight Russian fighters was sighted at a higher altitude. The leading *Schwarm*, of which I was a part, climbed to meet the enemy. Seconds later, the Soviets spotted the Germans; three or four of their number dived on the Stukas while the rest flew toward the German fighters. A Soviet fighter and I approached head on; when we were about 500 meters apart, the latter broke away. I emulated the maneuver by the Soviet pilot.

The Soviet pilot outmaneuvered me by carrying out a loop with a radius of about 800 meters. Completing a reversal, the enemy pilot approached me head on. At 350 meters the Soviet dropped his nose slightly. Then he pulled up again and I saw tracer reaching out toward me. I put the Messerschmitt into a climb, avoiding the burst, and then went into a left turn. The enemy pilot did likewise and once again the two fighters approached each other head on. Both pilots fired but failed to inflict lethal damage.

The dogfight continued with fast, steep turns and reversals, rolls and loops and many sophisticated horizontal and vertical maneuvers. Again and again the two fighters raced toward one another nose to nose and fired, before breaking away at the last moment. On one occasion, the Soviet fighter passed a mere ten meters over my canopy. Turbulence from the Yak 1's propeller rocked the Messerschmitt, but the enemy felt the same effect.

I entered a turn. I saw that my opponent was also in a turn. The Russian ended up not 350 meters behind me. I accelerated to "three madmen," as a member of the wing from the navy once characterized emergency boost, and pulled ahead to a relatively safe distance. I then carried out a gentle turn to the right before executing a reversal to the left. The enemy pilot fell for the ruse. I saw his opportunity to administer the coup de grace when a shrill voice called to me: "Wilhelm, Indians left and right!"

I instinctively reacted to the warning with the only correct action—I pushed the Messerschmitt's nose down and dove to 1,500 meters. Only then did I level off and look around for the enemy. I had escaped my two pursuers, but I had lost his opportunity to finish my attack on my clever opponent.

I gained altitude in a shallow turn. While climbing I could see dogfights going on in three different places at once and saw smoke trails from cannon and machine guns. The Messerschmitt climbed steadily until I was at the same height as my comrades. I looked around and saw that Leutnant Becker was in trouble. He had placed himself on the tail of a Yak 1, but another Soviet fighter was lining up for a firing pass on him from behind.

A fast pull-up with a subsequent roll brought me into firing position within thirty seconds. The enemy fighter was just about to open fire on Leutnant Becker who, for his part, had opened fire on the enemy fighter in front of him.

"Becker: Break right!" I called to my comrade. Reacting quickly, Becker changed course, giving me a clear field of fire. My cannon and two machine guns opened fire. Three streams of fire struck the left side of the enemy aircraft and walked into the cockpit. The aircraft began to burn; the Soviet pilot bailed out and swung to earth beneath his parachute. The blazing fighter preceded him, hitting the ground and exploding in a ball of fire.

"Thank you Wilhelm," called Becker. "Three more Indians ahead."

Both of us approached the enemy fighters. I climbed swiftly above the Soviets then half-rolled and dove on the formation. I opened fire as he flashed past; one of the Soviet fighters began to

smoke then rolled over and went into an ever-steepening dive that
ended when it struck the ground.

The fuel warning light on my instrument panel came on, which
indicated twenty minutes fuel remaining. I turned and set course
for home, still searching for further enemy aircraft, but there were
none to be seen. I instructed the members of my squadron, who
were all in the same fuel situation, to head for home.

I heard the individual voices of my men as they confirmed their
kills; without effective confirmation none of the kills they had
made would be recognized.

I felt a great sense of relief as I approached the airfield. I
rocked my wings three times as I came in to land. Once again I
had escaped with my skin intact, even though this time it had
required all of my reserves of strength to act and react in order to
avoid being shot down myself.

After landing Batz was lifted from the cockpit by men of the ground
crews and his mechanics and then placed carefully on the ground. Everyone clustered round him and celebrated his three latest kills.

Only his maintenance crew chief, Unteroffizier Höpfner, was somewhat unhappy. He had counted no fewer than nineteen bullet holes in the
airframe and he knew that that meant hours of work before the aircraft
was 100% serviceable again.

Wilhelm Batz still felt rather dizzy and his knees began to shake. On
entering the group area he was congratulated by Hauptmann Barkhorn.
This was followed by the obligatory mission debriefing. Everyone who had
taken part in the engagements on 29 April agreed that there were a number of real masters at work on the other side of the fence. Wilhelm Batz's
thoughts turned to the expert opponent he had met that day; later he
learned that it must have been Glinka or Golubev, most likely the latter.

✠

Three hours later Oberleutnant Batz's squadron took off again. This
time the mission was a low-level attack against a recently discovered Russian landing site. Following the course pencilled on their maps, Batz and
his men flew toward the target at only 1,500 meters. The landing site was
in a lagoon surrounded by trees and barely visible from the air. Batz spotted the dense birch woods that identified the target. He then led his men
into the attack.

The fighting began when the Russian light antiaircraft weapons guarding the landing site fired its first salvo. The Messerschmitts swept low over the bay. Batz made a slight correction with the rudder and raced toward several open boats tied up at a makeshift dock. Approximately twenty Russian soldiers were just climbing out of the boats. When the German fighter opened fire, they leapt into the lagoon and sought cover beneath the dock, even though the wooden structure offered little protection.

Wilhelm Batz saw the line of splashes from the impacting bullets walk through the open craft. There was an explosion as the gasoline tank serving the auxiliary motor—with which a number of the boats were equipped—went up. The mighty explosion blasted the boat apart. Planks and spars whirled into the air.

Batz's men followed him into the bay. When it was his turn for another pass, he took aim at a smaller dock and shot it to pieces. Three of the squadron's aircraft dived on the antiaircraft defenses and silenced them.

When there was no more movement below, the fighters followed the canal as far as they could. They discovered at least ten more such boats farther up the narrow waterway. The larger boats held twenty men, the smaller ones eight. As soon as the Messerschmitts opened fire, the Russians on the boats jumped overboard. Their mission completed, the German fighters turned and flew back to base at low altitude.

In the afternoon they were sent into action for a third time. This time they were to intercept a formation of Soviet bombers about to attack the German spearhead. The fighters found the bombers before they attacked but then became involved with the fighter escort. In the course of that fighting Batz shot down another enemy aircraft, raising his total for the day to four, his best so far.

The type of fighting seen on 29 April continued in the days that followed. In conclusion let us once again turn to the Soviet side.

The Soviet Air Force's 29th Fighter Regiment successfully fought the Luftwaffe on a number of occasions, especially on 3 May 1943 when it downed ten German aircraft and damaged two more. As on the German side, it was a handful of skilled pilots who accounted for most of the victories. In this case the pilot's name was Semenishin, a man whose bravery and skill were confirmed years after the war in the memoirs of Soviet Air Marshall Vershinin, who wrote:

Semenishin demonstrated outstanding skill and great bravery at the Kuban. Even though his victory total did not equal those of Pokryshkin, Kozhedub or Rechkalov, he was a great ace as well as a squadron leader in the 29th Fighter Regiment. He was wounded soon after his arrival at the front and returned to duty before his wounds had healed. Assigned to the 298th Fighter Regiment, Semenishin soon demonstrated his special abilities. He took over command of the *para* formation, which he led aggressively, achieving a respectable number of kills. But it was at the Kuban that he really excelled, securing the Golden Star of a Hero of the Soviet Union.

On 3 May 1943, 162 Soviet bombers of the 2nd Bomber Corps under Major General V. A. Ushakov attacked German artillery positions. They attacked repeatedly at intervals of ten to fifteen minutes. At the same time, Il-2s of the 2nd Mixed Flying Corps under Major General I. T. Yeremenko cleared a path for the Soviet armored spearheads.

The Soviet bombers and *Stormaviks* flew 2,243 sorties in four days. The Soviet 4th Air Army concentrated all available units in a 30-kilometer section of the 160-kilometer front in an effort to secure a breakthrough by Soviet ground forces.

In spite of the large numbers of enemy aircraft it destroyed, the Luftwaffe, led by the 52nd Fighter Wing, found itself overwhelmed. In this sector, the Red Air Force achieved air superiority over the front for the first time, although it was unable to extend this to air supremacy. That the Red Air Force failed to achieve its ultimate goal in spite of overwhelming numerical superiority was largely due to the 52nd.

In the period from 29 April to 10 May 1943, the Soviet 4th Air Army flew a total of approximately 12,000 sorties. It took part in 258 air engagements in which it claimed to have shot down 368 German aircraft. In spite of the heavy air support it received, the Soviet 56th Army failed to break through to Anapa on the Black Sea. The 52nd Fighter Wing played a major role in the German defensive effort, a success just as important as the many kills achieved by the leading aces of the unit.

✠

Also active in the Kuban area from April to June 1943 was A. L. Ivanov of the 57th Guards Fighter Regiment. At that time his regiment was largely

A Russian Pe-2 bomber forced down by German fighters.

equipped with Spitfire fighters. While the British fighter was fast in Ivanov's opinion, it possessed one serious shortcoming:

> Our English bird was too similar to the Me-109. Many of my comrades and I were mistaken for Germans and shot at by our fighters. Our antiaircraft guns also tried their luck against us with some success. After three months, by which time we had lost at least a dozen aircraft shot down or damaged, the Spitfire was withdrawn from the fight and sent elsewhere.
>
> In spite of this it can be said that this aircraft was a very good machine for me, and I shot down a number of enemy aircraft with it. I was forced to take to my parachute three times, luckily over our own territory, and I survived only because I came down on our side of the lines.

Political commissars spread the lie that Russian pilots who fell into German hands were shot immediately. This was not true, though it is known that a number of German pilots were shot out of hand by Russian soldiers after bailing out over enemy territory.

✠

By about 10 May the Luftwaffe regained air superiority in the area. New aircraft and several squadrons from other formations such as the 3rd Fighter Wing were thrown into the battle alongside the 52nd. In spite of the increased German fighter presence, the Soviet bomber forces remained as active as before. During the night of 26 May, for example, Russian night bombers carried out a heavy raid on German positions in the "Blue Line." The next morning Soviet infantry attacked the German line.

The Red Air Force committed 338 aircraft in support of the attack: 84 bombers, 104 close-support aircraft and 150 fighters. These concentrated their efforts on the narrow corridor selected for the breakthrough. Soviet armor broke through the German frontlines but, once in the rear, the tanks were attacked and destroyed by German dive-bombers and close-support aircraft. The tanks that had penetrated the German front were put out of action by antitank guns, assault guns and 88-mm Flak as well as by Pak sections. The Red Army lost more than 100 tanks that day.

The German counterattack began with a massed aerial bombardment involving more than 1,500 sorties. In the afternoon the formations of the 1st Air Corps flew another 600 sorties. This high number of sorties is an indication that every one of the relatively small number of available aircraft flew multiple missions that day. The men of the 52nd averaged five to seven sorties. The first wave of the Soviet air attack, which began at 0630 hours, consisted of 84 bombers. This was followed by the second wave of 38 close-support aircraft and a third wave of 49 Il-2s. A total of 150 fighters provided the escort for the bomber forces, and the whole day was spent in bitter engagements with the Bf-109s.

For the first time in the war in the east, Il-2 close-support aircraft laid smoke to cover the advance by the armored forces below. Following initial success, the Soviet advance was halted and German counterattacks destroyed those forces that had broken into the main line of resistance.

The Il-2 formations continued flying in spite of heavy losses. On 2 June, for example, Lieutenant N. P. Dedov led thirty-six Il-2s against German artillery positions near Moldavanskoye. Dedov had developed a new method of attack: Covered by thirty fighters, the close-support aircraft approached the target in groups of six aircraft at 800 meters. The attacking groups were about 400 to 500 meters apart. They formed a circle over the target area and began dive-bombing attacks. The Il-2s attacked one after another, dropping their bombs and strafing. They then made a left turn and returned to the protection of the circle. The unit's losses were minimal. Dedov's "circle of death" tactic was effective. The massed fire from the Il-2s prevented the German gun crews from serving their weapons.

Air Marshall of the Soviet Union Vershinin later ordered all Il-2 formations to adopt this tactic for ground attacks.

ALEXANDER POKRYSHKIN

One Soviet pilot very quickly made a name for himself in the skies over the Kuban, the Crimea and the Kerch Peninsula. His name was Alexander Pokryshkin.

Already a successful fighter pilot, Pokryshkin demonstrated his skills in this new combat zone by destroying twenty German aircraft. His legendary reputation was based on more than his success as a pilot. As a squadron leader, Pokryshkin worked out a number of new fighter tactics based on his own experience flying against German pilots. He assembled around him a group of good pilots, who went on to become known as the "Heroes of the Kuban" in Soviet military and aviation circles. Pokryshkin and his men succeeded in restoring the tarnished reputation of the Soviet Air Force.

Among the aces with Pokryshkin were the brothers Dimitri and Boris Glinka, who scored 21 and 10 victories there. G. F. Reshkalov, who went on to end up third on the list of Soviet aces with 55 kills, shot down eleven German aircraft over the Kuban region. He survived the war and was twice decorated with the Golden Star of a Hero of the Soviet Union.

In addition, there were such aces as Vadim Fadeyev with nineteen victories over the Kuban, N. E. Lavitski with fifteen kills in this area, A. L. Prokozhikov with twenty kills, N. K. Naumchik with sixteen, P. M. Beresnev with twelve, D. I. Koval with thirteen and V. I. Federenko with thirteen. Each of these pilots scored more than ten victories over the Kuban. Boris, the younger of the two Glinka brothers, was particularly successful over the Kuban region, with ten kills in a total of fifteen missions.

Serving alongside these "Heroes of the Soviet Union" were other noteworthy Russian pilots. One such pilot, who also saw action in the hunting grounds of the 52nd Fighter Wing, was Major A. A. Doroshenkov of the 43rd Fighter Regiment. On one occasion Doroshenkov led a group of six Yak 7B fighters in an attack on the German airfield at Anapa (this attack was described earlier in the text). On the morning of 26 May 1943 he carried out another attack on a German airfield, this time the one used by the 52nd's 2nd Group. The attack was carried out before sunrise. Doroshenkov succeeded in taking the Germans by surprise. The dawn patrol had just taken off. Instead of making a straight-in approach from the east, Doroshenkov flew south and came up on the airfield from the sea.

Nine of the group's aircraft were destroyed or damaged in the hail of bombs and machine-gun fire. This was a major loss that made itself felt for several days until new aircraft arrived, the improved G-series Bf-109s.

✠

The success of the Soviet fighter arm, in which General Novikov, the Commander-in-Chief of the Red Air Forces, had taken a special interest, continued to grow. The arrival of the first fighters from America, Bell P-39 Airacobras, was welcomed by Soviet aviators, even though the type was already considered obsolete in the USA. In the skies over Russia, the P-39 proved a powerful, well-armored fighter-bomber. When employed correctly, it also served well as an interceptor.

The location of the aircraft's engine—behind the cockpit—made the power plant less vulnerable to ground fire in low-level attacks. The centrally mounted 37-mm cannon proved an effective weapon against ground targets.

✠

In Alexander Pokryshkin the Red Air Force possessed a tactician who adapted his offensive techniques to meet the needs of the front. Pokryshkin studied every detail of his engagements and analyzed them thoroughly. The lessons he learned were passed on to his younger, inexperienced comrades, who were encouraged to adopt his tactics and techniques.

Marshall Vershinin said: "The effectiveness of Pokryshkin's theories was tested under fire."

Pokryshkin emphasized the advantage of superior altitude, which enabled the attacker to approach the enemy in a dive with a speed advantage, ensuring that he got in the first burst. Obviously, this was not easy against an opponent who had been taught this tactic in flight school. Nevertheless, the Russians were catching up to the Germans in this area as well. In many cases it was the Soviet pilot who was first to open fire by fractions of a second, which was often enough to decide the outcome of an engagement.

Pokryshkin also stressed the need to approach near to the enemy before opening fire. This view was shared by some of the prominent German aces over the Crimea and the Kuban such as Graf, Barkhorn, Hartmann and Batz.

Pilots who flew and fought over the Kuban, no matter which side they were on, state that both sides there fought with skill and fairness. There were no attacks on men in parachutes by either side.

Another prominent Soviet pilot over the Kuban area was Colonel N. Platonov. He adopted the *para* (two-man) formation. It is interesting to note that the two-man *Rotte*—element leader and wingman—was the basic tactical unit of the Luftwaffe's fighter arm. Colonel Platonov introduced a further variation in tactics: A frontal attack from superior altitude. According to his memoirs, Platonov scored three victories using this style of attack. He flew 155 combat missions, participated in twenty-six engagements, and shot down six German aircraft. Platonov received the Gold Star of a Hero of the Soviet Union on 1 May 1943 while serving in the Kuban area.

The Red Air Force's losses in the bitter battle over the Kuban are not listed in any Soviet accounts of the air war. German sources put Soviet losses in the months-long air battle at 2,280 aircraft by October 1943, when German forces had to be evacuated from the Kuban Bridgehead across the Strait of Kerch. The Red Air Force command gave the total number of missions flown over the Kuban as 35,000. It claimed to have shot down a total of 1,100 German aircraft. This figure is pure fantasy, as a perusal of Luftwaffe strength reports, especially those submitted by the 1st and 8th Air Corps, reveals.

The air fighting over the Kuban slacked off for a time beginning on 7 July 1943; the Red Air Force command moved all of its forces north into the area east of Belgorod/Kursk in July, where the German armed forces had launched their last great offensive in Russia.

After reading this chapter it should be obvious to the reader that the best Soviet fighter pilots were just as skilled as their German counterparts and that the notion that Soviet aircraft were "ripe plums" waiting to be plucked from the sky is nothing more than a fairy tale.

The Red Air Force was certainly a determined, aggressive opponent over the Kuban Region and elsewhere, even where the fighting was less intense. No fighter pilot from the western nations, whether French,

English or American, achieved near the number of kills as did the Soviet aces in the skies over the Kuban. And those kills were made against the best pilots Germany had, members of the 51st, 52nd, and 54th Fighter Wings, all experienced Eastern Front wings.

The highest-scoring fighter pilot of the Royal Air Force, Squadron Leader M. T. Pattle, a South African, scored forty-one victories over North Africa and Greece. Over mainland Europe the most successful was Group Captain Johnny Johnson with thirty-eight kills. The top-scoring US fighter pilot was Major Richard Bong with forty kills, all achieved in the Far East. The most successful American pilot in Europe was Colonel Francis Gabreski with thirty-one victories.

AT THE APEX: THE RISE OF WILHELM BATZ, COMMANDER OF THE 5TH SQUADRON, 52ND FIGHTER WING

For Oberleutnant Batz the summer of 1943 was an endless succession of missions over the Crimea. He and his squadron were given their assignments by Hauptmann Helmut Kühle. Batz and his wingman frequently took off alone to investigate the situation in the air while the rest of the squadron waited on strip alert on the ground.

Fighter sweeps over the Strait of Kerch often produced encounters with Soviet aircraft attempting to halt or at least interfere with German supply traffic to the Kuban bridgehead.

Helmut Kühle had taken over command of the 52nd's 2nd Group on 25 March 1943. He was to remain the group commander until 31 August. Kühle was popular with the men and never overplayed the fact that he was their superior. There was no need for heavy-handed tactics on his part; the group was a close-knit team.

One day in late May the morning patrol sighted a large formation of Il-2s. The headquarters *Schwarm* took off. It was led by Hauptmann Kühle. That was followed by Batz and his *Schwarm*.

"Everyone: Keep your eyes open," Kühle ordered.

The enemy formation was sighted, 800 meters lower and still far ahead. Batz instructed his *Schwarm* to climb. He flew over the Il-2 formation and reversed course. He then dove to the attack with each man selecting an enemy aircraft.

With their increased speed in the dive, the four fighters reached attack position very quickly. Batz had selected the Il-2 flying on the right side of

A Bf-109 G-14 of the 2nd Group at Neubiberg, Germany, 1945. J. V. Crow Collection

the formation. Approaching quickly, he put his first burst into the Il-2s fuel tank, which was located between the pilot and his gunner. Bright flames leapt from the tank. Batz fired again, this time from point-blank range.

In seconds the enemy aircraft was wrapped in flames. It flew on like a blazing torch for a few hundred meters. The last third of the fuselage then broke away, and the aircraft fell toward the sea. It struck the surface of the water, bounced once, then sank.

As Batz turned away he saw two more Il-2s on fire. An aircraft of his *Schwarm* was also burning; it turned toward land and set course for base.

The next day saw the squadron assigned to escort Stukas into the area northeast of Kerch. The fighters rendezvoused with the dive-bombers east of Anapa. Batz approached the lead Stuka; the pilot rocked his wings, a signal that he recognized the fighter escort. Direct communication between the fighters and dive-bombers was impossible because they were equipped with different types of radio. This situation remained unchanged throughout the war, even though direct communication would have made the job of escorting the dive-bombers much less complicated.

The flight to the target lasted about twenty minutes; there was no sign of Russian fighters. One after another, the Stukas peeled off and plunged toward the earth. Their target was troop concentrations, and the Stukas were armed with AB-500 bomb dispensers. Each dispenser contained approximately 200 antipersonnel bombs, each weighing one kilogram. The dispensers opened in midair, showering antipersonnel bombs over the target area.

A formation of Russian fighters appeared, and two of Batz's pilots veered toward them. Batz called them back; the primary mission of the fighters was to protect the Stukas and cover their return to German territory. The dive-bombers pulled out of their dives and climbed away in a wide, left-hand turn before assembling in the area west of the target for the flight home. Batz and his fighters followed the Stukas down to the target. It was a wild ride for the fighter pilots in their new Bf-109s.

Diving beside the two Stukas on the extreme flank, Batz suddenly spotted several LaGG 5 fighters. He broke away in a steep turn, rammed the throttle forward, and carried out a turn that would place him behind the closest enemy fighter.

The LaGG-5 was equipped for both the fighter and fighter-bomber roles. Powered by a 1,850 horsepower Shvetsov M-82F radial engine, the LaGG-5 was capable of a maximum speed of 644 kilometers per hour. It was armed with two 20-mm cannon and could carry a 150-kilogram bomb load.

The LaGG-5 was a difficult opponent as Batz was to discover. The Soviet pilot turned and approached head on. He opened fire and then dove away at the last second. The two fighters raced past each other at a distance of a few meters. Batz's Bf-109 had lost speed and it then lost altitude in a sideslip. As he passed the LaGG-5 Batz saw that the enemy aircraft had been hit.

Batz lost about 200 meters of altitude before regaining control. He turned toward the enemy aircraft that was trailing smoke at that point. Batz closed the distance quickly; apparently, the enemy fighter's engine had been damaged. He opened fire from a distance of 120 meters. The Soviet pilot abandoned his aircraft, which continued flying straight and level. The LaGG began to stagger and finally went down almost vertically. It exploded on striking the ground. The parachute came down in Russian territory; no German aircraft attempted to attack the helpless pilot.

The dive-bombers had set course for home. The group commander ordered the fighters to use the rest of the time remaining search for enemy. Batz led his squadron in the direction of the ferry landing. Several German fighters were already engaged with Soviet aircraft there. As they approached, the wild dogfight broke up into three or four individual engagements. Then another group of enemy aircraft appeared; it was more LaGG-5s, a group of four with four more keeping station about 500 meters above them. Hauptmann Kühle instructed Batz and his *Schwarm* to swing out to the right and attack. Wilhelm Batz led his fighters into a climb. When they had reached a suitable position from which to attack he radioed: "Let's go!"

The Messerschmitts dove toward the Soviet top cover. When they spotted the German fighters, the LaGG's broke formation and dove toward the lower group of four.

"Get them before they link up!" Batz called to his men.

He attacked the leading LaGG. Batz dived on the Soviet aircraft from behind and opened fire. Flames spurted from it. The other three members of the *Schwarm* each tackled one of the Soviet fighters. Another LaGG went down in flames while the other two turned to face their attackers. The Soviet top cover formation had failed in its attempt to join the lower group of fighters.

Batz turned toward the lower formation. The leading LaGG was in his sights as he dove. Suddenly, he noticed a shadow above him. His wingman shouted a warning: "Look out, Eagle 1! LaGG-5 behind you!"

Batz turned hard as the enemy opened fire. Most of the rounds went wide but several still hit his Messerschmitt. Batz realized that his aircraft was not responding fully to the controls. Then it was hit several times in the fuselage. After landing, Batz explained the situation:

> My right wing seemed to literally slide to the side. It pointed straight down. I stepped on the rudder with no result and then the machine rolled half onto its back and dived toward the sea. I recalled that one of my students had once encountered a similar situation.
>
> "Throttle back!' I shouted to myself. Suddenly, the Bf-109 righted itself and returned to a normal attitude. After testing the controls and finding that they responded to the slightest pressure, I reversed course in a shallow turn and was relieved to hear the voice of my wingman: "Have you in sight again, sir! I'm moving into position behind you. You disappeared all of a sudden."

Batz acknowledged just as the fuel warning light came on.

"Eagle 1 to everyone: Return to garden fence."

The flight back to base lasted about eight minutes. Batz swept over the airfield and waggled his wings twice before touching down. He taxied to his squadron's dispersal area where his two mechanics helped him from the cockpit.

The ground crew immediately set about servicing the Messerschmitt. The squadron painter arrived on the scene.

"That makes forty, sir," he said.

✠

During Operation Citadel the 1st and 3rd Groups of the 52nd Fighter Wing fought over the southern pincer and achieved great success. This was not enough to assure victory, however. The Luftwaffe's resources were inadequate for the task at hand. Nevertheless, by this stage of the war it was evident that formations trained for close-support missions were capable of stopping large armored formations and deciding a ground engagement from the air.

✠

Hauptmann Wiese scored his 100th kill in that sector. On 7 July Oberleutnant Paul-Hinrich Dähne scored the 800th victory by the 1st Group. Hauptmann Rall, commander of the 3rd Group, shot down three enemy aircraft, the last being the wing's 6,000th victory. After the departure of Major von Honin on 5 July 1943, Rall had assumed command of the group.

✠

The Soviets also fought hard during Operation Citadel. They took a toll of the Luftwaffe but their own losses were very heavy. The Red Air Force carried out a "preventive air strike" against the Luftwaffe at the beginning of Operation Citadel. A force of 132 Il-2s escorted by 285 fighters attacked eight German airfields. According to Soviet sources, 50 German aircraft were destroyed on the ground.

> Despite that, the opening missions by the Luftwaffe could not be stopped. They were of great intensity and took a heavy toll on the air forces of the 16th Air Army. (From a report by the 16th Air Army to the Soviet High Command).

During the advance by the 4th Panzer Army north of Belgorod there were 2,000 aircraft of both sides in the air. The two sides fought for air superiority over the battlefield. The skies above the Kursk front were frequently the scene of massive dogfights involving as many as 150 aircraft. On the first day of the German offensive, the Red Air Force lost 400 aircraft.

On the Russian side, the 8th Guards Fighter Regiment under Major General A. P. Galunov claimed no less than seventy-six victories on 5 July

1943. According to Soviet war correspondent I. V. Timokovich, three Soviet pilots—Lieutenants Belikov, Panin and Bulayev—each shot down four German aircraft on the first day of the battle.

According to its own sources, the 16th Air Army shot down 106 enemy aircraft. It flew 1,232 sorties against the German positions and was involved in 76 group-sized engagements.

General Rudenko, the Commander-in-Chief of the 16th Air Army, was ordered by General Rokossovski to carry out repeated strikes against German infantry in the central sector. The 9th Army under Generalfeldmarschall Model, part of the northern pincer, was forced to endure a hail of bombs and gunfire from aircraft of the Red Air Force. A total of 450 aircraft of the 6th Mixed Air Corps, the 2nd Guards Close-Support Division and the 299th Close-Support Division took part in those operations.

The star of Soviet fighter pilot Ivan Kozhedub rose during the Kursk fighting. He flew his first missions in a regiment of the 16th Air Army. He had served for a long time as a flight instructor up to that point, and his career thus bore some similarity to that of Wilhelm Batz. In November 1942 he joined a frontline unit in the Stalingrad area and flew his first combat mission in the La-5 north of Kursk. He first flew as wingman to one of his superiors. One day he lost contact with his leader. He then sighted several German fighters. Kozhedub dived to the attack. His bullets went wide and soon two Messerschmitts were on his tail. His aircraft was hit several times, and Kozhedub only managed to save himself by putting his aircraft into a steep dive, from which he pulled out only a few meters above the ground. In spite of damage to the leading edge of his aircraft's wing, he was able to land safely.

On the third day of Operation Citadel Kozhedub attacked a formation of Ju-87s. He shot down two of the Stukas before German fighters arrived on the scene. In the subsequent dogfight, Kozhedub shot down a Bf-109 with a few bursts, but a second German fighter proved a tougher opponent, scoring several hits on the fuselage of his fighter before it too went down in flames and crashed.

Kozhedub continued his success and, after the end of the Battle of Kursk, he received the Order of the Red Banner. At the same time, he was promoted to Lieutenant and was given his own fighter squadron. In the subsequent aerial engagements over the Dniepr crossings, Kozhedub shot down eleven enemy aircraft in ten days.

But it was not until the following year, the same year that Wilhelm Batz was enjoying his greatest success, that Kozhedub reached his best form in the skies over Romania, shooting down eight German aircraft in one week.

On 15 January 1945 Kozhedub even shot down an elusive Me-262. When the war ended, he was the top scoring Soviet fighter pilot with 62 enemy aircraft to his credit.

✠

The 52nd's 2nd Group remained in the Kuban Region. The numerically weak group was constantly overburdened with an endless succession of missions. Wilhelm Batz continued to score steadily—not spectacular multiple kills—but one or two enemy aircraft at a time.

The Bf-109 G6, which the wing had been using for some time, had a heavier armament than the earlier F model. Later examples had a larger fin and rudder of wooden construction. The G6 was powered by a DB-605 A powerplant producing 1,450 to 1,800 horsepower. Internal fuel capacity was 400 liters, which could be supplemented by a 300-liter tank carried beneath the fuselage.

Fuselage armament consisted of two 13-mm MG-131s above the engine. Each had a 300-round magazine. The G6 also had a 20-mm MG-151/20 cannon mounted between the engine cylinder banks (in later versions this was replaced by a 30-mm MK-108) with 100 rounds of ammunition. Two further MG-151 cannon, each with 150 rounds of ammunition,

A Bf-109 G-14 ("White 21") of the 2nd Group in Germany, 1945. J. V. CROW COLLECTION

were carried in underwing fairings. The standard gun sight was the Revi C 12 D (later the 16 D).

The Bf-109 G6 thus possessed enormous firepower, however, the extra armament had a deleterious effect on the aircraft's performance. Maximum speed at 2,000 meters was only 590 kilometers per hour. At 6,900 meters it reached a speed of 620 kilometers per hour. Rate of climb was seventeen meters per second; the G6 could reach 3,000 meters in two minutes and fifty-four seconds and 5,700 meters in six minutes.

Batz and his men flew steadily from Kerch, Uman and Reichshof before the group returned to Bagerovo on 20 December. Batz was one of the most successful pilots in the 2nd Group by then. Since 9 May 1943 he had led the 5th Squadron; as an experienced and capable aviator, he enjoyed the loyalty of his men. He was to lead the squadron for more than eleven months.

During that time Batz came to know every one of his men through and through. He confided to friends that he had complete trust in each of his pilots. The same applied to him; he was the squadron's "number one eagle," the first man into combat and the last one out.

Leutnant Erich Hartmann scored his 50th victory on 2 August 1943. On 1 September Hauptmann Gerhard Barkhorn became the group commander of the 2nd Group. On 30 November he shot down his 200th enemy aircraft. He was a great example to all his men and one of Wilhelm Batz's closest friends. The two men frequently discussed their operational experiences and compared notes on tactics.

Fighter sweeps over the east coast of the Crimean Peninsula were among the most common missions. The group command post, codenamed "Jumbo," worked hard to keep the fighters in the air supplied with the most up-to-date information. When the fighters were in the air, Major Barkhorn was rarely in his command post; he preferred to fly with one of his squadrons. Occasionally, when there was a large-scale operation, he led the entire group into action. The group's fighters often rendezvoused over Bagerovo with Stukas en route to attack Soviet positions and seaports. On one occasion, Il-2s attacked the 3rd Motor Torpedo Boat Flotilla's base at Feodosia. The 2nd Group put every available aircraft into the air. Led by Major Barkhorn and the headquarters *Schwarm*, the Messerschmitts flew toward the south coast of the Crimea.

"Eagle 1 to everyone: On our present course we will reach the coast about 30 kilometers east of Feodosia."

Everyone in the formation acknowledged. The Messerschmitts were still over the sea flying west when the Il-2s were sighted. High above them were eight Yak 9s—fast, maneuverable fighters.

Barkhorn gave the order to attack. The Messerschmitts dived on the Il-2s and Barkhorn shot one down on his first pass, hitting the enemy aircraft in the oil cooler. Batz and his men and the two pairs that made up the headquarters *Schwarm* selected their targets and opened fire. Batz closed with an Il-2 and caught the Soviet aircraft with a burst of cannon fire. The exploding rounds severed the Il-2s right wing; the Soviet machine spun to the ground and exploded.

The Il-2s had not yet begun their attack when they became involved in this wild dogfight. The eight Yak 9s immediately came down to assist. Batz became involved with the Soviet fighters and lost sight of the Il-2s, which had stubbornly held their course. The other German fighters were also engaged with the Yaks, leaving the Il-2s a clear path to their target.

The light Flak guarding the torpedo-boat base opened fire. The guns shot down one Il-2 and forced another to veer off, however, eight of the heavily armed close-support machines survived. They roared over the base—at that point also under fire from the guns mounted on the torpedo boats—and dropped their bombs. Two boats were hit. The Il-2s poured cannon fire into the remaining boats. By the time the Ilyushins had turned around for a second pass from the west, the German fighters had freed themselves from the Yaks. They raced to intercept the Il-2s.

"Nose to nose!" Barkhorn radioed.

The Messerschmitts opened fire. An Il-2 veered off course, but the others tried to repeat their attack on the torpedo boats, probably aware that they were in great danger if the Yaks failed to come to their aid again.

Batz passed 100 meters in front of one of the enemy aircraft. He pulled up, descended in a half-roll and ended up on the tail of the Il-2. He was too low for the Il-2s gunner to reach him, but he entered the gunner's sights with every meter he climbed.

When Batz opened fire he was still sixty meters and about twenty degrees below the enemy aircraft. He climbed and, allowing a small degree of deflection, opened fire. Batz saw the Il-2s oil cooler burst apart and a gray cloud emerged from the shattered tank. With a steep climbing turn Batz cleared the danger zone. Not a second too soon! The Il-2 exploded, scattering debris beneath the squadron commander's Messerschmitt.

In the meantime, Barkhorn and his wingman, Leutnant Heinz Ewald, who had only just joined the wing, had each shot down an Il-2. Barkhorn also downed one of the Yak 9's. The four Il-2s that survived to carry out a second pass shot up another boat before they turned and flew south to escape the Flak. Two more Il-2s and three Yak 9's were shot down as the Soviets withdrew.

This mission in defense of the Feodosia torpedo boat base was the prelude to a number of heavy blows the 52nd was to inflict on the enemy in the coming weeks.

Christmas was approaching. Oberleutnant Batz and his squadron moved to Bagerovo at the end of November. Flying from there, Wilhelm Batz was able to add to his victory total. Batz was recommended for the Knight's Cross by the wing commander, Oberstleutnant Hrabak, after his seventy-fifth kill. Weeks passed and Batz's score continued to rise.

The Soviets Pe-2s attacked Bagerovo with fighter escort. Several of the off-duty pilots scrambled with the alert *Schwarm*. One of them was Oberleutnant Batz, who was in the command post when the alert sounded. He ran to his aircraft where his crew chief held up one thumb, the signal that the aircraft was ready to go.

Assisted by the crew chief, Batz clambered into the cockpit of the Bf-109. He fastened his parachute straps as the mechanic cranked up the inertia starter. Batz tightened his straps and locked the canopy. Placing the ignition switches on M1 and M2, Batz pulled the starter. The 1,450-horsepower Daimler-Benz engine roared to life. Batz advanced the throttle slowly. He glanced toward the mechanic, who signaled that the chocks were clear.

The Bf-109 began to move. As he taxied to position, Batz saw that his wingman was in position on his right; he watched the entire headquarters *Schwarm* take off. After checking to ensure that the runway was clear, Batz pushed the throttle lever forward. The Messerschmitt danced over the bumps in the runway like a prima ballerina and then lifted off. Batz pushed the nose down slightly to gain speed. The undercarriage and flaps came up and he and his wingman sped east-northeast at low level.

Barely 10 seconds later Batz spotted the first Il-2s. They were headed for the airfield at treetop height and had already opened fire. The airfield Flak answered. Batz was at 450 meters when he sighted a Yak 9. Allowing just the right amount of deflection, he fired and hit the enemy fighter beneath the cockpit. The pilot of the Soviet machine rolled to the right and took a full burst that walked through the aircraft from engine to tail and caused it to explode.

Turning to avoid the wreckage of the downed Yak, Batz climbed above the approaching Il-2s. Looking up, he realized that his course was going to take him into the midst of a formation of Airacobras. He throttled back and dropped the radiator flaps to lose speed. Batz fishtailed and managed to reach a favorable firing position. One of the Soviet fighters carried out a Split-S maneuver in an effort to get in a shot. However, Batz reacted quickly. Pushing the nose down, he fired at the spot where he calculated the enemy fighter must pass beneath him. The Airacobra flew right through the burst of fire; it went down vertically and hit the ground. Batz pulled up, noting that the enemy aircraft had exploded on impact.

"Eagle 1: Indians above and behind you!"

Batz tried to turn to the right. He had just entered the turn when the first bullets hammered into the airframe. Batz continued to turn and simultaneously began to climb. He calculated that a half-loop would take him out of the line of fire while placing him in position to attack.

The Messerschmitt responded flawlessly in spite of the many hits it had taken. At the top of the loop Batz saw a Russian fighter climbing behind him. A half-roll returned him to horizontal flight. He fired two brief bursts as he approached the enemy and, seconds later, found himself in a turning battle with the Soviet fighter. After several full circles, the Soviet pilot carried out a reversal and headed east in a shallow turn. Batz was on the enemy fighter in a flash. A long burst struck the Yak. The Soviet aircraft seemed to rear up under the impacting cannon rounds. A wing came off, then part of the tail assembly. The Yak righted itself again, but then the right undercarriage leg came down. The aircraft contacted the ground. It rolled and slid about fifty meters before exploding in a ball of flame.

This was Batz's third kill in the German aerial counterattack. The Messerschmitts had arrived in time to prevent the enemy from fully deploying his forces. The cost was four aircraft damaged, one of which had to be written off. Wilhelm Batz's total now stood at ninety, fifteen more than when the Knight's Cross recommendation had been submitted.

✠

Christmas passed relatively quietly. The only enemy activity came on 26 December when several aircraft carried out nuisance raids on Bagerovo. Batz and his wingman scrambled several times and each downed an enemy aircraft.

By the end of 1943 only about half of the thirty-two aircraft with which the 2nd Group had arrived in Bagerovo on 30 October were left. Several more were repaired by the field maintenance section.

At the turn of the year 1944, the 4th and 5th Squadrons were transferred to Grammatikovo (west of Kerch). The 6th Squadron moved to Karankut for fourteen days.

✠

Hauptmann Barkhorn had achieved his 200th victory on 30 November 1943. On 28 November Major Rall shot down his 250th enemy aircraft. On 5 July he had relinquished command of the 8th Squadron to take command of the 3rd Group. He was the second German pilot to reach this figure. However, on 13 December another ace joined the list of greats. It was Erich Hartmann, who shot down his 150th aircraft that day.

✠

While flying from Bagerovo, the 2nd Group was responsible for guarding the airspace over Kerch, where the Soviet 8th Air Army had committed its main effort. One of its most frequent missions was escorting close-support groups which attacked and, on occasion halted, the Soviet armored spearheads.

The fighting continued in spite of the harsh winter. After a brief interlude of only a few days at Sarabus airfield on the Crimea, the 2nd Group returned once more to Bagerovo on 24 February 1944. On 27 February the group flew on to Grammatikovo and began flying missions from there the next day.

Flying from Grammatikovo on 24 March 1944 Wilhelm Batz downed three enemy machines to reach the 100 mark. Two days later he was awarded the Knight's Cross. The award recommendation had been submitted after his 75th kill, some time ago. In the next four months Batz's victory tally was to climb dramatically.

All of the 2nd Group was based at Grammatikovo effective 1 April 1944. The group achieved great success flying from this airfield west of Kerch. The bulk of the missions flown were offensive patrols and escort and reconnaissance flights. The group had by then achieved a reputation as something of a mobile fire-brigade, and it came as no surprise when it was moved to Khersonyes on 14 April to take part in the defense of Sevastopol. However, the group had to leave Khersonyes twenty-four hours later, leaving the airfield to the transport units evacuating important specialist personnel from the Crimea.

Major Barkhorn, who had 301 kills and was second only to "Bubi" Hartmann as the most successful fighter pilot.

The next stop was Toksanie and, thirty-six hours later, the group flew from there to Zilestea in Romania. The men of the 2nd Group flew as many as five sorties a day from Zilestea, helping cover the evacuation of German forces from Khersonyes across the Black Sea to Constanta. Battling Soviet high-altitude bombers, close-support aircraft and fighters, the group downed an average of 20 enemy aircraft a day in the period from 10 to 20 April.

Not a single day went by that Wilhelm Batz didn't manage at least one kill. Several times he shot down two and, on one occasion, five enemy aircraft in one day. As Barkhorn had predicted, Wilhelm Batz had become an indispensable member of the group. On 18 April 1944, however, Batz was forced to leave the group.

On 18 April Major Rall, who had commanded the 3rd Group with success, was assigned to duties in defense of the Reich. He was to take command of the battered the 11th Fighter Wing's 2nd Group. Rall took his old friend, Hauptmann Walter Krupinski, who commanded the 52nd's 7th Squadron, with him to Germany.

Oberstleutnant Hrabak summoned Major Barkhorn and Batz, recently promoted to Hauptmann, to the wing command post and explained the situation to them. He asked Batz to leave his group and take command of the 52nd's 3rd Group. At the same time, he promised him command of his former group, if the position should became vacant. Major Barkhorn, who held the position, nodded in agreement. He had already been informed unofficially that he had been selected to take command of a fighter wing in Germany, although that was to be some months in the future.

Hauptmann Wilhelm Batz left the wing command post as the new commander of the 3rd Group. At that time the 7th Squadron was commanded by Oberleutnant Eberhard Graf Treuberg, the 8th Squadron by Oberleutnant Friedrich Obleser, and the 9th Squadron by Oberleutnant Erich Hartmann. Batz was thus Hartmann's commanding officer for five months.

Soon afterward Batz was involved in a dogfight with an experienced Soviet pilot. He suffered a grazing wound in the shoulder and was forced to relinquish command of the group for a few days. Oberleutnant Hartmann stepped into the breach and led the group until 28 May.

On the evening of 28 May 1944 the German radio intelligence intercepted a Soviet operations order. When the order was decoded it was learned that the base of the 3rd Group at Roman, situated north of Yassy, was to be the target of a major attack. Further intercepts revealed that at least 375 Soviet fighters and 370 close-support aircraft and bombers were to take part in the raid.

The group's mechanics worked through the night to repair all the fighters in the unit's makeshift maintenance facilities. Hauptmann Batz had returned to duty from his wound; he issued his orders. The 1st Group would take off at first light accompanied by the group commander and his headquarters *Schwarm*.

All the remaining fighters would remain on the ground on strip alert. As soon as the enemy had been sighted, they would take off, thus eliminating any risk of being caught on the ground.

Batz and his headquarters *Schwarm* took off at first light and set course for the Russian frontline airfields. His aim was to spot and engage the enemy as early as possible and thus prevent them from attacking his own airfield.

The enemy aircraft were sighted in the red glow of the rising sun. Batz's first estimate was about twenty-four Il-2s escorted by approximately the same number of Soviet fighters. The information was relayed back to base, where the 7th Squadron took off at once.

Batz instructed his three pilots to climb to a position above the Russians before attacking their right flank. He wanted to force as many aircraft as possible to break formation. Batz's wingman was Oberfeldwebel Hellmers. The pair was flying about 600 meters above the escort fighters; they turned and positioned themselves behind the Soviets.

The two Messerschmitts swooped down on the group of eight Yaks and Airacobras, whose formation was rather ragged on the right side. They had not yet been noticed. The two Germans opened fire as they swept through the enemy formation. Batz had selected the Soviet machine flying on the extreme right; a long burst sent the enemy fighter down in flames. Then he turned right and pulled up into a three-quarters turn before diving on a Yak 9. Once again a single burst was enough to finish the Soviet fighter.

The first two firing passes by the four German fighters had cost the Soviets three fighters. As Batz prepared for his third pass, he saw Leutnant Evers engaged with a Yak 9. The two fighters twisted and turned until Evers finally downed his opponent; but his own aircraft had been hit in the cooling system, and he was forced to set course for home.

The remaining three Messerschmitts then began a turning contest with the four surviving Soviet fighters. Batz felt several bullets hit the fuselage of his Bf-109, but there was no serious damage. He turned quickly and caught the Soviet fighter that had attacked him from the side. A brief burst of fire, and the enemy fighter was shot down. Of the eight Soviet fighters flying top cover for the right flank of the formation, only one was left, and it quickly fled the scene. Batz called his pilots: "We'll turn back toward base and try to catch any stragglers from the 7th squadron's attack."

When they had covered half the distance they saw the 7th Squadron engaged with the Soviet fighters flying ahead and above the main formation. The Il-2s were still in close formation.

Batz radioed base and instructed the 8th Squadron to take off at once. The squadron's pilots had been sitting in their cockpits waiting for the order. They took off immediately and were able to attain sufficient altitude to make a frontal attack on the Il-2s before they reached the airfield. The Soviet formation was scattered. Batz engaged and shot down one of the Il-2s. Then he attacked a second, which turned away emitting smoke. Batz and his wingman couldn't see what happened to the Il-2. They had become involved in a dogfight between three Messerschmitts and several Soviet fighters. The Germans twisted and turned, dove on the enemy and were themselves attacked from several sides. Batz's wingman saved him by shooting down an Il-2 that had moved into position on his tail. Oberfeldwebel Hellmers opened fire a fraction of a second sooner than the Soviet pilot; his bullets struck the fuel tank of the Il-2, which immediately burst into flames.

The Messerschmitts landed on their last drops of fuel, but not before Batz overflew the field four times, waggling his wings to signal his four kills. Then he touched down and taxied to his dispersal area, where he received a tumultuous welcome. Four kills in a single sortie—that was something!

In the command post Batz received the combat reports from the other squadrons while the clerk copied down every detail. They had lost four aircraft; two pilots had taken to their parachutes and were safe.

The next Russian attack came two hours later. Batz was in the air once again, leaving his adjutant to take the necessary measures on the ground.

Batz closed the cockpit canopy. The engine's pitch grew to a roar as he prepared for takeoff. Just then, the first bombs exploded at the other end of the field. Batz and his *Schwarm* began to taxi. As they did, the four pilots saw that the first Il-2s were already over the field, spraying gunfire. As he taxied, Batz felt the shock waves from several bombs exploding nearby. The tail came up and the Messerschmitt picked up speed as it swept through the dust and smoke. Finally, the Bf-109 lifted off and climbed into the sky.

"Engage at will!"

The three pilots of the *Schwarm* acknowledged. To his right and left Batz saw the aircraft of the 9th Squadron, which had taken off earlier, in a duel with the enemy. As he reached 1,000 meters a Bf-109 moved into position behind him; it was his wingman, Hillers.

"Climb and turn toward the bombers!"

The gaggle of Pe-2 bombers roared past beneath the Messerschmitts. Batz and his pilots turned and dove on the leading group, which was no more than 4,000 meters from the airfield.

They opened fire from a range of 150 meters. Batz pulled out of the dive and fired again. He and Hillers each shot down a bomber. The other two members of the *Schwarm*, Steincke and Albertz, also downed a Pe-2 each. The leading group of Soviet bombers had been wiped out. The four Messerschmitts climbed and positioned themselves for another pass. Two more Soviet bombers began to burn. A third was hit and veered out of formation—straight toward the aircraft flown by Steincke. The German pilot sideslipped out of the bomber's path and hit it with a full burst from barely eighty meters away. The Pe-2 disintegrated. A piece of wreckage struck Steincke's machine, which went into a spin.

"Pull out, pull out!" Batz called to his pilot. As he watched, Steincke regained control and turned in the direction of home. Then he heard Steincke say: "Returning to garden fence."

More German fighters closed with the Soviet bombers until there were eight Bf-109s firing at the Pe-2s. Burning bombers, flying wreckage and crashing enemy aircraft marked the final phase of the second Soviet attack. It inflicted some damage on the airfield and its buildings.

Two of the Soviet bombers collided and then plunged to earth locked together. The enemy aircraft broke off their attack. Every German fighter with sufficient fuel remaining took up the pursuit in order to prevent as many bombers as possible from coming again.

The third sortie of the day saw Batz shoot down a Yak 7. On the way home he shot down a Soviet bomber. The enemy aircraft had already dropped its bombs and was trying to sneak home alone.

When Wilhelm Batz returned to base after his fourth sortie, it appeared that it was all over for the day. The 52nd Fighter Wing and several groups of other fighter wings had withstood the Soviet aerial assault. The group's base was still operational, although one runway had to be closed.

But the Soviets weren't finished yet. The alarm was sounded again at 1645 hours. Every serviceable aircraft of the 3rd Group took to the air. This time the enemy had sent a mixed formation of Il-2s, Pe-2s, and Yak 7 fighters. The fighting that commenced was the climax of the fighting on 29 May 1944.

The Messerschmitts buzzed about the gaggle of enemy aircraft. It seemed impossible that they didn't collide. Batz shot down a Yak 7, then turned and shot down a bomber. As he did so, he was himself attacked by a Soviet fighter. The enemy pilot was good, and Batz had to call upon all his skill and experience to fend off his opponent. Twice he was hit by the skilled Soviet, and he heard the bullets striking his aircraft. Instinctively, he turned away and raced toward a bomber from the side. Batz fired a burst into it and pulled up and over the enemy aircraft. Reversing course in a steep climbing turn, he saw the bomber crash. Once again, Batz came under fire from the same enemy fighter. Finally, after a three-minute dogfight, he got in a fatal burst and the Soviet fighter crashed in flames. The entire engagement lasted thirty minutes. Almost every German pilot came home with a kill. Batz had shot down three enemy aircraft.

By then Batz had lost track of how many he had shot down that day, however, the clerk had kept an exact record of everything.

Returning from the last sortie, exhausted and inattentive, Batz was almost shot down by an enemy fighter. But Hillers saved the day by shooting down the enemy aircraft. As soon as the fighters had landed, the mechanics set about rearming and refueling them. An hour later Batz's crew chief informed him that his aircraft was ready to go again.

Adolf Galland shakes hands with Walter Krupinski, Staffelkapitän of the 7th Squadron.

Then a report was received that yet another large formation of enemy aircraft was en route to the group's base. The group took off by squadron. The Messerschmitts intercepted the enemy just as they crossed the front lines. Each pilot selected a target as the Bf-109s swooped down on the enemy.

Once again Batz roared through the main enemy formation and shot down two bombers in rapid succession. He avoided an attack by a Yak 7. He turned and approached the enemy fighter head on. Both opened fire and then raced past one another wingtip to wingtip, missing by barely 100 meters.

Once again Batz demonstrated his outstanding skill and his virtuoso mastery of his machine as he completely outmaneuvered his opponent and subsequently shot him down. When Batz landed after his fifteenth victory, all of the men who could came over to his dispersal area and ringed his machine.

"Fifteen, sir!" shouted one of his mechanics. "Fifteen!"

Oberstleutnant Hrabak extended his hand to the hero of the day. "Unbelievable, Wilhelm! No one can match that."

"Thanks, Dieter," said Batz, wiping the sweat from his forehead. "I think that today was one of my best."

Hrabak, who had flown to Roman to attend the celebration that had been planned in honor of the new group commander that was scheduled to take place that night, placed his right hand on his friend's shoulder.

"You've exceeded all my expectations by far . . . I thank you," he whispered. "This day will go down in the history of our illustrious wing. Not only have you surpassed yourself, but you've come within two kills of the legendary Joachim Marseille."

Before the big celebration began that evening, Hrabak submitted a second recommendation for the Oak Leaves for Batz in recognition of his total of 175 victories. By the time Batz received the decoration on 20 July 1944, he had already raised his total to 200. The 200th kill came on 17 August, making him the 9th German fighter pilot to reach the magic figure.

✠

The group moved out of Romania when the Soviets launched Operation "Bagration" on 22 June 1944. It was an effort to counter Soviet air superiority over the central sector of the front. There were only forty fighters in the area of operations of Army Group Center—the 51st Fighter Wing and elements of the 52nd. The group arrived at Lida, its new base of operations, on 29 June following a stop at Parafino. Lida was about 130 kilometers west of Minsk.

The group achieved great success against the Red Air Force, as was reflected in Hartmann's victory totals in that period. Hauptmann Batz battled with unflagging elan and he was an example to the young replacement pilots—not just on account of his high number of victories, but because of his concern for each of his men. It was chiefly due to Batz's efforts that losses among the young pilots were surprisingly low, in spite of the hectic pace of operations.

The 3rd Group remained in Lvov (Lemberg) until mid-July; on 20 July it was forced to fall back to Zalliosc-Mokre. The next day the Red Army began its assault on Lvov, which led to the fall of the city on 28 July.

✠

The wing added 1,000 victories to its total in the period from 10 May to 2 September even though three squadrons had been assigned to Reich defense duties at the end of May. The summer of 1944 was marked by the withdrawal from one base to another in the face of the Red Army avalanche. The 3rd Group finally ended up in Krakow, where it joined the bulk of the 2nd Group.

"Bubi" Hartmann was also adding to his score. On 18 July 1944 he downed his 250th enemy aircraft. He added another 29 in the month of August alone, followed by 25 in September and 33 in October. His most successful day was 24 August, when he downed eleven enemy aircraft; the day before he had shot down eight. The last of his kills on 24 August raised his total to 301.

✠

On 16 August 1944 the 3rd Group was moved to Zilistea, not far from Ploesti. By then it had been reduced to 16 aircraft. From there it was to operate against American bombers attempting to destroy the oil production facilities at Ploesti. Its new opponents were B-17 and B-24 bombers. Flying in tight formations, the bombers could put up a heavy screen of defensive fire.

On 2 September 1944 the commander of the 1st Group, Hauptmann Adolf Borchers (who had received the Knight's Cross while serving with the 51st Fighter Wing), accounted for the wing's 10,000th kill. Seventeen days later Oberstleutnant Hermann Graf took command of the wing from Oberstleutnant Dietrich Hrabak. The latter officer had commanded the unit for twenty-three months through all the highs and lows of the Russian Campaign.

Hermann Graf was to lead this wing, in which he had begun his flying career as a young Leutnant, until the end of the war.

THE NEW WING COMMANDER

When the young Leutnant Hermann Graf downed his first enemy aircraft—an I-16 on 4 August 1941—the 52nd Fighter Wing was one of three "Eastern wings" in action at the Dniepr River. The wing was based at Biala Tserkov. Graf's tactical number was a yellow 9.

Born in Engen in Hegau on 24 October 1912, Graf trained as a pilot at the fighter school in Lechfeld (Bavaria). He first joined the 51st Fighter Wing as a Feldwebel before being transferred to the 52nd.

Victories came slowly in the beginning, however Graf began scoring steadily after shooting down a twin-engine DB-3 bomber on 30 August 1941. On 24 January 1942 he received the Knight's Cross after forty-two kills. Barely four months later, on 17 May, he received the Oak Leaves after increasing his score to 104 victories. Two days later Graf was awarded the Swords and was finally promoted to the rank of Oberleutnant. He became the eleventh German soldier to receive the coveted decoration. Finally, on 16 September 1942, Graf was awarded the Knight's Cross with Oak Leaves, Swords and Diamonds following his 182nd victory. It was only the fifth time that the decoration had been awarded.

Graf raised his victory total from 58 to 104 in a period of only seventeen days. He also received the four highest decorations for bravery within eight months.

The next great series of victories saw him increase his total from 127 to 202 in four weeks. Graf achieved his 150th kill on 4 September 1942 and his 200th on 2 October 1942. He was the first fighter pilot to reach the 200 mark.

Major Graf assumed command of the unit responsible for providing the Eastern Front fighter units with replacement pilots in 1943. Later he commanded the 50th Fighter Wing. On 6 September 1943 he shot down two four-engined B-17s over Germany. From November 1943 until the end of April 1944 he served as wing commander of the 11th Fighter Wing. That wing had a home-defense mission. He shot down another four heavy bombers and was injured when he rammed an American fighter during a dogfight.

On 1 October 1944, after his injuries had healed, Graf returned to his old wing on the Eastern Front. He served as wing commander of the 52nd until the end of the war. Together with the main body of the unit, which had withdrawn from Bohemia into Bavaria, he was taken prisoner by US forces. General Seidemann had sent an order for Graf and the commander of the 1st Group, Hauptmann Erich Hartmann, to fly back to Germany. The order stated:

> Graf and Hartmann are to fly to Dortmund at once in order to surrender to British forces. The remaining personnel of the 52nd Fighter Wing *will* surrender to Russian forces in Deutsch Brod (Czechoslovakia).
> /signed/ Seidemann
> Commanding General
> VIII Air Corps

"The Russians will probably put us up against the wall," said Graf. "Having shot down more than 550 Russian aircraft between us, we two are nothing more than objects of revenge to them."

"And what should we do? Follow General Seidemann's order?" asked Hartmann. Graf opened the tent flap and gestured outside, where there were more than 2,000 women, children, old people, wounded, and wing personnel.

"Do you think that I could climb into my crate and take off, Hartmann?" asked Graf.

"No, and I'm of the same opinion. Let's stay here and try to get to the Americans."

Under Hartmann's command all of the aircraft were blown up, all equipment was destroyed. The fuel dump went up in flames.

A convoy of trucks and cars set out toward the Americans. Near Pisek they met US armor. The tanks belonged to the 16th Armored Division and were accompanied by soldiers of the 90th Infantry Division. Everyone was placed in a camp near Schütthofen in Western Bohemia. The camp was soon filled to overflowing with 50,000 German prisoners and civilians.

On 16 May the Americans informed Graf and Hartmann, as well as Major Hartmut Grasser, the wing commander of the 200th Fighter Wing, that they were all going to be moved to Regensburg.

Loaded aboard trucks, the prisoners and civilians rolled straight into a Russian prison camp in a meadow only a few kilometers from the American camp. Everything had been prepared in detail. Hermann Graf and his men became prisoners of the Soviets. Graf was released in 1950; Hartmann remained a prisoner of the Soviets until October 1955.

Hermann Graf shot down 212 enemy aircraft in 830 combat missions, 202 of them in Russia. During his period of duty in homeland defense he shot down 10 heavy bombers.

TOWARD THE END

The 3rd Group moved to Lobellen in East Prussia on 8 October 1944. Wilhelm Batz had shot down his 200th enemy aircraft on 17 August 1944, barely one month after receiving the Oak Leaves. These were often hard-fought victories; Batz saw every engagement through to the end, even against skilled opponents. It is therefore not surprising that he was wounded in action seven times. Batz crash-landed his damaged machine on the German side of the lines a number of times, but only once was he forced to take to his parachute, again over German-held territory.

On 4 November 1944 Reichsmarschall Hermann Göring and his closest staff arrived unexpectedly at the group's base. Batz was in his command post when he learned of the arrival of the "fat one." He immediately ran outside, assembled all the aviators he could find, and reported to the Reichsmarschall.

A Bf-109 G-14 of the 2nd Group in Germany, summer 1945. A Hungarian
Bf-109 G is in the background. J. V. Crow Collection

Göring looked at the men, all of whom wore at least the Iron Cross,
First Class. He raised his field marshal's baton and called out, "Hail, aviators!"

"Hail, Reichsmarschall!" the pilots shouted back.

While preparations for the next mission went ahead, Göring, his officers and General Bodenschatz, his personal friend and adjutant, went into
the command post and talked with the officers. Göring congratulated Batz
on receiving the Oak Leaves and inquired as to the current state of the
wing's victory list.

After an hour Göring's SS guard, which had flown in with him, picked
him up and drove him to the next unit.

✠

On 28 December 1944 Major Gerhard Barkhorn, commander of the
2nd Group, shot down his 300th enemy aircraft. Soon afterward, on 16
January 1945, he became the wing commander of the 56th Fighter Wing.
Barkhorn spent the last few days prior to his departure briefing Batz on
the running of the group. On 16 January 1945 Wilhelm Batz assumed
command of the 2nd Group, then based in Hungary. From Budak, where
it arrived on 31 August 1944, the group had moved to Nagy-Rabe, Tisza-
Tardosch and Tiakta-Kanez. On 31 October it reached Feihegy near
Budapest and arrived in Veszprem in November. On 1 January 1945 the

group had moved to Bapolnapuszta. The next day there was a fighter sweep over Budapest, which was under attack by Soviet bombers. There were frequent scrambles. The group then moved back to the airfield at Veszprem, where Batz assumed command.

✠

In Veszprem the group and part of the group headquarters were quartered in a palace. However, Major Batz and his closest staff stayed in one of the nearby houses. Also there was the group flight surgeon, Stabsarzt Dr. Schwabe, the commander of the headquarters company, Hauptmann Mattholius, as well as the group adjutant, Leutnant van de Kamp.

One night the slightly tipsy members of the group paraded around the walls of the palace dressed in costumes they had found there. It had been snowing for several days, and the associated bad weather had grounded the group.

Major Batz stepped onto the balcony of the house and viewed the procession with astonishment. With him were the flight surgeon and all the others, who had been awakened by the noise.

"At least their morale is good, sir," declared the adjutant.

Batz nodded: "Couldn't be better."

"Are you going to do anything about it?" asked the commander of the headquarters company.

"Not on your life," replied Batz. "I'd be down there with them if they'd asked me." It was a reply that astonished the two staff officers.

Nevertheless, the procession was not without consequences. On the way back to the palace two officers shone a flashlight on the men. It was General Deichmann and his adjutant, who had set out to discover the cause of the racket. The participants scattered to the four winds. General Deichmann shouted after the fleeing men: "An officer and a senior NCO . . . report to me!"

No one came. Then finally a senior noncommissioned officer came trotting up and saluted smartly. He knew nothing about the matter so General Deichmann seized upon the several men he had recognized. One of them was Heinz Sachsenberg, a member of the 6th Squadron. He had recently been promoted to Leutnant and had received the Knight's Cross on 9 June 1944. Sachsenberg was confined to quarters for three days for causing a disturbance in the city of Veszprem. For Sachsenberg, that was an opportunity to take part in a running game of cards with Father Joschka, the group chaplain, and the flight surgeon.

Retaliation against the general was not long in coming. Everyone knew the house where Deichmann lived. A week after Sachsenberg's house arrest ended, an armored car and crew were requested from a nearby SS battle group. An SS-Untersturmführer (Second Lieutenant), was brought into the plot. As soon as the guard had passed he moved the armored car directly beneath the general's bedroom window and fired thirty rounds into the air from the vehicle's 20-mm cannon. He then roared away.

One of the general's sentries immediately sounded the partisan alarm. The entire guard rushed into the open and took up defensive positions, in the middle of which was the general. Freezing in his nightclothes, he ran around encouraging his men to withstand this nocturnal ambush.

✠

The air war over Hungary demanded the utmost of the group. Batz continued to fly regular combat missions. At the same time Hauptmann Hartmann took over the 1st Group, the group he was to lead until the end of the war.

On 6 March 1945, the 2nd Group flew to Papa, 40 kilometers northwest of Veszprem, before continuing on to Vat near Steinamanger the next day. On 18 April Batz led the group to Hörsching near Linz.

In the meantime Batz had continued to increase his score. On 24 April 1945 he downed his 237th enemy aircraft. Several days earlier, on 21 April, he had become the 145th German soldier to receive the Knight's Cross with Oak Leaves and Swords.

Wilhelm Batz shot down seven enemy bombers in fighting over Vienna. On 28 April his group moved to Eferding and, on 1 May 1945, to Hörsching. Three days later the group moved to its final base in World War Two: Zeltweg, sixty kilometers west of Graz. There the great hunt ended for the 2nd Group. The group hit the jackpot when orders came for it to withdraw to Munich early on 8 May 1945. It was General Deichmann who removed the unit from the clutches of the Soviets:

> Hostilities will cease at 2400 hours. All weapons will fall silent and we will have peace. The killing is over and so too, thank God, is the dying of the best sons of many nations. After 2400 hours your group, Major Batz, will take off on its last flight, which will bring you all back to Germany. The fighter group will take off and fly to Neu Biberg near Munich. The ground personnel will take all the serviceable vehicles and try to reach the German-Austrian border, with the objective of being captured by the Americans.

Major Batz bade a brief farewell to his men. He shook hands with each and every one of them. Then he gave his last official order as group commander: "Let's roll!"

Standing by the aircraft were the mechanics and the men of the "black company," forming a sort of lane through which the pilots walked.

First to take off was the group commander, followed closely by his wingman. After takeoff, the aircraft formed up into group formation and set course toward the northwest at 295 degrees.

When Munich came into sight the group flew around the city in a wide circle. The Messerschmitts flew on into the countryside and then landed smartly in Neu Biberg. They were in the American zone—they had escaped the Russians.

Batz and his men climbed out of their aircraft and were immediately surrounded by American pilots and technicians. The same evening they were taken to a bivouac site at Fürstenfeldbrück. The next morning, after receiving release passes, they were set free.

Ludwig Havighorst served with the infantry, the paratroops, and the Luftwaffe, flying fifty missions over Stalingrad.

Ludwig Havighorst: An Infantryman Joins the Luftwaffe

INFANTRY RECRUIT

On 1 October 1935 Ludwig Havighorst received the order to report for active service with the German Armed Forces. He joined the 26th Infantry Regiment, which was based in Rendsburg. Havighorst had never left his hometown of Ostbevern. The son of a blue-collar worker, be was his parents' seventh child. Havighorst's mother was born in the village of Senden, and both of his parents came from farm families. Three more children were born after the family moved to Ostbevern. The last, Franz, was seen as a late arrival. At the age of six, Ludwig was placed in the care of his grandparents and he enjoyed a happy childhood on the family farm. From there it was four kilometers to school, which young Ludwig usually bad to walk.

As the most gifted child, it was intended for Ludwig to go to secondary school, but the costs were too high and his parents were unable to realize this dream. Ludwig Havighorst was forced to give up the idea of continuing his formal education. Instead, he began training to be a baker in Haltern in 1929. His workday began at four in the morning and lasted until 1600 hours. In spite of the long hours, Havighorst managed to find time to go swimming with his friends in the nearby lake or participate in track and field in Lippe. Although he successfully completed his training, he had to give up any idea of pursuing a career as a baker as he had developed "eczema."

Havighorst then attempted to join the police. Following an initial rejection, he successfully passed the entrance exam in Bochum on his second try. In spite of that, he still was not accepted. Not until a third application was he accepted by the state police; however, several weeks later, the mailman delivered his draft notice. Together with several friends from Haltern, Havighorst traveled to Rendsburg where the barracks of the 26th Infantry Regiment were located. Each morning began with a 2,000-meter run around the barracks square while carrying a rifle. The routine was a tough one, but at least he got to sleep two hours more than when he was a baker's apprentice.

Where sports-related areas of training were concerned, whether crawling through barbed wire in full load-bearing equipment or scaling a two-meter-high wall, Havighorst was always at the forefront. Havighorst's company commander, Hauptmann Richard Daniel, saw to it that the training was hard. Daniel later rose to the rank of Generalmajor and commanded the 45th Volksgrenadier Division. He was to become decorated with the Knight's Cross and the Oak Leaves. Daniel paid particular attention to Havighorst. After initially having been drafted, Havighorst opted for a twelve-year enlistment. He recognized in the young man a high-quality junior leader. Havighorst became company, then battalion runner, and finally served in the same capacity with the regiment.

Havighorst and his comrades took part in an eighty-kilometer march to Eckernförde during a big exercise held in the summer. As runner to the individual staffs, he had to cover at least twice that distance, for he had to go from the company to the battalion to the regiment and back to the company. That evening, after the march was over, Havighorst sat writing a letter to his parents; his comrades had already fallen dead tired into their beds. Suddenly, Hauptmann Daniel appeared and asked what he was doing when his comrades were already sleeping. The young soldier explained and Daniel told him to "carry on." Not long afterward Havighorst was ordered to report to the Hauptmann. The latter asked him directly: "Schütze (Private) Havighorst, are you ready to join the Infantry Training Regiment in Döberitz near Berlin?"

Havighorst, who had heard of the army's elite regiment, replied excitedly that he was. Hauptmann Daniel told him why he had been chosen. Several soldiers from each regiment in the army were being transferred to the Infantry Training Regiment for specialized infantry training. When their training was complete, they would return to their regiments to pass on the skill and knowledge they had gained in Döberitz.

"Havighorst, make me proud!"

With that, Ludwig Havighorst was dismissed. In August 1936, with the Olympic Games in Berlin in full swing, Havighorst was transferred to the Infantry Training Regiment in Döberitz.

THE INFANTRY TRAINING REGIMENT

The regiment waiting for Havighorst was no more than a battalion in spite of all the detachments from other units of the army, although it was growing fast. In the beginning there were only three rifle companies and a heavy (machine-gun) company. Havighorst was assigned to the 3rd Company of the Infantry Training Regiment under Hauptmann Karl Grell. The commander of the Döberitz Infantry School was Hans Hube, then an Oberstleutnant. Despite the loss of an arm during the First World War, Hube rose to the rank of Generaloberst and became one of only 27 German soldiers to receive the Knight's Cross with Oak Leaves, Swords and Diamonds.

Conditions were cramped at Döberitz. At first forty soldiers were assigned to one large room. This all soon changed. As soon as the athletes left the Olympic Village, the Infantry Training Regiment moved in. The village, which had been constructed by the armed forces, was envisaged for such later use. The Olympic Village was built by the architect Werner March and garden architect Wiepking-Jurgensmann. It consisted of 140 massive single-story buildings surrounded by groups of oaks and birches. In the center was the village green, which bordered on a lake. On the east side of the lake stood a large blockhouse with a Finnish sauna.

Each of the 140 buildings had 10 to 12 double bedrooms, washrooms and toilets. The central point of each building was the day room with an open terrace. Each building bore the name of a German city. The students of the Berlin School of Art decorated the rooms with paintings depicting the history of each city. The houses were arranged in such a way that they corresponded to a map of Germany.

The approach road led directly to a command building located in one of the village quarters. A large dining hall for the athletes was located at the upper end of the village green. Later, it became the base hospital. The third main building was situated on a rise on the east side of the village. It consisted of a memorial hall dedicated to the late President Paul von Hindenburg, a large lecture hall and a number of practice areas. Situated in the northeast end of the Olympic Village was the sports field, which was built exactly to the scale of the Olympic Stadium. At the ends of the field were a field house and the water arena with a second sauna as well as baths and showers. The glass wall of the swimming pool enclosure could be opened, allowing direct access to the pool from the surrounding lawn.

The facility was unique among the military installations of the world. According to Havighorst, it was to become the home for "selected personnel, who were fully aware of their special role. They were to fulfil a very special mission. The purpose of the facility was to train capable replacement leaders and return them to their original or other units." He continued:

In the Olympic Village I belonged to the 3rd Company, which was trained as a close-combat company. We practiced fencing as well as fighting with fixed bayonets. There was also live firing practice with rifles and pistols in all positions. Our company commander, Hauptmann Karl Grell, trained with us day and night. We had to carry out twice as many night exercises and were soon called the "moonlight company."

Stationed near the Olympic Village was the "Richthofen" fighter wing, in which my brother Werner was serving. We often practiced antiaircraft defense with this unit, especially defense against low-level attacks.

On 10 October 1936 I was promoted to Gefreiter (corporal). I was present for several of Hitler's visits to the Olympic Village. The Führer came to see for himself the progress of our training. Whenever Hitler appeared, he always had Hans Hube at his side, who showed him everything and provided explanations.

My platoon leader at the time was Leutnant Helmut Becker-Broichsitter, an unlikely daredevil who received the Knight's Cross at the beginning of the French Campaign while serving as commander of the 14th Company of Motorized Infantry Regiment Großdeutschland.

The year 1937 arrived. Our training continued at a rapid pace. In the summer we carried out an exercise which included a demonstration of breaking into an enemy position. Adolf Hitler sat on the reviewing stand with several Japanese officers. The entire thing involved live ammunition! When the exercise was over, the Japanese officer nearest to me came over and said: "If you fight like that in a war, no enemy can ever resist you."

I became an Unteroffizier (sergeant) on 1 October 1937 and was designated a squad leader, after having been an acting squad leader.

During a joint exercise with the 26th Infantry Regiment the latter attacked our positions, playing the role of the enemy. I was in a favorable position with my machine gun. My old company came right toward my position, accompanied by an umpire on horseback. It was my former company commander, Hauptmann Daniels.

When I saw the Hauptmann stop a few meters in front of me I summoned up the courage to stand up. I took several paces toward him, clicked my heels together and reported: "Unteroffizier Havighorst. Please allow me to report to the Hauptmann that I served in the 3rd Company of the 26th Infantry Regiment in 1935."

He looked at me in astonishment. Then, obviously pleased, he got down from his horse, offered me his hand and said: "That's really wonderful that you reported to me, Havighorst! I'm really pleased. But now back to your place, quickly, so the war can continue." He climbed back on his horse and the war went on.

When Leutnant Becker-Broichsitter left the regiment in 1938 his place was taken by Oberleutnant Max Fabich. During the war Fabich rose to the rank of Oberstleutnant. He received the Knight's Cross on 19 April 1945 as the commanding officer of Armored Fusilier Regiment *Großdeutschland*.

In the summer of 1938 a training film was made in which Havighorst participated. It was entitled "Infantry in Close Combat." The instructional film was shown to each new class on its arrival. Shortly thereafter, the battalion moved to the Heuberg Training Area in Baden Württemberg for combined-arms training with tanks. The exercise taxed the men of the infantry to the fullest, but the officers in command were fully satisfied with the results of the exercise.

Ludwig Havighorst participated in the massive parade down the *Unter den Linden* held in honor of Adolf Hitler's birthday on 20 April 1939. The troops of the Infantry Training Regiment marched past the Führer in impeccable formation. Havighorst described the event:

Early on the morning of 20 April 1939 we were driven in trucks to the parade starting point. When the time came we marched off. As I was our company's pivot man. I was closest to Hitler—about four to five meters away—as we marched past.

Even while some distance away we saw that Hitler had his arm raised in the stiff-armed salute. We were surprised to hear that he held this pose for hours, almost without pause. We were to see him in this pose twice that day.

When the command "Eyes, right!" was given I found myself looking straight into Hitler's pale eyes. It seemed to me that Hitler was looking right through me. My comrades had the same impression. We goose-stepped past Hitler and his guests. After marching another 400 meters at a normal pace we were pulled out of the march column, directed into a side street and driven back to the starting point in trucks.

A good half-hour later we marched past Hitler for the second time. The process was then repeated for the third time. Many well-trained observers were fooled by this move. Each pass-in-review was a tremendous experience for us, something we can't forget to this day. Not until many years later did it become clear to me what sort of Führer we had served, but by then Germany was in ruins.

Ludwig Havighorst and comrades were present for the major riding and driving competition held in the *Deutschlandhalle* in the autumn of 1939. Havighorst:

> In the course of this exercise we also demonstrated our special antiaircraft vehicles.
>
> When the riding and driving competition was opened we were ready to go at the entrance. Adolf Hitler was already present when we marched in to the song "It's So Lovely To Be a Soldier." We were greeted by tumultuous applause. Our demonstration consisted of firing our twin machine-guns at an aircraft that was towed on a track suspended beneath the roof of the hall. We used blanks of course, but it caused a great sensation. Afterwards, we marched out of the hall accompanied by another song. This demonstration was repeated on five other days, each time at the beginning of the display, and received much applause.

Havighorst experienced another break in the service routine when he and his platoon went to the UFA broadcasting studio. There, directed by Feldwebel Gollasch, they sang soldiers' songs between news broadcasts that were carried over the entire German network.

At the beginning of August 1939 Hauptmann Grell informed his company that the Infanterie-Lehr-Regiment would not see action in case of a war. Everyone was speechless. Together with five Unteroffiziere, Havighorst subsequently volunteered for the Luftwaffe. According to a directive by Feldmarschall Göring, such requests had to be transmitted within twenty-four hours. Hauptmann Grell did his best to talk them out of it. Even the promise of an early promotion to the rank of Feldwebel failed to tempt everyone. Two of the men stuck to their decision and one of them was Havighorst.

TRAINING WITH THE LUFTWAFFE

Although Havighorst passed his aircrew suitability test, he did not go straight into the Luftwaffe. Hauptmann Grell, who had kept up the pressure to have his close-combat company see action, finally succeeded in having the unit assigned to a patrol operation in the Siegfried Line (*Westwall*). The operation took the patrol one kilometer into no-man's land. A French patrol was encountered, but there was no exchange of fire.

After cutting an opening in the barbed wire, the patrol crawled up to a French trench. On the patrol leader's order, the men threw hand grenades, which exploded about ten meters in front of the trench. Taking advantage of the resulting shock and confusion, the patrol stormed into the trench. The enemy troops manning the trench were completely overpowered. Several French soldiers were taken prisoner and the patrol returned with them through no-man's-land under enemy fire. One of the prisoners was a lieutenant. The success of this operation showed that the members of the Infantry Training Regiment were 100% fit for combat duty.

Havighorst's transfer to the Luftwaffe came through at the end of December following his unit's return to Berlin. He was ordered to report to the bomber school at Lechfeld on 1 January 1940 for training. The routine at the bomber school was a combination of navigation lessons, bombing and air-to-air firing lessons and training in the use of the radio. Every student there wanted to see action as soon as possible. The unit to which Havighorst belonged was transferred to Warsaw in February 1940. There he and two other students were put in control of an aircraft for the first time. The object of the exercise was to use the controls to keep the aircraft straight and level. The flight instructor was Unteroffizier Geisler. The Fw-58 took off and Havighorst was second in line to take over the controls.

"After an hour, I was deathly ill," he later admitted, "and it wasn't long before the pea soup from lunch was making its way upwards. The same thing happened to all the other students. But anyone who made a mess in the aircraft had to pay fifty Reichsmark for the cleaning. The threat helped!"

More and more flight training appeared in the schedule. Havighorst flew in the Fw-58, W-34, Do-17, Ju-86 and He-111. His training also included practice bombing and air-to-air firing. When the invasion of France began in May 1940, Havighorst and his fellow students were still in training; meanwhile, his old formation, the Infantry Training Regiment, was committed in France. Havighorst:

A year later while reading a newspaper I stumbled across the heading "Fallen for Greater Germany." Among the names was Unteroffizier Ulrich Hube, the son of my regimental commander. I had assisted him during the patrol operation in France, because he was night blind. I was shocked. "Little" Ulrich Hube. He had always struck me as hungry and in need of help. Now he had been killed in action as a nineteen-year-old Leutnant.

In July 1940 Havighorst's unit transferred to Quedlinburg, on the north side of the Harz Mountains. There the student crews completed their training with practice sorties and navigation flights. Then, in mid-August, Havighorst and his crew were assigned to 26th Bomber Wing based in Wittmundhafen. The wing commander was Major Martin Harlinghausen. At that time the wing was engaged in the anti-shipping role and flew mine-laying sorties against British ports. Ludwig Havighorst was about to begin his combat career.

MISSIONS AGAINST ENGLAND

Major Harlinghausen, was in the operations room when Unteroffizier Havighorst reported for duty at Wittmundhafen air base. After he had given his name and rank, Harlinghausen said to the Unteroffizier: "You can come along as our guest tomorrow evening, Havighorst. The target is Scapa Flow, where Prien scored his great success in U-47."

"Thank you, sir," answered the Unteroffizier nervously.

While settling in to his room, Havighorst learned that he was to fly with the crew commanded by Feldwebel Becker and that he would fly his first combat mission the next evening—19 August 1940. The next day Havighorst went to the briefing area with his comrades and sat down at the table reserved for Becker's crew. The squadron commander, Willrich, welcomed the men and, referring to aerial reconnaissance photos, showed them the route they would fly and the target. Then he said: "You must descend to 300 meters and drop your mines accurately."

The pilot and observer of the He-111 in which Havighorst was to fly discussed the best way to approach and bomb the target. After the briefing was over, the aviators collected their flight rations: a bar of caffeine-fortified chocolate, a thermos of good coffee and the obligatory trial mix. The flight to Scapa Flow and back was about eight hours long, right at the limit of what was possible with the equipment then in use.

When Havighorst and his crew walked out to the airfield, the crew chief informed Feldwebel Becker that the aircraft was ready to go. The two large mines beneath the fuselage, each weighing one ton, looked huge to Havighorst. Radio operator Ebbinghaus saw the new arrival's doubtful look and observed laconically: "Don't worry. Our bus will get us up, to the target, and back. There's nothing to it."

The pilot checked to make sure that the mechanic had removed the external control locks and then climbed into the aircraft. The pilot and observer sat up front. The flight engineer, seated behind the bomb cells, monitored the engines and checked his machine gun. The observer also checked over his weapon. Havighorst heard nothing of the conversation that was going on as he wasn't connected to the intercom. He watched as the pilot started both engines and pushed the two throttle levers forward. The noise inside the aircraft was unbelievably loud. With the engines at full power, the pilot could check to ensure that they were able to reach their maximum performance of 2,400 rpm and 1.4 atmospheres of boost. If during this so-called "run-up" either engine failed to reach 2,300 rpm or if boost pressure dropped, there was obviously a problem with the engine and the mission would be scrubbed.

Everything appeared to be okay; the pilot raised his hand. The crew chief pulled away the wheel chocks and signaled that all was clear to taxi. The He-111 began to move and taxied to the takeoff point where an officer of the wing headquarters was standing with the takeoff flag. He raised the flag, the signal that the aircraft was cleared for takeoff.

In his mind Havighorst pushed the stick—in the He-111 it was, in fact, a control wheel—as far forward as possible in order to raise the tail of the heavily laden machine. The He-111 accelerated as it rolled down the runway. The pilot, his full concentration on the takeoff, listened as the flight engineer called out the aircraft's speed. Takeoff speed was higher with the two mines and a full fuel load of 4,000 liters. When they reached 190 kilometers per hour, the pilot slowly pulled back on the control column. The He-111 answered the control input, lifted off, and then climbed into the sky. It swooped over the low trees surrounding the airfield.

The long flight to Scapa Flow had begun. The aircraft turned onto the designated course, the same one the following aircraft would be taking. The first leg over the North Sea was several hours long. On reaching the first turning point the He-111s made a gentle turn to the west, directly toward the Orkney Islands and Scapa Flow. The German bombers had to fly at 3,200 meters in order to clear the coastal balloon barrage. When the English coast came into view, the He-111 began a slow descent. There were no fighters to be seen and no antiaircraft fire. Almost silently the bombers approached their target. The observer gave the pilot several course corrections. Every member of the crew was at his station. The aircraft reached the ideal height from which to release its mines, 200 meters. They found the target marker and, as the Heinkel passed over it, the two mines were dropped. Relieved of its heavy burden, the He-111 soared upward like an elevator. The pilot applied full throttle and forced the aircraft's nose down.

Suddenly, the searchlights stationed around the sound came on. The antiaircraft guns opened fire. The He-111 accelerated as it raced away from the target only meters above the water. The aircraft escaped without being hit. After an eight-hour flight the Heinkel landed back at Wittmundhafen. Exactly twenty minutes earlier the radio operator had informed base that they were coming home. The He-111 received clearance to land as it swept over the harbor. Waiting by the runway was a staff car. It picked up the crew and Havighorst and took them to the command post. There Feldwebel Hecker clapped the newcomer on the shoulder: "Very good, Havighorst. You did well. No puking and no unnecessary noise. You can fly with us again!"

High praise from an old hand with the Iron Cross, First Class. After submitting its report and pinpointing the antiaircraft and searchlight positions, the crew was driven to the mess barracks where it had a good breakfast. Two more crews arrived while they were eating and there was a loud reception.

FIRST MISSIONS AS A CREW MEMBER

After two more flights with Becker's crew as an observer, Ludwig Havighorst joined the crew of Unteroffizier Hugo Greeven as its bombardier on the afternoon of 30 August 1940. Greeven had also received the Iron Cross, First Class. He exuded calm and confidence. This time the target was in central England. Derby was home to three large factories, one of them the Rolls Royce aircraft engine factory. Once again, they would fly over the sea before turning west when they were even with the Bay of Skegness. Powerful antiaircraft defenses were expected near Nottingham and, of course, around Derby. The chimney and twin water towers of the chemical plant—which was also to be bombed—would make the target easy to identify.

This time Havighorst sat in the seat to the right of the pilot. He put on the headset that connected him to the intercom. This sortie was a decisive point in Havighorst's flying career. He hung his parachute on a hook on the cockpit wall in front of him to his right; Greeven wore a seat-type parachute. Then he pulled back the curtain and looked at the equipment: the fusing system was still switched off to avoid the inadvertent arming of any of the bombs, if they should be released accidentally. The aircraft was armed with eight 250-kilogram bombs, all destined for the Derby aircraft engine factory.

Havighorst peered through the sight to ensure that it was properly aligned. Behind him the radio operator tuned his equipment. The aircraft took off at the prescribed time. Earlier, Havighorst had checked his machine gun and found it in order. The He-111 raced down the runway and lifted off. Climbing steadily, it soon reached cruising altitude and turned on course. Halfway to the target, they turned west. "The coast," said

Greeven. Havighorst saw the bright, narrow strip, which grew larger quickly. Below them they saw a line of barrage balloons. Suddenly searchlights flashed on. One of the brilliant beams held the aircraft for a few seconds. At once antiaircraft guns opened fire. Something struck the fuselage. Greeven calmly put the aircraft's nose down; the He-111 accelerated and raced away from the probing beams.

The antiaircraft fire intensified in the Nottingham area. Greeven skirted the antiaircraft zone and then returned to the previous course. The tall chimneys were the first features of the target area to become visible. Havighorst bent forward and peered through his bombsight. Directly over the target he pressed the bomb-release buttons. Eight 250-kilogram bombs fell from the bomb bay toward the factory. Greeven pulled the Heinkel into a left turn; far below Havighorst saw the flashes as his stick of bombs exploded.

"Bombs on target!" he reported. It appeared to him that they had hit the factory. He saw fires in two halls as well as a tall water tower. The fires soon disappeared behind them, and the only sign of the destruction they had wrought was the occasional tongue of fire leaping high into the sky.

British antiaircraft guns opened up again, and Greeven took evasive action. The exploding rounds sounded very close. Several fragments struck the fuselage, making a disturbingly loud noise. Then they flew into a heavy concentration of fire. They could hear the crash of the guns and the roar of exploding rounds.

"Hang on, I'm diving!" called Greeven. The bomber plunged toward the earth and swung into a turn to the east. The aircraft picked up a great deal of speed in its dive before Greeven returned it to horizontal flight. They roared over the outskirts of the Derby defensive zone at maximum speed and soon passed Nottingham—twenty kilometers to the south—receiving only sporadic fire.

On seeing bomb explosions and fires, they knew that their comrades had struck Nottingham. They were already over the sea, when suddenly the radio operator called out: "Fighter from behind. Above and to the right." It had to be a British night fighter that had taken off when Derby was bombed. It had waited for them over the coastline.

The radio operator's machine gun roared. Again, he shouted over the intercom: "Right!"

Hugo Greeven hauled the Heinkel around to the right and the burst from the night fighter's guns flitted past to the right of the aircraft. The Heinkel raced through the gradually lightening night at full throttle. The fighter disappeared as quickly as it had come.

Seconds later the radio operator called: "Now he's coming from above and left!" Once again the night fighter opened fire; the bomber's radio operator replied. After firing two bursts, the latter called breathlessly: "I got him! Left! Left!"

Greeven made a hard left turn. Then they saw the enemy fighter. It raced past them, almost close enough to touch. Havighorst saw it dive away trailing a long banner of smoke. The rest of the flight was uneventful, and the bomber landed safely twenty minutes after Havighorst reported to base. Greeven congratulated his new bombardier:

"Great job, Ludwig! You were right on target . . . you acted like an old pro."

✠

Finally, after much delay, clearance was given to attack the British capital. (Hitler had initially forbidden attacks on industrial targets in and around London.) Churchill had ordered attacks on Berlin after a German bomber mistakenly dropped its bombs in the defensive zone around London. Eighty-one twin-engined bombers of the RAF set out for Berlin on the night of 26 August 1940. Twenty-nine of them claimed to have found their target after a 1,000-kilometer flight. Ten bombs fell on Berlin. The British repeated the attack during the night of 29 August. Bombs fell in the residential area around Berlin's Görlitz Station, killing ten and injuring twenty-eight. Still, Hitler hesitated to retaliate.

The third attack on Berlin took place on the evening of 30 August. Bombs fell on Berlin (*Siemensstadt*) and the total of dead and wounded reached several hundred. It was obvious that the British had made the German capital their target. Hitler replied to the British raids on 4 September 1940 in a speech broadcast by German radio: "If they attack our cities, then we will eradicate their cities!"

On the morning of 5 September 1940, the wing commanders of the 2nd, 3rd, 26th, and 53rd Bomber Wings received orders to conduct the first attacks on London. As part of the 3rd Group of the 26th Bomber Wing, Ludwig Havighorst's squadron was also part of the first London raid. The crew took their places and Havighorst followed his own routine while the pilot went through the run-up procedure. He hung up his parachute and then laid out the target map and checked his machine gun. The loop in the River Thames would be their target. The balloon barrage there extended to a height of 2,200 meters.

This time everything happened somewhat faster; the target was closer than before. The intruders began taking antiaircraft fire as they crossed the coast. They were handed off from one searchlight to the next from there on in. Luckily for them they were flying in a long formation which prevented the antiaircraft guns from concentrating on a single machine, which would have been lethal. The bombers cleared the chain of barrage balloons by at least 1,000 meters. Beneath him, Havighorst saw the prominent features marked on his target map. The bend in the Thames appeared. The aircraft followed the river.

Havighorst called the pilot: "Hugo, the water tower!" They had reached the target area. As his aircraft was in the lead position, Havighorst broadcast the following message: "Squadron: Bombs on target!"

Havighorst was now in the nose of the aircraft and had already selected the mode of release. The bombs could only be dropped by the pilot by means of a bomb-release button. Havighorst took aim at the target. "Now!" he called to his pilot. Greeven released the bombs in train. In the mirror, Havighorst could see three of the squadron's aircraft behind them; he watched as they also dropped their bombs.

Behind Havighorst the radio operator transmitted a signal to the command post back at base to indicate that they had completed their mission. As the bomber turned away from the target, the crew saw their eight bombs explode far below and ignite a huge fire. The flight home was uneventful and the He-111 landed safely. On examining the aircraft, the crew chief found several holes in the aircraft's wings.

The first retaliatory strike against London had been flown. All of the attacking aircraft had reached their objective. When the last formation departed the target area, there were five large fires and a number of smaller one burning in the London docks. Sixty tons of bombs had fallen on London.

Another raid on London was scheduled for the afternoon of the following day. Reichsmarschall Göring, who arrived at the Channel Coast near Cap Blanc Nez accompanied by General Loerzer, assumed personal command of the air war. The "fat one" said to the assembled wing commanders, who were there to receive their orders: "The Führer considers the English attacks on Berlin a scandal, and we have decided on countermeasures. The 3rd Air Force will carry out the retaliatory attacks on London."

Turning to the commander of the 2nd Air Force, who was also present, he said: "You, Kesselring, will support this attack with your air force. We must attack today with at least 300 bombers."

"The arrangements have been made, sir. The wings are ready for action."

Three hundred twenty-four aircraft of the 2nd Air Force participated in the attack in addition to the 300 of the 3rd Air Force. The bomber formations—guarded by large numbers of single- and twin-engined fighters— were staggered at altitudes from 4,000 to 6,000 meters. The group of the 26th Bomber Wing participating in the attack took off from Wittmundhafen. The bombers circled for some time until all the squadrons had assembled into close formation. Most of the bombers were carrying eight 250-kilogram bombs. One of the other formations was armed with the first of the 1,800-kilogram bombs.

The Heinkels flew above the clouds. Greeven sat at the controls, holding position behind the aircraft in front of him. The bombers came under fire even before they reached the large bend in the Thames. Up ahead, several British fighters dived on the He-111s of the 26th's 1st Squadron.

The squadron commander radioed: "We are over the target! Release bombs!"

Havighorst passed the message to Greeven, who dropped the bombs. A fighter flashed past, and he directed a burst in its direction. Havighorst turned and saw the flashes from their stick of bombs. He scanned the airspace to the left and right; the aircraft of the 1st Squadron had already turned for home while those of the 3rd Squadron were still approaching the target, which was clearly marked by smoke and fire. Far above, English and German fighters twisted and turned. Soon the single-engined fighters would have to head for home, leaving the twin-engined Bf-110s to guard the bombers.

Suddenly, Greeven's He-111 came under fire from the right. The radio operator shouted a warning and the pilot began to weave. A shadow appeared behind them. Then Havighorst saw a Bf-110 approaching from the opposite direction. Flames spurted from its nose-mounted weapons. Tracer poured into the enemy fighter, which abruptly exploded in flames. Something struck the wing of the Heinkel with a dull thump. The jolt knocked the aircraft off course, but Greeven immediately made a correction. In minutes, the Heinkel was out of the danger zone.

They had not yet landed at Wittmundhafen when the squadrons of the 3rd Air Force took off. Navigation was simple for these aircraft; they needed only to head for the glow from the fires in the London docks.

More heavy bombs rained down on the dockyards. This was the opening act of the Battle of London, which the British referred to as "The Blitz"— it was to last sixty-five days.

THE MISSION FROM NANTES AND THE NEW SYSTEM

In the period from the 7 to 30 September 1940, Luftwaffe bombers flew 4,405 sorties against London, dropping 5,362 tons of high-explosive bombs and 7,499 canisters of incendiaries.

On 15 September, the day of the great air battle over London and the date that is known in British history as "Battle of Britain Day," Ludwig Havighorst was no longer with the 3rd Group. He and all the other newcomers had been transferred to the wing's replacement group. There the new personnel were used to form the 1st Group.

First, however, there was much training to be done. The crews had to learn to use a completely new type of high-frequency direction-finding equipment. Known as the X-System, it involved following a narrow beam transmitted by ground stations which led directly to the target. There were two transmitters, one at Vannes and another north-northwest of Paris. In Lüneburg Havighorst learned that the system had been developed by Doctor Plends at the Rechlin Research Institute in 1934.

The group's He-111 H3s were equipped with an X-System receiver. The pilot of the aircraft needed only to follow the beam to the target. As long as he heard a continuous tone from the beam in his headset, he was on course. If he heard a dot or a dash, it meant that he had veered off course to port or starboard and had to correct. A second X-System receiver indicated to the radio operator when the aircraft was 20 minutes from the target. This preliminary signal was sent by the second transmitter at 90 degrees to the first beam. On receipt of the signal, the radio operator activated an X clock. Ten minutes later, the radio operator received the main signal. He then set the second clock, which began running when the first stopped. The pilot had only to maintain speed, altitude and course. As soon as the second clock reached ten minutes, the contact closed and the bombs were released precisely on target. As Ludwig Havighorst listened to the briefing on the X-System, it all sounded like science fiction. Soon, however, he was to learn to his surprise that the system worked.

On 17 November 1940, a day before their transfer to Heiligenbeil, Havighorst and the others learned of his group's first mission from Vannes using the new system. The 100th Bomber Wing also took part in the raid. The target of the attack was the city of Coventry and its aircraft and armaments factories. The He-111s of the two formations dropped 500 tons of

A He-111 H at Bardofos, Norway, in 1940. J. V. Crow Collection

high-explosive bombs and 30 tons of incendiaries. The total casualties were 554 dead and 865 injured.

In justifying the attack on Coventry, the German government declared that it was a reprisal for the British practice of dropping bombs on German cities that had been going on for more than half a year. The German government stated it judged the enemy attacks on German territory to be contrary to the rules of warfare. It considered its own attacks as reprisals. As such, it felt them to be permissible.

The newly trained personnel return to the base of the 26th's 3rd Group at Nantes on 1 December 1940.

✠

Havighorst flew his first mission from Nantes—a mine-laying sortie to Plymouth harbor—a few days later. The aerial mines, which were lowered into the water by parachute, had to be released at a height of no more than 400 meters. But the pilot of Havighorst's new crew, Unteroffizier Dries, declared his intention to release the mines from 200 meters. A former chief pilot with Lufthansa, Dries was an experienced pilot well able to handle the He-111, even with a heavy load such as two 2,000-kilogram mines. The mines were carried externally and were released electrically by the bombardier.

The flight went smoothly. Dries skirted the French coastline and turned north-northeast after passing Brest. The aircraft flew into Portsmouth harbor unseen. Dries throttled back the engines at a height of 3,000 meters and approached the target in a steep glide. On reaching the ideal height of 200 meters, Havighorst released the mines. Dries advanced the throttles and put the aircraft's nose down to gain speed.

The He-111 accelerated rapidly, but the roar of the two engines gave away the aircraft's position. Seconds later, the first searchlights flashed on and fifteen beams were soon sweeping the harbor. The antiaircraft guns opened fire. The searchlights and exploding rounds made a hellish spectacle, but the He-111 escaped detection by flying low over the water. The antiaircraft rounds burst high above the machine.

Dries steered the Heinkel toward the sea and home, and landed at Nantes after 172 minutes in the air. During the mission debriefing, Dries' unmilitary behavior was again evident. The next morning the squadron commander, Hauptmann Auerring took Dries to task. He held out the possibility of a promotion if Dries could only be more military or, as the Hauptmann put it, "stop being so full of himself."

Dries observed dryly that he "liked the full feeling." This was met with laughter from his roommates and Hauptmann Auerring withdrew—half angry, half amused. Although Unteroffizier Dries was not a military man, he was an excellent pilot. Sadly, Dries was killed a few days later while flying the lead aircraft in a raid over London; a direct hit by antiaircraft fire brought down his aircraft over the English metropolis.

✠

Hauptmann Auerring was killed with Dries. Major Paul Claas became the new squadron commander. Claas was known for his audacity in action, leading many to question whether his actions were prompted by bravery or stupidity. Nevertheless, he was an excellent pilot and a commander who always had time for every member of his squadron. Claas later flew a number of daring missions over Stalingrad. He was shot down over the Sea of Azov on 28 June 1943. Claas received the Knight's Cross on 14 March 1943.

✠

The crew to which Havighorst belonged was once again tom apart in Nantes. Unteroffizier Ludwig Havighorst became bombardier in the crew of Hugo Greeven, with whom he had flown three missions in the summer of 1940. Havighorst flew twenty-four missions over England with Greeven.

On 11 December 1940 the target was Birmingham. They reached the target, which was easily identified by the fires set by a preceding squadron, and dropped their bombs. Greeven steered the Heinkel out of the antiaircraft zone and set course for the sea. Birmingham was hit hard. The 278 German bombers dropped 277 tons of high-explosive bombs and 685 incendiary canisters on the target. The biggest fire was in the Dunlop rubber plant. The return flight was uneventful.

The ports of Swansea and Liverpool were attacked on 20 and 22 December 1940. These were followed by the port of Southend on England's southwest coast. In each case, mines were dropped successfully. These last missions included something special. With a total flight time of five hours, the aircraft had to carry a maximum fuel load of 4,000 liters. Together with the two mines, this resulted in a total load of 8,000 kilograms. The bombers therefore had to employ takeoff-assist rockets to get airborne from Nantes' relatively short runway. Havighorst recalled the procedure:

> The rockets had to be attached to the wings. As the bombardier, I had to ignite the rockets as soon as we reached 120 kilometers per hour. The pilot said to me: "Ignite!" I then pressed the red button that simultaneously ignited the two rockets.
>
> During our first takeoff with the rockets, we in the machine felt a sudden jolt as soon as I pressed the red button. The pilot had to lift off at once. We made a left turn over the Atlantic, where the expended rockets were jettisoned. Afterwards, we took up our assigned course. Flying along the French coast, we reached the designated turning point and flew straight toward the target.

Havighorst described a raid on Manchester:

On 23 December we were part of a raid on Manchester by 171 aircraft. Shortly after takeoff we developed an engine problem. If we had continued we might have ended up in the drink, so we turned around. I informed base that we were going to land with full tanks and bomb load. When we turned on final approach, we saw the fire-rescue personnel and an ambulance waiting at the end of the runway. We touched down as smooth as silk and taxied to a stop. Hugo Greeven had got us down safely.

We were driven to the briefing room where we reported what had happened. The mechanics set to work at once and we learned the next morning that the starboard engine had been defective. It wouldn't have held out more than half an hour.

That evening we arrived in the briefing room five minutes before the briefing was to begin. Hauptmann Claas greeted us with the words: "Today is a big day. Our entire squadron is going to London. 250-kilogram bombs are being loaded. Our targets are the port oil facilities and the petrochemical industry. We will attack from the west and fly through as far as Tilbury. Secondary targets are the Ford factories in Dagenham and Maidstone."

The targets were marked on the maps that each bombardier taking part in the raid received. When we arrived at the aircraft, the ground crew chief reported it serviceable. Everyone took their places and carried out the usual pre-takeoff checks while the first aircraft, flown by the squadron commander, took off. Then our turn came. As soon as we reached 120 kilometers per hour I ignited the takeoff rockets. We were pressed back hard into our seats and we were over the sea in no time, where I jettisoned the empty rocket casings. Greeven accelerated to catch up with the squadron commander. When we caught up, he throttled back to maintain position. Using that method, we were able to avoid flying time-consuming circles while everyone joined formation.

On crossing the coast we came under fire from the batteries at Rochester and Grays. We changed course, which suggested that our target was not London, but Guilford or Reading. The first antiaircraft barrier was passed. We flew past London to the south on a westerly heading; twenty kilometers west of the city we made a 180-degree turn and headed straight for London. Soon we came under heavy fire from the city's antiaircraft defenses. Nevertheless, we got through unscathed and the squadron commander radioed: "All stations: Target ahead!"

I replied: "Identified!" All the other bombardiers reported sighting the target and then came the decisive command: "All stations: Bombs away!"

The bombs fell. As the leading aircraft veered away, I saw our target centered in my sight. I dropped the bombs in the prescribed sequence. They left the bomb bay, toppling in the initial phase of free-fall before stabilizing themselves. Then we turned and I saw our bombs exploding amid the fires started by the first bombs.

Several shell fragments struck the He-111. Havighorst turned in his seat and saw the fires ignited by their bombs. The next squadron was already approaching from the northeast. It soon dumped its bombs on the burning oil installation. The squadron broke formation. It was up to each machine to find its way home safely. When they were twenty minutes from home Havighorst reported their position. The Heinkel touched down after 225 minutes in the air. Then followed the standard ritual of the drive to the command post, where Hauptmann Schäfer was waiting. Major Claas landed right behind them. All of the aircraft returned safely from the mission to London, although several had damage from antiaircraft fire.

After 27 December, which saw 244 German aircraft over London, Havighorst and the rest of Greeven's crew flew another sixteen sorties over England. Among the targets were Cardiff, Pembroke, Liverpool, London, Paisley, Greenock and Campletown. The latter two—in the far north—involved a seven-hour return flight.

✠

Hugo Greeven was transferred out of the squadron. Once again Havighorst was assigned to a new crew. The pilot's name was Heinz Gericke. Their first mission was an attack on London. All went well on this occasion, but a subsequent mission to Pembroke was much hairier.

The weather was unfavorable and Gericke's crew's He-111—the *Toni Emil 1*—was carrying a full load of fuel. On reaching the target they found the Welsh city lying beneath a thick cloud cover. Their mission was to destroy the light industry located there which made equipment for the army and air force. Ludwig Havighorst described what happened:

We circled at low altitude over Carmathen Bay for more than half an hour, but we were unable to locate the crow's nest, as we called Pembroke. We headed back in the direction of Nantes with the bombs on board. As we approached base I reported we were landing in twenty minutes. We received instructions to divert to Rennes. When we reported twenty minutes from Rennes, we were ordered to divert to Melun.

"Can we make it?" Gericke asked me.

I set about measuring the distance with compass and protractor, in order to then calculate the compass heading, distance and flying time using the computer. A diversion to Melun meant another forty-two minutes. This was bad as we had already been in the air for six hours and still had our heavy bomb load. When I established contact with Melun, I was told that the weather was bad and the ceiling was forty-five to fifty meters with a visibility of about 200 meters. Air traffic control suggested we divert to Evreux, located northwest of Paris. As we approached Evreux, we learned that the weather there was just as bad. We had no choice at that point but to land. We were going to run out of fuel at any minute.

We descended through the dense cloud to a height of forty-five meters and suddenly Gericke shouted: "There's the field!"

Gericke banked steeply toward the airfield, simultaneously lowering the undercarriage. Our approach was good and we landed safely and taxied to a stop. Heinz Gericke had done a masterful job. The right engine stopped while we were still taxiing. I looked at my watch. It was 0639 hours. We were six minutes short of seven hours flying time. That was our early morning instrument flight of 18 January 1941. The next afternoon we took off for the flight back to Nantes at 1515 hours.

One of the next large-scale attacks took Gericke's crew—radio operator Unteroffizier Heinz Zwickler, flight engineer Feldwebel Wilhelm Waschewski and Havighorst—to Greenock. It was 7 April 1941 and another seemingly endless flight appeared to be in store. Havighorst, a Feldwebel since 1 April, looked at the target map. It showed the south bank of the Clyde on the west coast of Scotland with its shipbuilding and heavy industries. The route into the harbor was to be mined in an effort to block the flow of supplies—all of which came by sea—to these factories.

When they arrived over the target, there was nothing to be seen. They descended to 250 meters in the hoping of breaking through the layer of cloud, but in vain. Obviously, the cloud deck extended almost to the ground. The antiaircraft guns didn't fire a round to harass them; there was no sign of night fighters.

The He-111 flew around for an hour searching for targets without success. Checking the time, Havighorst realized that they had to turn back, if they were to have sufficient fuel to reach home and possibly divert to a secondary airfield. Havighorst reported this to the aircraft's pilot, who decided to reverse course. The Heinkel landed at Nantes after 500 minutes in the air. It still had its heavy mines, but it also had empty fuel tanks. Three of the squadron's machines had already landed, and Major Claas was not expecting any further detailed debriefings.

✠

On account of his experience, Feldwebel Ludwig Havighorst was designated the He-111 commander even though he was not the pilot. Under his command, the crew flew a sortie to Falmouth. The mission lasted five hours and six minutes and was uneventful. There were 150 German aircraft over Great Britain on 15 April 1941 when Havighorst and his crew mined the entrance to the harbor of Belfast. Other squadrons were tasked to hit Belfast's industries. The bombers approached the target over the St. George Canal and the Irish Sea.

The Heinkels crept up on the target, glided into the harbor and released their mines from a height of 230 meters into the middle of the harbor entrance. Not until the first aircraft climbed away did the searchlights go into action. Several random antiaircraft salvoes followed. Havighorst's He-111 turned away and climbed steadily. On reaching 4,000 meters, the crew began the most pleasant part of the mission—the flight home.

Suddenly, flames spurted from the port engine. Icy fear gripped the members of the crew. "Prepare to abandon aircraft!" Gericke ordered.

"Wait a minute!" interjected the radio operator. "Put the aircraft into a dive. Perhaps the slipstream will extinguish the flames."

"Go ahead, Heinz!" urged Havighorst.

Gericke closed both throttles and pushed the Heinkel's nose down. The aircraft gained speed as the dive steepened. Airspeed climbed to 500, then 600, then almost 700 kilometers per hour. The aircraft shook and vibrated. The wings held, but for how long? The situation looked critical. Havighorst instructed his pilot to bring the aircraft out of its headlong plunge. Gericke gently eased the control column back, bringing the aircraft out of its dive. He slowly advanced the throttles. The improbable had happened—the port engine was no longer on fire and it was even running quite smoothly again, though at reduced power.

Seven hours and fifteen minutes after taking off, Havighorst and his crew landed safely back at Nantes.

✠

On April 17 the group returned to London, which had been under heavy bombardment for months. A total of 685 aircraft dropped 890 tons of high-explosive bombs and 151 tons of incendiaries. The defenses were ready, and Gericke was frequently forced to take evasive action in an effort to avoid searchlights and antiaircraft fire.

The Heinkel was hit several times in the fuselage and wings. The crew held little hope of escaping the hellish fire alive. Flying at more than 4,000 meters, the crew was wearing oxygen masks. In spite of the cold, they sweated profusely. When Havighorst reported that they had dropped their bombs, he received orders to initially fly northwest—instead of south as planned—then turn northeast and head for Schiphol airport in Holland. The rest of the flight was uneventful, and they landed at Schiphol after 243 minutes flying time.

✠

On 21 April 1941 Feldwebel Havighorst received the Iron Cross, First Class, from the group commander, Major Holm Schellmann.

✠

Another mine-laying sortie to Plymouth was followed by missions on four consecutive nights, from 4 to 7 May. Barrow and Greenock were each visited twice, involving flights of seven and eight hours. Havighorst:

Those were nights we will never forget. The third and fourth missions were seemingly endless nightmares. On each occasion it was after sunrise before we landed back at base. This was followed by a few hours of restless sleep. Late in the afternoon came the next mission briefing.

After returning from the fourth mission, we were wakened shortly after noon. We were told that instead of the pass we had been promised, we would be flying to London again that night. The squadron commander promised that after we had returned a Ju-52 would fly us to Cologne, from where we could take our pass in Germany.

We sat down for the briefing and determined that on this mission we would dispense with the autopilot. In the event of a fighter attack, it first had to be disengaged before the pilot could take evasive action. This delay of a few seconds might be enough to cost the crew its lives. While still en route to the target, Gericke practiced breaking away several times after receiving a warning from the radio operator. A call of "fighter from the left!" was the signal for the pilot to apply full left rudder. The opposite applied for an attack from the right.

This time we approached the target from the east. After clearing the antiaircraft zone, we dropped our bombs on target. Gericke took up a course of 180 degrees—due south—and put the aircraft's nose down slightly to increase speed and cross the English south coast as quickly as possible.

The He-111 raced south through a cloudless sky at 450 kilometers per hour. Havighorst admonished his crewmates to stay alert and not let their guard down. Everyone scanned his assigned sector.

Suddenly, on the ground in front of us, I noticed four or five lights come on. Was this a signal to a lurking night fighter?

I instructed Gericke to alter course thirty degrees to the right. When he looked at me questioningly, I pointed downward. He also saw the lights and nodded. I noted the start of the course change and the number of degrees in order to be able to turn back to it later. Three minutes after the course change, direction lights again came on below us.

"Back to the old course," I ordered.

This time we saw lights on the ground again after two minutes. It was clear that the enemy had developed a new system to indicate the route of attacking or withdrawing aircraft to their night fighters.

Seconds later, Heinz Zwickler called: "Fighter from above left!"

Gericke turned the aircraft to the left immediately. Four streams of tracers flashed past the right wing of the He-111. We had escaped the line of fire just in time.

Zwickler had opened fire with his machine gun. One thing was clear to us all: Had we been thinking about the upcoming pass and dreaming about home in this situation, we would have been shot down for certain. The fighter attacked a second time, this time from above right. But Gericke hauled the aircraft around to the right in time and once more the burst from the enemy's guns went wide. The machine gun of flight engineer Waschewski joined the defensive fire. Gericke put the aircraft's nose down, in order to increase speed and leave the English coast behind us as quickly as possible.

The English fighter began a third pass.

"Hit!" called out radio operator Zwickler. Several seconds later the enemy fighter veered off, pouring smoke, and disappeared into the night.

We flew on toward the French coast at low level for a few minutes before climbing again. The *Toni Emil 1* landed safely back at base. Our crew chief found more than forty hits in our machine.

Unteroffizier Stubenrauch, the ground crew chief, cursed a blue streak. But he declined vigorously when it was suggested that he come along on the next mission and leave the repair to someone else. That quieted him down. The old saying was true—a soldier was never happy unless he was complaining—besides, he was a good mechanic.

Ludwig Havighorst received a week's leave, which passed all too quickly. He was scheduled to fly the evening following his return to Nantes. However, the scheduled mission was called off and he was placed on standby. He would fly that very evening. The target was Falmouth harbor, which was to be bombed and mined. The mission was completed without a hitch and the pilot flew back to base at maximum speed to avoid fighters. The aircraft landed back at Nantes after 300 minutes in the air.

What followed was a special mission to save the *Bismarck*. The German battleship had been cornered by a superior number of enemy warships in the Atlantic approximately 300 nautical miles west of Brest. They were to find the enemy armada and help the *Bismarck* escape.

Early on the morning of 27 May an endless stream of Ju-87s, Ju-88s, He-111s, and Do-17s began arriving at Nantes. That was the point of origin for the sorties in support of the *Bismarck*. Major Claas subsequently held a briefing for the crews in the squadron area. They learned that the *Bismarck* had left port on 18 May for Operation Rhine Exercise. Together with the *Prinz Eugen*, it had sunk the British battle cruiser *Hood* on 24 May, however, it had been hit by torpedo bombers while withdrawing into the Atlantic. Incapable of maneuvering due to rudder damage, the *Bismarck* was surrounded by a large number of enemy vessels.

The crews wolfed down their lunch and took off to begin the search. Each bomber was armed with eight 250-kilogram bombs and carried 4,000 liters of fuel. It was Havighorst's crew's first day mission. The air above the airfield and over the sea was full of aircraft. As soon as the enemy was sighted, they were to approach and bomb. The aircraft of the squadron took off at brief intervals.

The He-111s flew as far out to sea as they could. The crews spotted a dense curtain of antiaircraft fire ahead in the distance, but then everything disappeared behind smoke, probably laid by the enemy ships. The crews could not even see the surface of the ocean. After circling for some time, they were forced to head for home. Even before the French coast came into sight, the fuel warning lights came on. The crew made preparations to ditch at sea but, after a final course correction, they arrived at Nantes after eight hours and fifteen minutes in the air.

None of the German aircraft were able to drop their bombs. On 28 May the Wehrmacht daily report announced that the *Bismarck* had been sunk and that the fleet commander, Admiral Lütjens, had gone down with the ship.

✠

On the evening of 28 May Havighorst and his crew took off on a mine-laying sortie off the English south coast. After twenty-nine minutes of flight the engines began acting up and the mission had to be broken off. The pilot was just able to nurse the crippled Heinkel back to Nantes. The next mission also had to be called off over the Channel. Their "crate" was overdue for repairs, that much was clear.

Nevertheless, they took off in the aircraft again on the evening of 1 June. A total of 110 German bombers attacked Liverpool, the second largest city in England. Their targets included the airport, the Manchester shipping canal that linked the city with Liverpool, and a large vehicle factory. The attack went smoothly, in spite of the heavy antiaircraft fire they endured. On their return, the He-111 was sent for repairs. The mechanics carried out extensive work and, on the evening of 4 June, they took an almost new aircraft to Birmingham.

The antiaircraft fire was heavy and accurate; several salvoes exploded quite close. The crew knew that the ground crew chief would be livid if they brought the overhauled machine back with damage. During the return flight Havighorst was instructed to once again divert to Schiphol. The landing was uneventful. The crew went to supper and talked over the baffling events of late that had seen many aircraft and men—and not just from Nantes, but from bases all over—disappear. At first they thought they might be reinforcements for Africa, but it seemed hard to imagine that so many aircraft were being sent there. Following some minor repairs to their aircraft, Havighorst and his crew were supposed to take part in a major raid on the naval port of Chatham.

News that Duisburg and Bochum had been bombed the night before was enough to fully motivate them again. Ludwig Havighorst described the attack:

> We were greeted by a wall of fire from the antiaircraft guns as we approached Chatham. Our aircraft flew straight through. We reached the target and as soon as I had the arsenal building in my sight I pressed the bomb-release buttons. Four pairs of 250-kilo-gram bombs fell toward the target. Gericke pulled the machine around into a steep left turn, so that I could observe the fall of the bombs. I saw a series of flashes and then a garish ball of fire rose into the sky.
>
> "Bombs on target!" I called to my comrades. Zwickler informed base that we had completed our mission. We were again chased by a night fighter intent on shooting us down. After several bursts from Zwickler, it veered off and disappeared.
>
> We flew out of the antiaircraft defensive zone, however, several of our aircraft were shot down there by ground fire or fighters. In spite of these losses, the results indicated a major success. A number of important Royal Navy installations had been destroyed or badly damaged.

✠

At that point the majority of the squadron's personnel were sent on leave so that the aircraft, which were worn out, could be completely over-hauled. Ludwig Havighorst went home with the Combat Mission Bar in Silver on his flight jacket as well as the Iron Cross, First Class. He was proud and happy, as well as relieved and pleased to be away from the hell of the air war over Great Britain for two weeks. When Havighorst's crew returned to Nantes at the beginning of July they found only a rear detach-ment there. On 8 July 1941 Havighorst transferred with it to Melun, south of Paris.

Havighorst flew missions against the port of Great Yarmouth on the English east coast on two consecutive days. At thirty-two minutes after mid-night on 14 July he and his crew took off to lay mines in the mouth of the Thames. The mission was a success. After landing back at Melun, Havighorst received a musical reception provided by the base band in honor of his fiftieth mission over England.

The crew was back in the air again later on the evening of 14 July. Havighorst objected to the mission; the aircraft was carrying a full load of incendiaries destined for the Hull dockyard. If the bombs were off target, the whole city could go up in flames. The Heinkel took off at 2258 hours. The mouth of the Humber, with the cities of Hull and Grimsby, was considered a dangerous target. Heavy concentrations of antiaircraft guns guarded the area, but at least there was no long flight over land. Havighorst's machine carried a total of 1,444 incendiary bombs.

Havighorst called out several course corrections to the pilot. They arrived over the twelve-kilometer-long dockyard area and flew on as far as Saltend where the tank farm was located. The Heinkel descended to 1,000 meters to avoid the antiaircraft fire. Several fires were already burning in the target area and Havighorst used these as his aiming point. Visibility was extremely good, and the radio operator reported all bombs on target.

The dockyard and the valuable goods stored there went up in flames. After they cleared the antiaircraft zone, Havighorst received instructions to land at Wittmundhafen. That meant a flight of more than 500 kilometers to Germany. Havighorst's navigation brought the machine straight to the East Friesian Islands. Wittmundhafen's controllers refused them landing clearance, and they were instructed to land at Leeuwarden.

A He-111 H-11 used for towing the Gotha Go-242 transport glider.

Havighorst flew his last combat mission in Western Europe on 17 July. The aircraft carried eight 250-kilogram bombs, and the target was Hull. The mission was carried out much like those that preceded it. As the bomber turned away, the crew saw fires springing up on the ground. After six hours and thirteen minutes, Havighorst's aircraft landed back at Leeuwarden, where he and his men learned that the entire group was being transferred to Russia.

THE BOMBING WAR OVER RUSSIA:
THE GERMAN AIR FLEETS IN THE EASTERN THEATER

In the Führer Directive concerning Operation Barbarossa the Luftwaffe was given the following mission: "Destruction of the Soviet air forces on the ground and in the air. Direct and indirect support of army forces."

The 1st Air Force (Generaloberst Keller) was under the command of Army Group North. Army Group Center was supported by the 2nd Air Force (Generalfeldmarschall Kesselring), while the 3rd Air Force (Generaloberst Löhr) supported Army Group South.

On the morning of 22 June 1941, the German air fleets mustered a total of 1,945 aircraft. Of those, only 1,400 were operational. The fleet consisted of 510 bombers, 290 dive-bombers, 440 fighters, 40 twin-engined fighters and 120 strategic reconnaissance aircraft

Within twenty-four hours of the start of operations the Luftwaffe was able to score the greatest success in its history. More than 1,800 enemy aircraft were destroyed. Of these, 332 were shot down by German fighters and Flak. A further 1,500 were destroyed on the ground. German losses totaled 35 aircraft shot down. If the German estimates of the size of the Soviet Air Force had been correct, the Red Air Force would have been destroyed in a matter of days. But within days of the start of the invasion, the Luftwaffe was forced to admit that the number of Soviet aircraft was at least 8,000! And these were just the machines based in the western part of the USSR. Another several thousand had to be based in the eastern parts of the country. Generalmajor Hoffmann von Waldau, the Luftwaffe Chief-of-Staff, wrote in the war diary late on the evening of 22 June 1941: "The timing of the air attack on the Russian airfields on the first day of the attack was a complete success! These attacks opened the way for operations against the entire Soviet Air Force."

Typical of the reports released by the Commander-in-Chief of the Luftwaffe was this one submitted by the 5th Air Corps, which was committed on the left wing of Army Group South: "In the campaign against the Soviet Union, the 5th Air Corps destroyed more than 1,000 aircraft on the

ground in the period from 22 June to 3 July. On 29 June 1941 the Luftwaffe reported to the Armed Forces High Command that 4,990 enemy aircraft had been destroyed to date; it had lost only 179 of its own aircraft.
The Luftwaffe had achieved air superiority over the battle zone. Its subsequent mission was to support the advancing armored forces and eliminate
enemy resistance in the frontlines.

In the future that was to be the primary mission of the Luftwaffe in the
east.

FROM MELUN TO TIRASPOL

Havighorst provides details on the group's arrival in the east:

> Equipped with the most important things one needs as a soldier,
> we moved east with the rest of the group on 20 July 1941. We
> landed in Tiraspol on the evening of the first day; there we
> learned that we were now members of the 27th Bomber Wing.
> That wing bore the honorific of Bomber Wing "Boelcke" in honor
> of the First World War aviator, Oswald Boelcke, who was killed in a
> mid-air collision after his fortieth victory. Boelcke died unde-
> feated, as it was a collision with a German aircraft.
>
> From Tiraspol we flew daylight missions in pairs. At night the
> aircraft took off singly as before. The meager dugouts of Russia
> had replaced the noble accommodations of France. After six
> months our excellent aircrew rations disappeared and gave way to
> extra soup. Nevertheless, we no longer had to cover gigantic dis-
> tances as we did on the Atlantic—at least not at first. We attacked
> targets that were reached in a few minutes or an hour. As a result,
> we had to fly two or three times a day. Once we even flew five mis-
> sions in one day.

During the first large-scale mission against Moscow, the bombers
crossed the front near Smolensk. Havighorst and his crew took off at 2023
hours. The aircraft they flew was *Toni Ida + Kurfürst 1* (TI + K1); the crew
was the same. Havighorst had been told that he should fly no higher than
4,000 meters. As they passed overhead he drew the crew's attention to
Smolensk which was still burning. It fad fallen to German forces the day
before. Havighorst continued:

> This time the pilot released the bombs. That left me, lying me in
> the nose of the aircraft, free to fire on targets of opportunity with

the twenty-millimeter cannon we then had. After the run-up to the target, he merely had to press a button to release the bombs that had been armed by me.

We flew through the smoke and haze from the fires and then I saw the Smolensk-Moscow highway, which cut through the countryside like a bright stripe.

Suddenly, searchlights flashed on. Their number grew, and Gericke tried to escape the probing beams and the antiaircraft fire that soon began by changing course and altitude. This was the biggest display of fireworks we had encountered in any of our missions. Finally, I lost count of the antiaircraft batteries and ordered Gericke to climb to 4,500 meters.

As we were preparing to drop our bombs we saw a Ju-88 far beneath us; it was already in its characteristic dive toward the target. Several squadrons must already have bombed; fires were visible in several areas, and they were spreading fast.

Just as I was preparing the bombs for release, a warning call came from the radio operator: "Attention: Barrage balloon left!'

The radio operator wasn't imagining things. Over England the balloons reached 2,200 meters at most; here they floated at twice that height. I instructed the pilot to descend 500 meters. As we descended, the radio operator called out another warning: "Barrage balloons over the target area at 4,500 meters!" I dropped the bombs.

Seconds later we reversed course in a left turn so that I could observe the effect of our bombs. As I watched them explode, the radio operator called out: "Fighter from above right!" Then his machine gun opened fire.

The flight engineer opened fire as well. Suddenly, our attacker was transformed into a red fireball; pieces of wreckage rained down on our crate. The Russian night fighter plunged earthward in flames. We had shot down an enemy fighter on our first mission against Moscow.

The first mission to Moscow thus gave the unit, which was new to this theater, a great surprise—namely, the fanatical resistance of the Soviet armed forces, which had always been talked of rather disparagingly.

Havighorst's He-111 landed at its base on its last drops of fuel. During the subsequent debriefing, claims by both Havighorst's and the other crews concerning the number of searchlight and antiaircraft batteries were greeted with open skepticism, while the reports of high-level barrage balloons were written off as fantasy. Nevertheless, all the reports agreed and there was no longer any doubt that Moscow was well equipped to meet the German air assault.

The signals intelligence of Army Group Center soon discovered that the Red Army had set up 500 searchlight batteries in a defensive zone extending forty kilometers around the city. The city's antiaircraft guns were so plentiful that they could put up concentrated fire anywhere in the zone. Under Major General Gromadin the firepower of the Moscow air defense zone was increased considerably. Significant antiaircraft forces were moved in from the Far East by fast train.

On 22 July Havighorst's *Toni Ida + Kurfürst 1* took off for Moscow again. The 150 German bombers achieved good results, but they were little more than pinpricks, albeit painful ones, given the size of the metropolitan area and the dispersed nature of the targets. The third attack on Moscow was scheduled for 23 July. Havighorst and his crew flew around the antiaircraft zone east of Smolensk. They officially flew at 4,500 meters at that point; the cruising altitude of 2,500 meters they had used on the first raid had exposed them to heavy antiaircraft fire.

Once again, they were attacked by a Soviet night fighter. Waschewski and Zwickler fired for all they were worth. The pilot made the heavy He-111 dance like a ballerina—first left, then right, then finally down into a steep dive. After a long chase, the fighter was shaken off. The Heinkel dropped its bombs and returned to base.

On 23 July Oberleutnant Erich Thiel, the squadron commander of the 7th Squadron of the 27th Bomber Group, received the Knight's Cross. (He was later shot down and died while a prisoner of the Soviets.) Havighorst continued his narrative:

> We were assigned a special mission on 25 July—to attack the railway station at Briansk at first light. Heavy traffic with the detraining of troops and materiel had been reported there. This meant that we could fly to the target in darkness, but had to arrive there at dawn so we could see the target. However, this also meant that the return flight would be made in broad daylight, which would

make us easy prey for the enemy fighters, not to mention the anti-aircraft batteries east of Smolensk.

Our armorer and his section delivered the eight 250-kilogram bombs to the aircraft. Because of the special nature of the mission, we had to take along a war correspondent of the propaganda company. We took off at 2344 hours. My calculations as to our flying time and sunrise were correct; in the first light of day we spotted the Briansk rail station below us and several kilometers distant. I had set a ten-meter interval between bombs. The station was jam-packed with transport trains. We saw tanks and vehicles on open cars as well as guns and war materiel of all types.

"I'm going to bomb now!" I called to war correspondent, who was named Dressler. "Make sure you get everything with your camera."

The bombs fell away at the pre-set intervals. As we turned away they smashed into the rail cars one after another and pillars of smoke billowed upwards. Flying lengthwise down the long train, we had placed all our bombs on target. Everywhere one looked there was flames. Outside we could hear the furious staccato of the light antiaircraft fire and clusters of tracers rose toward us. Skilful evasive maneuvers by Gericke enabled us to evade the ground fire. We had scarcely left the danger zone when the radio operator called out enemy fighters.

The Soviet fighters were Ratas: Small, squat-looking machines but very maneuverable. No matter what maneuver Gericke carried out, the Ratas stayed with us. Not until we dove headlong into a cloudbank did we shake off our pursuers.

The same evening the squadron took off again for Moscow to visit "Uncle Joe." Further raids on the Soviet capital followed on the 26, 28, and 30 July. It was noteworthy that the Russian antiaircraft fire was then more accurate than it had been the first time. We were hit several times in the tail and fuselage by shrapnel but suffered no serious damage.

On the afternoon of 28 July our "black friends," as the men of the ground crews were called —without whom nothing flew from the base—loaded each of our machines with two BM-1000 aerial mines. In addition, 4,000 liters of fuel was pumped into each aircraft. Such a load made it difficult for our aircraft to get airborne from our forward base; nevertheless, everyone got off safely and we breathed a sigh of relief.

Our target on that occasion was an aircraft factory at the outskirts of Moscow. We approached in a wide arc from the south and the heavy bombs went hurtling down when we were over the target. Our two bombs landed right on one of the large factory buildings and the square behind it. Flames shot up and then a gasoline tank exploded in a burst of white flame. There were no night fighters but plenty of antiaircraft fire. It pursued us for some time as we set course for home.

As we approached base we were instructed to proceed to the holding area. Then we were told that there were enemy bombers over the field and possibly fighters too. We circled in a holding pattern and, when the red lamps came on, indicating that our fuel was running low, I asked: "Landing in five minutes?"

The answer was: "Wait!"

When the fuel situation became critical I instructed my pilot to head for the field and transmit the emergency signal. We approached the field and received landing clearance. After we landed and rolled to a stop the airfield lighting went out and we were in total darkness for a few seconds. After eight hours in the air we had landed on our last few liters of fuel.

✠

On 2 August 1941 the 2nd Group of the 27th Bomber Wing under the command of Hauptmann Günzel transferred to Bobruisk. There it took up residence at a former Soviet airfield that had been restored to service. All told, the group was to remain there for two months. The use of Bobruisk reduced flying times considerably. A flight to Moscow and back was now only five hours, which eased the strain on the aircrews.

From 11 August to 1 September Havighorst's crew flew thirteen missions to the railway stations at Bakmach, Toropets and Mena. In addition, troop trains, artillery positions and march columns were attacked and destroyed in the Chernigov and Loyev areas. Havighorst and his crew soon perfected the technique of attacking moving trains. In addition to their train-busting activities, the crew also flew further sorties against Moscow.

On 17 September Hauptmann Günzel, was awarded the Knight's Cross. He would later receive the Oak Leaves. One of the squadron commanders, Oberleutnant Wolfgang Skorczewski, received the Knight's Cross the same day.

Ludwig Havighorst was forced to leave his crew on 2 September. Unteroffizier Gericke was assigned a new bombardier and Havighorst joined the crew of Leutnant Heinz Bussemer. By that time he had flown more than sixty combat missions with his old crew. On 20 October Havighorst received the Operational Flying Clasp in Gold in recognition of his 100th combat mission. For a member of a bomber crew, it was a notable accomplishment.

Havighorst's first missions with his new crew were all daylight affairs against troop concentrations and truck columns, which they attacked at low level by dropping fragmentation bombs and strafing. During those sorties Havighorst manned the nose-mounted cannon. Other targets included moving trains and artillery positions near Chernigov, Nashin, Prikuli and Briansk. Havighorst:

We flew four consecutive missions to Moscow during the nights of 23–27 September. We had flown more sorties to the Russian capital by then than any other group of the 27th Bomber Wing. Given our lack of experience—Leutnant Bussemer and the other members of the crew had not seen action before—this was quite a feat and placed a great strain on our nerves. As the only experienced crewmember it was up to me to help wherever I could if we were to survive. It was a very difficult time and the young crew had to pass its test of fire in the heavily defended skies over Moscow.

After Moscow we were again ordered to fly missions against railway stations until 9 October. We attacked Mzensk as well as Kursk, Orel and Sukhinichi. The constant intervention of the Luftwaffe in the ground war was a matter of survival for our ground forces. However, we always returned to the relative peace of our bases, while our comrades of the infantry had to remain in their positions to meet the next Russian attack.

The one thing that made life especially difficult at this time, even at our bases, was the mosquitoes; we were situated at the edge of the Pripet Marshes.

On the morning of 10 October we moved up to Sechinskaya airfield, which was even closer to the front. It was from there that I flew my 100th mission on 10 October. During the pre-mission briefing the group commander said to me:

"In honor of this day you're flying with Oberleutnant Plümecke. Your target is two trains loaded with war materiel that air reconnaissance has located in the Kolomna area. You need only fly along the rail line and you can't miss them. Bring home a good report from your 100th combat mission."

The crew was driven to its dispersal area. The ground crew chief and armorer were standing by. There were no mechanical or system faults and the run-up revealed no problems with the engines.

The Heinkel took off and they found the train straight away. The pilot positioned the aircraft to attack the train from behind. At Plümecke's directive, Havighorst would drop the bombs and operate the cannon. As they swooped over the rail cars he released the thirty-two bombs and then opened fire with the 20-mm cannon.

The locomotive derailed, causing the rail cars to pile into one another. Several toppled off the tracks. Flames erupted from the tank cars. There were tremendous explosions as two cars loaded with munitions blew apart. The crew's radio operator informed base that they had successfully completed their mission. He reported direct hits with explosions and fires.

When the crew arrived in the debriefing room they found that preparations had been made to receive the newest member of the "One Hundred Club." Both the group commander and the squadron commander congratulated Havighorst. Eduard Skrzipek came up to Havighorst.

"Congratulations, Ludwig. You have been accepted into the train-buster's team."

Skrzipek had already destroyed more than twenty trains; later, he received the Knight's Cross while serving in the 27th's 5th Squadron. On 26 June 1944 he was decorated with the Oak Leaves.

Flight time from Sechinskaya to Moscow was only three hours. Four more flights to the Soviet metropolis brought Havighorst's total to eighteen. But things were not as rosy as Generalfeldmarschall Kesselring had seen them during a visit to Havighorst's group: "We need only fly four or five more missions against Moscow and the Russians will be finished. Their defenses are limited and the flight there is a walk in the park."

It was three months since the men had heard this, but any talk of the Russians being finished was premature. By the end of October Havighorst and his crew flew another twelve missions. The targets—which were in aid of the infantry—included Stalinogorsk railway station, troop concentrations behind the front and troop assembly areas in the rear. These missions gave credence to the maxim coined by British experts in relation to the bomber arm:

"The bomber arm is the soul of military flying. Only it is in a position to make a decisive contribution to victory. Everything else is elevator music." Once again Ludwig Havighorst:

One morning in mid-November, we were alerted to an attack by five Red Air Force bombers just as we were about to board the aircraft. They approached the airfield, and the bombs were already falling when we reached the slit trenches. It was a strange feeling to receive a demonstration of the effects of a bombing attack.

Several aircraft were hit by bomb splinters. However, the Russian bombers did not make it home again. A fighter pilot attacked with his Bf-109. He struck from below and shot down the first bomber. Then we saw him soar above the bombers in a climbing turn before swooping down from behind and shooting down the second bomber. The third, fourth and fifth enemy bombers suffered the same fate.

The spectacle that the fighter pilot had presented us was unforgettable.

For a time I flew with Oberleutnant Plümecke, the squadron commander. It was his habit to take a nap while in the air; he would lean back and say to me: "Take the thing!"

Not until after I had armed and set the bombs did I have to wake the "old man." He had to release the bombs. During the run-up to the target, I was in the nose of the aircraft, firing on the target with the cannon.

We had been using the new Lotfe 7 bombsight—a very precise aiming system that had been installed in our He-111—for some time. The device calculated forward angle as well as side drift. When the two contacts in the indicator lined up, it was time to release the bombs. As soon as one issued the pilot coarse heading adjustments—a turn to the left or right—the two contacts lay close together. All that remained were very minor corrections, which one could do oneself. The cross hairs of the Lotfe device were placed on the target, and a button was pushed which synchronized speed and drop angle. Of course, it was possible to encounter differing air currents at various altitudes. If this was the case the bombs did not fall on target. Instead, they landed several meters to the side, in front of, or beyond the target. But in all other respects the Lotfe was a 100% accurate bombsight.

✠

On 1 December 1941 Feldwebel Havighorst was transferred to the 5th Squadron of the 27th Bomber Wing. The wing commander at the time was

Oberstleutnant Hans-Henning Freiherr von Beust, who had received the Knight's Cross in Russia in July 1941. On arriving at his new squadron Havighorst learned that he was to hitch a ride to Nantes in an He-111 and from there go on leave. With only a minor deviation, the course which Havighorst plotted took them over Haltern. Bussemer flew a circle over the city and dam and then set course straight for Schiphol, where they landed.

On arriving in Nantes the aircraft was handed over and the crew left to take their leave in Germany. After their leave was over, the crew learned that their aircraft had already been picked up in Nantes. They were forced to remain there and carry out guard and other infantry-type duties. Not until 27 May 1942 did they leave to rejoin 27th bomber Wing in Russia. Havighorst:

> To this day it remains a mystery to me why this happened. We were out of action for six months, at a time when every crew was needed.
>
> When the five of us finally arrived in Poltava, our crew was torn apart. I became commander of a new crew. It included the brilliant but inexperienced pilot, Unteroffizier Ludwig Denz, and radio operator, Unteroffizier Helmut Wagner. The flight engineer was Oberfeldwebel Wilhelm Waschewski, an old hand with whom I had flown many missions. The gunner—added to the crew to deal with the increased fighter presence—was Obergefreiter (Airman Second Class) Otto Blaß.
>
> We found the 5th Squadron at full strength. The front had stabilized.

BETWEEN POLTAVA AND MILLEROVO

The new crew faced its first test on 10 June. It took part in an attack on enemy artillery positions behind the front. The target was reached within thirty minutes. When the bombers returned for a second attack they found that the enemy had strengthened his antiaircraft defenses. A total of five attacks were flown that day. Obergefreiter Blaß demonstrated his qualities as a gunner when the first enemy fighter appeared. He hit the fighter, which began to burn and was forced to break off its attack.

The Red Air Force had newer and faster fighters by then. The He-111s were therefore instructed to always fly in formation. It was thought that their massed defensive fire would give them a better chance of repulsing an attack by fighters. From that point on, the bombers flew in groups of three or six. The pace of operations remained hectic. Havighorst and his new crew flew thirty-four combat missions by 23 July. Their targets included troop concentrations, enemy airfields and railway stations in the rear being used by the Red Army. Also attacked were areas of the front near Alexandrovo, Liknoy, Losovaya Svoboda, Povozino, Nufoki and, especially, Voronezh.

During the same period Havighorst also flew six missions with his new squadron commander, Hauptmann Rupert Frost. Frost was a successful bomber pilot who had already been decorated with the German Cross in Gold. (Frost received the Knight's Cross on 25 November 1944 while serving with the 9th Night-Fighter Wing. These flights were made into the Voronezh area, where the Red Army was trying to hold on. The Soviets also launched counterattacks in an effort to regain lost territory.

Havighorst found that he had something left to learn from flying with Frost. Operations by the German air and ground forces were extremely successful. On the ground the 24th Panzer Division and the 16th Motorized Infantry Division were able to hold their own at Voronezh, dealing the Soviet 60th Army destructive blows. On one occasion Havighorst and Frost flew a mission in support of the 9th Panzer Division, and the 3rd Motorized Infantry Division as they attacked across the Don and Voronezh Rivers in the area of the 24th Panzer Corps.

MISSIONS FROM KURSK: FROM MILLEROVO TO STALINGRAD

On 23 July 1942 the 27th's 5th Squadron moved to Kursk. Ludwig Havighorst was now an Oberfeldwebel (Technical Sergeant), having been promoted on 1 March. By that time he had flown his 150th combat mission; on 15 March he received the Luftwaffe Honor Goblet.

From Kursk the squadron flew missions into the area east of Voronezh. These were followed by a series of flights in support of the German 6th Army as it advanced toward Stalingrad. The actions of the German bombers in the great bend of the Don contributed to the success of the army's advance. The wing focused its efforts in the area between Krimskaya in the north and Potenskinskaya in the south.

The 5th Squadron was forced to leave Kursk on 6 October. Its new destination was the base at Millerovo, approximately 300 kilometers west of Stalingrad. From there it would be able to reach important targets in the city and troop concentrations beyond the Volga River waiting to cross over to Stalingrad. The squadron reached Millerovo safely and the crews installed themselves in farm cottages at the outskirts of the airfield where the Russian aviators had once lived. The house into which Havighorst moved was still occupied by the wife of a Soviet pilot and her children; they had been left behind when the Soviet Air Force hastily abandoned the airfield. Havighorst:

> There we stole some potatoes from a potato pile while others distracted the guards and made the first proper roasted potatoes we had had for some time.
>
> The wife and children of the Soviet pilot were also enthusiastic about the cooking skills of their German guests and, of course, received a share of the food.
>
> Millerovo became something of a home to us aviators. We spent many months there. We flew nearly 150 missions from there to Stalingrad, the Caucasus and Astrakhan. We flew our first mission against trains in the Stalingrad area on 9 October 9.

✠

The mission given the aircrews was: "Smash the fleeing enemy. Support the army in its dash to Stalingrad."

Führer Directive No. 41 contained the following general order for the Luftwaffe:

> Apart from providing direct support to the army, the efforts of the Luftwaffe are directed at protecting the forces of the German Army in the southern area of operations and its staging areas. Especially vital are the railway bridges over the Dniepr. Additional air forces are to be assigned to protecting these.
>
> In the event of a concentration of Russian troops, their main routes and rail links from their assembly areas to the combat zone will be cut by our air force. These air attacks must reach deep into the Russian hinterland. In this event the destruction of the Don railway bridge will be required.
>
> The Luftwaffe will begin its offensive operations with concentric attacks, with massed strikes by our forces against all Soviet air forces and their ground organization within the attack zone. Preparations for rapid movement will guarantee optimal fighting conditions in the center and on the northern flank of Army Group South. The existing ground-support organizations necessary for these movements will be kept operationally ready.

It was this order that led the 4th Air Force to transfer the 8th Air Corps to Millerovo. The 27th Bomber Wing was to take part in the assault on Stalingrad.

The air fleet commanded by Generaloberst Wolfram von Richthofen included the 4th and 8th Air Corps. Richthofen had assumed command of this air fleet on 24 June 1942, the same day Generalleutnant Martin Fiebig took over the 8th Air Corps. On 2 August von Richthofen unleashed his forces against enemy columns and supply trains in the Stalingrad area.

On the other side, the Soviet High Command accelerated its build-up of the Red Air Force. It sent fresh forces with new aircraft to Stalingrad. General Novikov, the Commander-in-Chief of the Red Air Force, sent General Stepanov there to coordinate the defensive forces. On 20 August five long-range bomber formations were sent from Moscow to Stalingrad to help smash the German assault on the city. The 8th and 16th Air Armies stood ready to intercept the German bombers.

Havighorst recalled those times:

My crew and I flew our first mission to Stalingrad on 9 October. It was my 35th mission with that crew. Since 10 June, when we flew our first mission together from Poltava to Yurtshenko, we had become a close-knit team. The smooth cooperation and functioning of a bomber crew was its life insurance in crisis situations, where every action was vital. In such situations the airmen had to depend on each other blindly, and we five could do that. We had become a team in technical and tactical terms as well as in the carrying out of attacks—we wanted to survive.

On that 9 October 1942 we strafed and bombed the first train we caught near Stalingrad. Waschewski machine gunned the locomotive until it gave up the ghost. We turned away and, seconds later, Waschewski shouted: "Fighter from behind left!"

Denz reacted quickly and swung the aircraft to the left. The enemy followed. The radio operator, flight engineer and gunner all fired at the enemy fighter. The latter stubbornly held its course and kept firing at us. I heard bullets striking the aircraft. We flew every possible evasive maneuver, but they only took us out of the line of fire for a few seconds. The furious hornet behind us came closer.

Havighorst and the rest of his crew in front of a He-111 B-2. *From left:* Havighorst, Denz, Schilling, and Waschewski.

Once again bullets smacked into the wings and fuselage. Denz descended; the enemy followed. The fighter was firing its guns almost without pause. I told Denz to put the aircraft into a dive. He reacted at once, placing the Heinkel on its nose. The aircraft picked up speed. At 600 kilometers an hour the wings began to vibrate. There was a grinding noise in the airframe when we reached 650 kilometers per hour, but we had left the enemy behind. He didn't seem to be able to follow us at such speeds.

I shouted to Denz to pull out. He leveled off our heavy bird and we raced toward home—at that point significantly closer to the ground—at full throttle. The entire mission lasted only 250 minutes, but it seemed like we had been under fire for an eternity.

Mechanic Schlüter shook his head when he saw the state of our Heinkel. "You've wrecked the thing!" he said.

"You fly next time!" said Waschewski.

"No, thanks, I'd rather patch up your belly."

We had the whole next day off because our crate had to be repaired before it could fly again.

✠

On 14 October Havighorst's crew flew three missions back-to-back and returned without a scratch. The following day they attacked transport trains and tanks. The bomber crews soon became painfully aware that the latter had started to have antiaircraft machine guns mounted on their turrets. The men of the group subsequently flew to Morosovskaya, where another forward base had been established.

While returning from a mission on 22 October, Havighorst received instructions to land at Millerovo. From there they were to take off for Stalingrad itself on 23 and 24 October. Havighorst:

> That time we carried BM-1000 mines with which to strike the nests of Soviet resistance in the Red Barricade—where the Ivans were holding out in a part of the complex. It required at least ten kilometers before the aircraft reached the assigned altitude of 2,000 meters. We soon reached the target, however, care was required as the site below was partially occupied by our forces.
>
> We spotted the air identification panels immediately, and I guided the aircraft to the release point. A press on the button and the heavy bombs separated from the shackles and fell toward the target.
>
> We came under heavy fire as we turned away from the target. We dove out of the danger zone and raced home low over the steppe, landing after 120 minutes total flying time. We repeated this attack twice more. Stalingrad, which was always below us, seemed to be little more than a heap of ruins.

✠

On 23 October Havighorst's crew took off on a special mission. Not until they were airborne were they given their target. It was the oil refineries at Grozny on the Terek River. For some time the crew had been flying He-111 *Eins Gustav + Nanni Nanni* (1G + NN). Eight high-explosive bombs hung in the fuselage bomb cells. Havighorst:

> For hours we flew southeast at 4,000 meters. Only sixty kilometers from the target we received instructions by radio to change course and attack a secondary target. Called Chegem 1, it was a chemical plant located in the Caucasus.
>
> We found the large facility and dropped our bombs. They fell in the middle of the target and caused large fires that were visible for some time after we turned for home. We landed at Millerovo

after almost eight hours in the air. If we had been shot down en route we would have been finished. We had heard that the Russians made short work of aviators who fell into their hands, and all of us secretly prayed to be spared such a fate. We also had our loaded pistols with us. We gathered from conversations friend-to-friend, comrade-to-comrade, that almost everyone was of the same mind: If they were to be captured, then only dead.

✠

Although it has received scant attention from historians, the air battle waged by the Luftwaffe over Stalingrad was more intense than any it had been able to mount in the past. Not even the Battle of Britain saw a comparable pace of operations.

On 26 October Havighorst's crew attacked Maikop. After the bombs were dropped, two Soviet fighters latched on to the bomber and raked it with gunfire. Havighorst and his men nevertheless escaped and returned to base.

The next mission took Havighorst's crew to a large island in the Volga, which the Russians had transformed into an artillery base with more than 100 guns. The Heinkel was hit by ground fire, but Havighorst still dropped his bombs on the assigned target. Suddenly, searchlights illuminated the machine:

We veered away from the searchlight beams—dived away to gain speed. We then turned steeply, so steeply that the machine lost speed abruptly and hung suspended in the air like a ripe plum until the engines became fully effective again. The wings of our wonderful *1G + NN* were riddled like a Swiss cheese. In spite of this and other damage, we made it home safely.

When we were assigned the Volga Island as a target a second time on 28 October we knew what was waiting for us. Our unpleasant expectations were entirely fulfilled. The Russians had installed supply bases and a headquarters on the islands and these were guarded by a heavy concentration of antiaircraft guns and artillery.

In the period from 29 October to 1 November we flew four night harassment missions to Stalingrad. While en route we could see that the Red Army was moving strong forces up to the Don. There were huge columns, jam-packed with war materiel and weapons. We reported our observations to the group command by radio. We were already beginning to suspect what was in store for our soldiers in Stalingrad, and we hoped that the senior command would accept the proposed withdrawal of the 6th Army to positions in the rear. At this time it would have been possible without fighting and seemed to us to be the only right thing to do.

From 2 to 8 November we flew seven missions against Russian artillery batteries. Forward observers on the ground guided us straight to the target. There we were greeted by the antiaircraft fire that the Russians had set up to protect their heavy batteries.

We swept through the enemy fire toward our target. The bombs fell: Eight 250-kilogram weapons that did considerable damage to the target battery. Six times we raided these artillery positions hidden in the jungle of the large island in the Volga. Lying in the nose of the aircraft, I fired at the riverboats with the 20-mm cannon. The small vessels, which brought men and supplies to the island, tried to hide in the vegetation at the riverbank.

The last flight on that 8 November was my 200th combat mission. It turned out to be a hellish party for us. We were hit so hard that it was difficult to turn the aircraft away from the target. In spite of a rudder that was almost useless, Denz brought the aircraft home safely. None of the crew had been wounded.

Following repairs to the aircraft we flew two more harassment missions that day. Every crate that could get airborne was used. Four more nocturnal harassment raids against Stalingrad and enemy vehicle traffic followed in the period from the 9 to 12 November. It was clear to us aviators that something big was in the offing there; after all, it was plain to see. But apparently the senior commanders in the Stalingrad area had been struck blind and dumb, in that they simply ignored everything that was reported to them.

We subsequently flew five missions to Astrakhan, which placed a great strain on men and machines. The objective of these sorties was to sever road and rail traffic from there to Stalingrad. This time, however, we flew not as a small group of aircraft but with the entire wing, which at that time was still about seventy aircraft.

A full hour passed before all the aircraft became airborne and assembled into formation. Every pilot in such a formation had to maintain strict flight discipline, constantly making corrections in order to maintain position relative to the aircraft ahead of and beside him. The wing commander flew above the entire formation and passed along his instructions. He ordered the one squadron to move more to the left, or another to close up; and so it went.

We could calmly face an attack by dozens of fighters in that situation; we had become a single, heavily armed flying fortress. When the first enemy fighters appeared they soon discovered that they were faced with a new and dangerous proposition. They were nine red-painted La-5s. They were met by a wall of fire from 150 machine guns and seventy cannon. Three fighters, then two more, were hit and went down in flames. The rest turned away, climbed above our formation, turned again and tried to attack from the rear. Orders to fire came over the intercom. Once again every gun in the formation opened fire. A third attack was repulsed, and the two survivors of the nine machines veered off, trailing smoke. The other seven had crashed to the ground.

We arrived in the target area and overflew the enemy columns at a great height. Then we received the order to bomb. The bombs were dropped by squadrons. The Russian highway became a scene of chaos. After the bombs had been dropped, we descended and fired on anything that moved: horse-drawn vehicles were shot to pieces as they fled into the fields bordering the road; Russian infantry were cut down by machine-gun fire as they jumped down from their trucks. The seventy aircraft of the 27th Bomber Wing decimated the column.

The missions flown the next day were similar. On the fourth day our crate was moved from its previous position at the left rear of the formation as a result of my request to the squadron commander. Denz was suffering from serious pain in his left arm brought on by the nearly uninterrupted throttle adjustments needed to hold formation.

Our place was taken by Gottschalk's crew, while we moved into his former spot. This probably saved our lives; while fighting off an attack by Soviet fighters, Gottschalk was rammed by an enemy aircraft. It was a so-called *Taran* (intentional ramming) aviator. The enemy aircraft headed straight for Gottschalk's machine. In spite of the return fire, it bored into the target He-111 with a tremendous crash. Locked together, the two aircraft plunged to the earth.

✠

On 16 November 1942 Havighorst's crew flew three missions into the area north of Kletskaya and south of Perekopskaya:

The following attack was on rail targets east of Stalingrad, beyond the Volga. We approached the train head on and stopped it by shooting up the locomotive. Several cars were destroyed by direct hits. The antiaircraft guns, which were installed on the last two cars, opened fire on us. The aircraft took several minor hits, however, we had no difficulty reaching Millerovo.

The weather was poor on 19 November with almost zero visibility. None of our machines saw any action. After they woke us I was ordered to the group command post while my crew made preparations for the next mission. When I arrived I saw that the wing commander, Oberstleutnant von Beust, was there in addition to our group commander. Opposite him was a general who was staring at a map on the wall.

I reported to the wing commander, and Oberstleutnant von Beust informed me that the general—I have forgotten his name—had something to say to me.

I turned around, came to attention and the general began:

"Something's up down there," he said, pointing to the map. "We believe the Russians have attacked with strong forces. Do you think that you can take off in the prevailing conditions? Your commander tells me that you are an experienced aviator and can take off blind."

"Yes, sir, I will take off!" I replied.

I was instructed to note everything going on down there and to come home with the most extensive observations possible. We took off and set course for the great bend of the Don. Flying on instruments, we flew out of cloud and into the clear. Heading south, we soon discovered that the Red Army already had strong forces across the Don in several places and was heading for Stalingrad in three march columns.

We reported the number of columns and their length and density to the command post by radio. After the fifth report it was obvious to me that this was no shifting of forces; it had to be a major offensive.

Oberstleutnant von Beust instructed us to return. We were guided straight to the airfield. After we landed, I was driven to the group command post. The general was waiting for our report.

When I told him what we had seen with our own eyes he became
so furious that we feared for his health. He snapped at us:

"Are you crazy? That's not right! That's impossible!"

Oberstleutnant von Beust took two steps forward. "Sir," he said
pointedly, "if our Oberfeldwebel Havighorst tells you that there is
a tremendous build-up under way there, then you can be assured
that it is true."

"Yes, it is possible," admitted the general. "It's the Italians and
Hungarians down there."

When I left the command post Oberstleutnant von Beust told
me that we had just been placed on alert.

Our aircraft was refueled and rearmed immediately. A half-
hour later the squadron took off to attack the huge Russian
columns. We were in the thick of it again.

One of our aircraft and three machines from each of the other
two squadrons that took off were shot down. Our He-111 was hit a
number of times. The crew chief counted 151 holes. All of the
remaining aircraft had sustained similar damage.

In the following days our squadron lost six more aircraft in the
same way. They were written off as a result of heavy damage or
shot down.

The men of the 5th Squadron were in action constantly against tank
columns, troop transports and artillery positions in and around Stalingrad
until 28 November. Three or four missions a day were the norm. An indescribable feeling gripped the bomber crews. Havighorst:

We hit the enemy and the enemy hit back. Many comrades did
not return; all Hell had broken loose.

We kept flying as the Red Army's ring around Stalingrad grew
tighter and tighter, until the city, along with twenty German and
two Romanian divisions and a number of smaller units, was completely encircled.

THE SUPPLY FLIGHTS

On 28 November 1942 every available aircraft of the wing was sent to
deliver supplies to the 6th Army encircled in Stalingrad. The skies were
clear. Havighorst:

We of the 5th squadron flew the first mission from Millerovo on 28 November. On reaching a height of several-hundred meters, our crate suddenly refused to answer the controls and we could not hold course.

"Icing!" called Denz. "We're going to go down if we don't turn around at once."

The same thing happened to the other aircraft. We turned back and landed safely at Millerovo. Of all the aircraft assigned to deliver supplies, only twelve reached Stalingrad.

On 30 November all the aircraft got through. After penetrating the Russian antiaircraft barrier around Stalingrad we landed at Pitomnik airfield. We reached the end of the landing strip and were guided to the side of the airfield. Soldiers emerged from huts and tents, climbed into waiting trucks and drove over to us. They were men who had been wounded and several attached personnel who were being allowed to leave the pocket.

Unlike the formations that had been assigned a supply role operating from Tatsinskaya and Morosovskaya, the 27th Bomber Wing in Millerovo was returned to combat duty as of 1 December. Its target was Soviet forces on the Chir front that were attacking the Romanian forces there and threatening to bring about the collapse of the front. The 8th Air Corps was thus divided into combat and support formations, to the detriment of the effort to supply the 6th Army. There simply weren't enough aircraft suitable for the supply flights, and all the He-111s couldn't be used in this role without surrendering the entire front to the Red Army. The 27th Bomber Wing flew combat missions until 5 December 1942 and achieved some measure of success. On one occasion its bombs stopped the advance of a strong Russian armored unit.

The group took off on a single supply flight to Stalingrad on 6 December, the second day of Advent. Havighorst's crew had to remain overnight inside the pocket as they were to fly out a general of Army Group Don the next morning. The wounded were sent back to their tents. The next morning all the wounded were put aboard the aircraft at 0600 hours. The general arrived at 0640 hours. He was directed to his place between the bomb cells. The aircraft took off five minutes later and set course for home. Havighorst:

Our passenger was the Chief-of-Staff of Army Group Don, Generalmajor Friedrich Schulz. He had been sent into the pocket by Generalfeldmarschall von Manstein to see firsthand the situation in the city and the state of the 6th Army.

A Red fighter appeared behind us and opened fire. The men manning our guns returned fire. The general turned to me and asked: "What's going on, Oberfeldwebel?"

"Enemy fighter attack, sir!" He nodded and stared straight ahead.

We landed at Morosovskaya at 0739 hours. Generalmajor Schulz said good-bye to us and the wounded with a handshake. I thought it a noble gesture. He remarked that the flight "had made a deep impression" on him and wished us continued good luck when he left.

On the morning of 8 December we took off from Morosovskaya with supplies for the fortress. This time everything went smoothly and we returned to our home base at Millerovo an hour later, where we learned that we had once again been taken off supply flights. Forty-five enemy tanks had broken into the fortress' northwestern front and we had to help eliminate that threat.

For six consecutive days we flew three and four missions daily carrying eight 250-kilogram bombs. They were days that took us to Hell and back. Enemy fighters were always on our necks, and our fighters were nowhere to be seen. The sortie from Millerovo to Boguchar on 13 December was my 250th combat mission. Snow, ice and fog made things difficult, but we came through. Attacks by Russian bombers on the forward airfields of Tatsinskaya and Morosovskaya became more frequent. There were losses in men and machines.

On 14 December we flew another supply mission to Stalingrad. This time our cargo was gasoline and supply goods. We landed successfully, but dense fog prevented us from taking off. Once again we had to spend the night in a bunker at the side of the airfield. It was minus-twenty-four degrees Celsius, and we had difficulty starting the engines the next morning. The aircraft was packed to the limit with wounded. When it came time for us to take off there were still wounded men standing under the aircraft waiting to get on. We had to turn them away, because we were already over the maximum allowable load and had put aboard at least two more men than was prescribed. It was an appalling sight that went right to our marrow; we climbed aboard the aircraft and left that place of approaching death.

We flew the next supply mission early on the morning of 16 December. We began picking up ice at 500 meters. Denz had to call upon all his experience as a pilot to maintain height and hold the machine on course. Two Ju-52s crashed due to icing not far from us.

Pitomnik was socked in again when we arrived, and we were forced to drop the supply containers—so-called "supply bombs"—by parachute. Pursued by Russian antiaircraft fire, we turned and set course for home.

The weather improved later in the day and we set out once more for Stalingrad. This time we were able to land. The aircraft was soon unloaded and, once again, we saw the ambulances drive up from the tents and huts. The seriously wounded soldiers were packed into the aircraft. This time we took two more men; no more could fit due to the prone position of the wounded. We almost didn't make it out of the airfield, getting airborne only at the very last minute. It was my birthday and we celebrated it after landing. My squadron comrades came out and congratulated me.

More missions followed. The raids on Boguchar and Kantemirovka were flown en masse, and we fought off a number of attacks by Russian fighters and shot down several. On 20 December we were forced to evacuate Millerovo and fell back 150 kilometers to Starobelsk. Several days later, by which time the Russians had captured Millerovo, our 5th Squadron received orders to attack our former base and destroy the Russian aircraft stationed there. We took off and placed our bombs squarely on the target. We avoided hitting the houses, because we knew the civilians there, having lived with them for months.

On Christmas Eve we left Starobelsk for Urasov farther to the rear. Six to seven airmen were perched in each of our He-111s. We landed safely in Urasov; however, the aircraft behind us, which was carrying seven airmen, touched down just to one side of the runway. It rolled into a deep snowdrift and flipped over. A brilliant ball of fire rose above the billowing clouds of snow. There was nothing we could do. All seven men and the crew of the He-111 burned to death.

The bodies were recovered on Christmas Day and were laid out in front of our quarters. In spite of everything, we flew two more sorties on that 25 December in support of our forces surrounded south and southwest of us in Kantemirovka. They subsequently broke out and were able to reach our lines.

We had flown seven more bombing missions by 28 December. Each time we were attacked by Russian fighters. Two of these missions were flown from Urasov. By then we had flown 100 missions in this area, more than in any of our previous areas of operations. But even those uninterrupted missions failed to stop the enemy and our comrades of the 6th Army remained in the pocket.

✠

Meanwhile Oberfeldwebel Ludwig Havighorst had already been recommended once for the Knight's Cross in a submission made by the wing headquarters. The Knight's Cross was not forthcoming, however, because several of his fellow wing members were in line ahead of him. Instead, at the end of December, he was sent to officer training school at the suggestion of the wing. The higher pay he would receive as an officer would allow him to better support his family.

Havighorst received his assignment to Fürstenfeldbrück Officer Candidate School on 29 December. Havighorst:

I didn't want to leave my comrades in the lurch; nevertheless, I went. It wasn't often that a twelve-year volunteer was promoted to officer. I was proud that my superiors had selected me. Perhaps one day I might even lead my old famous 5th Squadron.

Joining Denz' crew as Havighorst's replacement was Feldwebel Hans Wolfersberger, already decorated with the German Cross in Gold.

The atmosphere at the officer school was one of deep shock over the end of the Stalingrad pocket and the 6th Army. I was the only course participant who had flown to Stalingrad, with more than 100 missions in that area. I was therefore called upon to give a block of instruction and describe the missions flown by my wing.

Everyone at the officer school, including the commander, listened spellbound. Havighorst learned second hand that the commander of his wing, Oberstleutnant von Beust, had once complained to Generalfeldmarschall Erhard Milch on the failings of the effort to supply Stalingrad from the air. Milch calmed him down and declared that things would be different from now that he was responsible for the Stalingrad airlift. He was going to bring in an additional fifty He-111 crews and twenty-five Ju-52s. This was certainly better, but it was too late.

The last radio message from Stalingrad reached Führer Headquarters on 2 February 1943. The next day in Fürstenfeldbrück Havighorst heard the Wehrmacht daily report:

> The Battle of Stalingrad is over. True to its oath of allegiance to the last breath, the 6th Army under the exemplary command of Generalfeldmarschall Paulus has succumbed to the superior might of the enemy and unfavorable circumstances.
>
> Generals, officers, noncommissioned officers and soldiers fought shoulder to shoulder to the last round. They died so that Germany might live. Their example will make itself felt for all time in the face of all Bolshevik propaganda.

Ludwig Havighorst went back to his room. He knew what was happening in distant Stalingrad at that hour. He had a premonition of the fate that awaited the prisoners. In spite of all the suffering and sacrifice, they had failed to save them. The Luftwaffe had lost 488 aircraft during the Stalingrad airlift. With them were lost more than 1,000 airmen. Five wings were virtually destroyed without being able to bring about a change in the situation. Total Luftwaffe losses in these missions amounted to more than 3,000 men.

Twenty army divisions were lost at Stalingrad along with the 9th Flak Division, the Romanian 1st Cavalry Division and the Romanian 20th Infantry Division. According to Soviet sources, 108,000 German soldiers were taken prisoner; of these, only 6,500 survived to return home ten to twelve years later. Several months after the German defeat, Stalin revised the number of 108,000 prisoners to 143,300. If this figure is true, it means that 136,800 German soldiers disappeared without a trace in the vastness of the USSR.

THE FIGHT GOES ON: THE LOTFE 7 D

On 5 December 1942 Ludwig Havighorst had received the 250-mission pendant to accompany the Operational Flying Clasp in Gold. When the recommendation for his Knight's Cross went nowhere, a submission was made for the German Cross in Gold—a consolation prize, so to speak. Havighorst received the decoration on 16 February 1943. He was called to the school office, where he received the medal from the commander's hand. That evening there was a big party with the other members of his course.

On 31 March Ludwig Havighorst learned that as one of the leaders of the course, he was to be promoted to Leutnant; officially, however, he was still an Oberfeldwebel. He returned to his squadron where he immediately began training on the Lotfe 7 D bombsight. The new equipment, which was fully electronic, was a miracle of technology.

Training sorties were flown in which cement bombs were dropped from 5,000 meters. Havighorst had rejoined his old crew in Munster, where the Lotfe 7 D training was being conducted. His friends told him of the end of the drama on the Volga, which had cost the lives of several of his comrades from the 27th's 2nd Group. Havighorst:

My squadron was the most active and my crew had the most missions. We were therefore first in line to drop practice bombs. We were rather nervous, as the young crews naturally expected great things of us.

We took off and climbed to 5,000 meters. At that altitude we had to put on our oxygen masks. Each crew was allowed four bomb runs; eight bombs were dropped each time. All four of our practice runs were successful. All bombs were on target. None of the other crews matched this feat. Of course, success did not just depend on the bombardier, my job. It also required a steady approach in level flight by the pilot.

As the acknowledged bombing experts, we spent the next few weeks helping the inexperienced crews eliminate their mistakes.

The period of rest and retraining on the Lotfe 7 D came to an end on 30 May. The 5th Squadron flew initially to Lemberg (Lvov) and from there on to Melitopol.

THE MONTHS LEADING UP TO OPERATION CITADEL

In preparation for the last major German offensive on the Eastern Front Reichsmarschall Göring placed the 4th Air Force in command of the 8th Air Corps. The latter was assigned to the southern group of forces taking part in the offensive. In command of the 4th Air Force was General der Flieger Deßloch. The 6th Air Force concentrated its offensive forces in the 1st Air Corps, which was to see action with the northern group of forces. The 8th Air Corps, commanded by Generalmajor Seidemann, readied its Stuka, bomber and fighter units for the start of the offensive. Seidemann's headquarters was located in Dniepropetrovsk. By the end of June 1943 the flying corps had more than 1,000 serviceable aircraft. In the northern sector the 6th Air Force under Generaloberst Ritter von Greim had 730 operational aircraft, concentrated in the 1st Air Corps, commanded by Generalmajor Deichmann. In total, the Luftwaffe assembled 1,830 aircraft for the offensive, its greatest concentration of aircraft on the Eastern Front since Barbarossa. The 8th Air Corps was well supplied with bombs, however, there was a bottleneck in the delivery of fuel. The shortage of fuel was even more acutely felt by the 1st Air Corps. The corps' Fw-190 formations had only 441 tons of C-3 aviation fuel against a requirement of 1,079 tons.

MISSIONS AGAINST KURSK, GORKI, YELETSK AND BELGOROD

The three groups of the 27th Bomber Wing, all equipped with the He-111, were based at Dniepropetrovsk and Zaporozhye. The wing was under the command of the 8th Air Corps.

The first mission of the 5th Squadron in preparation for Citadel was a small-scale raid on the railway station at Kursk. For the first time in six months Havighorst heard antiaircraft rounds bursting near his machine. The bomb load—consisting of thirty-two fifty-kilogram bombs—was dropped precisely on stationary trains and the station building. The return flight was uneventful.

This was followed by a solo visit to Kursk. The target on this occasion was the large, still undamaged, switch tower and the station building. The Heinkel carried eight 250-kilogram bombs. The Soviet air observers paid

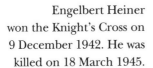

Engelbert Heiner
won the Knight's Cross on
9 December 1942. He was
killed on 18 March 1945.

little attention to the approach of the lone aircraft, perhaps believing it to be nothing more than a reconnaissance machine. When the antiaircraft guns finally opened fire, the He-111 was already over the target and Havighorst had dropped his bombs. As the aircraft turned for home, Havighorst saw that all the bombs were on target. He informed base by radio and then switched on the intercom: "We've done it! Now stay alert! Let's not be taken by surprise!" he warned the crew.

They came through with no problems and landed safely. Afterwards, Havighorst and his men learned that the squadron was to move to Orel. The first mission from Orel—a raid on the Russian tank factory at Gorki— took place on 4 June. The bombers timed their flight to arrive over the target at dawn, so as to avoid Soviet fighters. When they found that they could not reach Gorki before dawn, the bombers were ordered to attack their designated secondary targets and head for home. Further missions were flown on 5 and 6 June. Soviet resistance was stiffening and started to include night fighters.

Situated at the confluence of the Oka and Volga Rivers, Gorki was the site of the largest tank-producing factories in the USSR. The Gorki Kremlin, situated atop the Dyatkovy Mountains, was an obvious landmark, even at night; the moonlight reflected off its golden dome. The bombers' targets were beside the river. Havighorst and his comrades of the squadron attacked the tank factories on three consecutive nights. The bombing was accurate in spite of heavy antiaircraft fire.

There was a break in the action on 7 and 8 June. Suddenly, Russian bombers appeared over the airfield and dropped bombs and leaflets that read: "Murderers of Gorki! We will destroy you!"

On 8 June Hauptmann Bormann led the 5th Squadron to a new base at Olsufyevo. From there the He-111s could reach the well-known rubber plant at Yaroslavl. The squadron flew a night raid against this target on 9 June. In the bomb cells of each machine were thirty-two fifty-kilogram bombs. Situated on the right bank of the Upper Volga, the city stretched about thirty kilometers along the Kotorosl River, which emptied into the Volga.

The rubber plant was primarily involved in the manufacture of tires for the Soviet Air Force. The city was also an important target on account of its status as a transportation center and Volga River port. Havighorst placed his thirty-two bombs among the factory buildings. They caused large fires that spread rapidly. After all the aircraft had dropped their bombs, the two huge factory buildings were in flames. All aircraft returned safely to Olsufyevo.

The mission to Gorki on 10 June was much different. Heavy antiaircraft fire greeted the bombers even before they reached the target. One He-111 took a direct hit and went down in flames. On 13 June the squadron carried out a heavy raid on the tank factory in Gorki. Havighorst and his crew arrived over the target at the last minute before the planned bomb-release time. As soon as the bombs were dropped, both the gunner and radio operator identified a Russian night fighter. Havighorst:

> Denz swerved our crate to the left and the night fighter flitted past. As it did so, it flew into the first burst fired by Unteroffizier Blaß. The stricken machine turned away. Flames spurted from its belly, and it plunged to the ground, exploding on impact. This was our second night fighter kill in Russia.

The bombers visited the railway station at Yeletsk on 19 June. The attack was a success. In the days that followed, the formations of the wing, especially those of the 2nd Group, made preparations for a large-scale mission in support of the coming offensive. On 4 July the squadron and several others moved to Kharkov. Missions in support of the "Citadel" offensive began the next day.

Havighorst and his crew flew twenty sorties in the period 5 to 14 July, averaging at least two per day. It wasn't far to the targets, mainly troop concentrations in the area northwest of Belgorod. The German ground forces were meeting stubborn resistance and progress was slow. Soviet artillery positions behind the front were bombed as well. Other targets included freight trains, bunkers, railway stations, and tank columns approaching the front. Once they had dropped their bombs, the bombers swooped down on the enemy columns and strafed them. The Russian troops answered with everything they had—from antiaircraft guns to rifles. Even the small-caliber weapons were capable of inflicting serious damage on the He-111s. One mission was a special one for Ludwig Havighorst; it was his 300th! Havighorst:

> I flew my 300th combat mission on 14 July. It was from Kharkov into the area northwest of Belgorod. A triumphant reception awaited me and my crew on our return. Everyone of name and rank in the group was assembled in the briefing barracks. In the middle was the unmistakable figure of Generalfeldmarschall Albert Kesselring, who happened to be visiting old friends in the 4th Air Force and the 8th Air Corps.

Our group commander said a few words, after which Generalfeldmarschall Kesselring presented me with a large oil painting
titled "German Bombers over London." This picture has a place
of honor in my house today. It shows three He-111s over the
Thames Bridge and the Tower.

At this time my faithful comrades Ludwig Denz, Helmut Wagner and Wilhelm Waschewski received the German Cross in Gold.
Unteroffizier Blaß was recommended for the same decoration.
Several of my friends went so far as to suggest that I might want to
wash my neck (in preparation for receiving the Knight's Cross). I
dared not even think about it.

My crew and I had been through a lot together, as evidenced by
the fact that we all wore the Operational Flying Clasp with the 250
Mission Pendant. Such success would have been impossible without these men.

We flew a mission to Prokhorovka the same day.

✠

Prokhorovka was something akin to the "Waterloo" of the German
offensive for the southern pincer. It was there that Soviet General Rotmistrov's tank formations—the 5th Guards Tank Army—launched their
attack on Hausser's SS-Panzer Corps. Rotmistrov's 850 armored vehicles,
which included the heaviest Soviet assault guns, set out to destroy Generaloberst Hoth's 600 tanks. On that fateful 12 July 1943 the three Waffen-SS
armored divisions that made up the SS-Panzer Corps—SS-Panzer
Grenadier Division *Totenkopf* in the north, SS-Panzer Grenadier Division
Leibstandarte SS Adolf Hitler in the center, and SS-Panzer Grenadier Division
Das Reich in the south—met the massed Soviet tank forces on the plains
surrounding Prokhorovka. One thousand five hundred tanks and assault
guns clashed in what was to be the largest tank battle of the Second World
War. The Battle of Prokhorovka was a pitiless struggle between Tigers, Pan-
thers, and Panzer IVs and Soviet T-34s, KV-Is, and heavy assault guns.

But another major battle was being fought out in the skies above the
battlefield. Bombers, close-support aircraft and fighters from both sides
clashed in the air over the Kursk Pocket. Aircraft and tanks burned side by
side on the vast battlefield. In the evening the Waffen-SS divisions were
jolted by a fresh attack from the flank by the Red Army, which kept up its
pressure on the front as well. The He-111s of the 2nd Group were set

against this dangerous foe. The aircraft of the 5th Squadron flew in tight formation in hopes of successfully fighting off the Soviet fighters until the German fighters arrived.

The battlefield was a panorama of enemy tanks; there were fires everywhere. Havighorst sighted an enemy armored column. Seconds later, the squadron commander called: "Attack the enemy column approaching the battlefield from the east-northeast!"

The bombers turned north; seconds later they were met by heavy anti-aircraft fire. The bombs hurtled earthward, and Havighorst opened fire with the cannon as the Heinkel turned away. His two gunners likewise began firing at targets on the ground with their machine guns. The bombs struck the enemy column. Flames shot into the air. The sound of explosions could be heard inside the aircraft. They could see that a number of tanks had been hit. Ahead and behind them they could hear gunfire as the Bf-109's of the escort tangled with Soviet fighters.

When the 5th Squadron left the area of the battlefield, the enemy assault had been halted. The crews landed back at base, knowing that they would be going back to the same area at first light the next day. And, in fact, the next morning the crews were sent against a mass of Soviet armor spotted by a German reconnaissance aircraft south of Prokhorovka. The Soviet defensive fire was heavier than the day before, but the bombers had to fly through it, if they were to come to the aid of their infantry and tanks. This day witnessed a regrettable incident when another squadron of He-111s sighted concentrations of "enemy" tanks on the north bank of the Donets. The bombers attacked at once.

But the vehicles were not Russian; they belonged to the advance guard of the 6th Panzer Division under Major Franz Bäke, the commander of the 2nd Battalion of the 11th Panzer Regiment. The battalion had seized the north bank of the river in a surprise raid. Two officers were killed. The division commander, Generalmajor von Hünersdorff, and some of his officers, who had got together for a conference, were wounded.

On the afternoon of 15 July the 5th Squadron took off to attack Izyum. The next day it moved to Sechinskaya. The same evening it took off from there to hunt trains in the Kaluga area. Two trains were attacked and left burning. The war against the enemy's supply lines in the Kaluga area continued on 17 July. Railway stations and installations continued to be frequent targets of the He-111s. On the evening of 18 July the aircraft of the squadron bombed and set ablaze the station at Belev.

For Havighorst the next 100 missions in Russia were like a dream. Unfortunately, his logbook has been lost, but surviving photos show that he took off on his 400th combat mission on 4 October 1943. There was a reception when he returned with sparkling wine and beer. A band provided music and Luftwaffe female auxiliaries were invited for coffee. More than once during the celebration Havighorst was told that the 400th mission would mean the Knight's Cross for him. (Four hundred missions was the accepted figure for the awarding of the Knight's Cross to members of bomber crews.) No one else in the entire wing could match his total of combat missions, many of them of seven- and eight-hours duration.

Postwar research revealed that the wing command had put Havighorst up for the Knight's Cross. The proposal received the approval of the 8th Air Corps, which transmitted it to the next level of command. No one knows what happened to the submission after that. The only possible explanation why the wing did not pursue the matter was because Havighorst's 400th mission was also his last with his old crew. Hauptmann Bormann informed Denz that he would have to fly with Unteroffizier Toni Herbst as bombardier from then on. Bormann said of this: "The move was required because I needed Havighorst as bombardier in my machine."

Havighorst had to submit, like it or not. He flew his first sortie with the squadron commander on 14 October 1943. Flying with the commander, Havighorst lacked the prominence he had enjoyed as a crew commander. On 14 October two pairs of aircraft attacked Soviet rocket batteries. Havighorst was in the commander's aircraft; Denz and the rest of his old crew were in another. As the bombers climbed above a layer of cloud, they flew into the midst of an engagement between two Bf-109s and five Soviet bombers. The fighters mistook the Heinkels for the enemy bombers they were pursuing and opened fire. Approaching from behind, they attacked the trailing aircraft first. It was the one flown by Denz. The Heinkel was hit and lost an engine. The situation was critical; Bormann radioed over the bombers' frequency:

"German fighters attacking! All crews: Open fire on the attacking fighters! Denz: Drop your bombs and head for home!"

The fighters recognized their error and broke off the attack, and the remaining bombers continued to the Soviet position. The three aircraft each dropped eight 250-kilogram bombs on the rocket launchers and then went down to strafe the position. The Soviets returned fire and the Heinkels climbed away. They disappeared into the clouds and flew home. Ludwig Havighorst described the scene that awaited him there:

> When we landed at our base all we saw was worried faces. Everyone was strangely serious. Unteroffizier Wagner, one of the men from Denz' machine whom I knew well, came running toward me.

Visibly excited, he gesticulated wildly and shouted something. Not until he repeated himself did I understand what he was saying.

"They're all dead!" he shouted, tears running down his cheeks.

"What happened?" I asked sharply, already suspecting what Wagner meant. "A round from a German fighter stuck in our tail or close to it without exploding. When we reached home, the thing exploded and damaged our He-111 so badly that it crashed. I was the only one who escaped by parachute."

I was shocked. Ludwig Denz was not only a comrade, he was my friend and we had survived 251 combat missions together. And now he was dead; shot down by our own fighters! I also thought of Unteroffizier Toni Herbst, who had taken my place in Denz' crew. I later learned that he managed to bail out, however, his chute failed to open.

And then there was Oberfeldwebel Wilhelm Waschewski. He had been with the crew since England, always ready with an encouraging word when things got hot. Then I thought of Unteroffizier Blaß and his gift of gab. When he came back from leave he had told us great things about the nightlife in Saarbrücken. We had all survived 150 missions to Stalingrad and elsewhere in the course of barely a year. Now they were no more, killed as the result of an accident.

✠

The hectic pace continued. Bormann and his crew flew their fourth mission against the Soviet rocket batteries on 18 October. Havighorst:

Antiaircraft rounds burst nearby, shaking our aircraft. Hauptmann Bormann grimly held the machine on course toward our target. Then we were over the target. I kept it centered in the Lofte, pressed the release buttons when the moment came and called out "Bombs away!"

Seconds later we heard a mighty crash. Our aircraft was thrown hard off course and the left engine stopped immediately afterwards. Hauptmann Bormann immediately put the aircraft into a left turn, as was his habit. However, it was the wrong decision in this situation.

"Don't turn into the dead engine, sir!" I shouted. "Level off and trim it out!"

Hauptmann Bormann was obviously suffering from mild shock, which was understandable in view of the serious hit we had taken. But he recovered as soon as he heard my voice. I helped him set the trim to compensate for the dead engine. We stabilized the attitude of our crate, however, we had lost 1,000 meters of height by then and were within range of the light antiaircraft fire. The Russians opened fire at once, but we were fortunate and escaped with nothing worse than a few more holes in our crate.

I called the other aircraft, which formed up around us to give us cover against enemy fighters; with one engine out, evasive action would have been impossible. The landing was another potentially dangerous phase, a ground loop was likely as soon as we touched down in our situation.

However, Hauptmann Bormann brought us down in one piece. He set down so softly that the undercarriage did not collapse. As if nothing had happened, we had landed safely.

The burial of our four fallen comrades was supposed to take place on 19 October 1943. The entire squadron planned to gather at Mogilev cemetery to say farewell to its four dead comrades.

I found a seat on a winch in the back of a heavy truck. We set off in the direction of the cemetery. The driver pulled over at high speed to pass a slow-moving vehicle. The edge of the roadway gave way beneath the wheels on the left side of the truck, and it tipped sideways and rolled down into the bushes. I was trapped beneath the winch on which I had been sitting. What happened then I do not know.

I later learned that the others in the truck jumped down and helped remove the winch and free me. They took me to the nearest hospital. When I came to I was unable to move my legs or my right arm. The next day Hauptmann Bormann appeared in the hospital. My paralysis shocked him, but he concealed his feelings well behind a jaunty perkiness: "Havighorst, Havighorst," he said jokingly. "You've flown more than 400 combat missions and now you nearly end up in aviator's heaven on this silly trip. If you're going to go you should at least fly there."

Havighorst had suffered a number of serious injuries. A day later he was flown to a field hospital 200 kilometers farther west by one of the squadron's He-111s. After several days of rest, he was transferred to Prachatitz Reserve Hospital in the Bohemian Forest, where there were specialists who could treat his paralysis. During this time the squadron clerk arrived at the hospital to make a list of all of Havighorst's decorations, his missions and everything else about his career. The information was to form part of a third submission for the Knight's Cross, as Havighorst learned from the clerk: "Once again Oberstleutnant von Beust is going to give the application for the awarding of the Knight's Cross his full support. You are the only one the commander is recommending."

Havighorst knew that, at the latest, the commander of a bomber was supposed to receive the Knight's Cross after 400 combat missions. But this was not a rule and, even though he had 427 combat missions at last count, he still didn't believe it. He had heard of the two previous submissions via the rumor mill, but Havighorst wasn't sure that the rumors were true. But this time it was for real. What happened then is unknown. It is possible that the decoration became lost in the bustle of the Eastern Front and that after Havighorst's departure it was forgotten—out of sight, out of mind. However, all that is irrelevant; had he remained with the wing, he would have received the decoration there. While still at Prachatitz, Havighorst learned that Hauptmann Bormann had been killed in early October after his aircraft lost an engine. The aircraft had crashed into a hangar and all aboard were killed.

Carried out by Dr. Angerer at Prachatitz, the decisive operation was a success. All traces of paralysis disappeared. Havighorst was moved to Straubing Hospital and was then released at the beginning of July 1944. From there he went home; his fiancée Else picked him up at the station. Havighorst had just arrived home when his brother, Werner, who served with the 1st Fighter Wing "Richthofen," also arrived unexpectedly. An hour later there was another knock on the door and there stood his brother, Bernhard, a Leutnant with the 25th Infantry Regiment. Finally, after another hour, his brother, Franz, an Unteroffizier with a Flak regiment, also showed up. Four of the Havighorst brothers, of whom seven were in the services, were back with their mother. Of the seven brothers, six survived the war. Only Anton failed to come home; he was posted missing at the end of the war.

Leutnant Havighorst was married on 11 July 1944 in the St. Sixtus Church in Haltern. He wore a parade-dress uniform, providing proof that a highly decorated German soldier could be a devout Christian and publicly say so. On 20 July 1944, the day of the assassination attempt on Hitler, Havighorst received a telegram summoning him to the frontline aircrew collection point in Quedlinburg. There he learned that he had been promoted to Oberleutnant on 1 April. A medical examination in Quedlinburg revealed that Havighorst was no longer fit for flying duties. It was a heavy blow to the born aviator. He was never to see his faithful aircraft and his comrades again.

FROM NAVIGATION SCHOOL TO THE PARACHUTE TROOPS

Oberleutnant Havighorst was first sent to the Luftwaffe navigation school in Strausberg, east of Berlin, where he trained students in navigation. Several weeks later Havighorst was attached to the Luftwaffe Fortress Construction Battalion in Liegnitz an der Katzbach. Unknown to him and those who went with him, the latter was destined to become a paratrooper regiment.

The battalion entrained on 23 September 1944. The train left for the Western Front during the night. The troops disembarked at Hengelo. Havighorst oversaw the unloading while the battalion commander, Oberstleutnant Freiherr von Schenk zu Schweinsberg, went into the town to inspect the billeting area. Havighorst posted lookouts to watch for enemy aircraft. During the detraining one of them reported six bombers approaching from the west. Havighorst ordered everyone to take cover.

The British bombers attacked the railway station. The facility was devastated and all the railway workers, who had taken cover behind the rail cars, were killed. Those vehicles still on the cars were destroyed, however, none of the battalion's personnel were hurt.

In the days that followed, it was announced that the construction battalion was to form the core of the new 9th Paratrooper Regiment, the first companies of which were being raised in the Hengelo area. The regiment was part of the 3rd Paratrooper Division commanded by Generalmajor Walter Wadehn. Soon afterward the division was taken over by Generalleutnant Richard Schimpf.

Oberleutnant Havighorst, who had received a complete course of infantry training early in his career, was initially named platoon leader of the 1st Platoon of the 4th Company of the 9th Paratrooper Regiment. His company commander was Oberleutnant Grau. Havighorst became the acting company commander during the first major exercise involving the unit when Grau had become ill. When the exercise was over, Havighorst was summoned to the battalion commander.

Havighorst received lavish praise because he had been the only company commander who seemed to know what he was doing. When Schenk von Schweinsburg learned that he had served in the Infantry Training Regiment and was qualified in the use of explosives and combat-engineer techniques, he named Havighorst to command the 15th Combat Engineer

Company of the 9th Paratrooper Regiment. Havighorst assumed command of the company in the Cologne area on 15 November 1944 after completing a one-week combat-engineer course.

Ludwig Havighorst's career as a paratrooper began on 19 November. On 27 November the US 15th Infantry Division advanced past Frenzerburg in the Düren-Frenzerburg area of operations. Havighorst's company advanced toward Frenzerburg. There were a number of skirmishes with the Americans, in the course of which four of his men were wounded. The unit took over its assigned sector; Havighorst set up his command post on the outskirts of the town. Then a Sherman appeared. Havighorst described what happened:

> I took the *Panzerschreck* (German equivalent of the bazooka) and three men and ran into the citadel. I placed the antitank weapon on a table in one of the rooms so I could fire at the approaching tank through the window. The tank opened fire first; the armor-piercing round whizzed over our heads and struck the wall behind us. All they had to do was lower their sights and the next shot would sweep us off the table. I ordered a move to the next room. There we took aim at the tank and fired. After the smoke cleared, we saw that the tank had been hit; there were flames coming from the rear. The crew bailed out and was able to escape.

The fighting went on; some prisoners were taken. When an American attack seemed likely, Havighorst sent a patrol to scout a new defensive position about 1,000 meters to the rear. When the order to fall back came, Havighorst and his company pulled back to the new position along the railroad tracks. Finally, Havighorst received orders to fall back to the Lützeler Estate with his company. His company would be the regimental reserve. It had lost thirty-seven men killed or wounded in the previous 24 hours.

On 29 November 1944 the enemy began a heavy bombardment west of Lucherberg; four hours later he launched an attack by infantry with tank support. The attack was halted and repeated counterattacks drove the enemy from the former German positions. The 15th Combat Engineer Company was involved in bitter close-quarters fighting. Oberleutnant Havighorst was an inspiration to his men, leading the way in every engagement.

On the afternoon of that 29 November, Havighorst and the US officer in command arranged a cease-fire in order to recover the wounded. Soon afterward Havighorst's company was caught in an air attack; the village of

Elsdorf was carpet-bombed and completely destroyed. Casualties were heavy. Twenty-four dead and 32 wounded were buried beneath the rubble of houses.

What was left of the company moved to the western outskirts of Düren. From there it was committed in small assault detachments. The regiment set up its command post in the wrecked Düren district court house. On the evening of 15 December all of the regiment's officers were ordered to Jünkerath for a briefing. An order of the day from the Commander-in-Chief West was read out. The assembled officers were told that an offensive in the Ardennes was going to begin before dawn the next morning. "It's all or nothing," stressed Generalfeldmarschall von Rundstedt. "The hour has come for the troops in the West."

THE "WATCH ON THE RHINE":
IN ACTION WITH THE 3RD PARATROOPER DIVISION

The 15th Combat Engineer Company under Oberleutnant Havighorst took part in the last German offensive in the west. The 3rd division was attached to the 1st SS-Panzer Corps. Havighorst led his company into the jumping-off positions during the night. It was his 30th birthday and he was about to go into battle again.

At 0530 hours the Germans opened fire. Many hundreds of weapons of all types created a barrage the like of which the paratroopers had not seen since Normandy. The advance began. The attack made rapid progress. Heavy artillery fire began falling; there was hand-to-hand fighting as the paratroopers stormed through Merlscheid to Hüllscheid. The combat engineers reached Hüllscheid. The enemy fled and, by the evening, the company had reached its objective of Lanzerath. The German troops found that the enemy had abandoned their positions and had even left food on the tables. The rapid advance continued on 17 December, but resistance then began to stiffen. One hundred and fifty prisoners were taken in the fighting for Honsfeld, and there was a huge haul of vehicles and fuel. The paratroops then remained in place until 24 December. The advance had bogged down at Bastogne.

Havighorst, his company headquarters section, and the 1st Platoon had moved into a school in Ondenval. There were surprise artillery barrages and nightly patrols. After midnight on 1 January 1945, Havighorst and two members of the company headquarters section went forward to wish their comrades a happy New Year. They had gone scarcely 100 meters when the enemy artillery opened up. The firing was heavy, but Havighorst and his companions made it through. While inspecting the construction of bunkers by his company, he was ordered to the battalion command post. On the way Havighorst and his party were again caught by enemy artillery fire. One of his four men was killed, but Havighorst escaped injury.

Huge explosions woke the men of company on the morning of 13 January 1945. The entire regiment's sector was under heavy fire, and it was becoming heavier. Then American troops attacked. There was bitter close-quarters fighting in the main line of resistance. The Americans were repulsed several times, but the regiment was finally driven out of its positions in several places.

There was bitter fighting when a regiment of American troops entered Ondenval. Led by three half-tracks, Havighorst and his men counterattacked and recaptured a farm. Twenty American soldiers were taken prisoner. Havighorst and Oberjäger (Private First Class) Steckhahn took charge of the prisoners and led them to the rear. American artillery opened fire. Four rounds landed near the party, killing five of the prisoners and wounding Havighorst and Steckhahn. Havighorst was taken to hospital in Jünkerath. When his fever was gone, he was released to return to his unit. On the way, he was attacked by a British fighter-bomber that strafed his vehicle and fired rockets.

When the Battle of the Ardennes was over, the German Army had lost 10,749 dead, 22,388 missing, and 35,169 wounded in the bitter winter battle. The armed forces also lost nearly all its heavy weapons and material and a large number of aircraft. The "Watch on the Rhine" had failed to achieve its desired goal. The official figures revealed that the Anglo-Americans had also taken heavy losses. The American 1st and 3rd Armies lost 8,407 dead, 20,905 missing, and 46,169 wounded, while the British forces that took part lost *only* 200 killed, 239 missing, and 969 wounded.

FINAL FIGHTING BY THE PARATROOPERS

When Oberleutnant Havighorst returned to his regiment he learned that it had suffered very heavy losses during his two-week stay in hospital. Generalleutnant Schimpf had returned as division commander on 6 January. Havighorst became a liaison officer and spent the next few days working closely with Oberst Hoffmann. He led patrols and repulsed some from the other side. On 31 January the regimental commander was surrounded in Lanzerath. Havighorst led the attack that freed him. He and his men took part in fifteen close-quarter actions in a few days. In spite of this the German forces were steadily on the retreat. The 9th Paratrooper Regiment crumbled under the devastating blows of the enemy artillery and fighter-bombers.

Havighorst assumed command of the combat engineer company again and he received orders to cover the regiment's retreat to the Rhine at the end of February. This included securing the bridge at Bonn-Beuel. His company consisted of only sixty men at that point. On the morning of 4 March the regimental commander watched the last of his men cross the bridge. The very last was Ludwig Havighorst. The retreat continued from Oberpleis on the east bank of the Rhine. Oberst Hoffmann became ill and had to enter hospital. Hoffmann's place was taken by Hauptmann Graf Alfred von Freyberg. Before Hoffmann had left, he had recommended Havighorst for the Knight's Cross. Once again, the recommendation got lost in the shuffle. He had also recommended him for promotion to Hauptmann. It was only after his return home after the war that Havighorst discovered the promotion had been approved.

The next day Ludwig Havighorst was captured by American troops after a bitter street battle in Froitzheim. The town had initially been recaptured from the enemy but was on the verge of falling into their hands again. Ludwig Havighorst described what happened after his capture:

We entrained in Euskirchen on 7 March 1945. Belgian soldiers tormented an older Hauptmann who had a belly wound that had not completely healed. One of the Belgian soldiers struck down the badly wounded man with the butt of his rifle.

We were crammed into rail cars. We were given a cup of water once a day; there was nothing to eat. After a four-day rail journey we reached the camp at Cherbourg. The dogs who guarded us were the same everywhere: Men who had never smelled a shot of powder and wouldn't have been much good if they had.

All the officers were placed in a special camp. We were quartered sixty to a large tent, which was meant for thirty soldiers. The food was good, but there wasn't enough of it. In the morning, for example, each man received a cup of tea and a piece of bread. For lunch there was scrambled eggs, eleven teaspoons per plate.

The guards stole everything they could lay their hands on. They took my blanket, shelter half, and "bone sack"—the baggy paratrooper smock—during the coldest night of April 1945. On the morning of 9 May we learned that the war was over.

The day before we were joined by Oberst Hans-Ulrich Rudel. He was my tentmate for fourteen days. He was a man of unflappable character. When an officer of the guard ordered us to toss all our decorations and medals onto a shelter half, Ulrich Rudel provided the example for the rest of us. He smashed his decorations—including the Golden Oak Leaves with Swords and Diamonds—with a stone. We all did the same. When the man came to collect the shelter half, there was just a pile of junk lying on it. After its treatment with the stone, my German Cross in Gold was no bigger than a walnut.

In September 1945 a group of prisoners was assembled for transport to America. I was assessed "unfit for duty" on account of my wounds and was released together with fifty of my fellow prisoners. We former POWs were sent to Germany in open rail cars.

Near Liege we moved under a bridge. Some men hanging around on the bridge dropped a large stone. There was nowhere to run. One of my friends was struck. He fell to the floor covered in blood and died soon afterward. The British soldiers guarding the train raised their submachine guns and fired at those hate-filled assassins, who immediately ran for cover. In doing so they prevented an even worse disaster.

I arrived home on 12 September 1945. At the time I weighed 98 pounds (former weight 150 pounds). A few days later I was forced to enter the hospital for three months on account of jaundice.

In spite of all the degradation and all the pain over fallen comrades who flew with me, we all believed that we had to fight for a better future.

With 267 victories, Otto Kittel was the fourth most successful fighter pilot of all time.

Otto Kittel: From Pilot to Squadron Commander

PROLOGUE

Otto Kittel served with the 54th Fighter Wing his entire career as a fighter pilot. From 22 June 1941 until the end of the war the bulk of this wing was based in the northern sector of the Eastern Front.

He was born in Kronsdorf in the Sudetenland (Czechoslovakia) on 21 February 1917. From an early age Kittel was fascinated with aviation and longed to become a pilot. He joined the Luftwaffe in early 1939 at the age of twenty-two.

In February 1941, after completing all the necessary training, Kittel joined the 54th Fighter Wing. At that time he held the rank of Unteroffizier. The 54th was based at Le Mans and was responsible for the air defense of Normandy. However, the wing's 1st Group had remained at Jever, and Kittel was soon transferred there.

Kittel saw his first combat over Yugoslavia. His commanding officer, Major Hannes Trautloft, had already recognized his potential as a fighter pilot in Jever. Kittel wrote the following about his early career with the wing:

> After achieving zero success over Belgrade I went to Stolp-Reitz in Pomerania. There we received new aircraft in the form of the Bf-109 F. We carried out several practice flights until we were transferred to Trakehnen for Operation "Barbarossa."

When the German invasion of the Soviet Union began early on 22 June 1941, the 54th Fighter Wing went into action as part of the 1st Air Corps. Kittel shot down two enemy aircraft in his first mission over the Soviet Union, and his victory total climbed rapidly. Once he was himself shot down behind Russian lines; Kittel returned several days later disguised as a Russian *muzhik*.

Flying from Siverskaya, Kittel received the Iron Cross, First Class, after eleven victories. The victories came in rapid succession. By the time he had reached 100, he had already been recommended twice for the Knight's Cross. Neither was approved. He became a Feldwebel and then an Oberfeldwebel. Kittel was recommended for the Knight's Cross for the third time following his 120th kill; this time the submission was approved and he received the "tin tie" on 29 October 1943, by which time his total stood at 123 enemy aircraft.

From that point on the pace of victories quickened. Next came the Oak Leaves, awarded on 11 April 1944 after 152 kills. This followed close on the heels of a promotion to Leutnant for bravery in the face of the enemy. Otto Kittel received the 113th Knight's Cross with Oak Leaves and Swords on 25 November 1944. By then his victory total stood at 230 and he had been promoted to the rank of Oberleutnant—once again on account of bravery in the face of the enemy.

Kittel was known throughout Army Group North as the "butcher killer"—"butcher" being the name the German soldier gave the Soviet Il-2 close-support aircraft. On 13 February 1945 he shot down three aircraft, the last one bringing his total to 267. The next day Kittel dove into a formation of eight of the heavily armored Il-2s. He fired at and hit several of the Soviet aircraft but was then attacked and shot down by two Il-2s. His faithful Fw-190 crashed and exploded.

Otto Kittel had placed an unforgettable stamp on his squadron and the 54th Fighter Wing. The wing that produced sixty-eight recipients of the Knight's Cross had only one Kittel. He was the fourth highest scoring fighter pilot of all time. In his eulogy Oberst Trautloft said:

> Kittel's 39th victory was also the 4,000th by my wing. After a proud series of victories his name became known in every sector of the front. Honor his memory.

THE EARLY DAYS WITH THE 54TH FIGHTER WING

Unteroffizier Otto Kittel joined the 2nd Squadron of the 54th Fighter Wing on 12 February 1941. At that time the majority of the wing was based in Le Mans, having moved there from Dortmund and Delmenhorst in Germany. From that French airfield approximately 200 kilometers northwest of Paris the wing assumed responsibility for the air defense of Normandy. The wing also made use of a forward airfield at Cherbourg.

The wing's 1st Group, however, had remained in Jever in Germany. Kittel was sent to that group. He and his comrades spent the time in further training for combat, but the real thing wasn't far off. It was during this time in Jever that the wing held a gathering for all its pilots, at which the commander, Major Hannes Trautloft, "knighted" his men as fighter pilots. Kittel flew with many experienced pilots during his stay in Jever and learned a great deal from them about the art of being a fighter pilot.

On 6 April 1941 Kittel and the rest of the squadron flew across the Yugoslavian border. The fighters were flying escort for German bombers attacking airfields and military installations in the area of Belgrade. With their escort responsibilities complete, the fighters searched for targets of opportunity. In this way Kittel fired his guns in anger for the first time; the targets were enemy transport columns and trains.

Kittel and his group followed the rapid advance of the German ground forces, moving from Arad to Deta, from Fünfkirchen to Bilejkina, and from Pancevo—located on the Themis near Belgrade—to Semlin. By the time the Yugoslavian Army surrendered on 17 April 1941, the wing had raised its total of victories since the war began to 376.

During the fighting in Yugoslavia, Kittel flew several times as wingman for the squadron commander. His main role was to keep his commander's tail clear. As such, he had no opportunity to seek his own kills. The German fighter arm followed the proven practice of employing its fighters in pairs. The element leader was the more skilled pilot; it was he who got the first chance to engage the enemy. Although rank had nothing to do with who was element leader, Unteroffizier Kittel never got a chance to fire his guns at one of the scarce Yugoslavian aircraft in Yugoslavia. Nevertheless, he learned a number of valuable lessons that served him well in the future.

After the cease-fire in Yugoslavia the squadrons of the 54th gathered at the large commercial airfield at Semlin, where they handed all their Bf-109 E fighters over to the 77th Fighter Wing. From there the wing's personnel were sent to Stolp-Reitz in Pomerania. There the entire wing was equipped with the Bf-109 F. The transports carrying the wing's personnel arrived at the its new base on 12 May. Conversion to the new type was followed by intensive training; the many practice flights were used to familiarize the pilots with the latest tactical innovations and eliminate any teething problems with the new aircraft.

Beginning in mid-June 1941 the squadrons and groups began moving up to the airfields assigned them in preparation for the German offensive in the east—Operation Barbarossa. The wing headquarters and the 2nd Group took up quarters in Trakehnen, while the remaining two groups were based in Lindenthal and Blumenfeld. The 53rd Fighter Wing's 2nd Group was temporarily attached to the wing and was based at Gerlinden.

At the onset of Barbarossa, the 54th Fighter Wing was organized as follows:

Wing commander: Major Trautloft
  1st Group: Hauptmann von Bonin
    1st Squadron: Oberleutnant Koderitzch
    2nd Squadron: Oberleutnant Unger
    3rd Squadron: Oberleutnant Scholler-Haldy
  2nd Group: Hauptmann Hrabak
    4th Squadron: Oberleutnant Philipp
    5th Squadron: Oberleutnant Mütherich
    6th Squadron: Oberleutnant Stangel
  3rd Group: Hauptmann Lignitz
    7th Squadron: Oberleutnant Scholz
    8th Squadron: Oberleutnant Egger (Oberleutnant Hausmann)
    9th Squadron: Oberleutnant Schneider (Oberleutnant Bob)

A number of the wing's pilot had already received the Knight's Cross. They included: Dieter Hrabak, Hans Philipp and Arnold Lignitz.

THE WAR AGAINST THE SOVIET UNION: FIRST MISSIONS
The 54th Fighter Wing took off on its first mission against the Red Air Force at 0300 hours on 22 June 1941. The 120 aircraft of the wing overflew the border at 0305 hours; their mission was to escort the bombers en route to their targets, the Soviet airfields at Kovno, Kedainai and Poniewesch.

The 1st Air Corps under General Helmuth Foerster and the Commander of Air Forces Baltic, Oberst Wolfgang Wild, had been instructed to attack all Russian-occupied airfields within the range of their bombers and destroy the Soviet air forces on the ground and in the air. The objective was to prevent the enemy from attacking the German ground forces from the air.

Other targets for the German bombers included Soviet road, rail and other traffic networks, the Baltic Fleet and its ports, and marine traffic on the White Sea-Baltic Sea canal. If the Luftwaffe could wreck the locks at Proventum—the highest part of the canal, at ninety-eight meters above sea level—the Soviet Navy would be unable to move its forty-six submarines, fifteen destroyers, and a number of minelayers from the Gulf of Finland to the Arctic Ocean (Siberian Sea).

✠

There were several encounters that first day with Soviet Polikarpov I-16 *Rata* fighters. On the second mission that morning Otto Kittel was scheduled to fly with the squadron commander as his wingman. The group headquarters had received word that Russian bombers were attacking the roadstead and gas works at Königsberg. Hauptmann von Bonin immediately scrambled the wing's 2nd Squadron, which was on strip alert.

Sitting in the cockpit of his machine, Unteroffizier Kittel watched Oberleutnant Rumpf, who was the acting commander of the squadron, taxi to the takeoff point. Then it was his turn. He performed all the functions that had become second nature by now: Fuel cock open, throttle lever at one-third power, starter pump on, cooling flaps closed, propeller pitch set on automatic. The two mechanics began cranking up the inertia starter. Kittel switched on the ignition and the starter began giving off its characteristic high-pitched whine.

The mechanic gave the all clear signal. Kittel nodded and engaged the starter. The propeller began to turn and the motor started at once. Advancing the throttle, Kittel heard the deep, regular drone of the engine, a sign that everything was in order. Every pilot developed an ear for the sound of the engine and could often tell at once if something was wrong.

Scanning the instruments, Kittel saw that oil and fuel pressures, boost pressure and fuel flow were all in order. He raised his right hand in a thumbs-up signal and nodded to the mechanics for a job well done. He then taxied to the takeoff point. Oberleutnant Rumpf was already in the air when he reached the takeoff area. Kittel tightened his straps and then advanced the throttle. The Messerschmitt accelerated down the runway, lifted off and climbed away. Kittel retracted the undercarriage and flaps; all that was left to do was trim the aircraft. Then he switched on his reflector sight and checked the radio.

He heard the voice of the squadron commander: "Parrot to everyone: Close up, tight formation!"

Kittel moved in closer. He saw Rumpf turn around and signaled that everything was all right. Rumpf nodded and turned the other way to look for the two aircraft of the second *Rotte* (a two-man team consisting of element leader and wingman). The other two Messerschmitts moved in closer.

Rumpf called his pilots: "We'll try and cut them off on their way home."

They flew a course that Rumpf hoped would bring them to the bombers in about twenty minutes. They spotted seven of the ten reported SB-2 bombers and then several fighters, which Kittel identified as Yak-1s.

"Enemy fighters at two o'clock. They're flying about 1,000 meters above the bombers."

"Identified!" replied Rumpf. "Attack the bombers!"

The Messerschmitts overtook the enemy bombers rapidly and began taking return fire. Looking up, Kittel saw the Yak-1's diving toward them.

Oberleutnant Rumpf also saw the enemy fighters and turned behind the bombers, causing the first bursts from the Yaks to miss.

Kittel closed in fast on the bomber flying on the extreme right of the formation. At 200 meters he pressed the firing buttons for the two machine guns and the cannon. The first burst was high. Kittel lowered the Messerschmitt's nose and fired again. This time there were flashes on the SB-2 as his rounds struck home. After a third burst the enemy bomber plunged to the ground. It crashed and exploded in a ball of fire.

Kittel broke left and saw one of the Yaks open fire as it dove toward him. He turned tighter and tried to get on the enemy's tail. However, the pilot of the Soviet machine turned just as tightly and Kittel was unable to close the distance. The two fighters flew three complete circles before Kittel, at the recommendation of the squadron commander, put the Messerschmitt's nose down and dove out of the "carousel." He leveled off six-hundred meters lower. The Russian had obviously lost sight of him and turned back toward the now decimated bomber formation. Kittel approached the unsuspecting Soviet from behind and below. When he had closed to 140 meters, he opened fire. The enemy aircraft blew up and pieces showered Kittel's aircraft. He ducked involuntarily when a piece of wreckage struck the cockpit windscreen.

The enemy formation had been all but wiped out; Oberleutnant Rumpf gave the order to head home. Unteroffizier Kittel waggled his wings twice as he flew over the airfield. He had opened his score with the enemy, and he had the squadron commander to thank for allowing everyone to engage the enemy.

✠

The struggle went on, and the 54th, known as the "Green Heart Wing" on account of its unit emblem, followed the advancing German armies. The green heart was the symbol of Thuringia. It had been selected as the wing's emblem by its first commander, Hannes Trautloft. In his book on the wing Trautloft said: "The green heart is the emblem of my Thuringian home, to which I feel a close attachment."

✠

During the march through Latvia, Estonia, and Lithuania toward the city of Leningrad the wing moved in succession to the airfields at Dünaburg, Pskov, Ostrov and Luga, spending a week or two at each. The

The commander:
Hannes Trautloft.

first large-scale air engagement against the Soviet Air Force occurred over Dünaburg on 30 June 1941. A large force of Soviet bombers was reported heading for the German front line. The bombers were escorted by approximately forty fighters of various types.

The entire wing scrambled to intercept, taking off by groups. The 1st Group was the first airborne; Kittel was again flying on the squadron commander's wing. When they reached the area of the German frontlines they could see the flashes of exploding bombs. With the Soviet bombers were LaGG-3 and Yak-1 fighters. Kittel heard Oberleutnant Seiler, the commander of the 1st Squadron, give his men the order to attack. Then the voice of Oberleutnant Rumpf rang out in his headset: "All stations: Let's roll!"

He watched as Rumpf turned, positioned himself behind a bomber, and shot it down. Kittel recalled what the pilots who had experience with the Il-2 had told him: Position yourself behind and somewhat below it and try to hit it in the unprotected underside. Otherwise, it won't go down.

Kittel was still approximately 2,000 meters above the low-flying Il-2s that were plastering the infantry's trenches with bombs. He turned and descended toward a gaggle of about ten machines that had not yet dropped their bombs. As he dove, Kittel flashed through a scattered formation of enemy fighters. He moved so rapidly they had no chance to fire. Then he saw two Il-2s directly in front of him. He dropped beneath the Soviet aircraft and was only 300 meters above the ground when he began climbing into attack position. He closed the distance quickly; the maximum speed of the Il-2 with its bombs in place was 400 kilometers per hour. At 200 meters the Stormavik almost filled the entire windscreen. Kittel wanted to fire, but he overcame the hunting fever that had gripped him. He closed to 100 meters and fired. The Russian aircraft seemed to literally blow apart. Kittel turned away at once and slipped beneath a second Stormavik that was preparing to drop its bombs. He opened fire from 200 meters. The Soviet aircraft veered off, jettisoned its bombs in an effort to gain speed, and turned toward Kittel. He heard several bangs as bullets struck his Messerschmitt, but the clumsy enemy aircraft was no match for the maneuverable fighter.

Kittel fired and saw his rounds ricocheting off the armor of the enemy aircraft. He moved in closer and fired again. Pieces flew off the Ilyushin's wooden skinned wings. The next burst sent the Il-2 plunging earthward, where it crashed and exploded. Dogfights were going on above and in front of him. Numerous smoke trails marked the end of Soviet bombers. Kittel fired at a Yak but missed when the enemy aircraft evaded at the last second. Oberleutnant Rumpf's voice came over the radio: "End of the line, it's time to go home!"

The pilots landed and went into the wing barracks to file their claims. When they had been tallied up, Major Trautloft banged his fist on the table.

"Gentlemen," he announced, beaming, "our wing has scored a total of sixty-five victories in the air today."

Everyone was excited and enthused, not least Kittel, who received the Iron Cross, Second Class for his efforts.

By 5 September the 54th had arrived at Siverskaya; several days later it moved to Gatchina, near Krasnogvardeysk. Together with Staraya Russa and Ryelbitzi, these airfields were to be home to the wing for nearly two years. The wing remained exclusively in the northern sector of the Eastern Front.

On 24 August 1941 Oberleutnant "Fips" Philipp, the commander of the 4th Squadron, had become the first member of the wing to receive the Knight's Cross with Oak Leaves. It followed his 62nd victory. Philipp had earlier received the Knight's Cross on 22 October 1940 after downing 20 enemy aircraft in the air war against England.

In contrast, Otto Kittel's score climbed slowly. He was increasingly called on to fly wing for one of the group's prominent pilots. This earned him a reputation as a dependable wingman who could be counted on to keep his element leader's tail clear in any circumstance. In spite of his limited opportunities, Kittel raised his score to eleven enemy aircraft by the winter of 1941–42. He was very proud when he was awarded the Iron Cross, First Class.

On 30 September Hauptmann Lignitz, the commander of the 2nd Group, was shot down over Leningrad. His men saw him bail out successfully. Lignitz came down in the city and was never heard from again, but rumors that he had been killed by the citizens there refused to go away. His successor was Hauptmann Seiler; Oberleutnant Heinz Lange assumed command of Seiler's 1st Squadron. When the commander of the 1st Group, Hauptmann von Selle, was transferred, Hauptmann Eckerle assumed command of the group. Command of his 6th Squadron passed to Oberleutnant Sattig.

The Red Air Force attacked Siverskaya early on the morning of 2 January 1942 and destroyed ten aircraft on the ground. It was a serious, but not fatal blow. Fortunately, the human cost was limited to minor injuries to several ground personnel. Starting the engines of the Bf-109s was almost impossible at minus-forty-five degrees Celsius. Everything froze, even the grease with which the guns were lubricated after every cleaning. This resulted in a number of weapons failures at critical moments.

Hauptmann Eckerle was killed in combat on 14 February. His successor as group commander was Hauptmann Philipp. Oberleutnant Wengel assumed command of Philipp's 4th Squadron. A further change in personnel resulted from the serious wounding of Hauptmann Schmoller-Haldy; his place was taken by Hauptmann Koall, who had led the wing's fighter-bomber (*Jabo*) squadron for a time.

✠

Otto Kittel scored another double in mid-March. He and three other pilots from the squadron intercepted a formation of Il-2s while on a fighter sweep. The Soviet aircraft were in the process of attacking a road leading into a salient in the front. The four Messerschmitts arrived on the scene just as the first bombs were falling, but this time there was a surprise waiting for them. Unlike the Il-2s they had encountered before, these ones had a rearward-facing gunner sitting behind the pilot. This addition made the sturdy, heavily armored Il-2 an even tougher opponent.

"We'll fly over them, turn in behind them and attack from below. If you hit the oil cooler, it's all over."

The four fighters overflew the gaggle of Il-2s, which was heading west toward its target. The enemy saw them of course but, assuming that they were on their way to a destination behind Soviet lines, ignored the Messerschmitts.

On reaching a position four kilometers behind the Il-2s, Kittel and the others turned and descended toward the Soviet aircraft. They closed rapidly with the slow-moving bombers. When tracers began racing past their ears, they realized that they were dealing with a new type of Il-2 and that things were going to be more difficult. Nevertheless, the German fighter pilots knew about the Ilyushin's Achilles heel. Kittel saw the squadron commander descend even lower. He followed, veering slightly to the left to line up on the enemy aircraft to the left of the one chosen by his commander. Kittel approached his target from behind and about 20 degrees below. The rear gunner suddenly stopped firing. Kittel knew why: He was in his opponent's blind spot. If the gunner tried to hit him, he would riddle his own tail surfaces.

Kittel saw the wing root of the enemy aircraft fill his gun sight. He descended slightly, then raised the nose ten degrees and fired his cannon and machine guns. Pieces flew from the wooden skin of the Ilyushin's wing and several bullets pierced the armor on the floor of the cockpit. The Il-2 pitched downward and struck the ground in a matter of seconds. The tremendous explosion produced a large crater.

Kittel immediately turned left and climbed away at full power. He ascended to a point about 700 meters above the enemy before diving on the next Il-2. Kittel followed the same procedure as before, diving beneath the Il-2, then climbing swiftly—while braving the fire from the rear gunner—to position himself for the attack. The Soviet pilots, obviously inexperienced, were taken by surprise by this maneuver.

The bullets and rounds from Kittel's guns struck the Il-2s oil cooler. Oil gushed from the ruptured oil tank and some splattered onto the windscreen, blinding Kittel. Unable to see, he turned away from the enemy formation and began to climb. Soon the oil on the windscreen thinned and he was able to see better; Kittel called his squadron commander: "Windscreen covered with oil; I'm returning to base."

"Well done, Kittel, I saw both of your kills. The second machine is going down in flames. Go home."

After Kittel had landed, he remained sitting for a few seconds and leaned back. He breathed deeply. Both of his mechanics were there in no time. "Something wrong, sir?" they asked (Kittel had been promoted in December).

"That was number 13 and 14, sir," said one of the "black men." "It's going up," he added.

Kittel nodded to him gratefully.

"Slowly, slowly, I fear. But in the end, you want to come home in order to keep going for a long time."

That was his motto: Take the safe route and avoid ill-considered and wild offensive tactics. In the end that alone produced success and all that went with it. Risking himself and his aircraft for a single victory was not Kittel's way.

In the weeks that followed the temperature rose and early morning takeoffs by the Bf-109s were possible without a great deal of work on the engines. Otto Kittel was in action almost constantly, flying as wingman and element leader. It was during this period that he first tackled Il-2 close-support aircraft alone. Kittel was always ready to respond to a call for help from the infantry, whether he was officially sitting on strip alert or just waiting around the group command post for someone to come looking for a replacement for a man who couldn't fly.

It was mid-May and Kittel's victory total had climbed to seventeen when he was once again "turned loose" to go hunting on his own. He had just left the wing command post and gone to that of the group. Both were scantily furnished; in the group command post two telephones sat on a pair of empty bomb crates. One was to the wing and the other linked the group to its subordinate squadrons. Behind the phones in a corner sat the radio operator at his set. He monitored radio traffic, received messages from the wing and passed them on to the squadrons. The men on duty there were not very confidence inspiring. Their boots were dirty and many of them wouldn't have dared to be seen in Germany with uniforms like those they were wearing. But things were different there. Only those things related to flying and shooting down the enemy counted. That was the bottom line in a frontline formation.

Just as Kittel was about to leave the command post, he heard a call come in from a pilot: "Attention base! My engine is on fire. Keep the runway clear."

Hauptmann Eckerle acted immediately. He simply looked at the duty officer. The latter picked up the flare pistol and ran outside. He fired three red flares, the signal to keep the runway clear. Anyone on approach to land would have to pull up and go around and await further instructions. Everyone else ran outside. Moldenhauer, one of the staff clerks who was blessed with extra-keen vision, called out: "There he is!" In seconds everyone could see the Bf-109; it was trailing a cloud of black smoke. Already very low, it altered course slightly to line up with the runway.

The fire trucks were already on their way to the landing site. As the onlookers watched, the pilot of the Messerschmitt set his aircraft down gently. The Bf-109 had rolled about 100 meters when it suddenly swerved, slid sideways, and came to rest at the edge of the field. Fortunately, it had not flipped over.

Within seconds, the pilot had jumped clear and ran toward the fire trucks. He had not yet reached them when a jet of red flame shot up from

A fine study of a Bf-109 E-4 of the 54th's 3rd Squadron, flown by Anton Döbele.

the aircraft; then the ammunition exploded, sending bullets in all directions. The pilot threw himself to the ground. Then he raised to a crouch and kept going. A piece of burning wreckage fell in the grass beside him. Sparks flew and set his flight suit on fire.

The fire brigade was ready, however. Two men ran over to the pilot and extinguished the flames. Then they dragged him out of the danger zone. The fire truck drove closer to the aircraft and began putting out the fire. All this had happened in a matter of seconds, and Kittel was still thinking about the tremendous explosion when the alarm was sounded from the group command post.

"Second squadron: Strip alert! Russian bombers with fighter escort on the way."

"Off you go, Kittel" said Hauptmann Eckerle.

Kittel ran to the dispersal area. Everything was just as he wished it. His crew chief held his thumb in the air, signaling that the aircraft was ready to go. Kittel climbed in, fastened his parachute straps, and was first to taxi to the takeoff point. Although he was officially a wingman, he was free to take off without regard to any set formation whenever the commander ordered a *freie Jagd* (open hunting). He taxied to the takeoff point; the officer standing there raised the takeoff flag. Kittel carried out a textbook take-off—passing 200 meters by the still-smoldering Messerschmitt—and set course for the front.

At first Kittel flew at half throttle to allow his squadron mates to catch up. Soon he saw the first aircraft appear behind him. The squadron commander confirmed that they were free to seek the enemy and Kittel spurted forward. He flew over the front; below, counterbattery fire was raging on both sides of the front. Kittel continued to climb. He had put on his oxygen mask and reached 4,800 meters when he sighted the first group of enemy bombers. The Soviet aircraft, SB-2 medium bombers, were directly ahead and at least 1,800 meters lower than he was. There was also a fighter escort, at least forty strong.

Kittel alerted the rest of the squadron: "Attention! Indians above the bombers!"

"Bombers have priority, Otto," the squadron commander called back. Kittel counted about forty bombers as he flew over the formation. He reversed course in a wide arc and positioned himself behind the tight formation. The Messerschmitt closed the distance and was soon within attack range. A gentle nudge on the stick and the Messerschmitt's nose went down. Ignoring the six or seven I-16s that remained above and behind him, Kittel raced toward his first target.

He flew through several bursts of gunfire without being hit. The first enemy aircraft appeared in Kittel's sight; he throttled back somewhat, made a slight course correction, and pressed the firing buttons. The enemy bomber took the full burst; as soon as he saw hits flashing all over the SB-2 Kittel turned sharply to the right and climbed. Seconds later, the Soviet bomber exploded; the blast rocked Kittel's fighter. Pieces of metal showered in all directions, fortunately without striking the Messerschmitt. The bomber's starboard engine whizzed past it like a comet, complete with a fiery tail.

Kittel then found himself confronted by two Ratas; one dove straight at him while the other tried to head him off. A steep turn in the opposite direction shook off the second Rata, but the first opened fire and bullets struck the fuselage of Kittel's Messerschmitt. The dogfight that developed drifted ever farther behind the bombers and their escorting fighters, and they were over Russian territory. If he were to be shot down at that point, he would be in big trouble.

Otto Kittel tried to gain ground toward the west. The fighters turned in ever-decreasing circles. Twice the maneuverable Rata was able to pull enough lead to fire, but Kittel escaped serious damage on both occasions. While in a right-hand turn, Kittel suddenly dove away steeply. He carried out a 360-degree turn and then climbed steeply; several minor corrections were enough to position him behind and beneath his opponent. The Soviet pilot had been unable to follow Kittel when he dived and was now unsure as to where his opponent was.

Kittel took advantage of these seconds of uncertainty on the part of the enemy pilot. One final correction—then he opened fire from a distance of 200 meters. Kittel closed the range rapidly. His last two bursts struck the Soviet from only 80 meters. The Rata's port wing broke away. While the Soviet fighter spiraled to earth, Kittel set course for home and began to climb in preparation for crossing the Soviet frontlines.

He crossed the lines at 3,000 meters. No sooner had he cleared the danger area from the enemy antiaircraft defenses when his red fuel-warning lamp came on. Kittel landed back at base on his last drops of fuel. He had raised his personal victory total to seventeen, but this time the engagement had demanded everything of him. He pulled off his helmet and wiped the sweat from his brow. Then he leaned back until his crew chief climbed on to the wing. After opening the Plexiglas canopy, Kittel let the mechanic help him from the cockpit. He noted his legs still felt like jelly.

That exhausting engagement had showed him that the Russians had pilots who had analyzed German fighter tactics and had changed their own tactics in response.

THE DRY SPELL

After May kills were hard to come by for Otto Kittel. It seemed that everything was working against him. In spite of that, he kept trying. He downed
the occasional enemy aircraft, but the intervals between victories were
long. It was the men in black—as the ground crews were called—who
helped keep his spirits up during that dry spell.

✠

It was the summer of that eventful year 1942; the 54th Fighter Wing
was still in the northern sector of the Eastern Front. Feldwebel Riedl was
on duty in the command post. Riedl had just finished eighteen hours of
answering telephones and recording data; the tired staff-duty noncommissioned officer had just finished his shift and was about to retire to his tent
when the field telephone rang:

I picked up the receiver. On the other end of the line was a certain "Wittgenstein." I was already rather sleepy and didn't understand him. I replied: "What kind of 'Stein'?" The answer was
precise and well articulated:

"This is Major Prince zu Sayn-Wittgenstein!"

Of course, at that time I knew nothing of the existence of such
a prince in the air force and thought to myself: One of the boys is
trying to pull my leg. So I answered back smartly: "So, you're
Prince zu Sayn-Wittgenstein. This is Count Coke of the gasworks!"

The prince lost his composure. "You must be mad, you idiot!"
There was a click as he hung up.

I thought I had settled the matter. Several minutes later I
turned to another of the men on watch, Unteroffizier Karl Kraus,
one of the "command-post experts," and asked: "Have you ever
heard of a Prince zu Sayn-Wittgenstein?"

"Of course! He's the commander of the night fighter unit
based here. I'm sure you'll hear from him in the morning at the
latest, perhaps even sooner."

It turned out to be sooner; shortly afterwards the phone rang.
On the line was Major Trautloft.

"Feldwebel Riedl, you are to report to the command post
immediately!" He said rather sharply.

Karl Kraus grinned impertinently. "You haven't been in the
clink here yet have you? You'll soon get to know the cubby hole,"
he said.

I buttoned my tunic, pulled on my boots, put on my tin hat, and marched off. By then it was dark. The sky overhead was clear and starry and, in spite of the daytime summer heat, it was pleasantly cool. On arriving in the wing command post I clicked my hobnailed boots together and mimicked the impeccable soldier: "Feldwebel Riedl, reporting as ordered!"

The commander seemed unimpressed and began speaking at once:

"Man, have you taken leave of your senses? Talking to an officer on the phone like that is simply impermissible!"

The candle on the nearby table flickered brightly as the Major took a deep breath. Then another Major standing to his left joined in. I could see the Knight's Cross at his throat.

"That's enough, Trautloft," he declared casually. Then he turned to me: "So you are Count Coke of the gasworks. I'm happy to make your acquaintance. I am Prince zu Sayn-Wittgenstein."

"Please, sir, allow me to explain," I stammered. "I thought some friends were playing a joke on me, and I would like to officially apologize. I had absolutely no idea who you were."

"Very well, Feldwebel, I accept your apology. The matter is closed."

The prince was really a prince from head to toe, but Major Trautloft was no less gracious.

"Very well then, Riedl, more discipline on the telephone in the future. Dismissed!"

I saluted, made a smart about face and left the commander's tent. As soon as I was outside I heard raucous laughter from the tent. The two majors were treating the whole thing as a laughing matter. They understood fun and knew that it was worth its weight in gold in the current situation.

"Count Coke" was one small amusing episode in difficult times.

This episode, which turned out favorably for Feldwebel Riedl, was followed some time later by a second unusual occurrence that initially caused wild terror but then resulted in relieved laughter. The story became known as the "attack on the heart john." The heart john was a tiny rectangular wooden shack in whose front door a heart had been cut out for ventilation. It was, in official military parlance, a "screened provisional toilet installation."

Naturally, each squadron had such a hut somewhere in the steppe near the dispersal area for pressing needs. At the time of the incident, in July 1944, the 54th's 2nd Squadron was stationed at the airfield at Polotsk, near Dünaburg. There was always something going on in that area, as the events of those weeks showed. The following incident took place on 10 July.

Not far from the command post bunker there was one of those one-man latrines. Under the circumstances and times, it was quite comfortable. Made of sturdy tree trunks it was about two meters high and 1.2 meters square.

On that day Feldwebel Helmut Claus, a member of the command post personnel, was sitting in the shack, having felt the "call of nature." Several Russian fighters were already buzzing about, and they suddenly turned straight toward the airfield and began to strafe. One of the Soviet pilots obviously took the shack to be a secret dugout. He bore down on the wooden shack and while everyone dove for the slit trenches. The good Feldwebel was left to his fate.

The men in the trenches watched in horror as the Russian fighter swooped down on the shack and began firing. Boards and beams flew in all directions. The shack was demolished, and when the fighter had left there was Feldwebel Helmet Claus sitting on the toilet seat for the entire world to see. He was obviously unscathed. As we were rubbing our eyes in amazement, he roared angrily: "Haven't you ever seen an airman taking a shit?"

That did it. The laughter must have been audible as far as the Russian front lines. Seconds later—as if it had heard the distraught Feldwebel shout—the Russian fighter came back and made another pass. The Feldwebel pulled up his pants and ran to the nearest trench. He dove in headfirst and then, turning to me, declared: "The Russians don't even have the decency to let one do his business in peace."

In spite of the situation, this brought forth another outburst of laughter.

Someone said: "Be glad that your rear end is still in one piece. It could have turned out differently."

✠

The emblem of
the 54th Fighter Wing.
Top left: 1st Group.
Top right: 2nd Group.
Center: 3rd Group.
Bottom: 4th Group.

Riedl continued:

Things did turn out different for the Soviet fighters, which were
covering the eight close-support aircraft. By then the German
fighters that had scrambled when the first attack came were high
enough to attack the Soviet fighters and bombers from above.

Once again it was Otto Kittel who provided us with a brilliant
demonstration. By then he was known as a great flier and had
worked his way to the top of the list among the wing's aces with
150 kills.

He dove past three or four fighters and poured several bursts
into the belly of his first victim, which immediately went down and
crashed not two kilometers from the airfield. Then, like a rocket,
he swooped upward in an unbelievable turn. He rolled the
machine onto its back and dove onto the tail of an Il-2. He was so
close when he opened fire that we thought he was going to collide
with the enemy aircraft, but then it too went down in flames and
crashed.

Once again, Kittel climbed like a comet and turned toward the
enemy machines that were already heading for home. In two minutes he shot down two more of the enemy, including another Il-2.
The show, which was like a tragedy after the burlesque, ended
with four kills in, at most, ten minutes. One of our pilots collided

with an Il-2 but was able to escape by parachute and got off with only a broken leg.

But back to events in the summer of 1942 . . .

Otto Kittel continued to increase his score. Oberstleutnant Trautloft kept an eye on his record. The wing commander was certain that Kittel would win the Knight's Cross. In his opinion, he had already earned it. In addition to his victories, Kittel had flown more than 100 missions as a wingman, during which he had saved numerous comrades from being shot down by Russian fighters.

Otto Kittel was not one of those overly exuberant young types found in air forces everywhere, who let his first victories go to his head. Instead, he was one of the quiet ones. If it hadn't been for the reports by his comrades confirming his victories or reports on aircraft shot down from forces on the ground, he would never have caught anyone's attention. He was just there; he fought and won and his quiet devotion to duty was an inspiration to everyone in the wing.

Although he had only received the Iron Cross, First Class, Kittel had become one of the squadron experts and was acknowledged as a fighter and a comrade. 1942 had been a year of combat and victory for Kittel, but no matter how difficult the situation was, he always came through. In spite of the fact that he had shot down his thirty-ninth enemy aircraft, Kittel was dissatisfied with himself in February 1943.

He and a friend came back from a difficult mission, tired and worn out. Seeing how downcast Kittel was, the other pilot said to him: "What more do you want? We're still alive and I think that we'll be entered on the victory list more often in the future. Remember 14 February last year when Hauptmann Eckerle got it and "Fips" Philipp took over our group. He got the Swords on 12 March."

He went on to remind Kittel about the outstanding successes of the wing. Philipp had 100 kills (31 March); the wing then got its 2,000th kill (4 April 4). Oberfeldwebel Klemm was the lucky shooter. He continued to encourage Kittel: "Perhaps it will be your turn soon to get our 4,000th kill."

Otto Kittel grinned slightly. "That's possible . . . I looked in the wing logbook; the 4,000th must be due soon."

On the morning of 19 February 1943 the 2nd Squadron took off to intercept Soviet bombers. Escorted by a squadron of fighters, they were reported attacking forward German positions. Kittel and his squadron were on strip alert when the alarm was sounded. The Messerschmitts took off one behind the other and set course toward the enemy. After approximately three minutes, Kittel sighted the first Russian bomber. He headed straight towards it and opened fire as soon as he was in position. He saw the lances of flame from the bomber's nose guns. Kittel broke right, passed the bomber, reversed course and prepared to make a second pass. Kittel opened fire. There were flashes all over the bomber's wing and then the starboard engine exploded. The enemy aircraft's port wing dropped before it went down almost vertically and crashed.

"Well done, Kittel," called his squadron commander. Seconds later someone called out a warning and Kittel pulled up into a vertical climb, avoiding a burst of fire from a Russian fighter. He cut in front of one of his comrades and continued to climb. He fired at another Russian fighter as he passed; the enemy aircraft began to smoke but could not be claimed as a kill.

The enemy formation was ravaged in the engagement. The Soviets lost thirteen bombers and seven fighters. Kittel flew over the airfield and waggled his wings before coming in to land. His mechanic raised his arms in joy; his friend Kittel had had a successful mission, something all of them had been hoping for. As soon as he had landed, Kittel was instructed to report to the squadron commander. He presented himself as ordered and reported one enemy bomber shot down. The squadron commander nodded.

"Well done, Kittel. You're to report to wing at once. The motorcycle is waiting."

In his mind Otto Kittel went over the possible offenses he might have committed, but he found nothing to warrant a summons by the wing. Kittel knew as soon as he faced Oberstleutnant Trautloft in the wing barracks that there was nothing bad in the air. A glance at the table in the background revealed several bottles of French champagne complete with glasses.

"Feldwebel Kittel, reporting as ordered!" he declared smartly.

"Thank you, Kittel, stand at ease!"

The wing commander allowed his gaze to wander over the pilot standing in front of him. This serious and calm man radiated reliability and readiness to serve, even when standing at ease. Trautloft knew that Kittel could be much more if he could just bear in mind all the things he told his pilots. True, Kittel had downed two enemy aircraft that morning, but Trautloft knew that the young warrior was capable of much more than the fifteen kills he had achieved from autumn 1941 to May 1942 seemed to indicate. Kittel stood before his commander, square-jawed and taciturn. When would he finally begin, he asked himself. Kittel had no idea that the commander was trying to evaluate him.

He had long since ceased to be a wingman, pulling the chestnuts of the more high-profile pilots out of the fire. He had made a name for himself as an Il-2 killer and was known to the soldiers at the front. Trautloft had known for a long time that Kittel was one of the most reliable men in his wing and that he was deserving of the highest expectations.

The man standing in front of him embodied the best traditions of German soldiery, even if he contradicted his concepts of a fighter pilot. Otto Kittel was a gifted hunter, a pilot who could handle any situation, as he had already demonstrated in numerous instances by attacking far superior enemy formations.

"Kittel, I have happy news to tell you. Your thirty-ninth victory was also the wing's 4,000th. Before you took off this morning, it was 3,997. Two scored kills before you, but you brought down the 4,000th. On that we all congratulate you."

Trautloft extended the Feldwebel his hand. The latter shook it firmly. Immediately he was surrounded by friends and superiors, all eager to congratulate him.

"Keep it up," his group commander, Hauptmann Philipp, said while clapping him on the shoulder. "I think that you'll want to begin catching up now."

Philipp was also referring to himself; he had received the Knight's Cross with Oak Leaves and Swords on 12 March 1942 and was coming up on his 100th victory.

"But I need about sixty kills to catch up, sir," replied Kittel.

"That won't take long. I have instructed that you're no longer to be assigned as wingman. Instead you're to be sent out to get your own kills whenever there's an opportunity."

"Thank you, sir."

Otto Kittel was very grateful to his group commander. He didn't care much for playing nursemaid. Kittel stood poised to make a run at the victory leaders, but there was another factor that would then influence his career. In January 1943 the 1st Group was transferred to Krasnogvardeysk to reequip with the Fw-190.

✠

The group underwent conversion training on the new type in Heiligenbeil. Kittel was enthused by this powerful, well-armed machine. After a few practice flights, it was as if he had never flown another aircraft. The Focke-Wulf fighter was powered by a 1,700-horsepower BMW-801 radial engine, which conferred on the aircraft a maximum speed of 660 kilometers per hour and a service ceiling of 11,000 meters.

The Fw-190's range was 800 kilometers, but its greatest advantage was its armament of four 20-mm cannon and two 7.9-mm machine guns. This made it better able to deal with the Il-2, Kittel's favorite target. The new aircraft was an immediate hit on the Eastern Front and Kittel's score began to climb rapidly.

✠

On 1 March 1943 the 1st Group of the 54th Fighter Wing was organized as follows:

Group Commander: Hauptmann Philipp
Adjutant: Oberleutnant Dutel
Maintenance officer: Oberleutnant Dieball
Operations Officer: Hauptmann Haase
Transport officer: Oberleutnant Lemme
Headquarters Company Commander: Oberleutnant Jullmann
Headquarters Company First Sergeant: Oberfeldwebel Biemüller
Headquarters Administrative Noncommissioned officer: Oberfeldwebel Raß
Classified Material Custodian: Feldwebel Riebl
Assistant Operations Noncommissioned Officers: Unteroffizier Claus and Unteroffizier Kraus
Headquarters Company Maintenance Sergeant: Oberfeldwebel Kilian
Maintenance Section leader: Oberfeldwebel Wirth
<u>1st Squadron</u>
Squadron Commander: Oberleutnant Nowotny
Squadron First Sergeant: Hauptfeldwebel (Master Sergeant) Ertl
Squadron Maintenance Chief: Oberfeldwebel Schröder
<u>2nd Squadron</u>
Squadron Commander: Oberleutnant Nowotny
Squadron First Sergeant: Hauptfeldwebel Ertl
Squadron Maintenance Chief: Hauptfeldwebel Bähner

3rd Squadron
Squadron Commander: Hauptmann Koall
Squadron First Sergeant: ?
Squadron Maintenance Chief: Hauptfeldwebel Putz

BATTLING THE IL-2 "BUTCHER"

The battle zone east and northeast of Staraya Russa, the city at the western edge of the Demyansk Pocket, had been under heavy Russian artillery fire since 28 November 1942. The Soviet Air Force also attacked tirelessly with medium bombers and the armored Il-2 close-support aircraft, the best they had. The latter swarmed over the German front lines, attacking dugouts and bunkers. The only support the ground units had in their struggle with the Soviet Air Force was the 54th. Flying from Krasnogvardeysk, it strove to provide the infantry with some relief from the attacks by Soviet bombers and close-support aircraft.

Soviet Marshall Semyon Timoshenko had under his command the 11th and 27th Armies. With those forces he was to pierce the narrowest part of the pocket in the area east of Staraya Russa and Ramushevo, due west of the Lovat River. He sent the 1st Shock Army from the south. The northern group of Soviet forces consisted of thirteen rifle divisions, nine

The 1st Group on parade. *From left:* Hauptmann Koall, Leutnant Fischer, Hauptmann Haase, Waffeninspektor Hecht, Stabszahlmeister Erz.

rifle brigades, and a number of tank elements. In the south the 1st Shock Army included seven rifle divisions, four rifle brigades, and armored elements with 145 tanks.

Holding out inside the pocket was the 2nd Army Corps with the 8th Light Infantry Division and the 81st and 290th Infantry Divisions. Opposite them, on the other side of the pocket, was the 126th Infantry Division. The German forces totaled 100,000 men but had no tanks.

By 27 February 1943 the German forces had managed to clear the Demyansk Pocket and the corridor with help from outside. The 54th Fighter Wing played a major role in the successful evacuation. Not one artillery piece was left behind. Nevertheless, the graves of approximately 10,000 German soldiers remained in the pocket. What followed were five major battles in the Staraya Russa area initiated by the Red Army. This renewed offensive on the part of the Red Army marked the beginning of a period of hectic action for the wing.

SCRAMBLES

The alarm was raised on the morning of 4 March 1943. Soviet bombers were approaching Staraya Russa. The 54th's 2nd Squadron, which was on strip alert, immediately scrambled its first two flights. Among the eight were Otto Kittel and his squadron commander Hans Götz. When the bombers came into sight Götz instructed his men to attack from above in close formation: "Tackle the bombers first!"

Otto Kittel saw the first two small formations of bombers pass by beneath him. He reversed course, placing him behind the enemy. Exploiting his altitude advantage, Kittel dove on the bombers of the right-hand formation, while Hans Götz and two other pilots tackled the group on the left. Kittel moved onto the tail of a Pe-2. From a distance of 200 meters he pressed the firing buttons. There were flashes all over the Pe-2. It sheared out of formation and tried to escape in a wide turn. Kittel followed and delivered another burst. The Soviet bomber lost its starboard wing and went down vertically. Turning away sharply, Kittel soon found himself facing a Soviet *Rata* fighter. The Soviet pilot reacted quickly to avoid the German's first burst of fire. The Soviet turned and tried to get on Kittel's tail. The experienced Kittel noted that the Soviet fighter could be a serious opponent when flown by a good pilot—in spite of its inferior speed. And this one was good!

The two fighters jockeyed for position until Kittel positioned himself for a decisive burst. The Rata took several hits in the cockpit and went down burning. Kittel saw the enemy aircraft hit the ground and explode.

He tried to catch up with the first bomber formation by flying at full throttle. In the distance he could see that his comrades had shot down another enemy aircraft and had engaged the third and last formation. Kittel closed in on a bomber, which opened fire on him with its two rearward-firing machine guns. Two bursts were enough to send the Soviet aircraft falling from the sky.

Not until the red fuel-warning lamp came on did Kittel set course for hone. He flew over the airfield, waggled his wings three times, then came in and landed; Kittel received an enthusiastic reception from his ground crew. After debriefing in the group's debriefing shack Kittel first went back to his two ground crew in order to ensure that they were at work repairing the bullet holes in his aircraft. There was a brief conversation, typical of Kittel:

"How does it look, Rupprecht?" he asked the crew chief.

"Good, sir. It will be refueled, rearmed and ready to go in an hour."

"Thanks, Rupprecht. Carry on."

Kittel went to his quarters and freshened up for lunch. That was one of his constant worries: Always being fresh and rested. He always tried to lay down for a half-hour after eating. This time he was awakened before his nap was over. There was an alert. Kittel rushed to the dispersal area and his aircraft. There were fresh areas of paint on the airframe where the ground crew had made its repairs.

He caught up with the squadron commander: "What's going on, Hans?" he asked.

"The 1st and 3rd Squadrons are already in the air, so we're taking off. Russian close-support aircraft are working over the infantry."

Kittel was second into his aircraft, after his friend Götz. The fighters taxied for takeoff and received clearance immediately. He accelerated down the runway, feeling the power of the BMW engine. He then lifted off into the Russian sky.

"Directly northeast, at the Lovat," called Götz.

A total of five aircraft formed up and headed toward the target area. They were at 1,800 meters when they saw tracer streamers and explosions in the German trenches far below. The fighters dived on the Il-2 close-support aircraft and opened fire. As they climbed away after the first pass they flew over the Russian lines and were greeted by antiaircraft fire.

"Reverse and make another pass!"

Kittel was flying at 300 meters. He began taking small-arms fire and veered away, which placed him in an Il-2's line of fire. He climbed steeply out of the danger zone. Looking around, Kittel sighted a second Il-2. Only

fifty meters above the ground, it was flying along the main line of resistance at right angles to his heading and was firing into the German positions.

Kittel aimed at a point in front of the Il-2 and opened fire. The enemy
aircraft flew through the streams of rounds. It took one hit behind the
engine and several dozen in its armored flank. Smoke began pouring from
the Ilyushin, which nosed down and struck the ground. As he swept over
their heads, Kittel saw the infantry standing in their trenches with their
arms raised. He then made a steep turn and caught another Il-2, which
likewise went down after several bursts. But by then it was time to return to
base, where he landed safely.

There were frequent calls for help from the infantry in the days that
followed. Fortunately, there were several forward observers in the frontlines
who could provide a measure of early warning of the approach of enemy
aircraft. In that way the fighters of the wing were able to get into the air and
intercept the enemy bombers before they could drop their bombs.

EIGHTY KILOMETERS BEHIND ENEMY LINES

Flying from one of the forward airfields near Staraya Russa, Otto Kittel
fought several impressive engagements in the days leading up to 14 March.
On the morning of 15 March 1943 he took off as part of a *Schwarm* (a
flight of four) led by Oberleutnant Götz. No enemy aircraft had been
reported, but the four Germans stumbled onto a formation of twenty
Soviet aircraft after patrolling the area for ten minutes. Most of the enemy
aircraft were LaGGs, but several were Airacobras, provided by the USA.

"Attention everyone: Attack individually!"

Oberleutnant Götz and Feldwebel Brönnle dove on the LaGGs and
were engaged in a wild dogfight in seconds. Both shot down a LaGG. Kittel had selected one of the Airacobras. They circled cautiously and
exchanged several bursts, with no damage inflicted on either side. Kittel
tried one of his favorite maneuvers—a "slip through"—whereby he went
from a circle into a figure eight and ended up on the enemy's tail. He
fired and saw pieces fly off his opponent's tail. His excess speed took him
so close to the enemy that he dared not fire for fear of being struck by
debris if the aircraft broke up. The enemy pilot evaded desperately and
Kittel found himself in his line of fire for a second. He heard bullets strike

his aircraft but nothing critical was hit. Then he found the range. His bullets struck the cockpit area and he must have hit the pilot, for the enemy aircraft went down vertically.

Kittel reported his victory, hoping for confirmation.

"Seen and noted," replied Oberleutnant Götz.

The enemy aircraft struck the ground and exploded in flames.

"All the Russians have taken off. We'll turn and head back, perhaps we'll run into some others on the way."

Otto Kittel hadn't gone far when he suddenly detected a change in the sound of the engine. Then it began to sputter, a sure sign that it was about to give up the ghost.

"Calling Sunflower: I have engine trouble."

"We'll stay with you," answered Götz. Meanwhile, Herbert Brönnle moved in close enough for Kittel to see his face.

"Hang on, Otto. You can make it. If you must come down, then hide yourself immediately. Travel only by night. A compass heading of 255 degrees will take you right to Staraya Russa."

"Thanks, Herbert," replied Kittel. He was aware of course that Brönnle knew what he was talking about; in the fall of 1941 he had been shot down near Leningrad, after which he covered more than 20 kilometers on foot and returned through the Russian lines. (On the previous day, 14 March 1943, Brönnle had received the Knight's Cross after his 57th victory. On 4 July 1943, after a transfer to the 2nd Squadron of the 53rd Fighter Wing, he stalled over Catania airfield and crashed from 300 meters following engine failure. Brönnle died in the crash.)

Kittel's aircraft was losing height rapidly, and he knew that he would have to force-land somewhere.

"I've got to come down. Go home, I'll get through."

Oberleutnant Götz was well aware that the nearest German strongpoint was sixty kilometers away as the crow flew.

The propeller stopped turning. Kittel sought a favorable place to put his Fw-190 down. When the propeller finally stopped he was over a treeless, snow-covered field. To the right were several houses; he would have to come down as far away from them as possible. He reached for the map and stuck it in the knee pocket of his flight suit. Then he removed the dashboard clock—pilots were under orders to bring them back whenever possible.

The Focke-Wulf descended lower and lower and finally touched down gently on the snow-covered surface. The aircraft slid only 150 meters before coming to a stop. Kittel released his straps, leaving the parachute pack in place, and slid back the canopy. He stepped onto the wing then jumped down to the ground. The snow was frozen hard.

He immediately turned toward the forest. When he reached it, he saw two women running from the area of the houses toward his Fw-190. A number of children, at most eight to ten years old, followed; there were no men in sight. Kittel tramped through the forest, the floor of which was covered with snow. His flying boots became wet and heavy.

Gradually, he felt his strength leaving him. To his dismay, he realized that he had left his emergency rations in the aircraft. The Russian women would get to enjoy them. Fortunately, he had a bar of chocolate in his jacket pocket. He ate one of the round, fifty-gram pieces and took a long rest before continuing on his way. The going was hard and Kittel was forced to rest often, but at least he could travel by day in the forest.

Later he stopped and sat down, his back resting on a tree trunk. Kittel fell into an uncomfortable sleep. When his head fell forward he woke up and continued his journey. An hour before dawn he came to the edge of the woods; peering into the darkness, he saw several houses, part of a settlement. He was determined to find something to eat there.

He called out in Russian—as a native of Southern Germany he spoke Czech, and he had picked up some Russian in the course of many months in the Soviet Union. When no one answered he entered the nearest house. He found nothing to eat there, but did discover a worn fur cap and a walking stick as well as a moth-eaten sheepskin coat. So attired, he left the

Trautloft in the cockpit of his Bf-109 G-6.

house. He almost looked like a Russian peasant. At that point, all he had to worry about was mimicking an old man if he were challenged. Kittel skirted the settlement; by the time it was light he had come to another forest that matched his general direction of travel. He kept walking until afternoon, when he crawled beneath a dense wall of brambles and other vegetation covered with a roof of snow. He intended to rest there for a few hours.

It was already midnight when the cold woke him. In spite of the double layer of clothing, he was frozen stiff. Laboriously, Kittel resumed his trek. By the time darkness came again, he was so exhausted that he could scarcely go on. Soon afterward, however, he saw lights shimmering in a large clearing that had been cut out of the edge of the forest. He worked his way nearer and discovered that it was a barracks in which Soviet aviators were quartered.

He had to find something to eat. He therefore walked through the broad entrance to the camp, which was marked by several posts stuck in the ground. He bent over and leaned heavily on his stick. The nearest sentry didn't even take his rifle from his shoulder. He merely called casually to Kittel, who answered in Czech. That seemed to satisfy the guard. He gestured that he might pass and Kittel, no longer looking like a German soldier with his thick layer of stubble and dirt-smeared face, tramped through the camp. He reached the exit and was about to leave, but the guard there was more suspicious. He asked Kittel several questions that the latter answered passably in a mixture of Czech and Russian. It was enough to satisfy the sentry.

Several hundred meters farther he came upon a group of men camped outside, obviously road workers. They were sitting around a fire, over which a spit was turning. The enticing smell of roasting meat reached his nose. The men called to him and asked him to stay, but he begged off. A rather old man came over and looked into his face. Kittel thought he saw something like recognition in his face, but it disappeared immediately. He gave Kittel a crust of bread smeared with some unidentifiable fat and then furtively made the sign of the cross.

Kittel gratefully took the bread and walked on. He feared that he would hear the old man call out a warning at any moment, but the Russian remained silent. He began to eat the bread, and he felt his strength renewed when he had finished. That couldn't be from the crust of bread alone. It was something else that gave him the unshakeable confidence that he would make it.

Kittel walked all night and he came to one of the many streams that flow out of Lake Ilmen at first light. He saw a Russian patrol on the far bank and ducked into the nearest bushes. It was obvious that crossing this open terrain and the stream by day was out of the question. If he tried it, he ran the risk of being shot at from one side or the other. In that open area, that was as good as a death sentence.

He crawled under the dense covering of bushes, which the heavy snow had pressed down to about thirty centimeters from the ground. At noon he spotted a Russian patrol walking along the shore of the lake. German artillery began shelling the area and the patrol scattered in all directions. Two men at the end of the patrol ran his way. One ran past him, but the second crawled under the bushes and lay there, five meters from Kittel. Kittel could hear the man's heavy breathing. The smell of his unwashed body assaulted his nose. He felt the urge to sneeze but overcame it by concentrating all his willpower. Finally, the patrol leader called to the two men to come back; the two set off at a trot and disappeared. In spite of the cold, Kittel could feel sweat on his face. That had been a close shave. What could be more dangerous than this near confrontation?

When it was dark Kittel left his hiding place and inspected the shore of the lake. He found a well-worn path leading to a ford and stepped into the water, which was ice cold. Step by step, he worked his way across the stream. In the middle the water was up to his chest. Once he sank up to his neck and he felt as if he were bathing in ice water. Kittel kept moving toward the far bank. When he arrived he found that there were no positions of any kind. After 200 meters he came upon the first German position, the combat outpost of an infantry battalion.

Then a voice called out: "Halt, who goes there? Advance and be recognized!"

Kittel heard a click as the challenger released the safety of his rifle.

"German airman. I was shot down behind Russian lines three days ago and I have walked this far."

"Don't tell us stories, just say the password."

"Asshole!" thought Kittel. "I have been in Russian territory for three days. My name is Feldwebel Otto Kittel of the 2nd Squadron of the 54th Fighter Wing."

"Then come closer, but no pistol or other nonsense. We know about Kittel."

Kittel opened the tattered sheepskin, and the soldier saw the decorations on his flight jacket.

The man turned and shouted: "It's him, sir!"

"Very well then, welcome home, Kittel!" said the Leutnant and returned his pistol to its holster.

They shook hands. Kittel followed the Leutnant into his dugout. The latter gave one of the men a wave; he brought over the coffeepot that had been bubbling away on a stove and a cup. He poured Kittel a cup of coffee, which smelled suspiciously like real bean coffee, which in fact it was.

"Thanks. If I could also have something to eat . . . I haven't eaten in two days."

He was given a thick slice of bread covered with an almost equally thick slice of meat from a tin. He took a bite and washed it down with coffee, while the Leutnant called the battalion command post. He reported the arrival of the Feldwebel and asked that the wing send someone to pick him up. An hour later a wing Kübelwagen arrived. Kittel was dozing in a corner of the tiny command post. Oberleutnant Götz stormed into the bunker and hugged his friend.

"Man, Otto, thank God you're still alive!" he shouted in relief. He hugged the Feldwebel again then pinched his nose and declared: "It smells a lot like Ivan here, are you sure it's you?"

"You should have seen me in my cap and sheepskin," replied Kittel with a grin.

"You won't want to return to the group without those fine things," observed Götz. "The comrades will want to take your picture as an Ivan."

"Fine, but you're responsible."

Kittel pulled on the sheepskin jacket and placed the fur cap on his head.

"I walked through a huge Russian camp with these," he said, grinning.

"We thought he was an Ivan trying to spy on us," interjected the infantry Leutnant.

Kittel said goodbye to the soldiers and promised to shoot down at least two "butchers" the next time he saw action. Then he climbed into the Kübelwagen beside Oberleutnant Götz, who took him back to the airfield.

When Kittel got out in front of the command post he found everyone who could walk assembled there—his mechanics, friends, even Rex, the wing commander's dog. He was highly amused when Oberstleutnant Trautloft asked "where Kittel was." It took the commander a moment to recognize his successful pilot. Also there to help celebrate were Oberfeldwebel Brönnle and Oberleutnant Hans Götz. (Only a few months later, on 4 August 1943, Hans Götz, victor in eighty-two combats, would be killed in the Karachev area while attacking Il-2 close-support aircraft. He lost control of his machine and crashed inverted into a wood, where he died in the subsequent explosion and fire.)

There were two events to celebrate in Krasnogvardeysk on that eventful 17 March 1943. One was the return of Oberfeldwebel Kittel from behind enemy lines, the other the 203rd victory by Major Hans Philipp, who had become the most successful fighter pilot in the Luftwaffe for a short time.

Kittel sat down with the two great aces, wing commander Trautloft and group commander Philipp, at the "birthday table" set up in honor of his fortunate return. Personnel in the operations center had meanwhile calculated that he must have walked eighty kilometers on his trek to freedom.

THE WING COMMANDER—HIS MEN

Otto Kittel was one of the most reserved pilots in the entire wing. Despite that, he was considered a good comrade by his friends on account of his unshakeable calm, his presence of mind and his sense of duty. He was also treated with the utmost respect by his superiors. For his part, Kittel had found a number of role models in the wing. Heading the list was the wing commander, Hannes Trautloft. His wing had shot down more than 4,000 enemy aircraft by early 1943—no mean feat. Such success required strict leadership and capable planning. He had forged the iron core of the wing from a handful of individualists. Everything that made such a closely-knit formation was rooted in the person of the wing commander.

Hannes Trautloft had served in Spain. Prior to that, he had been an instructor and trainer of fighter pilots in Schleißheim. By the time the 4,000th victory came, he had been in command of the 54th Fighter Wing for three years. Trautloft was a born flier. His special interest was sports—skiing, climbing and, above all else, handball. He created an almost civilian atmosphere for his men when they were off duty. He knew everyone, down to the last armorer, and many of their families as well.

Trautloft's greatest service, however, was the time he spent toward the training and welfare of the replacements. This had made Otto Kittel an experienced fighter pilot, helping him live through many ticklish situations to fight again. They were all united under the emblem of the "Green Heart."

✠

Kittel respected the many personalities within the group, but he developed a special friendship with one. It was Hans Philipp, who commanded the wing's 1st Group and had previously led the 4th Squadron. "Fips," as Philipp was called, and Kittel talked frequently. The subjects were usually home and flying. Philipp had been in the Luftwaffe since 1936. He received the Knight's Cross on 22 October 1940 and the Oak Leaves on 24 August 1941. The months that followed witnessed his most successful period. By 17 March 1943, the day Kittel returned from behind the lines, he had raised his victory total from 63 to 203. He was thus the most successful of all German fighter pilots at the time.

When Kittel came over to personally congratulate his friend on his 203rd victory, Philipp—a Major at that point who was soon to be promoted to Oberstleutnant—said: "You'll get there too, Otto. You have what it takes, you're one of those who won't let rapid victories make him careless. And that is the key to victory."

"Man, Hans, I don't even have the Knight's Cross, and I don't even dare think about it."

"But you will. With thirty-nine kills you're almost due."

"I fear that you're completely mistaken. Surely, I will have to bring down at least 100 of the enemy before they even notice that I'm here," said Kittel without resentment and with a trace of a knowing smile. "You also know that we—in spite of all our comradeship—have several officers with terrible sore throats and a big mouth." (The expression "sore throat" was used by members of the armed forces to refer to someone eager to obtain the Knight's Cross, which was a neck award.)

"Yes, of course I know that. Everyone beats his own drum, and you've made quite a name for yourself with your flight across half of Russia."

"True, but remember it was quite involuntary. If only I could get some leave. I've got a wife at home who wants to have her first baby."

Kittel and Major Nowotny (center) review the assembled members of the unit.

"Don't worry, Otto. I'll see to it that you're one of the first in the group to get leave. Then you can go home and take your 'long-distance wife' in your arms. With best wishes from me . . . after all I did serve as your 'pastor.'"

Both men fell into silence, recalling a scene at the base at Krasnog-vardeysk in June 1942. Otto Kittel was standing in front of a table bedecked with the Reich war flag. He stood at attention as his commanding officer and friend conducted the proxy wedding ceremony between him and his fiancée. The witnesses were his squadron colleagues. The administrative sergeant noted everything with the time and date. When it was over, Kittel was a married man. To the left and right behind the men, directly opposite Kittel, stood two aircraft. One was his own, the other belonged to a com-rade. Siegler, Guth, Forbrig, and Oberleutnant Götz were also there to offer congratulations on behalf of the 3rd Squadron. Kittel longed to finally take his young wife—whom he had known and loved for many years—in his arms. Major Philipp kept his word in that respect. After sev-eral missions in March and April, Otto Kittel received a well-earned leave and was able to rest at home with his parents and wife.

Soon after their conversation Major Philipp was forced to leave the wing. On 1 April 1943 he was to take over command of the 1st Fighter Wing, based in Germany. The tide of events ended the comradeship between Kittel and Philipp. The latter was killed in action on 8 October 1943. At the time of his death, Philipp knew that Kittel had reached 100 victories and still had not received the Knight's Cross.

FIFTIETH VICTORY

When Otto Kittel returned from leave, Hans Philipp was no longer the group commander. In his place was a pilot who had earlier received the Knight's Cross with the 9th Squadron and who was rapidly making a name for himself: Hauptmann Walter Nowotny. He was a brilliant aviator who was racking up kills at an impressive rate. Nowotny and Kittel hit it off straight away. If there was anything Nowotny especially valued, it was courage and level-headedness.

As the Russian summer began, Oberfeldwebel Otto Kittel was one of most successful pilots of the 3rd Squadron. On 3 May there was an alert: Soviet bombers were en route to attack the base. Kittel and another pilot took off before the bombers—DB-3s with a strong fighter escort—reached the airfield. The second pair of fighters that made up the *Schwarm* took off right behind Kittel's *Rotte*. By the time the enemy aircraft were nearing Krasnogvardeysk, the four fighters were above them. All four dove on the escort, which scattered. Machine-gun and cannon fire rang out. The Focke-Wulfs flashed past the escort and opened fire on the bombers. Kittel's chosen target fell after two bursts. Someone called out that the bombers were jettisoning their loads. Kittel looked and saw the DB-3s release the bombs suspended beneath their fuselages. They fell to earth and exploded.

Three bombers had gone down when Kittel's wingman called out a warning: "*Rata* behind you, Otto!"

Kittel swerved left out of the danger zone. The enemy fighter flashed past him and began a reversal, which placed him right in front of Kittel's machine.

The two fighters approached each other head on and simultaneously opened fire from 200 meters. The Russian pulled up just before he fired and his rounds missed the target. Kittel put his aircraft into a steep turn. This time the Soviet pilot had flown too far before turning; he took a full burst from cockpit to tail. The *Rata* blew apart and pieces whirled through the air. The bombers turned toward the east. One pair of Focke-Wulfs dived on them as they turned. Flames belched from the fuselages of two of the bombers; both Russian machines crashed and exploded. Kittel and his wingman set out after the *Ratas*, which had likewise turned for home. One of the enemy pilots obviously mistook them for his own. They were probably no more than shadowy outlines in his rear-view mirror.

"Cover me," Kittel called to his wingman and raced closer and closer to the enemy aircraft. At only seventy meters he pressed the triggers. Hits flashed all over the I-16; it staggered, went down vertically and crashed.

"That was your third, Otto," called Kittel's wingman, who had noted the time and place of all three kills.

As they flew back to base, the two pilots suddenly spotted a bomber in front of them. It had obviously lost an engine; it was flying very slowly. Kittel sheared out of formation and dove towards the bomber. The enemy gunners opened fire from at least 400 meters. Kittel heard bullets tearing the metal skin of his aircraft. He felt something strike his knee and realized that his engine must have been hit. Seconds later, oil covered his windscreen. The engine sputtered and Kittel tried to keep it from dying.

Kittel called the group: "I've been hit . . . have engine damage. Must land."

"Use 122's airfield. It's the most favorable," came the answer from the group not a half minute later. The group operations section was referring to the airfield used by the 122nd Army Support Aviation Group. Kittel knew the airfield, but he hadn't thought of it until then.

"I'm landing there," he informed his pilots. "Send someone for me."

"Understood, Otto! Break a leg!"

Kittel turned in the direction of the army airfield; it was about four kilometers away. His engine was on its last legs. Kittel called the airfield and received permission to land. A red flare showed him the exact way and also told any local reconnaissance aircraft that might be preparing to land that an emergency was in progress and that they should remain clear.

Kittel saw the airfield; as he descended, he also saw an ambulance driving to the end of the runway. The engine sputtered and then quit. Kittel set the propeller blades in the gliding position and just managed to reach the touchdown point. The aircraft rolled and bucked like mad and he jettisoned the canopy to enable a quick exit if it should catch fire.

The Focke-Wulf finally came to a stop at the far end of the field. A fire truck rolled up and pointed its two nozzles at the aircraft. Kittel placed both hands on the cockpit side and vaulted out. He ran the few steps to the ambulance and jumped inside. The ambulance drove away from the aircraft, while the fire truck hosed down the engine, which had begun to smolder.

The Hauptmann in command of the reconnaissance group greeted him: "Congratulations, Kittel. They'll be here to pick you up at any moment."

The staff car arrived five minutes later and Kittel jumped in. They drove to the command post, where he filed claims for his three victories, which had already been reported by his wingman. Then he had to tell about the "Sunday salvo" from the Russian; he then learned that his wingman had subsequently attacked and shot down the bomber.

✠

The next day Kittel took off in a "borrowed" airframe; his own had not been returned yet and would need repairs before he could take it into the air again. Kittel scored further kills in the days that followed. He was getting ready for the next mission on the morning of 10 June, when his mechanic said hopefully: "Surely, we'll be able to paint on the 50th today, sir!"

"No predictions, Wölm," Kittel said to the ground crewman. "We will see!"

The mission given Kittel and the others was a fighter sweep over a Soviet airbase that was home to a *Rata* regiment. He and Tietze and the other two members of the *Schwarm*—Heutin and Krutzke—had worked out a plan for luring the *Rata*s into the air. It was 1030 hours when the

Schwarm took off. Visibility was good, approximately twenty-five kilometers. The only cloud cover was a thin layer at a height of about 3,500 meters. They watched as the Russians took off. Kittel estimated the number of *Rata*s at about ten. They timed the bounce perfectly and hit the Russian fighters while they were climbing. A turbulent dogfight broke out. Kittel's wingman pulled up into a climb, trying to draw an enemy fighter with him. It worked immediately; there was a *Rata* on his tail in seconds. By flying at full throttle, Tietze was able to keep the enemy at a distance.

He called Kittel and the latter answered. Tietze knew that Kittel was in position. He flew straight ahead, passed the airfield antiaircraft defensive belt, and then made a gentle left turn. Kittel was sitting behind Tietze's pursuer at that point; he moved his hand forward to cover the firing buttons. Kittel waited until he had closed to within eighty meters; then he fired, just as the Soviet pilot realized that he was in danger. The I-16 spun around as it took the full weight of the burst. The Soviet aircraft went down trailing a stream of fire. It crashed and exploded.

"He's gone, Tietze," called Kittel.

Two minutes later Tietze also shot down an I-16. There was only one Soviet aircraft left in the air, and the three remaining pilots saw it. Kittel was the first to engage. It must have been the leader of the Soviet squadron, a very experienced pilot, who had taken off. The two aircraft looped and rolled, fired inverted, and dove. The two went round and round in a carousel that must end in the death of one of them. Kittel later described that engagement to his friend Oberleutnant Götz:

> Suddenly, he was on my tail and opened fire from 200 meters. I put the nose down and, glancing at the airspeed indicator, saw that I had 600 kilometers on the clock. The BMW held out. I gained some breathing space and climbed back up to 3,000 meters. My opponent attacked. He wanted to send me to Hell; that was certain. There wasn't any point in taking off, if you didn't have that unshakeable will.
>
> We had already been circling for twenty minutes and had both fired without success.
>
> When I saw the red light come on, I knew that I had to end the engagement immediately, either by shooting down my opponent or taking to my heels as fast as I could go.
>
> I tried diving once again. I pulled up at 1,200 meters. I climbed above him in a loop and ended up on his tail. I was then 100 meters behind my opponent, who broke to the right. More

expecting this reaction than seeing it, I also turned right and opened fire with my cannon. The engine and cockpit hood flew away under the impacts. I watched as the enemy aircraft spun down in a steep spiral and crashed.

I heard Tietze's voice: "You got him, now let's go home."

We still had forty kilometers to fly. I had just enough fuel to reach our base and land - not without first waggling my wings, of course.

My mechanic came running. "You got fifty!" He shouted, his face beaming. I just nodded and let him unfasten my parachute straps. I thought of my opponent and, somehow, I felt sorry. After all he was only an aviator as well; it was just that he was on the other side of the fence.

This illustrates both Kittel the aviator and the man; even though he was happy to have achieved that important victory, he felt respect for his defeated opponent. He acknowledged his ability as a pilot and felt regret at his death.

✠

Otto Kittel had reached fifty victories. The wing would soon see action in the Battle of Kursk. It was to be an ordeal that demanded the utmost of every member of the 54th Fighter Wing. It was in that area of operations that Otto Kittel would begin his meteoric rise to become the top-scoring pilot in the wing, and one of the leading pilots in the fighter arm.

THE 54TH FIGHTER WING
AS THE "FIRE-BRIGADE OF THE FRONT"

Beginning in the spring of 1943, the wing under Oberstleutnant Trautloft was increasingly called upon to undertake relief actions on the Eastern Front. The two groups still in the east, the 1st and the 2nd, were sent to threatened areas of the front like a sort of flying fire brigade. They appeared for a short time over Finland, as well as over the southern and central sectors of the front. The 54th fought over the Ukraine and the Crimean Peninsula. The lack of sufficiently strong fighter units on the Eastern Front caused the rapid transfers to new theaters of operations. The fronts in Italy and France, and especially in defense of the homeland, were all crying out for fighters. German fighter forces were insufficient to meet the many needs placed upon it.

A downed Soviet Polikarpov I-16 fighter.

In the spring of 1943 the "Green Heart" fighters were operating over the army units in the Vyazma-Bryansk area. From April to May 1943 the 4th Group took part in the struggle against the growing strength of the Red Air Force over the Crimea. The pilots of the 54th flew from bases at Orel, Vyazma, Bryansk, Vitebsk, Kiev, Kharkov, and Poltava. They were also based at Mamaia Orsha and Nevel, Vinnitsa and Zhitomir, Polotsk, Dünaburg and, finally, also in Dorpat.

VICTORIES

Oberstleutnant Trautloft was forced to leave his pilots when Operation Citadel began. His transfer to the post of "Inspector East" on the staff of the General in Command of Fighters had been decided long before. Nevertheless, Trautloft would have preferred to remain with his wing; it was facing unprecedented burdens in those days.

The new wing commander was Major Hubertus von Bonin. He had also participated in the Spanish Civil War, where he shot down four enemy aircraft. He later destroyed nine enemy aircraft while flying with the 26th Fighter Wing over the English Channel. On 1 January 1940 von Bonin was named to command the 1st Group of the 54th. He was then transferred to the 52nd Fighter Wing's 3rd Group, where he became the group commander. He returned to the 54th as a Major. Von Bonin had received the Knight's Cross on 21 December 1942 after his fifty-first victory.

Major Reinhard Seiler commanded the 1st Group. He was an experienced pilot, having achieved nine victories in Spain. He had received the Knight's Cross on 20 December 1941, when he was the commander of the 3rd Group. (Seiler shot down his 100th enemy aircraft on 6 July 1943. He was seriously wounded in action soon afterward and was evacuated to Germany. Although seriously handicapped, he returned to the front and assumed command of the 104th Fighter Wing in August 1944. His ultimate total was 109 victories. After his 100th victory he was the 419th member of the armed forces to receive the Oak Leaves.)

The 5th of July saw the 54th's 1st Group in action over the northern pincer of the Kursk Front, where elements of the 9th Army under Generaloberst Model were attacking. Hitler's directive for this attack read:

> The objective of this attack is to encircle and destroy the enemy forces in the Kursk area by launching a highly concentrated and rapid thrust by two armies from the areas of Belgorod (southern pincer with the 4th Panzer Army and Army Detachment Kempf) and south of Orel (9th Army).

Generalfeldmarschall von Kluge, Commander-in-Chief of Army Group Center had selected Generaloberst Model and the 9th Army for the northern pincer; Generalfeldmarschall von Manstein led the southern pincer. The eastern flank of the 4th Panzer Army was to be guarded by Army Detachment Kempf.

Warned in advance of the coming German offensive, the Red Air Force launched a preventive strike from five airfields in the Kharkov area aimed at destroying the German air forces on the ground on the morning of 5 July 1943. The Soviet air commanders had obviously learned something of German air-war doctrine. According to Soviet sources, 132 Il-2 close-support aircraft and 285 escorting fighters took part in a single raid on the German bases on 5 July. They attacked eight German airfields and claimed fifty aircraft destroyed on the ground.

✠

The alarm woke the men of the 2nd Group of the 54th Fighter Wing from their sleep at approximately 0330 hours on 5 July 1943. The day before and throughout the past week they had flown several attacks against the surprisingly inactive Soviets. Otto Kittel had raised his victory total to fifty-six. He and the other members of the 3rd Squadron ran to their aircraft, which had been readied by the mechanics.

"All clear, sir," declared the mechanic as he helped Kittel into his parachute harness. Kittel closed the Plexiglas hood and saw the squadron commander and the lead *Rotte* taxiing for takeoff. Exactly 20 seconds later he was given the flag signal to taxi with the next *Rotte*. Within seconds of receiving clearance for takeoff Kittel was racing down the runway. The Focke-Wulf soared into the pale morning sky, and Kittel could see the rising sun on the horizon to his left as he reached 2,000 meters.

Oberleutnant Götz informed his pilots of the contents of the urgent message he had seen in the group command post: "Squadron commander to everyone: Fighters and butchers reported approaching Orel. They took off from Samodurovka and Bobrik."

They crossed the Russian front south of Trossna and were fired on ineffectively by several antiaircraft batteries. Then Oberleutnant Götz' wingman reported a formation of Il-2s. Kittel and several others confirmed the sighting. Götz instructed his pilots to spread out on line and prepare for a squadron attack from above.

The Fw-190s dove on the Il-2s from 2,000 meters above. The Soviet bombers stubbornly held their course. As he dove toward the gaggle of squat, heavily-armored Il-2s—each of which was carrying two 250-kilo bombs—Kittel saw the Soviet fighters above the bombers break formation in order to intercept the attacking Germans. Kittel had completed his reversal and found himself 1,000 meters behind the gaggle. Suddenly, he was fired on from behind. He veered hard right and then turned again after several hundred meters. He then turned once again to avoid a burst fired in his direction.

He then raced toward his first target; the Il-2 grew larger and larger in his gun sight. Kittel fired all weapons and saw yellow flashes as his rounds struck the fuselage of the enemy aircraft—and bounced off! Kittel put the Focke-Wulf's nose down. He still had an escort fighter on his tail. At that point, he was at about 1,200 meters altitude and 200 meters beneath a formation of three Il-2s. Overhauling the bombers rapidly, Kittel put the Fw-190 into a gentle climb. The firing behind him began to die down; the enemy pilot was probably holding his fire to avoid hitting his own aircraft.

At that point only 100 meters behind the Il-2, Kittel was out of the enemy gunner's field of file. He closed until he was sure he could not miss and opened file. Cannon rounds smashed the Ilyushin's oil cooler. Kittel veered right immediately, which was just as well. A stream of oil spewed forth from the enemy aircraft and ignited, forming a fiery comet's tail that followed the Il-2 as it plunged to the ground. He was then at the same height as the enemy. Kittel turned again and was hit several times by return fire. Jinking wildly, he evaded the fire from the gunners of the two

Il-2s and then dropped into position beneath one of them. Kittel scored several hits on the Soviet aircraft, which went down and crashed.

Kittel pulled up into a climb, passing several enemy fighters as he did so. One of these scored several hits on the German fighter. Kittel then swooped upward into a high loop, which put him behind the Soviet. He dove on the enemy fighter and, using his infallible sense for calculating the required amount of lead, pressed the triggers at precisely the right second. The Soviet fighter flew through the stream of rounds and blew apart. Kittel flew on and chased a Russian fighter off Oberleutnant Götz' tail. The red fuel-warning light came on and Kittel turned for home. He waggled his wings four times as he passed over the airfield. Kittel landed safely and taxied over to the dispersal area where his two mechanics and the armorers would be waiting to refuel and rearm his aircraft.

The first to congratulate him was Hauptmann Seiler. Kittel saw that two members of the squadron had already landed, his friends Tietze and Lanzenbacher. The latter was already showing promise of becoming one of the good pilots. Kittel had a few sips of coffee in the canteen and ate some of the leftover breakfast before going to his quarters. There he lay down on his cot, took several deep breaths and was sound asleep in less than two minutes. It was afternoon by the time he woke up. There had been another alert and the 2nd Squadron, which had been on strip alert, had taken off. The 3rd Squadron was going to strip alert at that point. The pilots walked out to their aircraft.

"Everything's in order, sir," declared Grünberg. A few scrapes . . . weapons oiled and ready . . . ammunition belts filled and likewise clear."

The pilots sat down on the chairs and cots and let the sun shine on their faces. It was 1625 hours when the order to take off was given. Russian bombers were on their way to attack units of the 20th Panzer Division that had advanced as far as Gnizez. Kittel and the others took off in pairs. Flying with him on that occasion was Tietze.

The Focke-Wulfs gained height rapidly and set course toward the southeast. Near Tagino an officer of the XLVII Panzer Corps fired the predesignated signal flare, the signal that they were to turn south. Two minutes later they saw the first exploding bombs from the enemy attack. The fighters split up and attacked the bombers that had not yet released their loads.

Kittel approached a bomber head on and took aim at the cockpit. He must have killed the pilot; the bomber went straight down and exploded among the forward Soviet defensive positions like a flying bomb. A minor course correction placed another Soviet bomber in his sights; it also went down in seconds. The other members of the squadron shot down six more enemy bombers.

When 5 July came to an end and the total of enemy aircraft shot down was tallied, it was revealed that the Soviet 2nd and 17th Air Armies had lost 120 of the more than 400 aircraft which they sent into action that day. Otto Kittel alone had accounted for six of them. The day was not without cost to the German side, however. Several members of the 54th Fighter Wing were killed in action on 5 July.

✠

The 6th of July was another day of hectic action and, once again, Kittel was in the forefront of the operations, downing three Soviet aircraft. It was on that day that the group commander, Major Seiler, was seriously wounded. His place was to be taken by Major Gerhard Homuth. Homuth would come to the group from the 27th Fighter Wing, the wing which had achieved such success in Africa and which produced the most successful of all German pilots against the Western Allies, Hans-Joachim Marseille. Homuth didn't reach the Eastern Front until 1 August 1943; until then the individual squadron commanders took turns leading the group.

Otto Kittel was kept extremely busy during the "Citadel" operations, when the wing was frequently called upon to assist the ground troops under attack by the "butchers." Victories came so fast that Kittel had difficulty keeping track. Only his iron will to give his all and yet survive enabled him to come through.

The primary role of the fighter pilots operating in the north was to provide air cover for the forces of the northern pincer. The northern group's forward progress was stopped at Hill 272 north of Molotytschin and at the rail junction at Ponyri. With the major objective in the extreme east—Maloarchangelsk—still in enemy hands, the northern pincer's attack bogged down. Even repeated attacks on enemy positions using 50- and 250-kilogram bombs did nothing to change the situation.

The new group commander, Major Homuth, was shot down and killed on 3 August. Once again Oberleutnant Götz filled in. Sadly, Kittel's friend was shot down and killed in the Karachev area on 4 August. At the time of his death, Götz had 82 kills to his credit. He had been awarded the Knight's Cross on 23 December 1942. Hauptmann Nowotny, former commander of the 1st Squadron, assumed command of the group on 10 August.

On 17 July 1943, Feldwebel Meißner had recorded the wing's 5,000th victory, an indication of the continued success enjoyed by the Green Heart

Wing. The 6,000th would be achieved by Hauptmann Nowotny on 9 October 1943.

Otto Kittel's performance in the engagements that followed surpassed anything he had done so far. He was in the air whenever possible. With the Battle of Kursk over, it was vital that the German forces hold onto Orel, which was under assault by Soviet forces. The old Tsarist city was prepared for demolition; it was only a matter of time before it was overrun by the Soviets. A large number of German and Russian soldiers died in the Orel Salient. According to German sources, the Soviets had lost 5,015 armored vehicles and 1,854 aircraft since fighting began there on 5 July.

The last great concentration of German aviation forces had fought a tremendous battle. In addition to the 2nd and 17th Air Armies, the Soviets threw the 16th Air Army under General Rudenko into the struggle. That air army had concentrated its attacks against the 9th Army. The 6th Mixed Flying Corps and the 2nd Guards Close-Support Division halted German infantry and armored attacks until they were driven off by the few German fighters.

It was in the Kursk area of operations that Otto Kittel's star began its dramatic ascent. The rising star on the Soviet side was Captain Ivan Kozhedub. During his first mission over Kursk, Kozhedub, who flew an La-5, was

A Bf-109 of the 54th Fighter Wing. It returned safely to base in spite of flak damage to its port horizontal stabilizer.

shot up by two Fw-190s. Although the German fighters shot off one of his aircraft's wingtips, he managed to return to base and land safely. On the third day of "Citadel" he shot down two Ju-87s and then destroyed two escorting Bf-109s. At the end of the Battle of Kursk he received the Order of the Red Banner and was promoted to squadron commander.

One of the prominent Soviet bomber units was the 1st Bomber Corps under Colonel I. S. Polbin. It attacked concentrations of German armor at Prokhorovka. Its 291st Close-Support Division inflicted heavy losses on the German forces.

The Luftwaffe lost 487 aircraft in the Battle of Kursk; this figure climbed by a further 785 machines in the period of the Soviet Orel offensive which lasted until the end of August. Total German losses in that sector were thus 1,272 aircraft. Such severe losses could no longer be made good, especially of trained pilots and crews.

When the Soviets launched their Orel counteroffensive, the Red Air Force committed more than 3,300 aircraft against an estimated 1,100 German airframes. Three Soviet air armies attacked Orel from three sides: the 1st Air Army from the western front; the 15th Air Army from the Bryansk front; and, the 16th Air Army from the central front. Stavka, the Soviet High Command, sent selected formations to the front. The 2nd Bomber, 2nd Close-Support and 8th Fighter Corps were assigned to the 1st Air Army. The other two air armies also received adequate reinforcements.

It was as part of the counteroffensive by the Soviet land forces in August that the Red Air Force launched its first full-scale air offensive. General Novikov, the commander-in-chief of the Soviet air forces, committed his formations to the maximum possible degree.

As a result of these large-scale air attacks and Soviet attempts to destroy the German airfields and deprive the Luftwaffe of its bases, the men of the 54th Fighter Wing were simply overwhelmed. In spite of that, they continued to take to the air and fight. In a sensational run of victories that saw him shoot down at least one enemy aircraft every day, Otto Kittel had raised his victory total to ninety-four by 4 September. For most pilots that would have been more than enough to be awarded the Knight's Cross. But Kittel kept flying and fighting; he had no use for self-promotion. It was Hauptmann Nowotny who interceded with Major von Bonin on Kittel's behalf. On 4 September 1943 Nowotny had became the 293rd recipient of the Oak Leaves after his 189th victory. Kittel himself knew nothing of what was happening in the background. His first concern was to survive the struggle in order to return to his wife and son, who had only recently been born.

In the course of his second mission on 15 September, Kittel and several comrades ran into a large formation of enemy bombers. He shot down two bombers and was then jumped by two Soviet fighters. Kittel evaded the fighters and managed to shoot one of them down. When he landed—again with several dozen holes in his "pelt," as he called it—he was greeted by his crew chief, who was holding up a placard. On it Kittel saw a stylized wreath of laurel leaves. Inside it in large characters was the number 100.

Only then did he realize that his three kills had raised his total to that magic number. In spite of his objections, Kittel was raised onto the shoulders of his two mechanics, who carried him toward the group command post in a triumphant procession. Hauptmann Nowotny stepped outside. Kittel straightened himself up and reported to his commander.

"Thank you, Kittel. You are playing an important part in the defensive fighting. A report just came from the front from the 352nd Infantry Division, which wishes to thank you."

"Thank you, sir, but there's not much to talk about. I merely jumped in and took apart two Il-2s."

That was the hard language of the front, a language spoken by everyone to avoid being overwhelmed by events. It was a defensive mechanism of the body and spirit to ensure continued and ultimate survival. Nowotny clapped his best Oberfeldwebel on the shoulder. "The report that's been lying around at wing because of all the changes will be sent out today, I promise you that."

"A few days rest wouldn't be bad either, sir," replied Kittel. But rest was the only thing he couldn't get in those turbulent days.

The fighting went on, as did the killing and dying. On 19 August 1943 Oberleutnant Max Stotz, victor in 189 air battles and recipient of the Oak Leaves—which he received after 100 kills—was shot down in combat against Soviet fighters over Vitebsk. He was seen to bail out and as he came down in enemy territory and was posted missing in action. This illustrates the inconsistencies in the evaluation of victories displayed by the higher levels of command. While Max Stotz received the Oak Leaves after 100 victories—and deservedly so—Kittel was still without the Knight's Cross after 100 kills.

On 22 September 1943 Hauptmann Nowotny received the swords after 218 victories. A few days later, following his 220th kill, he became the first member of the wing to receive the Knight's Cross with Oak Leaves, Swords and Diamonds.

THE KNIGHT'S CROSS

Otto Kittel continued to score in the days and weeks that followed. Once his aircraft was badly shot up in a dogfight. He just managed to reach German territory, where he made a forced landing. Kittel escaped just before the aircraft exploded. The infantry took him "home" to their bunker in a triumphal procession. They showered him with honors and gifts. The battalion commander had already reported his arrival to the regiment and soon Oberst Kaellner was standing in front of the airman. "I'm pleased that this unintentional landing has brought you to us, for it gives us the opportunity to thank you personally for your many efforts on our behalf. You've saved the lives of many comrades of the infantry and, indeed, often saved the entire sector for us."

Kittel half raised his hands in desperation, but then let them drop again. "Thank you, sir. If we do our duty in the air, your soldiers do the same here in the foxholes. But compared to you, we live in the land of milk and honey."

"Nonetheless, Kittel, you should know that if you were in my regiment you wouldn't be walking around without a collar," he said, referring to the Knight's Cross, like the one worn by his battalion commander.

After an opulent lunch and a cup of coffee a staff car arrived to pick up Oberfeldwebel Kittel and take him back to his unit. He received an enthusiastic reception when he arrived. There was an aircraft available—its regular pilot was ill—and that afternoon Kittel took to the air again and shot down an enemy aircraft. Major von Bonin had already submitted a recommendation for the Knight's Cross for Kittel, but von Bonin's patience was to be sorely tested as well.

October was almost over when, on the 26th, Otto Kittel took off to intercept an attack by Soviet ground-attack aircraft. There were 123 victory bars on the tail of his aircraft at that point. He also had at least 30 unconfirmed victories in his log book—aircraft shot down or damaged in the course of his numerous solo missions when there was no one there to witness his kills. Kittel didn't report those victories. He wasn't in favor of unconfirmed kills, especially since he had no desire to appear to be more than he really was. All of his 123 kills had been confirmed several times.

When Kittel and the others arrived at the dispersal area they saw the unit mascot, a mongrel dog they called "Ivan," standing beside Feldwebel Becker. The dog was wagging its tail gratefully as Becker fed it corned beef from a tin. The dog was extremely fussy, turning up its nose at lesser treats, meat paste on bread, for example. Kittel's latest victory had been chalked up on the rudder of his aircraft the day before. He strolled over to his comrades, who were standing around listening to the squadron jokester. In those days they usually flew to the Dniepr, where the Red Army had forced a crossing some weeks ago.

On 10 October the intelligence battalion of the Luftwaffe High Command placed the number of Soviet combat aircraft stationed in the Nevel area at 747, of which 300 were fully serviceable. The Russian attempts to break through on both sides of the Smolensk-Orsha highway were frustrated.

In the distance smoke could be seen rising from the burning cities on the Dniepr River; He-111 formations had bombed them as part of the effort to halt the Soviet assault. Then a forward observer sounded the alarm. The pilots clambered into their machines. Just as he was about to take off, Kittel sighted four or five enemy aircraft. He raced across the grass surface of the airfield, lifted off and then put his aircraft into a steep turn in the direction of the five approaching aircraft. He was the first off the ground and took it upon himself to engage the enemy until help arrived. His Fw-190 was pointed at the middle aircraft, a Yak-3. Seconds later it filled his illuminated sight and Kittel fired. His bursts rocked the enemy machine. Flames licked over its canopy, and a cloud of dark smoke poured out from beneath its tail. Then the canopy flew away and a dark figure fell clear. Seconds later a parachute billowed in the Russian sky.

"Got him, Otto. He's finished!" called his wingman.

Leaving the four remaining enemy aircraft to the others who had followed him into the air, Kittel flew on. He gained altitude and then spotted the next enemy formation; they were LaGG-3 fighter-bombers, not as fast as the Yaks. He flew toward the enemy formation, jinking left and right to avoid the enemy tracers. He then climbed even higher.

By the time he turned in behind the enemy formation he was at least 1,000 meters higher. Reversing course, Kittel dove on the LaGGs from above. He scored solid hits on one of the enemy fighters; it began to burn and turned away. Two Soviet fighters tried to engage him in a head-on pass. Kittel evaded by putting his aircraft into an upward roll, leveling out and firing again. The LaGG-3 pulled away, executed an unbelievably tight turn and opened fire. Kittel pulled the stick back as far as it would go, putting the Focke-Wulf into a steep climbing turn.

He felt the airframe vibrating, a sign that the aircraft was on the verge of a stall. He looked back and saw the LaGG behind and beneath him. The Focke-Wulf stalled at the top of the loop and began to spin toward the earth, leaving the Soviet fighter even farther behind. Kittel carefully brought the aircraft out of the spin and pulled back on the stick to bring it out of its dive. A glance at the altimeter revealed that he was 2,000 meters above the ground. Then he froze; three MiG-3s were approaching from directly in front at about the same altitude.

Kittel tramped on the left rudder pedal and changed course. He continued to descend at full power and watched as the needle of the airspeed indicator climbed to 590 kilometers per hour, then to 620 kilometers per hour. It finally stopped at 700 kilometers per hour. At five-hundred meters Kittel began to pull out of the dive; the Focke-Wulf leveled out at only 250 meters above the ground. The enemy aircraft had been left far behind. Kittel began to climb and reversed course in a shallow turn. Continuing his climb, Kittel reached a position above the flight of MiGs. He opened fire from 120 meters and put two bursts into a MiG-3 before he was forced to veer off by two others. When his red fuel-warning light came on, he turned away and raced for home. As he filed his combat report, Kittel realized that he had raised his victory total to 127.

Eric Rudorffer shot down 224 enemy aircraft, including 11 heavy bombers. He had 86 victories in the West (12 in the Me-262) and 138 in the East.

The next day Kittel came down with a severe case of diarrhea and was unable to fly. The following day, when he was fit to fly again, he was summoned to the wing command post. When he arrived he saw a man from the air corps staff standing beside Major von Bonin. He had no idea why so many of his friends were there, including several from other squadrons. Not until he was ordered to step forward and face the assembled squadron did he begin to suspect something was up. Then it finally happened; Major von Bonin presented Otto Kittel the Knight's Cross in the name of the Führer.

Otto Kittel felt no triumph or special joy arise in him. When von Bonin asked why he wasn't happier to finally receive the coveted decoration he replied: "I'd almost given up believing it would happen." Then he added: "I was beginning to think that I wasn't included in the roster of wing personnel."

There was a lively celebration. When the alarm was sounded the men around Kittel almost had to physically restrain him; he always wanted to be the first into the air.

Kittel wrote to his wife, telling her that he had received the Knight's Cross. A week later he received a letter back from her, in which she said:

> Dear Otto, my beloved husband!
> I share your joy. Your comrades, who have passed on your greetings to me in the past weeks, tell me that you have earned this decoration.
> Please take good care of yourself!
> I love you very much.
> Your wife.

✠

Otto Kittel was then released by the wing. He was sent to Replacement and Training Group East, where new fighter pilots were indoctrinated into the ways of air combat on the Eastern Front. As an instructor, Kittel was to pass on his knowledge and experience to the next generation of pilots. This activity was a necessary one; it spared blood and machines. Nevertheless, Kittel was not happy in his new job. His promotion to Leutnant came through in January 1944. He submitted a series of requests for transfer back to his old wing, but all ended up in the garbage can. However, the wing's losses had been heavy. When a new squadron commander was needed, Kittel was recalled.

Kittel rejoined the wing at the beginning of March 1944. The 1st Group was based at Wesenberg in Estonia. He reported to the new wing commander, Oberstleutnant Anton Mader, a Knight's Cross recipient who had come over from 77th Fighter Wing. Even though he had remained in touch with his wing during his absence, Kittel was dismayed by the many new faces, which suggested that many of the old ones were no longer there. Major von Bonin had crashed east of Gorodok in the Orsha sector on 15 December 1943 after a ten-minute flight. He and his wingman ran into six Il-2s and six Yak 9 fighters. Von Bonin attacked a straggling Il-2 without effect. He was then jumped by an enemy fighter as he set up for a second pass. Major von Bonin's aircraft was hit and went down from 900 meters in a left-hand turn. It crashed at 1339 hours. The body of the wing commander was recovered on the German side of the lines. This outstanding wing commander, this fatherly friend to his fighter pilots, was buried with military honors at the cemetery in Orsha (South) on 20 December 1943. Kittel was shaken when he learned of von Bonin's death from the wing adjutant, Reymann. He also owed the wing commander a great deal and his grief was deep and true.

There was a series of other, less tragic, changes before Kittel rejoined the wing. Hauptmann Nowotny, his former group commander, had been transferred to Germany to form an experimental jet-fighter unit. His place had been taken by Oak Leaves recipient, Hauptmann Adameit. (Adameit was forced down in enemy territory with engine damage on 8 August 1944 and was not seen or heard of again. Following his death, Hauptmann Eisenach led the group until the end of the war.)

Leutnant Otto Kittel was placed in command of the depleted 3rd Squadron. As squadron commander he continued to lead the way, scoring steadily. On 4 April 1944 he encountered his first enemy aircraft following his forced absence from the front. Kittel reacted as always and quickly downed the Soviet fighter. After he had landed, the armorer discovered that he had fired only six rounds from his cannon.

Kittel was in action up to three times a day until 8 April. The precision with which he shot down enemy aircraft—whether bombers, close-support aircraft or fighters—was uncanny. If he returned without waggling his wings, it meant that he had not found the enemy or that the enemy had flown away from him. Otto Kittel scored his 150th victory on 8 April. Several days later he shot down two more enemy aircraft. On 11 April 1944 he became the 449th German soldier to receive the Knight's Cross with Oak Leaves.

What then followed was an uninterrupted string of victories. Otto Kittel's aim was unerring and true. He knocked the enemy out of the skies in droves. By 23 September 1944 he had 200 victories; the Swords seemed the only logical recognition of his success. Kittel continued to fly and fight in the northern sector of the front, saving numerous forward positions from destruction at the hands of the Soviet Air Force. He shot down entire formations of Il-2s and waded into the enemy's bombers with his handful of fighters.

✠

By then the wing had been reduced to two groups in the northern sector of the Eastern Front. The 3rd Group had been transferred to Germany, where it suffered heavy losses serving in the defense of the homeland. Formed at Jesau on 1 July 1943 under Hauptmann Rudorffer, the 4th Group initially saw action in the north. At the end of November 1943 Hauptmann Sinner assumed command of the group. Sinner was replaced by Hauptmann Schnell in February 1944. Following Schnell's death the group was led by Hauptmann Koall. In mid-April the group was transferred to the southern sector of the Eastern Front, where its fighters flew escort for He-111 formations operating over the Dnestr Front. This left only the 1st and 2nd Groups of the 54th Fighter Wing in the north of Russia.

✠

In October 1944 Otto Kittel and his handful of fighters faced a foe who was vastly superior in numbers. On one occasion, large numbers of Soviet bombers attacked the German front. Kittel took off to intercept the leading formation. As soon as he and the five aircraft of his squadron reached firing position, Kittel took aim at the first bomber. The enemy gunners opened fire from 350 meters. Kittel dove under the fire and then climbed steeply. He hit the bomber in the wing root with his first burst. The wing of the enemy aircraft immediately began to blaze fiercely. He pulled back gently on the stick and climbed. As he did so he crossed the path of two fighters diving from above. He evaded those and took aim at the next bomber. It also went down in flames.

Kittel then became involved in a turning contest with an enemy fighter. Outmaneuvering his opponent, he positioned himself on the enemy's tail, which sealed his fate. Turning once again, Kittel plunged into the midst of the group of bombers on the right. He shot down the first bomber, then circled round the second and opened fire from the side. Braving the stream of return fire, Kittel raked the Soviet bomber from nose to tail. It also fell from the sky. Soon the red fuel-warning light came on and Kittel set course for home. He waggled his wings four times as he flew over the field; on the ground, his mechanics tossed their caps into the air.

Otto Kittel had shot down his 250th enemy aircraft; he was one of the top German fighter pilots at that point. When he had brought the aircraft to a stop, he sat back for a minute to collect himself and allow the excitement from the bitter air engagement to recede. His men knew that this was his custom and they allowed him a few minutes alone. Not until Kittel climbed down from his aircraft did his men swarm over him and lift him onto their shoulders. They carried him to the group command post where he filed his report.

After offering his congratulations, the group commander said to him: "If you hadn't been away for three months, Kittel, you'd have surely reached 300 by now."

"That's possible, sir," replied Kittel, "but those three months were like a rebirth for me. I was able to experience the birth of my daughter and take a proper vacation."

"But now you're back," observed the commander with a smile. "You know the wing has recommended you for another necktie party [the Swords]."

Kittel shook his head. "You know, sir, all that's not so important any more. When one of us prevents three bombers from dropping their bombs, as I did today, it means life for dozens, perhaps hundreds of soldiers. They're down there below us in the muck, and it cheers them up when we fly low while chasing the butchers. They can see the crosses on our machines and know that they're not alone. If we only had a few more aircraft, then we'd show the Ivans."

✠

On 25 November 1944, Kittel shot down two Soviet close-support aircraft, raising his victory total to 264. He returned to base, made the usual victory pass and landed safely. Kittel was called to the wing command post. There he learned from the wing commander that Hitler had awarded him the Knight's Cross with Oak leaves and Swords.

After 264 victories he had achieved what many of his comrades who lacked his fantastic numbers of enemy aircraft shot down had won before him. Kittel did not begrudge it to them, however. In any case, he had now entered the phalanx of the best fighter pilots in the world. For a simple son of the Sudetenland it had been a long, arduous journey marked by countless struggles and engagements and countless battles with his own fear. Kittel was skeptical when the group clerk, who maintained the list, informed him that he had surpassed his revered former group commander, Walter Nowotny. Nowotny had reached 258 kills. But it was true. The only pilots in front of him were "Bubi" Hartmann, Major Barkhorn and Major Rall.

He received one final leave. He flew to Führer Headquarters to receive the Swords. From there he went straight home to his family. His old friends and the older people of the town treated him like a king, something he didn't want. He and his wife and children withdrew to a winter sports hut where they could be alone. When he returned to the wing in January 1945, Kittel took over the reformed 2nd Squadron. By 13 February he had raised his victory total to 267.

✠

On 14 February 1945 Otto Kittel took off from one of the airfields in Dzukste to intercept a flight of Il-2 close-support aircraft. His comrades reported that he dived into a group of eight Il-2s and opened fire. He hit one of the enemy aircraft; the Il-2 did not go down. Instead it disappeared over the Russian lines, on fire and in trouble. His dismayed comrades then watched as two Il-2s drove Otto Kittel toward another flight of approximately four Il-2s. Kittel's machine was hit hard and, seconds later, burst into flames. His faithful Fw-190 A-8 went down. It trailed a long banner of flame and crashed. Otto Kittel had no chance to take to his parachute.

The foe with which Otto Kittel had fought throughout his career—the Soviet Il-2 close-support aircraft—had claimed his life on his 583rd combat mission. The most successful fighter pilot of the 54th Fighter Wing and the fourth most successful in the entire Luftwaffe was no more. A large percentage of the enemy aircraft he had shot down had been Il-2s. They had taken a bitter revenge.

Otto Kittel was one of the few top fighter pilots to rise from the bottom. He had to work for every kill. He spent the early part of his career as wingman to numerous established aces. He was killed in combat against a numerically superior foe; but attacking superior numbers of the enemy was standard practice for Kittel. Many times he had feared for his life, but each time he managed to escape even the most difficult situations.

He was gone. But he lived on in his old squadron and the new one he had led; his spirit lived on in all of the men who had known him. He had placed his indelible mark on the squadron and his group, giving them the impetus to achieve unbelievable feats. The 1st Group had produced no fewer than thirty-two recipients of the Knight's Cross and a good dozen more who deserved to win the decoration. On the evening Kittel's death was announced, one of his friends said: "Soldiers like Otto Kittel don't die. They merely leave us. But they live on in our hearts and become flying legends."

THE FATE OF THE 54TH FIGHTER WING

The last chapter in the story of the 54th Fighter Wing, a wing with more than 9,600 victories to its credit, began on 8 May 1945 with the retreat from Kurland (Courland). The ground personnel escaped just before the door was closed; they fled to Flensburg, the seat of the German government after 8 May, in navy vessels or in transport aircraft. Soviet air raids on the airfield and port of Libau inflicted heavy losses during the evacuation.

On the morning of 8 May the pilots of the wing took off in pairs and fours for the final flight to Flensburg, where an advance party of 200 men of the ground services were waiting. This advance party had left Neuhausen airfield near Königsberg (Kaliningrad) in mid-January with orders to reach Schleswig-Holstein via Pillau, Stolp, Prenzlau, Güstrow, Lübeck and Kiel.

During the flight back to Germany on 8 May Oberleutnant Gerhard Thyben, commander of the 4th Squadron, shot down a Soviet Pe-2 reconnaissance aircraft over the Baltic west of Libau. It was the last victory claimed by the wing. British soldiers were waiting for the pilots when they landed at Flensburg. A few days later the bulk of the ground personnel, who had traveled by ship, arrived in Flensburg via Kiel. The wing was assigned quarters in the town of Odderage. There the final formation was held in July 1945. Following a brief speech, the wing commander, Oberst Dieter Hrabak, disbanded the wing. One by one, the members of the wing were released; by September 1945 all had left Schleswig-Holstein.

The 54th Fighter Wing, which had fought from the first day of the Second World War to the last, was no more.

THE WING COMMANDER'S EULOGY FOR OTTO KITTEL

Upon the death of Otto Kittel, the wing commander, Oberst Hrabak, spoke the eulogy at his funeral:

Otto Kittel was one of the best men produced by our country. With 267 victories, he was the most successful fighter pilot of the 54th Fighter Wing.

Otto Kittel was born in Komotau on 21 February 1917 and joined the wing's 2nd Squadron in autumn 1941. He wasn't a big man—and actually much too quiet and serious—but he very quickly learned how to fight in the air. On 23 February 1943 he scored his 39th victory, which was also the 4,000th of our wing.

On 15 March 1943 he flew in the *Schwarm* of Oberleutnant Hans Götz, his squadron commander, on a fighter sweep into the area northeast of Staraya Russa. After a victory by Oberleutnant Götz and another by Feldwebel Kittel, the Russians withdrew to the east. The German machines turned for home, but Otto Kittel didn't get far. His motor failed. He must have been hit in the engine during the engagement with his opponent.

He informed his *Schwarm* leader by radio that he had to crash-land. Kittel's machine lost height and Oberleutnant Götz saw the Fw-190 land in open, snow-covered terrain without flipping over or going up in flames. His comrades could not help him. Kittel disappeared into the forest and struck out toward the west.

After three days he reached the southern run-off from Lake Ilmen. He crossed it and reached a German infantry position on the south side of the lake. He had covered 80 kilometers, including detours. Soon he was back with his 2nd squadron in Staraya Russa.

Scarcely had he recovered from the trials of his long trek when he returned to action. He continued his success. On 29 October 1943 Oberfeldwebel Kittel finally received the long-deserved Knight's Cross.

A proud series of victories then started. The Russian air forces grew steadily in strength. Numerically, they were far superior to us and they had also learned a great deal about air combat.

By April 1944 Kittel had reached 150 victories and was promoted to Leutnant for bravery in the face of the enemy. Soon afterward, he was made acting squadron commander and, a little later, became commander of his old 2nd Squadron.

In the fighting in Kurland battles this gifted aviator's name was known on every front. It was there that he met a fighter' pilot's death on 14 February 1945. In the meantime, he had been promoted to Oberleutnant for bravery in the face of the enemy.

Attacked by a large number of Soviet Il-2 close-support aircraft in the Zabeln area, he was able to shoot down one Il-2 before a bullet from the Il-2s rear guns struck. His Fw-190 crashed in flames.

With a total of 267 victories, decorated with the Knight's Cross with Oak Leaves and Swords, he was the most successful fighter pilot of the 54th Fighter Wing and the fourth most successful of the entire Luftwaffe.

Honor his memory!

With 121 night victories in 164 combat missions, Heinz-Wolfgang Schnaufer
was the world's most successful night-fighter pilot.

Heinz-Wolfgang Schnaufer: A Night Fighter Ace

Heinz-Wolfgang Schnaufer joined the Luftwaffe in early 1941 after graduating from high school. After completion of basic training and a number of specialized courses, he was assigned to night fighters in early 1942 Schnaufer scored his first night victory on 2 June 1942 while flying with The the 2nd Group of the 1st Night Fighter Wing. In mid-August 1943 he assumed command of the 1st Squadron of the 1st Night Fighter Wing. By that time Schnaufer had shot down 21 enemy aircraft by night using the various interception methods.

In spite of bad weather, Schnaufer took off to intercept the British bomber stream crossing the breadth of Germany on its way to Berlin on 16 December 1943. In the ensuing engagement, he shot down four Lancaster bombers. A ceiling of only 35 meters made it almost impossible for the night fighters to take off and land, but some risked it. Of the 450 British aircraft that dropped 1,815 tons of bombs on the German capital, 25 were shot down and a further 29 so badly damaged that they were destroyed in crash landings at their home bases.

Schnaufer scored his 50th victory on 25 March 1943. Two months later, on 25 May, he shot down five Lancasters in a span of 14 minutes. Schnaufer registered a total of 39 night victories in the period from 20 January to 25 May 1944. When 1944 came to an end Heinz-Wolfgang Schnaufer was at the top of the list of German night-fighter pilots with 106 victories. He had even surpassed his late friend Oberst Helmut Lent, who died as the result of a flying accident with 102 night and 8 day victories to his credit.

Schnaufer assumed command of the 4th Night Fighter Wing on 10 November 1944. In just four years he had risen from airman to wing commander. In the three hours after midnight on 21 February 1945 he shot down two Lancasters from the groups of bombers returning from bombing Nuremberg. That evening he took to the air again. 373 bombers were attacking Duisburg and another 349 were striking Worms. Heinz-Wolfgang Schnaufer, the "Knight of the Night," shot down seven more bombers.

This feat is all the more remarkable inasmuch as the entire engagement lasted only seventeen minutes.

When the war was over, Schnaufer's aircraft, which had been captured by the Allies, was displayed in Hyde Park in London. Today, a fin and rudder from the aircraft, on which all of Schnaufer's kills are marked, is on display in the Imperial War Museum.

Schnaufer was always the first to give credit for his success to his crew:

> It was my comrades. I always depended on them: On Rumpelhardt, who guided us to the enemy, and on Gänsler, who held the enemy at bay and knocked out the machine gunners in the bombers. When it comes to the necessity of interdependence, there is nothing to compare to a night fighter crew.

Everyone knew that Schnaufer was the heart and brain of this closeknit fighting team. His aggressive spirit was unprecedented, and his inspiration and feeling for special situations made his Bf-110 G4 into a deadly instrument of the night.

SCHNAUFER, THE YOUNG AIRMAN

The gifted Heinz-Wolfgang Schnaufer was graduated from high school at the age of seventeen. Since the age of fourteen his only wish was to become a soldier. Schnaufer easily passed the officer candidate entrance tests.

Schnaufer had an opportunity to fly almost every type of aircraft in the course of his training. His superiors recognized that he had a natural ability and they pushed him to excel. His initial training was as a fighter pilot, and Schnaufer passed the course the first time around. This was followed by a course in instrument flying on heavy fighters, single-engined fighters and Stukas. All these were vitally important assets for a perfect nightfighter pilot. Training in night-fighter tactics rounded out his comprehensive training.

✠

On 1 April 1941 Heinz-Wolfgang Schnaufer received the shoulder boards of a Leutnant. He was subsequently transferred to the new 1st Night Fighter Wing, where he was assigned to the 2nd Group of the 1st Night Fighter Wing. His baptism of fire came late on the evening of 2 June 1942; British bombers were heading toward Duisburg and Oberhausen.

The command center reported large numbers of enemy aircraft. The size of the raid took the German fighter controllers by surprise. (This was the second of the 1,000-plane raids launched by the RAF; the first was on Cologne. The RAF had combed the training units and 347 aircraft of the Operational Training Units took part in the raid.)

For the first time in his life Heinz-Wolfgang Schnaufer was vectored toward an enemy bomber. He and radio operator Fritz Rumpelhardt, who had been assigned to Schnaufer on account of his experience in night fighters, scanned the sky in front of the Messerschmitt. As they closed the distance, they spotted the glowing exhausts of the enemy bomber. Suddenly, several streams of tracer spewed forth from the tail turret.

Schnaufer instinctively dove under the lethal burst and then climbed to approach the bomber at an angle of 25 degrees. When the enemy aircraft filled his sight, he pressed the firing buttons. Schnaufer fired two bursts from his cannon and machine guns. Flames shot from one of the bomber's engines and then there was an explosion. The next burst struck the area of the wing root; the British machine tipped over and went into a vertical dive. It finally crashed and exploded. Schnaufer tried to locate another bomber but without success.

Rumpelhardt consoled his pilot. "Good for your first kill, sir. Perhaps next time it will be more."

Minutes later, Schnaufer landed at the group's base. Of the 726 British aircraft that reached their targets, 32 were shot down. The rest dropped 1,235 tons of bombs on Duisburg and Oberhausen.

Major Streib, the commander of the 1st Group of the 1st Night Fighter Wing, congratulated the Leutnant on his first night kill at the subsequent debriefing.

"Continue to be cautious, Schnaufer, and more victories will follow," said Streib.

✠

In the months that followed, Schnaufer engaged the British bomber fleets on a number of occasions. He scored five more kills in rapid succession and was awarded the Iron Cross, First Class, of which he was most proud. Schnaufer soon learned that locating and attacking the enemy at night was a nerve-wracking business in spite of all the technological aids. In addition, there were the British gunners, men who he knew fought desperately in the knowledge that they were the only defense the bombers had against the prowling night fighters. The night fighters also had to run the gauntlet of their own Flak as they closed with the enemy bombers.

As he gained experience, Schnaufer became more successful. Several double victories helped raise his score and he received the German Cross

A Bf-110 of the 1st Night-Fighter Wing in 1942. Note the "Englandblitz" emblem.

in Gold after fifteen kills. By then he was also commanding the 12th Squadron of the 1st Night Fighter Wing. Schnaufer and the crew of his Bf-110—radio operator Rumpelhardt and gunner Wilhelm Gänsler—soon earned an enviable reputation. They flew in all types of weather. Neither fog nor rain could keep them from taking to the air to seek out the enemy bombers attacking German cities. Schnaufer's crew trusted him implicitly; he could lead them anywhere. Schnaufer himself said of his comrades in arms: "I would have been nothing without them. Only the team produced victory."

Radio/radar operator Rumpelhardt was with Schnaufer for 100 of his victories. Gunner Gänsler was present for 98. On 27 July 1944 Rumpelhardt, by then a Leutnant, received the Knight's Cross. He had joined Schnaufer in 1942 and went on to become the fourth most successful radio/radar operator in the entire German night-fighter arm. All told, he took part in 130 combat missions. Oberfeldwebel Wilhelm Gänsler was the most successful gunner in the German night-fighter arm. He was famous throughout the force for his fantastic vision. Gänsler began his career with Hauptmann Ludwig Becker, one of the pioneers of the night-fighter arm, before joining Schnaufer's crew in the winter of 1942. At the time, Becker was the squadron commander of the 12th Squadron. He and his radio operator, Oberfeldwebel Straub, who had taken part in 40 kills, were posted missing on 26 February 1943. The day he died, Becker had been the 198th member of the armed forces to receive the Knight's Cross with Oak Leaves. After taking part in 80 night victories with Becker and Schnaufer, Gänsler received the Knight's Cross on 27 July 1944.

Heinz-Wolfgang Schnaufer flew a total of only 164 combat missions, in the course of which he shot down 121 enemy aircraft, 114 of them four-engine airframes. Schnaufer was involved in a car accident in France on 13 July 1950; he died of his injuries two days later.

NIGHT FIGHTER MISSIONS

1943 saw Schnaufer constantly in action; the only break was a leave that he spent at home with his mother. The 16th of December 1943 was a very special day for him and his crew. Four hundred fifty British bombers were on their way to Berlin to pound the capital. Berlin was the stated objective of the British winter bombing campaign.

The German night-fighter crews were standing by when the Freya radars began picking up the enemy aircraft over the North Sea. Schnaufer was sitting in the squadron's radio shack. He and his men had been forbidden to take off because of dense fog. Then the report came through: "Enemy bombers over the North Sea!"

Schnaufer jumped to his feet and grabbed his things. "They're coming!" he shouted and his eyes flashed. He almost ran to the door and called back over his shoulder: "Take off, take off!"

Schnaufer and his crew ran to their aircraft. The two mechanics were waiting to help start the engines; Schnaufer was the first to taxi. He steered the Bf-110 toward the end of the runway. The fully loaded fighter raced down the runway through the dense fog. Climbing at full power, the Messerschmitt soon broke through the layer of cloud. Suddenly, they were in the clear.

"Look at that, boys!" called a relieved Schnaufer. "It's as clear as glass up here."

Seconds later Gänsler spotted the first enemy aircraft with his fantastic vision. The aircraft was flying alone.

"The master of ceremonies, sir," shouted Rumpelhardt excitedly.

"The master of ceremonies" was the name the Germans gave the lone aircraft that flew ahead of the main force to mark the target with illumination and incendiary bombs and pyrotechnics known as "Christmas trees." The main force dropped their bombs using these visual cues. If the master of ceremonies were shot down, the enemy bombers were forced to bomb semi-blind, giving the defenders a real chance of saving the target city from serious damage.

"We'll take the pathfinder," said Schnaufer.

They closed the distance rapidly. The crew of the Lancaster seemed unaware of the approaching danger. For his part, Schnaufer knew that he had to get in close to be certain of delivering a lethal burst. There was no question that approaching an enemy bomber at night entailed a certain risk. If the gunners, especially the one in the tail turret, spotted the night fighter, things could get very hot in a hurry.

Schnaufer was sure of one thing: This enemy aircraft had to be brought down. The silhouette of the bomber grew larger and larger until it filled the entire windscreen. They had closed to within 50 meters and were flying behind and beneath the bomber. Schnaufer pressed the firing buttons. The sound of the cannon firing rang out above the roar of the engines. Cannon rounds poured into the enemy bomber, but it stubbornly held its course. All three members of the crew saw flashes sparkling on the Lancaster; there was no fire. Another burst produced an explosion; the Lancaster lurched hard to the fight and disappeared from its pursuer's field of view. Schnaufer pulled hard on the stick, turning left to avoid pieces of wreckage from the stricken bomber. The pathfinder's entire load of incendiaries and pyrotechnics exploded in a garish display of color. Sev-

Generalmajor Josef Kammhuber, commander of the 1st Fighter Division (right), after awarding the Knight's Cross to Leutnant Hahn, the most successful long-range night-fighter pilot (twelve night kills, the majority over British bomber bases). Hahn was killed over England in October 1941.

eral "Christmas trees" fell slowly, marking the site of the pathfinder's destruction.

"Now, the next one," declared Schnaufer. He made a wide, shallow turn, reversed course and discovered another lone machine; not far behind it was the main force. Schnaufer turned behind the leading Lancaster. Finding the correct approach angle, he maneuvered into position beneath the Lancaster. From there he could make use of the *schräge Musik* (literally: "slanting music") installation: Two 20-mm cannon mounted at a 72-degree angle in the fuselage aft of the cockpit. This practice had two advantages: The pilot avoided being blinded by the muzzle flashes, and the attacking fighter was out of the rear gunner's field of fire.

As soon as he reached the proper firing range, Schnaufer pressed the firing button for the two cannon. Rounds smashed into the belly of the Lancaster. The bomber nosed down into a steep dive and the tail gunner opened fire. He continued firing as the bomber's dive steepened into a vertical plunge from which there would be no recovery. That was number two. The first groups of aircraft belonging to the main force approached.

Schnaufer turned behind the nearest bomber. Slowly and deliberately he moved into firing position. Again the two vertically mounted cannon roared. Rounds poured into the long fuselage and starboard wing of the bomber. It flew on, apparently oblivious to the many hits it had taken. The bomber neither changed its course nor left formation; there was also no sign of fire.

Schnaufer moved in closer. He was now right on the enemy's tail and opened fire with his forward-firing weapons. The bomber took more hits and small flames licked out from the rear fuselage. The enemy aircraft continued to fly on, but the fire was spreading rapidly and Schnaufer instinctively moved away. Seconds later, the bomber went up in a mighty explosion. Schnaufer was just on the periphery of the blast. He felt the shock and the tremendous heat wave generated by the explosion. The Messerschmitt fell like a stone, but Schnaufer remained calm. He regained control of the aircraft after descending 300 meters.

"That was damned close, sir," remarked Gänsler.

"And that will be enough for this night," seconded Schnaufer. He was exhausted; he had shot down three enemy bombers. Schnaufer turned the Messerschmitt toward home. Halfway through the turn, Gänsler called out: "Lancaster at six o'clock!"

"Here we go again," said Schnaufer optimistically. He felt the sweat running down his back beneath his flight suit. But this bomber couldn't be allowed to escape. He hauled the Bf-110 around and fired at the enemy aircraft. Just as he fired the enemy pilot put his aircraft into an evasive maneuver and both bursts went wide.

"Damn it! The bastard's good" declared Schnaufer. A warning signal flashed in his head, telling him to be extra careful. And well he should be: In the next second the rear gunner opened up with his four machine guns. Schnaufer reacted instantly and steered the Messerschmitt out of the line of fire.

"He's corkscrewing, sir!"

Gänsler read the intentions of the enemy pilot as soon as he began his evasive maneuver. The huge Lancaster turned and dove. He then climbed again. It was a critical maneuver for a heavily loaded bomber, but the pilot had to risk it in order to escape the enemy on his tail. Schnaufer didn't try to follow every maneuver by the British pilot; instead, he followed the general path of the corkscrew and waited for his chance. He closed rapidly and dove away from the next burst from the rear gunner. He then pulled back on the stick. Suddenly, he found himself sitting only fifty meters behind and below the Lancaster. He opened fire as the bomber reached the apex of the corkscrew. The 20-mm cannon rounds riddled one of the enemy's fuel tanks. Schnaufer saw the gray banner of escaping gasoline and broke away. Seconds later the bomber burst into flames and went down like a huge torch.

That night mission had lasted no more than thirty minutes; but they were thirty minutes in which every second counted and could have made the difference between life and death. The result was a special accomplishment, and Schnaufer was happy when he had landed the aircraft and taxied it to the dispersal area.

In autumn 1943 Reichsmarschall Göring visited the 1st Night Fighter Wing. Heinz-Wolfgang Schnaufer was among those waiting to greet him. He was there when Oberstleutnant Streib welcomed the "Fat One" and saw him shake hands with the group commanders, including his commander, Hauptmann Jabs. In Göring's entourage were Generalmajor Josef Kammhuber and his friend from the First World War, Generaloberst Lörzer.

Schnaufer stood to the right of Hauptmann Jabs in the ranks of the assembled aircrews. On his right were Oberleutnant Drewes and Oberfeldwebel Vinke; the latter had received the Knight's Cross on 19 September 1943. (Vinke was posthumously awarded the Oak Leaves on 25 April 1944. He was shot down over the North Sea by a Spitfire while on an air-sea rescue mission. At the time of his death, Vinke had 29 night victories.) Next to Vinke was Feldwebel Pfeiffer, another highly decorated night-fighter pilot who had received the German Cross in Gold.

As he stood before the "Fat One," Heinz-Wolfgang Schnaufer had *only* the Iron Cross, First Class, and the German Cross in Gold. That would change on 31 December that year when he received the Knight's Cross after forty-two night victories. Schnaufer's run of victories, which had already increased, was to continue at a faster pace in the new year. In January 1944 he took off on a mission that was to be the beginning of a run of success that was to make him the talk of the night-fighter fraternity.

DIFFERENCES IN THE COMMAND OF THE NIGHT FIGHTER ARM
Before turning to the events of January 1944, a brief detour that concerns the command of the night-fighter arm will shed light on the supreme command. In addition, it will serve to illustrate the difficulties faced by the night fighters in this the period of their greatest success.

In the first half of 1943 Generalmajor Kammhuber had built a "roof over Germany" from Jutland to the Mediterranean in the form of the "dark night-fighting method" and *Himmelbett* zones (four-poster-bed zones). In these zones there were five night-fighter wings with a combined total of 400 aircraft. They were designed to contest the ever-increasing weight of the night-bombing offensive. A sixth night-fighter wing was to be formed in the near future. Obviously, this was not enough to shield Germany from the Allied bomber fleets; the enemy's strength was growing steadily. For this reason, Generalmajor Kammhuber pleaded for the forced expansion of the night-fighter arm from 6 to 18 wings. Instead of just a narrow belt in the west, that would allow fighter-control centers to be established throughout Germany and allow the defenses to deal with airborne threats anywhere at any time.

Plan-position indicators and new radio guidance systems were to supplement the costly radars. Each night fighter was to be equipped with airborne radar that would increase its chances of success. It was a program that would quadruple the size of the electronics industry.

Generalmajor Kammhuber's proposal foresaw the creation of a fighter fleet, similar to the British Fighter Command, which would include the following formations:

> 3 fighter corps, each with 2 fighter divisions
> 3 night-fighter wings in each fighter division and
> 4 night-fighter groups with 30 airframes each in each night-fighter wing.

This meant the formation of eighteen night-fighter wings with 120 aircraft each—a total force of 2,160 night fighters. On 21 May Kammhuber put his case before the Reichsmarschall and received Göring's unreserved approval. With Göring on his side, the program then had to be put to Hitler for a decision. Generalmajor Kammhuber was ordered to Führer Headquarters on 24 May 1943. The meeting began. Hitler picked up Kammhuber's memorandum and pointed to a section underlined in red.

"General Kammhuber, you say that the Americans will be building 5,000 military aircraft each month. If this were true then you would be right!" After a brief pause, Hitler continued: "I would have to withdraw the Eastern Front aircraft immediately and commit all forces to air defense. But these numbers are not correct. I won't stand for such madness!"

Neither the Chief of the armed forces, Feldmarschall Keitel, nor Göring bothered to correct Hitler's view that these numbers were products of Kammhuber's imagination. They wouldn't tell him that they had been compiled by the intelligence staff of the armed force high command and were absolutely reliable. Hitler categorically rejected Kammhuber's pro-

Luftwaffe female signals auxiliaries in the "bleachers" in a fighter control center. They played an important role in guiding the night fighters to the enemy bombers.

posal. He declared that the night-fighter arm was already shooting down enough bombers and that this would soon have the effect of scaring the British off. Generalmajor Kammhuber was dismissed in disgrace. Later Göring took Kammhuber to task and accused him of compromising him— the Reichsmarschall—with his "meglomaniacal demands." He conveniently forgot that he had originally agreed with Kammhuber's proposals. Göring even went so far as to say to him: "If you want to swallow up the entire Luftwaffe then why don't you sit down in my chair!"

In a typical move, the memorandum from which Kammhuber had got his figures was immediately cancelled and replaced by a new memo with lower production figures. Kammhuber was relieved as commander of the 12th Air Corps and replaced by Generalmajor "Beppo" Schmid, former chief intelligence officer of the Luftwaffe Operations Staff.

In was mid-November 1943 before Kammhuber was relieved as General in Command of Night Fighters. The man who had built the German night-fighter arm and who wanted to turn it into a really potent and victorious weapon, was shoved off to Norway. During this period of stagnation the commander of the 300th Fighter Wing, Major Hajo Hermann, developed a new night-fighting method: the *wilde Sau* (the "wild boar").

Major Hermann was concerned by the fact that far too many bombers were still breaking through the *Himmelbett* system to devastate German cities. Over the target area they were caught by searchlights and sometimes held in their beams for minutes. In his opinion, that was the time and place for the fighters to attack. The entire procedure would be conducted visually, requiring no electronic aids.

The events of July 1943, which culminated in the destructive raids on Hamburg, caused Göring to consider Hermann's idea. Göring summoned him on 25 July, the day after the first Hamburg raid, and ordered the 300th Fighter Wing brought to immediate operational readiness. Formation of the wing was already well under way at Rheine, Bonn (Hangelar) and Oldenburg. Hermann promised that the first combat-ready squadron would see action immediately. Hermann and twelve of his fighters were ready when the second Hamburg raid took place on 28 July. The single-engined fighters engaged enemy bombers over the searchlight zone.

"Wild-boar night fighting" replaced the *Himmelbett* method very rapidly. The Berlin area, with its huge searchlight belt, represented an ideal hunting ground for the "wild boars." Conditions were ideal on the night of 24 August 1943; 56 heavy bombers were shot down. Forty-seven British bombers were shot down a week later—once again over Berlin. A total of 123 four-engined bombers were shot down in RAF Bomber Command's raids on Berlin on 24 August and 1 and 4 September. Following these successes, an air of cautious optimism spread through the Luftwaffe command in Berlin.

In September 1943 Oberstleutnant Hermann received orders to expand his fighter wing into a air division of three wings. The division was organized under the newly promoted Oberst Hermann as follows:

30th Fighter Division
300th Fighter Wing (Bonn-Hangelar): Oberleutnant Kettner
301st Fighter Wing (Neubiberg): Major Weinreich
302nd Fighter Wing (Döberitz): Major Mössinger

These wings flew regularly in the rainy, foggy fall and winter weather that prevailed in late 1943, taking off even in conditions of poor visibility. There was a total of sixteen major raids on Berlin in the period from 18 November 1943 to 24 March 1944. In the words of the head of RAF Bomber Command, Air Marshall Arthur Harris, "Berlin will be wrecked from end to end. This operation will cost us 400 to 500 bombers, but it will cost Germany the war."

The losses suffered by the "wild boars" were catastrophic; after its comet-like ascent, single-engined night fighting was in decline by March 1944. The 30th Fighter Division was disbanded on 16 March 1944. By then the twin-engined night fighters had received a new airborne radar, the Lichtenstein SN-2, which was not affected by the chaff dropped by the British. This and other electronic aids made it possible once again for the night fighters to pursue the bomber streams using the *zahme Sau* ("tame boar") method.

Heinz-Wolfgang Schnaufer and his veteran crew often took to the air after the bomber streams in early 1944. These missions were to prove extremely successful, partly on account of Schnaufer's drive, but also because of the multitude of targets offered by the massed bomber streams, which were then vulnerable. The following account describes Schnaufer's first mission in 1944, in the course of which he shot down his 40th and 41st victims.

HUNTING IN THE BOMBER STREAMS

It was 15 January 1944, a fateful day for Germany. For that was the day a British cabinet committee headed by Deputy Prime Minister Attlee submitted a plan for the future division of Germany into zones of occupation. The proposed boundary between East and West Germany followed a line Lübeck-Helmstedt-Eisenach-Hof. The American and Soviet governments agreed three days later. That same night a force of 472 bombers successfully skirted the *Himmelbett* zones and dropped 2,005 tons of bombs over Braunschweig. When the order to scramble came, Oberleutnant Schnaufer and his squadron were the first to take off. They flew in the direction of the enemy for a time, in order to be able to engage the bombers over German territory for as long as possible.

The crew of three was on high alert. Behind Schnaufer, facing aft, sat radio/radar operator Rumpelhardt. The gunner, Feldwebel Gänsler, was responsible for watching the area behind the night fighter. Schnaufer was navigating toward the nearest radio beacon when suddenly Gänsler called out: "Look out! Look out! A heavy bomber right above us. It's flying away from us to the left."

Schnaufer turned his head in the specified direction. He hadn't expected to meet the enemy yet. Obviously, that was one of the leading bombers that had already dropped its bombs. Schnaufer turned west and Rumpelhardt switched on the new Lichtenstein FuG 220 SN-2. The two circular radarscopes came to life. The one on the left showed the azimuth, the one on the right measured the elevation of the target.

"Several targets on the scopes, all in different directions," reported Rumpelhardt.

"They've already been engaged and have split up," replied Schnaufer briefly.

Rumpelhardt guided his pilot toward the nearest target. They turned on to a westerly heading and Rumpelhardt called his pilot again: "We must be in the midst of the bomber stream now, sir. Targets everywhere."

Schnaufer followed his radar operator's instructions as they closed in behind the selected bomber.

"Where is he?" he asked Rumpelhardt.

"He should be right in front of us," replied the radar operator.

Seconds later, Schnaufer spotted four dull red exhaust flames. They grew larger quickly, indicating that they were very close. Then the outline of the bomber appeared against the lighter background of the sky.

"Range 600 meters!" Rumpelhardt called out.

The SN-2 had worked perfectly; but another 100 meters and it would have been useless; its minimum range was 500 meters. Schnaufer slowly closed in on the enemy. He was aiming for a position slightly below the bomber, from where he could use his *schräge Musik*. The Lancaster grew larger and larger. The enemy was still unaware of the fighter's presence, perhaps having relaxed his vigilance after having dropped his bombs and on the way home. Schnaufer matched the speed of the bomber. Having descended too far he then began to climb meter by meter. The Bf-110 glided ever closer to the enemy.

Schnaufer's gaze was fixed firmly on the enemy bomber. The other two members of the crew also stared at the giant. It and its seven-man crew had just completed another terror raid against a German city and its civilian population. It was to be its last. The Lancaster was then only fifty meters away. Beneath its fuselage Schnaufer saw the small Plexiglas bubble of its air-ground radar. There was no sign of any defensive action; the Lancaster had no belly turret and was therefore blind and defenseless against an attack from below.

But, Schnaufer thought, the women and children of Braunschweig were defenseless, too. They were now laying beneath the rubble of their homes or had been burnt to ashes by the incendiaries being dropped by the British. He always had to keep that thought in mind when he attacked: That this bomber should never again be permitted to drop its deadly load over Germany. Schnaufer saw the outline of the bomber through the reflector sight attached to the cockpit roof. He aimed at the port inner

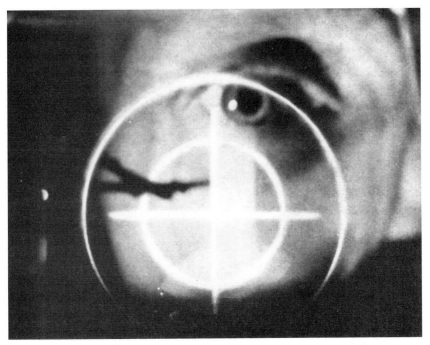

A bomber in the illuminated gunsight of a German night fighter.

engine of the Lancaster. The gun sight was aligned for the oblique weapons mounted aft of the cockpit.

"Now, sir!" called Rumpelhardt, his voice vibrating with suppressed excitement.

But Schnaufer had already pressed the firing buttons. The cannon of the *schräge Musik* bellowed. Small flashes on the wing of the enemy bomber showed that he had aimed well. He dared not fire into the fuselage of the enemy aircraft; if it exploded the night fighter would be lost.

The entire wing of the Lancaster was ablaze within seconds of being hit. "He's finished!" Rumpelhardt declared. One of the engines sputtered and stopped, trailing a long fiery tail behind it. The burning Lancaster held its course for five minutes; finally, almost entirely engulfed in flames, it pitched forward into a dive. The bomber's angle of descent became steeper and steeper. The wings came off and it crashed and exploded. The size of the explosion suggested that the Lancaster still had its bombs on board; perhaps, it had turned back early and had not yet found a place to jettison its load. Schnaufer put the Messerschmitt into a climbing left-hand turn toward the east in the direction of the bomber stream. Ahead of them in the distance the crew saw a number of blazing torches falling to earth:

Their comrades were scoring as well. They flew a 360-degree turn and allowed a group of about twenty bombers to pass. They then turned in pursuit of their next victim. They were so close that they could fly visually.

"That was number forty just now, sir," reported Rumpelhardt. "Are we going after another?"

"By all means, Rumpel," replied Schnaufer, shortening the name of his radar operator.

They moved closer, but this time the enemy must have seen them. Before they could descend beneath the bomber, the four machine guns in the rear turret of one of the bombers opened up on them. Several bullets struck the Messerschmitt's fuselage, but the aircraft descended quickly under the turret's field of fire. Pulling up from below, Schnaufer positioned himself in the most favorable firing position under the nearest Lancaster before pressing the firing buttons. Two streams of 20-mm cannon rounds sawed into the wing of the Lancaster. The big bomber tipped up on one wing as it turned to flee. Schnaufer's Messerschmitt was right behind it. His second burst caused an engine to explode, then the fuselage blew apart into a number of pieces. Schnaufer turned and flew back to base. After landing he received congratulations on his 40th and 41st victories. When the congratulations were over, the wing commander, Werner Streib, who himself was a recipient of the Oak Leaves, said: "That's the Knight's Cross for you at last, Schnaufer."

Streib was right. Schnaufer was awarded the Knight's Cross on 15 January. The decoration was presented by Generalmajor Streib. On 10 February Schnaufer was named the group commander of the 4th Group of the 1st Night Fighter Wing. He replaced Major Jabs, who soon afterward became the wing commander. Jabs subsequently lead the wing until the end of the war.

FOUR TIMES FOUR

What then followed was a great run of success against the enemy bomber flood. Schnaufer shot down four bombers on his next mission and repeated that feat three nights later. By 25 March 1944 he had raised his victory total to 50. There was a break in operations due to bad weather, and it was 11 April before he took off again to engage the enemy. Two bombers fell to his guns that night.

The next mission for Schnaufer's crew came on 25 April; once again, they succeeded in infiltrating the bomber stream. But the first attempt to knock down one of the leading bombers did not go well. The Messerschmitt was hit several times by return fire and Schnaufer veered away. After checking the instruments, he found that all was normal and decided

An armorer at work on the machine guns of a Bf-110. The "Englandblitz" emblem is shown in detail.

to try again. This engagement against the RAF, whose target on the night of 24–25 April was Munich, was to be one of Schnaufer's crowning successes. More than 500 bombers reached the target area; there they dropped high-explosive and incendiary bombs on the city.

Schnaufer and his crew had long since become a deadly combination. Their teamwork developed from experience and knowledge. The many missions they had flown together gave them a sense for every type of danger. They had been molded into a close-knit team in a way that only these three men in their light twin-engined machine could have. Schnaufer's actions were based on his skill and especially sharp intuition. He flew with his two comrades through thick and thin.

His name was increasingly used by the propaganda ministry. The legends surrounding this young man, both a skilled aviator and determined fighter, grew and grew. The name Schnaufer was often mentioned in the broadcasts aimed at England and he was well known there by early 1944. The British respectfully gave him the name "the Night Ghost of St. Trond," referring to the airfield from which he flew most of his missions. It is known for a fact that Heinz-Wolfgang Schnaufer on occasion disobeyed orders in order to engage and destroy enemy bombers—if possible before they dropped their deadly loads on German cities.

Everyone in Germany should remember that his destruction of 121 bombers saved thousands of families from suffering, lingering disabilities and death.

THE FIFTH "FOUR"
Oberleutnant Schnaufer gunned the engines and sent his new Bf-110 racing down the runway. A large force of British bombers was attacking Munich. It was 25 April 1944.

The Bf-110 gained altitude rapidly. Ground control provided initial vectors until Rumpelhardt switched on the SN-2. St. Trond, their base in the Netherlands, was already far behind them when Schnaufer saw bright flashes in the sky ahead. Some of their comrades had made contact with the bomber stream. He advanced the throttles to the stop and felt the aircraft accelerate. The Messerschmitt closed the distance quickly and came under fire from three aircraft flying to one side of the main stream. Schnaufer cursed as he dodged the enemy fire. He flew a 360-degree turn and positioned himself at least 100 meters beneath the last group of bombers.

Rumpelhardt guided his pilot to the enemy. They came nearer and nearer until the decisive second came. The obliquely mounted cannon roared briefly. The bomber was hit in the port wing; rounds walked toward the fuselage and set the inboard engine on fire.

Schnaufer flew beneath and behind the bomber for several minutes until he saw it shear off and begin its final plunge, wrapped in flames. Several hundred meters below the Messerschmitt the enemy aircraft exploded. Schnaufer turned back toward the stream. He approached slowly and fired at another bomber. The enemy aircraft went down immediately to crash and explode. They had intercepted the bomber stream far from Munich. Then something began that would remain forever in Schnaufer's memory. Everywhere he looked he could see tracer and the flashes made by exploding cannon rounds. One of the night fighters was hit by return fire and dove away steeply. Had he really seen parachutes or was it his imagination?

"They got out, sir," called Rumpelhardt.

Breathing a sigh of relief, Schnaufer turned his attention to the bombers in front of him. Several times other night fighters cut in front, forcing him to take evasive action. He saw them falling out of the sky: Ten, fifteen enemy bombers! The sky in front of and over Stuttgart was filled with falling wreckage. Flames from the stricken bombers seemed to blot out even the Christmas Trees.

Suddenly, a bomber was shot down not 400 meters to Schnaufer's right. A gentle pressure on the rudder pedal and the Bf-110 moved away from the scene of the engagement. Schnaufer made another course correction and positioned himself beneath the nearest bomber. The burst of cannon fire struck the Lancaster, which immediately went into a steep turn. Schnaufer followed and saw that this was just a ruse. After descending several hundred meters the bomber resumed its original course.

"You won't get away from me, asshole!" Schnaufer shouted furiously. He turned to follow, closed slowly and fired again when he had reached the right distance.

That time he fired two bursts from the *schräge Musik*; immediately the starboard wing of the Lancaster separated from the fuselage. The bomber lurched to the side and began to fall. Five parachutes were seen to open. The blazing wreck of the Lancaster fell past the five men hanging beneath their chutes. One was hit by a piece of burning wreckage. In seconds, the canopy above the man turned dull red and he plunged to earth as if drawn by an invisible hand.

As they maneuvered for their next attack, the crew could already see Munich burning. Red mushroom clouds marked the explosion of high-explosive bombs, and there were huge fires ignited by the incendiaries. Schnaufer attacked and damaged a Lancaster. It veered off course and jettisoned its load in an empty field. So lightened, it tried to escape by going into a corkscrew.

"We're not going to chase him," declared Schnaufer. "He's going to come down somewhere later anyway." The Messerschmitt turned toward the stream again. Seconds later, Rumpelhardt called out: "To our right . . . about 400 meters higher . . . a group of bombers headed back."

"They've already bombed," added Gänsler.

"Let's get them," said Schnaufer. He decided to attack these bombers; he could see from all the tracers, condensation trails and blazing bombers that there were still numerous engagements going on up ahead.

"If we go there we might be shot down by one of our own."

Schnaufer allowed the bombers to pass. He then turned and positioned the Messerschmitt beneath them. Suddenly, they came under fire from ahead and to the right. Bullets struck the Bf-110. Where was the firing coming from?

"An enemy straggler, sir."

Schnaufer had acted instinctively and hauled the Bf-110 out of the way of the enemy fire without being badly hit.

"Everything alright?" he asked. Both crewmen checked their equipment and confirmed that all was normal.

Schnaufer resumed his pursuit of the enemy bombers. He caught one of the withdrawing heavies and moved into position beneath it. The twin obliquely mounted cannon roared and the Lancaster seemed to shudder under the impacts of the rounds. Schnaufer pulled the nose of the aircraft up, then dove again; as the bomber passed through the line of fire of the forward-firing guns, he pressed the firing buttons. There were bright flashes as the rounds struck home. The bomber burst into flames and lurched downward. The entire crew bailed out.

Suddenly, the red fuel-warning light came on. "We must return to St. Trond," Said Schnaufer.

"That's four again, sir," called Rumpelhardt.

"Three of them never got to bomb Munich. That counts for double, guys."

On the way back to base Schnaufer and his crew encountered another small group of bombers that had obviously become separated from the main stream. He risked another attack. When the twin cannon of the *schräge Musik* jammed, he tried a conventional attack with the forward-firing guns. The Messerschmitt was hit by return fire. That was enough; Schnaufer turned away and set course for St. Trond. Schnaufer landed safely. They had shot down four enemy bombers on five consecutive mis-

All the information was displayed on the "Seeburg Table" with friendly and enemy aircraft depicted as points of light.

sions. After the debriefing, the wing commander shook the young officer's hand. The stress of the past few hours was obvious in his face.

"Congratulations, Schnaufer, that's more than any other night-fighter pilot before you."

"But perhaps it was too little, sir."

"Possibly, Schnaufer. But you should be satisfied and pleased with your success."

Other successful pilots from the 4th Group of the 1st Night Fighter Wing that night were Oberfeldwebel Grofe with two kills and Oberleutnant Greiner, the commander of the 11th Squadron of the 1st Night Fighter Wing. Greiner shot down a Halifax.

Schnaufer went to his quarters, where his enlisted orderly had hot coffee waiting. Schnaufer nodded gratefully. He gestured for his men to sit down; over coffee they went over every phase of the attack in order to eliminate any weaknesses. Only when they had finished did they retire to their beds.

✠

The Allied force that attacked Munich lost thirty-one bombers, most of them to night fighters. A further nineteen were badly damaged; twelve of these were wrecked in crash-landings at their bases in England, while the remainder spent lengthy periods under repair and were subsequently assigned to training units.

In England the voices warning that a continuation of this murderous battle might bring Bomber Command to the brink of defeat were growing in number. But the order were received from the British Prime Minister, Winston Churchill: "Keep bombing, keep bombing!"

Churchill had promised the British Empire blood, sweat, and tears, and he kept his word.

THE BALANCE ON THE BRITISH SIDE

The British command drew up the balance sheet for the Battle of Berlin. In the period from 18 November 1943 to 31 March 1944 RAF Bomber Command had flown 9,111 sorties to the German capital. The city had been deluged with 16,000 tons of high explosives and incendiaries, the most dropped on any German city so far. The five attacks in the period from 18 November to 3 December alone claimed 2,700 RAF dead.

Of the aircraft that took part in the Berlin raids, 367 Lancaster and 111 Halifax heavy bombers had been shot down. Seriously damaged were 745 Lancasters (of which 69 were total losses due to crash-landings in England) and 199 Halifaxes (25 of which were written off on landing). The German night-fighter arm lost 90 aircraft in the frightful battle in the skies over the German capital. An area of 9.5 square kilometers in Berlin was totally destroyed by the bombardment. Tens of thousands of dwellings lay in ruins; buried under the rubble were just as many dead and injured. In spite of the devastation, the industries of metropolitan Berlin were scarcely affected.

RAF Bomber Command had, of course, attacked other targets in Germany in the specified period. A record 20,224 sorties were flown. 1,047 bombers failed to return and another 1,682 were severely damaged. RAF personnel losses in this period were on the order of 10,000 men. The British leadership under Winston Churchill promised that this sustained bombardment of Berlin and its civilian population would make Germany ready to sue for peace by 1 April 1944 at the latest. This prediction was first made at a general staff conference by Air Chief Marshall Harris.

The British bombing offensive was temporarily halted in April 1944. The official reason was preparations for the upcoming invasion of France. The more likely reason, however, was because of the enormous losses suffered by the RAF. April was the month of the US 8th Air Force, which continued the work of destruction by day.

A BIG NIGHT FOR SCHNAUFER'S GROUP

The nights immediately following the raid on Munich were somewhat quieter in St. Trond. Nevertheless, Schnaufer took off several times to intercept enemy aircraft, such as on the night of 11 April 1944 when the British attacked Aachen. Two Lancaster bombers fell to his guns that night.

The heavy raid on Cologne on the night of 21 April was considered "a birthday present for Hitler" from "Bomber Harris." Schnaufer was able to shoot down a bomber, but then his own aircraft was hit by return fire. It took all his skill as a pilot to get the damaged aircraft back to base.

"We were just about ready to bail out," he told his superiors after landing. The mechanics immediately set about repairing the shot-up night fighter.

During the night of 23 April the RAF attacked targets in Northern Germany. This time Schnaufer returned empty-handed. Both of the Messerschmitt's engines began to falter, and he was forced to return to base immediately. The only member of the group to make contact with the enemy was Oberleutnant Greiner, who shot down a Halifax.

Schnaufer's machine was serviceable again by the afternoon of 24 April. He took the Bf-110 up for a test flight and determined that everything was working to his satisfaction. Schnaufer and his crew were in the air on the night of 27 April. They infiltrated a group of about 40 bombers and shot down two Lancasters.

The next day several of the group's aircraft took off to intercept RAF bombers, whose target areas included the outskirts of Paris. The first kill went to Leutnant Potthast, who shot down a Halifax. Other victories went to Oberleutnant Augenstein and Heinz-Wolfgang Schnaufer, who destroyed a Lancaster with two bursts. The fighting continued. Schnaufer's machine was hit several times by return fire, and he was forced to break off the pursuit of further bombers. Two other members of the group, Leutnant Pengler and Oberleutnant Greiner, scored successes against the RAF. Pengler downed a Halifax and Greiner shot down a Lancaster and then a Halifax. On 2 May Greiner and Augenstein each shot down an enemy bomber.

The 9th of May saw Schnaufer and his team in action against minor raids by groups of Halifax bombers. Schnaufer, Pengler, Greiner, Drewes and Potthast all brought down enemy bombers. Potthast destroyed a second Halifax at an hour past midnight.

The group continued to enjoy success. Oberleutnant Greiner destroyed a Lancaster on the night of 12 May. The following night Oberleutnant Augenstein and Leutnant Pengler each shot down a Lancaster. On the night of 13 May it was again Schnaufer's turn to shine. In fact, the month of May 1944 was one of his most successful ever, culminating in his great success of 25 May. More about that shortly. First, however, let's look at some of the raids launched by the Luftwaffe in early 1944 to extract revenge for the RAF's nighttime bombing campaign and its horrendous cost in German civilian casualties.

THE GERMAN REVENGE RAIDS

Hitler had promised the British government revenge for Berlin. He ordered an immediate resumption of air attacks on London and other targets in England. Late on the evening of 21 January 1944, bomber units of the 9th Air Corps under Oberst Peltz took off in two waves for London. It was the first large-scale German raid for some time. A total of 447 aircraft participated; only a small percentage of these were heavy bombers. The operation was repeated on 30 January; 285 aircraft took part, of which 60 were heavy bombers. The raiders dropped a total of 310 tons of high-explosive bombs and 715 tons of incendiaries. The two attacks cost the Luftwaffe 57 aircraft.

The 9th Air Corps launched another large-scale raid on London on 19 February 1944. Eleven of the 187 aircraft that took part in the attack failed to return.

✠

In February 1944 the German day and night-fighter arms lost a total of 1,217 aircraft. These numbers reflect the bitterness with which the air war over Germany was fought. The fighting cost the Luftwaffe some of its best pilots; here are several examples:

Oberstleutnant Egon Mayer, the wing commander of the 2nd Fighter Wing, received the Swords on 2 March 1944. The same day he was killed in combat with Thunderbolts over Montmedy. At the time of his death Mayer had achieved 102 victories in the West, including 24 heavy bombers. He was the first fighter pilot to reach 100 victories on the Western Front.

Four days later, Hauptmann Hugo Frey, known in the 2nd Squadron of the 2nd Fighter Wing as the "Viermot killer," was shot down by the tail gunner of a bomber he had just shot down. Twenty-six of Frey's thirty-two victories were heavy bombers; he was awarded the Knight's Cross posthumously on 4 May 1944.

The nocturnal air battle has begun. Anti-aircraft guns fill the sky with tracer.

The next to fall was Oberstleutnant Wolf-Dietrich Wilke. Known as the "Prince," he had been the wing commander of the 3rd Fighter Wing since September 1942 and had received the Swords on 23 December 1942 after 155 victories. He was shot down in combat with Mustangs near Schöppen-stedt on 23 March 1944. Wilcke had 162 kills to his credit when he died.

✠

Ninety aircraft of the 9th Air Corps under Oberst Peltz resumed the offensive on the night of 25 March 1943.

On 18 April the German bomber commander scraped together every-thing he could find in order to pay back the British with a major strike against London. Peltz assembled a force of 125 aircraft: 60 Ju-88s, 29 Ju-188s, 13 Do-217s, 5 He-177s, and 10 Me-410s. Compared to the raids carried out by the Western Allies, however, it was a pinprick, especially since most of the aircraft involved in the attack could not carry nearly as heavy a load as the Anglo-American bombers.

One hundred seventeen bombers of the 9th Air Corps attacked Bristol on the night of 24 April. Ninety-one bombers attacked the same target on the night of 15 May; thirteen failed to return. On the night of 26 April

1944 193 aircraft bombed shipping in Portsmouth harbor. Two nights later the Luftwaffe sent 60 aircraft to drop aerial mines on the same target. A further attack on Portsmouth by 78 aircraft took place on 27 April. Finally, on the night of 30 April, 101 German bombers attacked installations in Plymouth harbor. A force of 106 aircraft struck Portsmouth on the night of 16 May 1944. They left part of the dockyard in rubble. The attack was repeated a week later by a force of 104 bombers, of which eight were lost.

Torquay was the target for 65 German bombers on 28 May, while on 30 May only 51 aircraft of the 9th Air Corps were in action over England. Their target was Falmouth. Antiaircraft fire brought down two of the attackers. This attack ended the German aerial offensive against England. At the same time, the RAF resumed its attacks on Germany with renewed strength and vigor at the end of May.

MAY 1944: THE 4TH GROUP OF
THE 1ST NIGHT FIGHTER WING IN ACTION

It is now time to examine in detail the successes achieved by the 4th Group of the 1st Night Fighter Wing during the period 2–24 May 1944. They have already been alluded to several times. In addition to Heinz-Wolfgang Schnaufer and his crew, the group—indeed the entire wing—had many experienced and successful crews, some of whom had been with the night-fighter arm from the very beginning.

One of the most successful pilots was Oberleutnant Hermann Greiner, commander of the 11th Squadron of the 1st Night Fighter Wing. Greiner had scored his first night victory on 26 June 1942. Greiner began the group's series of successes on 2 May when he shot down a Halifax. That same night Oberleutnant Hans-Heinz Augenstein brought down a Lancaster. Augenstein had been a member of the 7th Squadron of the 1st Night Fighter Wing since the end of 1942, and his performance in May 1944 was to win him the Knight's Cross on 9 June.

Augenstein had assumed command of the 12th Squadron of the 1st Night Fighter Wing in February 1944 when Schnaufer left to become the group commander. The two men were friends. Schnaufer was certain that Augenstein would soon reach forty victories, which was enough to guarantee him the Knight's Cross. Schnaufer shot down a Halifax on 9 May. Victories were also claimed by Oberleutnant Greiner and Leutnant Fengler, thus raising the group's total by three. On 10 May Leutnant Potthast shot down a Lancaster and a Halifax. Two nights later it was Oberleutnant Greiner's turn again to bring down an enemy bomber. Augenstein also shot down one of the raiders on 12 May. Schnaufer and Fengler were still in the air when Augenstein landed. Leutnant Fengler destroyed a Lancaster and just avoided being knocked out of the sky when the bomber exploded. Schnaufer scored a perfect three: all Halifax bombers. The last to land at St. Trond, he received an enthusiastic welcome home.

Oberleutnant Greiner destroyed a Halifax on the night of 22 May. He later reported that the Halifax put up a stubborn fight. Greiner was forced to make two firing passes before the British bomber veered out of the bomber stream, went down in spirals and crashed. That same night, at 0100 hours on 22 May, Schnaufer came upon a group of bombers on their way home from bombing Duisburg. Two of the Lancasters were shot down. Schnaufer's machine was hit several times by return fire, and he was forced to return to St. Trond.

The group was in the air again during the night of 23 May. Schnaufer and Augenstein each shot down two Lancasters. The kills are listed in the group's victory list—which is arranged chronologically—as follows: Augenstein, Schnaufer, Augenstein, Schnaufer.

Oberleutnant Augenstein was subsequently awarded the Knight's Cross, which he received on 9 June 1944 after forty-six night victories. Forty-five of them were four-engined bombers. (On 6 December 1944 Augenstein was shot down and killed by a British long-range night fighter flown by Flight Lieutenant Hedgecoe.) On 25 May Schnaufer flew a mission which saw him shoot down five enemy aircraft his best single mission to date.

THE ATTACK OF 25 MAY 1944

As described in previous sections, Schnaufer and his crew of Rumpelhardt and Gänsler had flown a series of successful missions in April and May 1944 but had failed to eclipse their best result of four bombers. That was to change on 25 May. The entire crew was given a brief leave. This gave the men a chance to rest and regenerate themselves after the stresses of a prolonged period of night actions.

Schnaufer had long known that the key to success in night combat was to approach as near to the enemy as possible and deliver the killing burst from close range. Obviously, that was an extremely difficult maneuver, especially on a dark night. Nevertheless, the pilot of the night fighter had to weigh the risk of collision against the danger of being spotted early by the enemy and fired upon. Experience had made that type of attack a matter of routine for Schnaufer and his crew. This might have led to inattention and overconfidence, but Schnaufer approached each attack as if it were his first.

The German night fighters usually received their first warning that British bombers were coming shortly before they took off from their bases in England. The German signals intelligence picked up transmissions from the bombers as they tuned their transmitters to match the frequencies of the ground-based receivers. It then notified the night-fighter organization that an attack was highly probable.

The call signs of the ground stations and the bomber groups were known to the Germans, and they usually knew which formations were going to be in the air on a given night. Radio silence was ordered for all bombers during flight. Only those aircraft that were forced to return early with mechanical trouble were permitted to signal their return using a three-figure X-group code.

By the time the bombers were located by ground-based Freya radars, the first night fighters were already in the air. Ground controllers vectored them toward the bomber stream until the radar operators in the fighters could acquire the enemy on their SN-2 sets and guide their pilots in. On the evening of that 25 May 1944, signals intelligence had reported the first squadrons tuning their radios two hours before the probable takeoff time. The night-fighter crews were immediately placed on alert.

By the time Hauptmann Schnaufer's group received the order to take off, the first crew was already on strip alert. Schnaufer's crew chief pulled the chocks from the wheels of the Bf-110 exactly one minute after takeoff clearance was given. The aircraft began to taxi. It then raced down the runway and lifted elegantly into the air.

Schnaufer was assigned a west-southwest heading by ground control. If they maintained that heading they would soon be over Aachen. Rumpelhardt received an update on the position of the enemy from ground control along with a course correction, which he passed on to his pilot.

"They're coming," he said. "If we maintain this heading we should spot the first group to our right. I'm switching on the radar."

Schnaufer was intensely focused. He tried to pierce the blackness with his eyes, but he could see nothing but the small clouds high above them. The sky was otherwise clear—good flying weather. Near Aachen they were handed over to the next fighter controller. Three minutes passed with no sightings.

"I have a bogey," Rumpelhardt reported suddenly. "One more . . . another! Numerous bogeys bearing 280 degrees!"

Schnaufer altered course to the southwest.

"Heading is good, we're closing and . . ."

"I see them!" called out Gänsler. "Directly to our right!"

Schnaufer turned his head and saw dark shadows passing through the night sky.

The Würzburg-Riese radar provided early warning of incoming raids.

"Target in sight!" he called. Meanwhile, Rumpelhardt had passed on the location and heading of the bombers to ground control. Schnaufer turned northwest, behind the first group of bombers. He estimated that there must be 200 machines. There was as yet no sign of the next group.

In a wide turn Schnaufer approached a group of about twenty bombers on the left flank of the stream. He tried to scan the night sky with his eyes. Were there any escort fighters with them? He saw none. Were there more bombers beneath him? Nothing to be seen there either. Gänsler reported all clear on the right side.

"We're attacking!"

Schnaufer moved beneath the lowest aircraft and reduced speed to almost match that of the enemy bomber. The Messerschmitt closed in meter by meter. At a distance of 45 meters Schnaufer pressed the firing buttons for the *schräge Musik*. The aircraft shook gently as the guns fired. In the same second rounds struck the port wing and engines of the bomber. Ten seconds later it veered off course. Descending in a wide arc, the Lancaster lost height and then exploded in a ball of fire.

"Number one, sir," called Rumpelhardt.

Schnaufer returned to the relative safety of the airspace beneath the bomber stream. All three members of the crew were on maximum alert. The victory came at 2259 hours; Rumpelhardt noted the time and location, so that the wreck could be inspected the next day. The Messerschmitt was soon in firing position again. The cannon roared and the second bomber fell out of the sky as quickly as the first. At 2301 hours the blazing torch that had been the British bomber began its final plunge. Schnaufer's third pass was interrupted by four bombers approaching from the right on a collision course. Gänsler called out their position and opened fire from 200 meters. All four enemy aircraft opened up on Schnaufer's Bf-110. The aircraft was hit several times and Schnaufer put the Messerschmitt into a descending turn. Once beneath the bombers and out of sight, he flew a 270-degree turn. On completing the turn, Schnaufer found himself at least 400 meters beneath the enemy bombers, which were closing on the left flank of the stream.

Schnaufer began to climb and steered the Bf-110 toward the bomber farthest away from the stream. By the time he was in firing position, four minutes had passed since the first sighting of the four bombers. As usual, Schnaufer's aim was good and the British bomber went down in flames before it could drop its bombs on a German city. That time Schnaufer turned away to the left instead of to the right. Rumpelhardt guided him behind the leading group of bombers in the second wave, which flew past about 600 meters to the side.

"We're attacking again!" announced Schnaufer.

He wiped away the sweat that was running into his eyes. The exhaust flames of many bombers were visible in the clear night sky. The rumbling sound of explosions to the west was a sign that other night fighters were engaging the enemy before they reached their targets. Schnaufer reached firing position. Though they had experienced this many times, the three men stared at the heavy bomber that dwarfed their Bf-110 as if transfixed. Flames shot from the bomber's starboard wing as the cannon rounds struck home. Seconds later, it separated from the fuselage of the doomed aircraft. The enemy aircraft veered off course, just missing one of its number, and then spiraled nose-first toward the ground.

"Number four, sir," said Rumpelhardt. "We should think about heading home."

"Why not five this time, Rumpel?" asked Schnaufer.

Schnaufer approached another bomber but was fired on from below and had to break off the attack. He never risked continuing an attack once discovered. Only in an uninterrupted approach could he make use of the Bf-110's superior speed. Veering away from his selected target, Schnaufer saw a Lancaster at his one o'clock position open fire. Something struck the wings of the Messerschmitt. Schnaufer pushed the aircraft's nose down and dove under the Lancaster's fire. Allowing plenty of lead, Schnaufer opened fire at the Lancaster. Although the chances of hitting the target in such situations were slim, he did manage to score hits on one of the bomber's turrets, which abruptly ceased firing. Schnaufer circled back. Unable to find the Lancaster again, he moved into position behind the next British bomber.

One minute after beginning his approach, Schnaufer opened fire with his forward-firing weapons. He scored hits, but not enough to bring down the Lancaster. He guided the Messerschmitt to a position under the bomber from where he could administer the coup de grace with the *schräge Musik*. The Lancaster was hit again and fell from the sky. Rumpelhardt checked the time; exactly fourteen minutes had passed since their first kill.

"Back to base," said Schnaufer, leaning back slightly in his seat. He felt the tension in his body and noticed the sweat running down his back and face. They landed safely back at St. Trond. Schnaufer and his crew had destroyed five British bombers before they could drop their bombs on a German city. All together, the 4th Group of the 1st Night Fighter Wing accounted for ten enemy aircraft that night.

This was a great victory for Schnaufer's group; it also showed what was possible given an efficient, well-organized ground-control system and a well-trained crew.

FURTHER NIGHT VICTORIES FOR SCHNAUFER

The last week of May and first week of June 1944 witnessed a marked reduction in activity in the skies over Germany as the Allied air forces concentrated their efforts on preparatory attacks for the invasion of France scheduled for 6 June 1944. The next victory for Schnaufer and his crew came on the night of 12 June, when the RAF attacked the hydrogenation plant located in Gelsenkirchen.

From Wehrmacht daily reports and the rumor mill, the airmen of the 1st Night Fighter Squadron learned of the beginning the revenge attacks on Britain with the V-1 unguided missile. The campaign was initiated on the night of 13 June 1944 by the 155th Flak Regiment commanded by Oberst Wachtel. A total of 144 V-1s were launched at the greater London area on the night of 16 June. The missiles inflicted some damage, however twenty-one were shot down by RAF fighters. Of the 2,000 V-1s fired at London by 30 June, approximately half reached the city. British fighters claimed to have shot down 661.

The 24th of July was to be a night unlike any the night-fighter crews had experienced before in their war against the bomber streams. It wasn't one night but three nights separated by brief intervals. As soon as the first reports of radio activity on the part of the RAF bomber squadrons were received, the duty crews at St. Trond were ordered to strip alert. The remainder were placed on alert status. The Freya search radars reported individual penetrations by enemy aircraft, however, none of these entered the area allocated to the 4th Group of the 1st Night Fighter Squadron. But then a report was received from a Würzburg radar located farther to the south: "British formations believed to be heading for Stuttgart."

Schnaufer listened to the report and cursed softly to himself. Once again, large numbers of enemy aircraft had escaped detection by the long-range radars and were already on their way to Stuttgart. He had to try and intercept and break up this British formation before it reached its target.

"I'm going alone. You others remain here in case things heat up here too."

Heinz-Wolfgang Schnaufer and his crew took off and headed southwest in pursuit of the enemy. Rumpelhardt received heading information from a *Himmelbett* station. He passed course corrections to Schnaufer as further reports were received. When it became obvious that Stuttgart was in fact the target, Schnaufer increased speed and flew straight toward the city. Rumpelhardt had by then turned on the SN-2. He watched the cathode ray tubes intently, feverishly searching for the telltale blip that would indicate the presence of another aircraft. A target appeared to the east; obviously another German night fighter racing toward Stuttgart, it soon disappeared. They were approximately forty kilometers from Stuttgart when Rumpelhardt reported the first enemy aircraft: "Directly ahead! Range approximately 800 meters. Appears to be a bomber."

Involuntarily Schnaufer bent forward slightly. He peered through his reflector sight but could see nothing. Rumpelhardt called out the range as 600 meters.

"I have him," Schnaufer said softly. He descended slightly and began his approach.

As the distance between the two aircraft closed, Schnaufer reduced power to more closely match the speed of the enemy aircraft. Still closing, he reached optimum firing position undetected. A single burst was enough

Major Schnaufer and his crew. From left: Gänsler, Schnaufer, and Rumpelhardt. All wore the Knight's Cross.

to send the bomber falling from the sky. Skirting the bombers, Schnaufer quickly passed the front of the group. Then Rumpelhardt spotted a lone aircraft flying 4,000 meters ahead of the rest.

"The pathfinder, sir," he reported.

"We have to get him!"

Shooting down the target marker, the harbinger of catastrophe for German cities, was always a prime objective of the night fighters. If the pathfinder were shot down, the main force would have a more difficult time finding the target and bombing accurately.

Radar operator Rumpelhardt kept the enemy aircraft in the center of his screen. But apparently a member of the bomber's crew spotted the fast-closing fighter and sounded the alarm. The British pilot put his aircraft into a series of evasive maneuvers known as the "corkscrew" in order to shake off its pursuer. But Schnaufer stayed with the bomber. The British gunners opened fire from 400 meters. Schnaufer descended beneath the return fire and continued to close the distance. At 80 meters both Rumpelhardt and Gänsler shouted: "Now, sir!"

Schnaufer fired at the very moment they reached optimum range. The pathfinder was hit hard. It turned slightly toward the east but flew on. Schnaufer fired again, this time with the forward-firing guns. He raked the bomber from nose to tail. Suddenly, there was a bright flash. Was the bomber about to explode?

"He's dropped an illumination (photoflash) bomb, sir," called Gänsler, who hadn't been blinded by the flash. The enemy obviously hoped that the flash would blind the crew of the night fighter and allow them to escape. But the bomber would not escape from Schnaufer.

The bomber's rear gunner opened fire again. The first burst struck the radio and radar equipment. Schnaufer instinctively shoved the stick forward and quickly flew beneath the rear turret's field of fire. He halted the Messerschmitt's descent after several hundred meters and began to climb again.

"Where is he?" he asked Rumpelhardt.

"Can't say. The radar's out, sir."

"Damn! Look for him, look!"

Schnaufer held the course that the pathfinder had been flying. His hunch soon proved to be right. Rumpelhardt was the first to spot the bomber's exhaust flames. Then Schnaufer sighted the Lancaster; the Messerschmitt was bounced about in the turbulence from its four propellers.

He warned his crew: "I'm attacking!"

Schnaufer descended beneath the bomber and then climbed toward the correct firing position. As the Bf-110 climbed slowly, the crew could see the mighty fuselage of the bomber. Its bomb bay was filled with target markers and other pyrotechnics to guide the main force to its target. Schnaufer prepared to fire the *schräge Musik*. At the same instant, one of the bomber's gunners opened fire but missed. The four guns in the rear turret maintained a steady stream of fire. It looked as if Schnaufer was flying right into it but, with the sure instincts of an experienced night-fighter pilot, he saw that the bursts would pass above him.

As soon as he reached the most favorable position, he opened fire. One burst was enough to set the enemy aircraft on fire. Its load of pyrotechnics illumination and incendiary bombs exploded. The master of ceremonies went down in a tremendous display of fireworks. Two members of the crew bailed out, but their chutes were already in flames when they opened. The rest of the crew died in the blazing bomber.

Some of the burning wreckage struck Schnaufer's Messerschmitt. Then Gänsler reported: "Our starboard engine is on fire!"

Schnaufer immediately switched off the ignition. Flying on one engine, the Messerschmitt was as good as crippled. He tried to get out of the bomber stream. Then, suddenly, the shadow of a Lancaster appeared in the glare of burning Christmas Trees and exploding target markers.

"A little faster, sir, and I can shoot him down."

Schnaufer advanced the throttle. If Wilhelm Gänsler said to do so that was reason enough for him.

Seconds later the gunner's machine gun began to rattle. Gänsler held the triggers down. Seconds later, there was a tremendous explosion. Looking to his right, Schnaufer saw the enemy aircraft going down.

"Well done, Wilhelm," Schnaufer called.

The bombers flying behind Schnaufer reached the area illuminated by several parachute flares. They were obviously confused, as it appeared as if several target markers had been dropped at the same time. First one Lancaster, then others, began dropping their bombs where the pathfinder had met its end. Only one small group held its course toward Stuttgart. Most of the bombs fell in wooded areas near Renningen, Malsheim, and Münklingen. The bombs caused little damage apart from an unfortunate suburb on the outskirts of the city, which was hit by four or five bombs and wiped out.

The bombers turned and set course for home. By then, however, they had to run the gauntlet of the other night fighters that had meanwhile taken off to intercept the Stuttgart raiders. Several more of their number were shot down by these. Schnaufer requested and received permission to land at an airfield northwest of Stuttgart. He made a successful engine-out landing and taxied to the apron. The local mechanics promised that the aircraft would be fit to fly back to St. Trond the next morning. He quickly made contact with the wing and reported his two kills, including the pathfinder, and the enemy aircraft shot down by Gänsler.

Schnaufer then phoned his mother in Calw. As soon as she answered, he could tell by her voice that she had not slept. "Mother," he said, "the Tommies tried to attack Stuttgart, but we spoiled things for them."

"That's good, my boy, take care of yourself."

"Good night, mother. Go to sleep, nothing more's going to happen tonight."

After evaluating the target photos, the British repeated their attack on Stuttgart. The results achieved by the 614 bombers that reached Stuttgart failed to satisfy Harris, and he scheduled another raid for the following night, 26 July. A third was to follow on 27 July.

Harris intended the raids on Stuttgart to be a second Operation "Gomorrah," the code name for the destructive attacks on Hamburg in 1943. The results were not as bad, yet bad enough when one considers that 898 people lost their lives in those three nights in Stuttgart. A further 1,916 inhabitants of the city were injured, some seriously. After the three-night inferno, 100,000 people in the city were homeless.

A SPECIAL OCCURRENCE

On 27 July 1944, Schnaufer's crew stood in front of the wing's headquarters area. The group commander, Hauptmann Schnaufer, and the wing commander, Oberstleutnant Jabs, stepped outside. The two officers walked over to Schnaufer's two crewmen, who were standing at attention. On the right side of their tunics shone the German Cross in Gold, on the left the Iron Cross, First Class and the Operational Flying Clasp. The two officers stopped five paces in front of Rumpelhardt and Gänsler. Oberstleutnant Jabs turned to Fritz Rumpelhardt standing on the right.

"Leutnant Rumpelhardt, on behalf of the Führer I present you the Knight's Cross of the Iron Cross."

Then he turned to Wilhelm Gänsler. "Oberfeldwebel Gänsler. I also present you with the Knight's Cross of the Iron Cross on behalf of the Führer."

With the help of the adjutant, Oberstleutnant Jabs placed the decoration on both members of Schnaufer's crew. Schnaufer was the first to congratulate both his comrades. There was emotion in his voice as he turned to Rumpelhardt: "Fritz, you've been there for my 89 kills, stood by me every night, and faced every danger without wavering."

Then Schnaufer turned to Gänsler: "And you, Wilhelm, were there for seventy-two of my victories. My thanks and special congratulations to both of you."

Heinz-Wolfgang Schnaufer had scored seventeen victories before Gänsler joined his crew, twelve with Leutnant Bahro as gunner, and five with Erich Handke. Feldwebel Handke, who was now Hauptmann Drewes' gunner and an officer candidate, also received the Knight's Cross that day. Drewes had commanded the 2nd Group of the 1st Night Fighter Wing since March of that year and was a good friend of Schnaufer's. Handke was also on hand to shake Schnaufer's hand. Hauptmann Drewes was also among those being decorated, standing in the second row, shoulder to shoulder with his gunner. On 17 April 1945 Drewes would receive the Oak Leaves after fifty-two victories, forty-two of them by night.

The entire wing celebrated. During the festivities, the commanding general of the 1st Fighter Corps, Generalmajor Schmid, whispered to Schnaufer that he might want to "wash up," as a certain high-ranking gentleman wanted to see him. That could only mean Hitler! On 30 July, only three days after the decoration of his two crewmen, Hauptmann Heinz-Wolfgang Schnaufer was awarded the 84th Knight's Cross with Swords. He flew to Rastenburg to receive the coveted decoration from Hitler at his *Wolfsschanze* headquarters.

Another of Schnaufer's contemporaries, Prinz Sayn von Wittgenstein, in front of his Ju-88.

In Hitler's East-Prussian headquarters Schnaufer met Erich Hartmann, who became the most successful fighter pilot in the world. Hartmann, who had been awarded the Swords on 2 July 1944, described life on the Russian Front. He was the commander of the 9th Squadron of the 52nd Fighter Wing. Hartmann would become the commander of the 52nd's 1st Group on 1 February 1945.

Following the announcement of the Swords, and before his departure for Rastenburg, Schnaufer received a real, live good-luck pig from several of his comrades: Hauptmann Drewes, Leutnant Gräfe, the group flight surgeon, Dr. Schreiber and Major Rotter. Drewes even came up with a bouquet of carnations. The pig—*Schwein* in German—was symbolic of the German saying *Du mußt Schwein haben*—"You've got to have luck!"

During his return to the wing Schnaufer stopped off in Dortmund. He was immediately surrounded by a throng of airfield personnel, who pressed him for details of his nocturnal battles with the bomber streams. Afterward he posed for a group photo in front of a Do-215.

TO THE BITTER END

By 16 October 1944 Heinz-Wolfgang Schnaufer had raised his victory total to 100. He received the 21st Knight's Cross with Oak Leaves, Swords and Diamonds and was subsequently promoted to Major for bravery in the face of the enemy. At twenty-two he was the youngest Major in the Luftwaffe. The Wehrmacht daily report declared:

> During the night 9–10 October Hauptmann Schnaufer, group commander in a night-fighter wing, whom the Führer has decorated with the Knight's Cross with Oak Leaves and Swords, scored his 100th night victory.

Schnaufer and his group continued their relentless pursuit of the Allied bomber streams. His victory total continued to climb. Schnaufer was always ready to go as soon as incoming bombers were reported. Schnaufer had always been ready to jump in and take the place of any aircraft that developed mechanical trouble. One of those "replacement" flights had occurred on the night of 24 October 1944. Nine hundred fifty-five bombers of the RAF were in the air that night; their target was the Krupps armaments factories in Essen. On that occasion Essen was devastated by an inferno from the sky. No less than 4,538 tons of bombs and incendiaries rained down on the city, with 90% of the tonnage high explosive (including 509 4,000-pound "blockbusters"). The raid left more than 600 dead, numerous injured, and tens of thousands of homeless.

Schnaufer caught up with the bombers as they retired. He shot down two of the eight bombers lost on the raid. He flew his last mission with the 1st Night Fighter Wing on 5 November, shooting down a bomber from a force attacking the Dortmund-Ems canal.

On 10 November he left to take command of the 4th Night Fighter Wing. Major Schnaufer replaced Oberstleutnant Thimming, who had been wounded. In spite of all the paperwork and technical matters associated with the position of wing commander, Schnaufer kept flying as often as he could. On the night of 21 November Schnaufer took off to intercept a force of bombers attacking the synthetic fuel plant in Homberg-Meerbeck. This followed an unsuccessful attack the night before. The enemy lost three bombers, one of which was accounted for by Schnaufer.

✠

Schnaufer and his crew saw action twice in December 1944. Each time he shot down an enemy bomber, raising his victory total to 106.

In spite of the extra demands then being made of him as a recipient of Germany's highest decoration, Schnaufer had increased his victory total to 106 by the end of 1944. He was then at the head of the list of German night-fighter pilots, passing Oberstleutnant Helmut Lent. Lent had become the 15th German soldier to receive the Diamonds on 31 July 1944 after shooting down his 100th enemy aircraft. Sadly, he was involved in a landing accident and subsequently died of his injuries. Before his death, Lent had been promoted to Oberst for bravery in the face of the enemy. A close friend of Schnaufer's, Lent ran into trouble while landing his Ju-88 G—D5 + AA—at Paderborn on 5 October 1944.

An engine developed trouble at the most inopportune moment. His aircraft struck a high-tension wire and crashed. Lent was badly injured and died two days later. Killed with him were his long-time radar/radio operator, Leutnant Walter Kubisch, who had participated in 80 of Lent's night kills, as well as Oberleutnant Klöß and Leutnant Kark. Helmut Lent had downed 113 aircraft—8 by day and 105 at night—including 61 four-engined bombers and one Mosquito.

Members of the 3rd Night Fighter Wing, which he commanded, stood guard at Lent's grave. Among the other leading figures of the night-fighter arm present to pay their last respects was Heinz-Wolfgang Schnaufer.

THE LAST GREAT SUCCESS
On 16 February 1945 the Allied military radio station in Calais sent best wishes to Schnaufer on his twenty-third birthday.

On the evening of 20 February 1945 the RAF sent a force of 994 bombers on multiple raids to Dortmund, Düsseldorf, Monheim and the Mittelland Canal. Every available German night fighter was scrambled to intercept the raiders. Shortly after midnight Schnaufer received the first report of the incoming raid. He was at Gütersloh with the wing headquarters. He immediately scrambled his few serviceable night fighters, which caught up with the bombers as they withdrew after bombing. Compared to other recent raids, it was a comparatively costly night for the RAF with a total of twenty-two aircraft lost.

Even before Schnaufer and his crew reached the combat zone they could see burning aircraft and tracer fire. He transmitted the order for all aircraft to attack, then moved in on the closest bomber. The engagement lasted four minutes. The pilot of the RAF bomber threw his machine about the sky in an effort to shake off the night fighter. Schnaufer scored several hits with his forward-firing guns on his first pass and then succeeded in positioning himself to use his *schräge Musik*. The enemy aircraft was literally shot to pieces. Both wings separated from the fuselage, then one of the engines ripped free of its mounts and soared through the air like a glowing comet. Wreckage rained down on the ground.

Schnaufer attacked a second bomber less than three minutes later. It was a textbook kill. The bomber shed a wing after the third burst and went down vertically.

The next attack ended prematurely when the upward-firing guns jammed. Schnaufer came under fire from the bomber, which holed his machine in several places. He broke off the attack and landed at Gütersloh, where his mechanics were waiting to repair the aircraft for the next sortie and to paint on two new victory bars.

After the debriefing, the three men had breakfast and retired to their quarters to sleep. There wasn't much time to rest. They were again placed on alert the next evening. Schnaufer—ignoring the pleas of his staff—decided not to stay on the ground. He wanted to "dive into the fray," as he put it. Large numbers of enemy bombers were reported bound for Germany. An hour later the first night-fighter crews were ordered to strip alert. The controllers reported that the bombers were bound for Stuttgart and Duisburg. Schnaufer decided to attack the southern group. After taking off, he was informed that several hundred bombers were also attacking Kiel.

Using information from a giant Würzburg radar, the fighter controller guided Schnaufer toward the enemy bombers until his own radar operator could take over. Rumpelhardt soon acquired a contact and directed his pilot toward the first bomber. It was precisely 2315 hours when Schnaufer made his first attack. He approached from directly behind and came under fire. Schnaufer pulled himself together; he would have to remain cool if he were to defeat the enemy.

Two bursts from the upwards-firing guns eliminated the first enemy bomber. The enemy long-range night fighters flying above the bombers had not yet noticed that a German night fighter had infiltrated the bomber stream. The second enemy bomber was brought down by a textbook attack. After taking evasive action to avoid return fire, Schnaufer closed in to within 100 meters of a third bomber. The RAF pilot put his air-

The port fin of Schnaufer's Bf-110, displaying his victories.

craft into a corkscrew in an effort to shake off the fighter. Schnaufer followed for at least five minutes before he was able to position himself for an attack with his forward-firing guns. Then Gänsler opened fire on a fourth machine that was sighted at the Messerschmitt's two o'clock position. Just as Schnaufer's third victim fell from the sky, Gänsler's target blew apart with an explosion that lit up the night sky.

"That makes four, sir," called Rumpelhardt.

"And the fifth will soon follow," declared Schnaufer. He rammed the throttles forward and the Messerschmitt climbed like a falcon toward the enemy bombers.

Schnaufer's next burst riddled the fuel tanks of a Lancaster. He turned hard to avoid the fuel streaming back from the crippled machine. Shrouded in flames, the bomber flew on. Several parachutes appeared, but they were immediately consumed by the flames. The crew of the Lancaster had no hope of escape. They had shot down five enemy aircraft, but Schnaufer was in no hurry to head for base. They had ammunition left and the aircraft was answering the controls perfectly.

Following a brief encounter with an enemy night fighter, Schnaufer moved toward the bomber stream again. Approaching from below, he positioned himself beneath the fat belly of the sixth bomber. The stream of cannon rounds struck the forward fuselage of the bomber. The British tail gunner continued to fire as the doomed aircraft took its final plunge.

"Home, sir?" asked Rumpelhardt when the fuel-warning light began to glow red.

"We still have five minutes. How does it look?"

"Target at one o'clock. Range 1,000 meters."

"We can get him then."

Schnaufer increased power and set out after the still invisible enemy. He acquired the bomber visually and accelerated further. The tail gunner opened fire. Eighty meters . . . seventy . . . fifty! The twin upward-firing cannon roared. Cannon rounds smashed into the starboard wing and outboard engine, which burst into flames. The bomber curved away from the stream with Schnaufer in hot pursuit. He climbed until the Messerschmitt was level with the target and then unleashed his forward-firing weapons.

The night fighter came under fire from two sides and bullets struck the airframe. Gänsler also opened fire. The bomber exploded and went down in flames. Schnaufer turned away and set course for home. All seven kills had taken seventeen minutes.

Schnaufer landed and filed his combat report. In the twenty-four hour period from shortly after midnight on 21 February to just before midnight on the 22nd he had destroyed a total of nine Lancaster bombers out of a total of fifty-six RAF bombers lost. It was a unique accomplishment and there was an appropriate celebration.

✠

The previous two nights demonstrated that the Luftwaffe night-fighter force was still capable of inflicting heavy losses on its enemy. Heinz-Wolfgang Schnaufer managed to shoot down several more enemy bombers in the weeks that followed, but most of his time was spent on the ground. Entire groups were tied to the ground by lack of fuel and ammunition.

In subsequent weeks the 4th Night Fighter Wing took to the air on a few occasions and Major Schnaufer was able to raise his victory total to 121, all night kills. His last victory came on his 164th combat mission.

The German night-fighter force was increasingly hamstrung by fuel and ammunition shortages. Missions over Germany by the RAF and the USAAF were now almost unopposed. In addition, the night-fighter arm's strength had sunk to one-quarter of its authorized level. Like the German day fighters, the night fighters were unable to prevent German cities from being senselessly destroyed, literally until the final day of the war. Civilian casualties were severe. As American forces advanced into Germany from the west they overran the airfields used by the night fighters.

Schnaufer shot down a bomber during a devastating RAF area-bombing raid on Pforzheim on the night of 24 February. One of the last concerted efforts by the night fighters took place on 4 March 1945. More than 100 German aircraft took off to intercept RAF bombers attacking the Ladbergen aqueduct on the Dortmund-Ems Canal. One of them was flown by Schnaufer. Seven Lancasters were destroyed, two of them by Schnaufer and his crew. The first at 2155 hours and the second at 2204 hours; his 117th and 118th victims.

On 12 March a force of 1,107 British bombers—748 Lancasters, 292 Halifaxes, and 68 Mosquitos—dropped 4,851 tons of bombs on the unfortunate city of Dortmund. Schnaufer was in the air again that night and managed to shoot down one of the two Lancasters lost. This was the largest number of Bomber Command aircraft striking a single target during the war and also the record tonnage of bombs dropped. Dortmund was totally devastated and all war production ceased.

This same night the Luftwaffe mounted its last major night intruder effort over Britain, Operation Gisela. One hundred and forty-two Ju-88 Gs from the 2nd, 3rd, 4th, and 5th Night Fighter Wings attacked returning Bomber Command aircraft over their airfields, shooting down 20 bombers and causing many others to crash land.

✠

In March 1945 Schnaufer test flew the unique twin-engined Do-335 *Pfeil* ("Arrow") which was being developed as a night fighter. Had it been available to the units, this high-speed machine—800 kilometers per hours—would have been an excellent long-range night fighter. Designed as a high-speed bomber, the prototype Do-335 first flew in the summer of 1943 and was sent to Rechlin for flight testing. After much discussion, it was decided to use the aircraft in the day fighter and fighter-bomber roles.

The first prototype of a night-fighter version, the Do-335 V-10, was finally rolled out in 1944. Proposed armament was two 20-mm MG-151/20 cannon and an engine-mounted 30-mm MK-103. Major Schnaufer was enthusiastic about the aircraft's performance, however, it was developed too late for quantity production.

✠

Major Schnaufer flew his last combat mission on 9 April 1945. He took off from Faßberg and headed north. The RAF's target that night was Kiel. Schnaufer initiated the pursuit of a Lancaster but was forced to break off his attack when an enemy night fighter appeared. Thus his 122nd victory eluded him. His final flight took place on 19 April. Schnaufer flew top cover for the base at Eggeberg while part of the wing took off for Faßberg. It was a last desperate effort, but Schnaufer didn't want to abandon the people of Germany to their fate. He and his men fought until the last day. Finally, on 8 May 1945, he issued the final order of the day and disbanded his wing.

Command Post, 8 May 1945

To my proven the 4th Night Fighter Wing

Men of my wing!

The enemy is in our land. Our proud aircraft have been handed over. Germany is occupied and has surrendered unconditionally. Comrades, these depressing facts bring tears to our eyes. The future lies uncertain and merciless before us, it can only bring us worry and pain.

But something will always remain in us, my men: The tradition of our wing and our accomplishments! This tradition will give us the necessary backbone if we should be humbled. It will hearten us and allow us to look clearly and proudly into the future.

Once again I will call to mind the history of our famous wing, which was feared by the enemy. The cornerstone of our wing was laid on 18 April 1941 when Oberst Stoltenhoff formed the 2nd Group of the 4th Night Fighter Wing from the 2nd Group of the 26th Destroyer Wing. Formation of the entire the 4th Night Fighter Wing took place exactly three years ago, on 1 May 1942. Its mission was at first to protect Southern Germany from the major night raids that were then beginning.

Our first bases were Mainz-Finthen, Laupheim, Jouvincourt and Laon-Athies; in 1943 Florennes, St. Dizier and Coulommieres were added. But more than mere place names mark our path.

The end of a hunter. A Bf-110 G, Werk No. 160750, near Bad Kösen, Germany, June 1945.

The soil of France and Germany is marked with many small patches that mark the crash sites of the heavy bombers shot down by us.

Five hundred seventy-nine bombers—three complete bomber divisions—were shot down by the 4th Night Fighter Wing in difficult air battles under the most severe conditions. Successful night ground-attack missions in all weather on Avranches, on Nijmegen, on motor vehicle columns and trains in the rear cost the enemy hundreds of vehicles and locomotives.

The long-range missions over England were the final blow by our wing. The destruction of the pontoon bridge near Wesel was a worthy end to our glorious, difficult struggle.

Comrades, these great successes were achieved only through your unshakeable attitude, through your diligence and through your belief in Germany. Many times our wing came close to being crushed by the enemy's great material superiority, but we got back up after every blow and, with determined courage, hit back just as hard to the very end.

This unequal struggle has demanded great sacrifices of us. One hundred two flight crews with 400 officers, noncommissioned officers and enlisted personnel failed to return. Some were killed in fighting on the ground in true fulfillment of duty, others while defending against enemy air attacks. They gave everything for

Germany and for our wing, and they have the right at this moment to demand that we remain decent and upright German men.

I bid farewell to my wing today with a feeling of nostalgia—but also one of pride—and I thank all of you for the trust you have shown me in times of crisis.

If you are now once again called upon to work hard in another Germany, you can, my men of the 4th Night Fighter Wing , carry within you the feeling that you did everything humanly possible to win this war for Germany.

Long live our beloved Fatherland!

/signed/ Schnaufer

Wing Commander

4th Night Fighter Wing

✠

After the surrender the British wished to question Schnaufer about his missions, tactics and technology. He was sent to England along with other prominent fighter pilots. The English also took his Bf-110. This historic aircraft with its 121 victory markings was displayed in Hyde Park. Astonished Londoners paused to read the placard in front of the Messerschmitt:

> This Messerschmitt 110 was flown by the most successful night-fighter pilot in the world, the 23-year-old Major of the German Air Force, Heinz-Wolfgang Schnaufer

Schnaufer's aircraft remained on display for weeks. Afterwards the fin and rudder bearing the victory markings were removed. Today, they may be seen in the Imperial War Museum in London.

EPILOGUE

Heinz-Wolfgang Schnaufer returned to Germany in 1946. During his wartime career he had survived 164 night missions, braved return fire from enemy bombers and his own Flak. At the age of twenty-four he had his whole life before him. He returned to his home where he became involved in the family business and helped expand it. Schnaufer took in many former members of his wing and gave them work when they needed it.

In spite of the prevailing attitude toward former soldiers, he enjoyed the respect of most of the inhabitants of his hometown. He worked like a horse at the family business, which developed into a major concern within two years.

Soon he was able to afford a new car, in which he made business trips, just like when he was the wing commander. On 13 July 1950 Schnaufer was making a quick trip from Biarritz to Bordeaux. Suddenly, a truck pulled onto the highway from a side road. Schnaufer slammed on the brakes and skidded in an atternpt to avoid the truck. The two vehicles collided and the Mercedes flipped over. Schnaufer was thrown clear and landed in a ditch. He was not injured in the crash itself, but the load of oxygen bottles the truck was carrying rolled on top of him, breaking almost every bone in his body

Heinz-Wolfgang Schnaufer fought for his life in a French hospital for forty-eight hours, but the highest-scoring night-fighter pilot in the world lost his last battle on 15 July 1950. No one in the hospital knew that the young man was "The Night Ghost of St. Trond." As far as the doctors were concerned, he was a young German who had had the misfortune to die in an auto accident in which he was not at fault.

An anonymous French truck driver had accomplished what hundreds of the enemy had failed to do during three years of war.

Reichsmarschall Hermann Göring, Commander in Chief of the Luftwaffe.

The Luftwaffe:
A Brief Examination
of Its Branches

THE FIGHTER PILOT

In general, the World War Two fighter pilot was an airman who was strongly individualistic. He tended to prefer to do things on his own—including fighting—as well as bearing direct responsibility for others. He preferred practical activity and technical matters to theoretical studies. The source of the fighter pilot's strength and energy was partly physical and partly mental. The desire of these men to become aviators sprang from the enthusiasm of youth and from the joy of living, and they were always ready to surrender themselves to the ecstasy of flying and fighting.

In their fast, maneuverable machines, fighter pilots experienced the magic of flight with an intensity several times greater than did any other pilots. Apparently immune to the laws of gravity, free of all earthly cares, they flew at dizzying heights. Consciousness of the power of their machines melded with the awareness of their own strength. All this allowed them to reach the unparalleled results they achieved in combat.

Even though fighter pilots were basically lone warriors, the experience of flying and fighting welded the individual squadrons, groups and wings together, causing the pilots to feel part of a close community.

Fighter pilots were warriors: Clever, fine-nerved hunters or powerful, single-minded daredevils. Several of their number bore the stamp of genius. Just as nature from time to time produces one of its creations with unparalleled perfection, so some fighter pilots displayed completely unexpected abilities that simply allowed them to become the best.

In addition to certain mental and physical characteristics, every successful fighter pilot possessed the two qualities most vital to success: Piloting skill and vision—the Alpha and Omega of fighter piloting.

There was also an immeasurable quality: Determination decided every engagement! All in all: The formula for a successful fighter pilot was a

Werner Mölders, fighter commander and first recipient of the Diamonds.

Adolf Galland, general in charge of fighters, December 1941 to January 1945.

Gordon Gollob, Galland's successor as general in charge of fighters.

Hans-Joachim Marseille, the "Star of Africa."

Factory-fresh Fw-190 A-3 fighters.

combination of courage, lightning-fast reactions and a skilled mastery of one's machine. All successful fighter pilots shared the same attitude toward their deadly trade, which could be formulated as follows:

> In aerial combat it is not a question of you *or* me! It is simply: *You must fall, not me.*" (See O. Haase: *The Essence of the Fighter Pilot*)

The entire magnitude and frightfulness of the war was concentrated into the few minutes of an aerial engagement, and the victor was usually the one who kept his nerve and displayed an iron will.

As soon as the fighter pilots closed their canopies they were alone and, as Adolf Galland once put it, "they fought until they fell." Among the best were Erich "Bubi" Hartmann, Gerhard Barkhorn, Günther Rall, Heinz Bär, Hermann Graf, Otto Kittel, and the unforgettable "Star of Africa," Hans Joachim Marseille. The top 100 German fighter pilots accounted for more than 24,000 enemy aircraft.

MEDIUM- AND LONG-RANGE BOMBER PILOTS

The Commander-in-Chief of the Luftwaffe knew that the success of the bomber force, which was decisive to the outcome of battles and the campaign, was achieved only because the flight crews and the technical personnel carried out the tasks given them almost to the point of exhaustion. The strategic forces were drawn into the army's battles in order to fill gaps in the ranks of close-support aviation.

There is nothing to add to Generalfeldmarschall Kesselring's words about the German bomber force. It never really developed a long-range capability—indeed, that aspect of air power was almost completely ignored in the formation of the Luftwaffe—and its relatively small bomber forces were generally relegated to operational-level commitment as opposed to strategic operations. Although strategic missions were mounted, they were mere pinpricks compared to the massive air campaigns launched by the British at night and the Americans by day. Kesselring's words illustrate the fate toward which the bomber and close-support forces were drawn as the war progressed: Ultimate defeat and destruction.

Just as the enthusiastic aggressiveness of fighter pilots is an accepted fact, one can say that, in general, bomber pilots were a more analytical and flexible type of aviator. What characterized them best was unshakeable calm and a philosophical/contemplative outlook on life. Many bomber pilots were daring but also determined fliers—a fact acknowledged by

Albert Kesselring, Commander in Chief of the 1st and 2nd Air Forces and later Commander in Chief South.

their comrades and even the fighter pilots. Combined with their unshakeable calm, this allowed them to achieve great things. For example, the determination needed to dive or fly into a curtain of enemy antiaircraft fire was decisive to a bomber pilot's success.

The bomber pilot himself operated no weapon. Instead, he left the defense of his aircraft against enemy fighters to his gunners, the radio operator, the bombardier and the flight engineer. His main contribution to the defense was maneuvering his aircraft in such a way as to evade enemy attacks.

This does not mean that bomber pilots did not have to carry out direct attacks as well. In many cases—and Joachim Helbig in this book is an outstanding example of this—bomber pilots displayed great courage and offensive spirit in attacks against heavily armed warships and other types of point targets. They had to dive straight through heavy antiaircraft fire to deliver their bombs. They had to get the bomber and its crew to the delivery point of the ordnance.

This pinpoint attack was not typical for bombers, however. It was more usually associated with the dive bombers. Nevertheless, it can be said of level-bombing attacks that a cool head and imperturbability, indeed even stubbornness, were the essential factors in addition to daring and aggressiveness. Once again, a bomber pilot had to his bomber and its crew to the delivery point of the ordnance. Everything else was meaningless to him.

Obviously, the notion of the bomber pilot cannot be seen entirely in narrow guidelines and stereotypes. It is indisputable that the bombardiers, gunners, flight engineers and radio operators played just as great a role in combat as did the pilots. The latter were not and never could be lone warriors; teamwork was an essential factor in every bomber. It was upon this team and the combination of forces in the aircraft that success depended. The pilot was only a part of a group—a small one to be sure—which itself was a part of a larger formation, usually operating in close formation. Contrast this with the fighter pilot. Even when flying as part of a squadron or group, the fighter pilot often retained a degree of independence that was anathema to the bomber force.

During their frequently lengthy flights to the target, bomber crews had more time for reflection than did Stuka and night-fighter crews or fighter pilots. The bomber crewman was thus in many respects the direct opposite of the fighter pilot. The typical bomber pilot was a steady, powerfully self-confident person with both feet planted firmly on the ground.

Because of the mission of the bomber pilot—putting ordnance on a distant target—formation flying was essential in order to survive. It was

The Do-17 provided a significant portion of the Luftwaffe's bomber strength in the early years of the war and played a major role in the Battle of Britain.

only in a tight formation that the less maneuverable and highly vulnerable bombers—fuel and bomb laden as well as being a significantly bigger target—could survive. Survival was determined by a team effort and the concentrated firepower of all of the formation's machine guns united against intruders.

The Heinkel 111 was the workhorse of the Luftwaffe's bomber units through the entire war. When the war began, eighteen of the Luftwaffe's twenty-seven bomber formations were equipped with the He-111. The He-111 H served as the Luftwaffe's standard medium bomber until late in the war.

As the war progressed the Western Allies produced growing numbers of medium and heavy bombers whose performance first equaled and then surpassed that of the He-111. The fate of the He-111 crews was soon sealed. As a result of several elementary failures and miscalculations, Germany never succeeded in producing in quantity an aircraft with a performance significantly better than that of the He-111.

Eight hundred He-111s were placed in service in the years before the war; a further 452 machines of this type were added in 1939. The subsequent years saw the production of 756 (1940), 950 (1941), 1,337 (1942) and 1,405 (1943) He-111s. In 1944 only 756 were delivered. With this low output and the heavy losses suffered by the groups, it proved impossible for the Luftwaffe to maintain the force of bombers with which it had entered the war

Oberst Werner Baumbach, one of the best-known German bomber pilots (30th Bomber Wing) and the sixteenth recipient of the Knight's Cross with Oak Leaves and Swords once said in that regard: "We took off in the He-111 against Polish targets on the morning of 1 September 1939. We flew the last attacks of the war with it—using remotely controlled bombs against the Russians' Oder bridges in April 1945."

Among the most significant bomber pilots were Werner Baumbach, Dietrich Peltz, Hermann Hogebach, Dr. Ernst Kühl, Dr. Ernst Kupfer and Hans-Georg Bätcher (658 combat missions over France, England and Russia). Others included Martin Harlinghausen, Eduard Skrzipek, and Hans Emig.

DIVE-BOMBER PILOTS

The missions of the dive-bomber were generally simpler than those of the conventional bomber and were marked by a certain monotony. Hauptmann Rudolf Neumann, at the time a squadron commander in the 2nd Squadron of the 2nd Stuka Wing, said in that regard: "Apart from minor differences—such as the prevailing antiaircraft and fighter defenses—the missions carried out by our arm, the dive-bombers, are invariably the same."

One consequence of this fact may be that Stuka pilots were less ready than other members of the Luftwaffe to talk about their operational experiences.

A man who was well-qualified to comment, Hauptmann Kurt Kuhlmey, the group commander of the 3rd Group of the 3rd Stuka Wing, once answered this question as follows: "My experiences were nothing special."

Kuhlmey, who became known as the "Prince of Bir Hacheim" in the war in Africa and who may be considered one of the most experienced and successful Stuka pilots, agreed with Oberleutnant Kurt Riegel, the squadron commander of the 5th Squadron of the 3rd Close Support Wing, who said: "We Stuka pilots are the poorest swine of the century."

Only by turning as tightly as possible could a Ju-87 evade a much faster enemy fighter. The aircraft's gunner could fire at the attacking fighter from a steep turn. In general, however, unescorted Stukas were easy prey for the attacker; they lacked the speed necessary to flee.

A very great deal was expected of the Stuka pilot in performance and devotion to duty, and he could expect little recognition in return. Nevertheless, those who served in a Stuka group stayed on and did not press for a transfer to another branch of the Luftwaffe. As with most other aviators, Stuka pilots developed a loyalty and love for their branch that made the thought of becoming some other type of pilot incomprehensible.

A Bf-109 G-6 of the 27th Fighter Wing. This variant is a bomber destroyer with 20mm cannon pods under the wings.

Bf-109 Es in Russia, 1941–42.

In spite of a high feeling of self-worth, Stuka pilots in general were sensitive to any injury to their status. The classic picture of a Stuka pilot: Cool, well balanced almost to the point of being phlegmatic, conscious of duty and sober. The Stuka pilot was not without vitality, however, and an aggressive spirit.

As Oberstleutnant Kuhlmey wrote: "The decisive factor in the success of a Stuka pilot was his character. We found out after about seventy missions whether one was going to last."

Kuhlmey, the "Prince of Bir Hacheim," was one of the outstanding leaders of the Stuka arm. It was due to his bearing that his men elevated him to the status of "Prince." His soldierly bearing was reflected as much by his constantly friendly nature and his cautious reserve, as by his feeling of self worth, his inner stability and in his mental prowess and acuity.

Someone who also came close to this ideal was Oberleutnant Riegel. On one occasion his squadron sustained heavy losses of almost fifty percent in the course of a mission. Before the next sortie, a calm and composed Riegel said to his men: "You all know what happened yesterday! Anyone who doesn't stay in formation is done for. I will fly slow enough so that everyone can hold tight formation. Good luck!"

Every member of the squadron flew like the devil, stayed in tight formation and together they fought off several fighter attacks.

Some of the most prominent Stuka pilots were Oskar Dinort, Hubertus Hitschhold, Walter Sigel, and Karl Henze. The most highly decorated member of the German armed forces in World War II was also a Stuka pilot: Hans-Ulrich Rudel.

NIGHT FIGHTERS

Following early experiments during the First World War, the German night-fighter arm developed very slowly. Some limited testing was begun in 1936; however, results were disappointing. There was little cause for alarm, however. At that time no one could foresee the need for a night-fighter arm to combat the scale of enemy bombing raids that lay in the future. Indeed it was Reichsmarschall Hermann Göring who said: "We have no need for night fighters!"

Events were to prove him wrong. The first night missions—actually flown at dusk—were carried out in April 1940 against incoming and outgoing bombers of the Royal Air Force. They were launched after the initiation of Operation *Weserübung*—the invasion of Norway and Denmark—by the 1st Group of the 1st Destroyer Wing under Hauptmann Falck. In May of 1940 Falck was called upon to brief Luftwaffe Generals Udet, Kesselring

A Bf-110 D of the 26th Destroyer Wing "Horst Wessel," escorting Ju-53 transports to Tunisia, 1943.

A Messerschmitt Bf-110 G-4 night fighter with FuG 220 SN2b and FuG 219 C1 radar aerials.

and Milch on this specialized branch of the air force, before meeting with Reichsmarschall Göring for the same purpose on 26 June 1940.

As a result of his discussions with Falck, Göring—then convinced of the need for night fighters—ordered the formation of the first night fighter wing. Hauptmann Falck was named to command the new formation. On 19 July 1940 the 1st Night Fighter Wing was formed.

Oberleutnant Werner Streib scored the first night victory during the night of 20 July 1940, using the so-called *helle Nachtjagd*, or "illuminated night-fighting," method. Streib enjoyed a phenomenal career, rising to command the 1st Night Fighter Wing with the rank of Major and becoming the 54th recipient of the Knight's Cross with Swords. Streib was Heinz-Wolfgang Schnaufer's superior officer and mentor; he played a major role in the success of Schnaufer, who went on to become the highest-scoring night-fighter pilot of the war, receiving the Oak Leaves, Swords and Diamonds in the period from 24 June to 16 October 1944. Helmut Lent was also a member of that legendary night-fighter wing.

The illuminated night-fighting method employed operational zones in which were positioned a searchlight unit, three night fighters and a Luftwaffe signals company. The latter's Freya radar located approaching enemy bombers. Würzburg radars then took over the enemy aircraft from the Freya equipment and informed the command posts of the appropriate searchlight batteries. These illuminated the bombers' flight path, making it visible to the lurking night fighters. Of the three night fighters stationed in each zone, one was always in the air, a second was held on strip alert and the third was kept in reserve. Success was limited compared to resources expended. The enemy soon recognized the threat posed by the defensive zones and either penetrated them in a shallow dive or simply flew around them.

The illuminated night-fighting method was replaced by the so-called combined night-fighting method. The new system was based on a concentration of forces in the airspace surrounding Kiel, Hamburg, Bremen, Duisburg, Cologne, Frankfurt, Darmstadt/Mannheim and Munich. In principle, the procedure of locating the enemy aircraft, holding it in a cone of searchlights and attacking it remained the same as the illuminated method. The difference was that the Flak control officer in each zone passed data from the Würzburg radars to the searchlight and Falk batteries, while the fighter-control officer guided the night fighter to the enemy. It was not uncommon for the night fighter to run into the fire from the Flak, which were permitted to fire up to a height of 4,000 meters within the defense zones.

Equipped with fighter versions of the Ju-88 and Do-17, the 1st Group of the 1st Night Fighter Wing under Hauptmann Heyse was the first to undertake long-range night-fighting missions. The 2nd Night Fighter Wing evolved from that group. The long-range night fighters attacked enemy bombers over the sea, over England or even over their own bases. Other fighters infiltrated the returning bomber formations before attacking. But since bombers that were on their way home had already dropped their bombs on Germany, Hitler soon forbade that type of anti-bomber mission.

A new system, the Himmelbett method, was introduced in the summer of 1941. The principal elements of this system remained in use until the end of the war. Circular defensive zones were set up, whose size was based on the ranges of the available radars. The Würzburg set had a range of 35 kilometers, while the Würzburg Riese (giant Würzburg), which entered service in 1942, had a range of sixty to seventy kilometers. The following is a brief description of a Himmelbett interception:

A Freya search radar located the enemy at a distance of about 150 kilometers. The enemy formation was then handed off to a Würzburg Red. That was the name of the radar that maintained contact with the enemy. The radar that guided the night fighter to the enemy was called a Würzburg Green. During the detection phase, the night fighter was supposed to circle in the waiting area at the altitude of the approaching enemy. A radio beacon was installed in each waiting area as an orientation point. A second fighter was held on strip alert, and a third on general alert. A fighter-control officer guided the night fighter to the enemy by referring to a so-called Seeburg Table. The positions of friendly and enemy aircraft were displayed on the table's glass plate by means of colored dots.

This system, which was limited to only one night fighter in action in a zone at one time, was later modified and made more efficient, but without changing the entire system.

The use of night fighters in a daylight role against enemy bombers in 1943 and 1944 was a senseless sacrifice. The Bf-110 was no match for the American escort fighters, and losses to them and the defensive fire from the bombers were heavy.

The development of more advanced electronic aids improved the night fighters' chances of success considerably. The FuG-227 homing device, known as the Flensburg, was designed to home in on the transmissions of the "Monica" tail warning radar used by British bombers. The device that was supposed to protect them spelled doom for many RAF Lancasters and Halifaxes.

An infrared optical search device, the so-called Spanner, was also introduced but proved disappointing. The first airborne night-fighter radar was

Reich Defense: The death throes of a B-17 Flying Fortress.

Reich Defense: A stricken B-24 Liberator after a direct hit from an 88mm Flak shell.

the FuG-202 Lichtenstein BC. This device and later improved variants closed a gap that existed in the interception process. It allowed the fighter's radar operator to issue fine corrections to the pilot during the final 2,000 meters of the approach to the enemy aircraft, where the Würzburg-Riese ground-control radar was ineffective. The minimum range of the FuG-202 Lichtenstein was 350 meters, close enough to put the night-fighter pilot in visual contact with the target.

Even though the German night fighters were engaged in a completely unequal struggle, they nevertheless inflicted grievous losses on the enemy, mainly due to their unshakeable willingness to fight on. The inability of the night-fighter arm to prevent Germany's cities from being reduced to ash and rubble was due to the overwhelming weight of the bomber streams and their supporting aircraft, not to a lack of skill or willingness to fight.

Among the most highly decorated night fighter pilots were Wolfgang Falck, Helmut Lent, Hans-Joachim Jabs, Werner Streib, Günter Radusch, Manfred Meurer, and Egmont Prinz zur Lippe Weißenfeld.

CLOSE-SUPPORT PILOTS

Generally speaking, the close-support pilot was a determined daredevil who, in carrying out his range of missions, combined his aggressiveness with a good eye and a sure hand. On the part of the Luftwaffe the first close-support missions were flown by the Legion Condor in Spain. It was there that the idea of employing the air force to directly support the army was born.

During the opening stages of the Second World War the Luftwaffe's close-support formations were equipped with the Hs-123 biplane. These were succeeded by another Henschel airframe, the twin-engined Hs-129. In addition, the Ju-87, and, to a limited degree, the Ju-88 were also used. In the final years of the war close-support versions of the Fw-190 (F and G) came to predominate.

While Germany was on the offensive, the task of the close-support formations was to smash the first breach in the enemy lines. During the great battles of encirclement in Russia they bombed encircled enemy forces and helped smash attempts by trapped enemy forces to break out. Additional targets of the close-support groups included enemy supply lines, railroads, highways, rail stations and depots.

In Spain the He-51 was relegated to the close-support role after the arrival of the first Bf-109s. The 3rd Squadron of the 88th Fighter Wing under the then Oberleutnant Galland had flown close-support missions in the He-51, which carried six ten-kilogram fragmentation bombs under the

A Ju-88 A-5 bomber just after takeoff. On the starboard bomb rack is a PC 1400 "Fritz" armor piercing bomb.

fuselage. The He-51's successor, the Hs-123, was also an open-cockpit biplane, but it had been designed specifically for the close-support role, It was capable of absorbing a great deal of punishment and could also carry a greater payload.

In the summer of 1938 the 8th Air Corps was formed under the command of Generalmajor Wolfram Freiherr von Richthofen as a "close-support flying corps." It consisted of the 10th, 20th, 30th, 40th, and 50th Close Support Groups. These groups were equipped with the Hs-123, the Arado 66, the He-45, He-46, and He-51. On 1 August 1938 the 10th Close Support Group was equipped with the Ju-87 and was redesignated as a Stuka Group. In the beginning, the close-support and Stuka groups flew almost exactly the same type of missions.

In September 1943 a new office was created by Generaloberst Günter Korten in which all close-support and Stuka units were combined under the command of the new General in Charge of Close-Support Aviation. From that point on, all dive-bomber, close-support, high-speed bomber and antitank formations were considered close-support aviation. The General in Charge of Close-Support Aviation was directly subordinate to the Commander-in-Chief of the Luftwaffe.

According to the instructions given him, he was to "ensure all the necessary conditions existed in order to achieve and maintain the maximum degree of readiness and efficiency on the part of the close-support formations, in conjunction with the Luftwaffe General Staff and the High Commands of the Army and Navy."

Additionally, Korten was directed as follows:

> Oversee the planning and direction of the technical development of close-support aviation's aircraft, weapons and equipment; oversee the planning required to ensure the delivery of weapons and equipment. Guarantee the delivery of personnel replacements to close-support formations.

Korten's office evaluated all the operational reports submitted by the close-support formations. These were then evaluated and the lessons learned were passed on to the force as operational guidelines. The office oversaw the implementation of new tactics and the training of close-support pilots.

On 1 September 1943 the Luftwaffe High Command named Oberstleutnant Ernst Kupfer, the wing commander of the 2nd Stuka Wing "Immelmann," as the first General in Charge of Close Support Aviation. Kupfer had been awarded the Knight's Cross with Oak Leaves while commanding the Stuka wing. Several weeks after his appointment, Kupfer was killed when the aircraft in which he was flying crashed in the Belasia Mountains in Greece. On 11 April 1944 he was awarded the sixty-second Knight's Cross with Oak Leaves and Swords posthumously.

Secret Command Matter No. 11125/43, which was issued on 5 October 1943, laid down general regulations and guidance for the creation of close-support wings. According to the directive, all flying formations engaged in directly supporting the ground forces were to be renamed close support wings. The unfortunate death of Oberst Ernst Kupfer prevented him from putting his ideas into practice. His successor was Oberst Hubertus Hitschhold. Hitschhold accelerated the process of reequipping the close-support formations with the Fw-190.

There were numerous outstanding personalities within the ranks of the close-support wings. One of the most interesting was Hauptmann Robert Weiß, whose career is outlined in this book. The dominant figure in the field of Luftwaffe close-support flying was undoubtedly Hans-Ulrich Rudel. Among this legendary figure's exploits was the destruction of 547 enemy tanks.

Once they had dropped their ordnance, German close-support pilots eagerly engaged opposing enemy fighters—and with great success. With

Ernst Kupfer,
the first General in Charge of
Close-Support Aviation, who
died in November 1943.

the German ground forces constantly on the defensive after 1943, the primary tasks of the close-support groups were aiding the army in its efforts to halt the onrushing flood of enemy armor and supporting local counterattacks. Effective support by the heavily armed Hs-129s and Fw-190s was often the decisive factor that enabled the hard-pressed German infantry to master crisis situations. Losses were heavy, and the close-support pilots faced the grim prospect of being shot down and captured by the Soviets daily. There are numerous accounts of desperate escapes to safety through enemy-occupied territory.

The close-support forces adopted the Infantry Assault Badge (*Infanteriesturmabzeichen*) as their emblem, an indication of their close ties to the infantry and their dedication to supporting them in their desperate struggle. It was an awareness that they were often the last hope of their infantry comrades on the ground that enabled them to achieve the enormous feats that they did.

Index

Page numbers in italics indicate illustrations.